THE PREHISTORY OF BRITAIN AND IRELAND

This book presents a new interpretation of the prehistory of Britain and Ireland and is the first in many years to consider both regions together. Richard Bradley begins the account when Britain became separated from the Continent and ends with the integration of the two islands into a wider European network shortly before the Roman Conquest. Using both textual and material documentation, he also distils the results of recent fieldwork, much of it funded by commercial developers, which has greatly expanded the quantity and variety of excavated evidence. Bradley also compares the archaeology of both islands and discusses the varied ways in which their inhabitants lived their lives. Intended as an interpretation rather than a manual, this book is primarily concerned with settlements, landscapes, monuments, and the evidence for regional variation. All of these topics are discussed in relation to contemporary approaches to prehistory. Treating Britain and Ireland on equal terms, Bradley also aims to avoid emphasizing a few well-researched areas, an approach that characterized previous accounts of this subject.

Richard Bradley is a professor of archaeology at the University of Reading. A Fellow of the British Academy and recipient of an honorary doctorate from the University of Lund, he is the author of *Ritual and Domestic Life in Prehistoric Europe, The Past in Prehistoric Societies: An Archaeology of Natural Places, The Significance of Monuments,* and *Rock Art and the Prehistory of Atlantic Europe.*

CAMBRIDGE WORLD ARCHAEOLOGY

SERIES EDITOR

NORMAN YOFFEE, *University of Michigan*

EDITORIAL BOARD

SUSAN ALCOCK, *University of Michigan*
TOM DILLEHAY, *University of Kentucky*
STEPHEN SHENNAN, *University College London*
CARLA SINOPOLI, *University of Michigan*

The *Cambridge World Archaeology* series is addressed to students and professional archaeologists and to academics in related disciplines. Each volume presents a survey of the archaeology of a region of the world, providing an up-to-date account of research and integration of recent findings with new concerns of interpretation. Although the focus is on a specific region, broader cultural trends are discussed and the implications of regional findings for cross-cultural interpretations considered. The authors also bring anthropological and historical expertise to bear on archaeological problems and show how both new data and changing intellectual trends in archaeology shade inferences about the past.

BOOKS IN THE SERIES

RAYMOND ALLCHIN AND BRIDGET ALLCHIN, *The Rise of Civilization in India and Pakistan.*
CLIVE GAMBLE, *The Palaeolithic Settlement of Europe.*
CHARLES HIGHAM, *Archaeology of Mainland South East Asia.*
SARAH MILLEDGE NELSON, *The Archaeology of Korea.*
DAVID PHILLIPSON, *African Archaeology* (second revised edition).
OLIVER DICKINSON, *The Aegan Bronze Age.*
KAREN OLSEN BRUHNS, *Ancient South America.*
ALASDAIR WHITTLE, *Europe in the Neolithic.*
CHARLES HIGHAM, *The Bronze Age of Southeast Asia.*
CLIVE GAMBLE, *The Palaeolithic Societies of Europe.*
DON POTTS, *The Archaeology of Elam.*
A. F. HARDING, *European Societies of the Bronze Age.*
NICHOLAS DAVID AND CAROL KRAMER, *Ethnoarchaeology in Action.*
JAMES WHITLEY, *The Archaeology of Ancient Greece.*

CAMBRIDGE WORLD ARCHAEOLOGY

THE PREHISTORY OF BRITAIN AND IRELAND

RICHARD BRADLEY

University of Reading

CAMBRIDGE
UNIVERSITY PRESS

CAMBRIDGE UNIVERSITY PRESS
Cambridge, New York, Melbourne, Madrid, Cape Town, Singapore,
São Paulo, Delhi, Dubai, Tokyo, Mexico City

Cambridge University Press
32 Avenue of the Americas, New York, NY 10013-2473, USA

www.cambridge.org
Information on this title: www.cambridge.org/9780521612708

First published 2007
Reprinted 2007, 2008, 2009, 2010

A catalog record for this publication is available from the British Library.

Library of Congress Cataloging in Publication Data

Bradley, Richard, 1946–
The prehistory of Britain and Ireland/Richard Bradley.
  p. cm. – (Cambridge world archaeology)
Includes bibliographical references and index.
ISBN-13: 978-0-521-84811-4 (hardback)
ISBN-10: 0-521-84811-3 (hardback)
ISBN-13: 978-0-521-61270-8 (pbk.)
ISBN-10: 0-521-61270-5 (pbk.)
1. Prehistoric peoples – Great Britain. 2. Prehistoric peoples – Ireland. 3. Excavations
(Archaeology) – Great Britain. 4. Excavations (Archaeology) – Ireland. 5. Antiquities,
Prehistoric – Great Britain. 6. Antiquities, Prehistoric – Ireland. I. Title. II. Series.
GN805.B6954   2007
936.1 – dc22   2006016080

ISBN 978-0-521-84818-4 Hardback
ISBN 978-0-521-61270-8 Paperback

For Tim Phillips and Dave Yates, without whom this book could not have been written.

"At a very early period, probably soon after the general dispersal of mankind, and division of the earth among the Noachidae (an event which took place . . . about 2100 years before the Christian area) the descendants of Gomer, the grandson of Noah, passed the Thracian Bosphorus, and gradually spread over the various countries of Europe, still proceeding onwards towards the west, until some of their families reached the coast of Germany and Gaul, and from thence crossed the sea into Britain.

These Nomadic wanderers, the Aborigines of Europe, went under the general denomination of Cimmerians or Celts; and as their progress was uninterrupted, except by natural causes, – for they had no hostile armies to encounter, but merely waste and uncultivated countries to traverse, which some remained to colonise, whilst others, as the population increased, ventured forward, – we may reasonably infer, that within the space of four or five centuries from the first migration of the Gomerites out of Asia into Europe, or about sixteen hundred years before the birth of Christ, the British Isles were inhabited."

Matthew Holbeche Bloxam (c. 1840), *Fragmenta Sepulchralia*

CONTENTS

Illustrations		*page* xi
Preface		xv
1	The Offshore Islands	1
2	A New Beginning	27
3	North and South	88
4	Ploughshares into Swords	178
5	The End of Prehistory	226
Bibliography		279
Index		307

ILLUSTRATIONS

Frontispiece: Ireland seen from the coast of Scotland.   *page* xviii

1.1. The world according to Hecataeus of Miletus.   3

1.2. Ptolemy's map of Britain and Ireland.   5

1.3. The offshore islands of Britain and Ireland.   9

1.4. Stages in the separation of Britain from the Continent.   11

1.5. Places, regions, and rivers mentioned in Chapter One.   12

1.6. Land over 200 metres in Britain and Ireland.   13

1.7. Riverine connections in Britain and Ireland.   18

1.8. Distances between different parts of the shorelines of Britain,
     Ireland, and the near-Continent.   19

1.9. Sea routes between Continental Europe, Britain, and Ireland.   21

2.1. Places and regions mentioned in Chapter Two.   28

2.2. Artefact types mentioned in Chapter Two.   31

2.3. Earlier Neolithic houses at Corbally and Lismore Fields.   39

2.4. Settlements and tombs at Céide and Bharpa Carinish.   45

2.5. Groups of Earlier Neolithic pits in East Anglia.   47

2.6. Mortuary house at Lochill and chambered tomb at Carreg Samson.   48

2.7. Portal tomb at Poulnabrone.   49

2.8. Four Irish court tombs and associated houses.   51

2.9. Earlier Neolithic houses and chambered cairns in Orkney.   53

2.10. Court tomb at Creevykeel.   55

2.11. Mortuary structures and related features.   56

2.12. The long cairns at Street House and Pipton.   57

2.13. The treatment of houses and bodies in England and Ireland.   62

2.14. Bank barrows at Cleaven Dyke and Auchenlaich, timber structures
      at Littleour and Claish, and an enclosure at Douglasmuir.   63

2.15. Outline plans of the Rudston and Dorset cursuses.   66

2.16. Five cursus monuments and the enclosures associated with their
      terminals.   67

2.17. Four English causewayed enclosures and other nearby earthworks.   70

2.18. The possible Neolithic enclosure on Carrock Fell.   71

2.19. The relationship between causewayed enclosures, cursuses, and
      bank barrows.   77

2.20. The relationship between oval and circular mounds and enclosures.   79
2.21. The structural sequence at Eynesbury.   83
2.22. Round barrows and associated enclosures at Duggleby, Howe and
      Maxey.   85
3.1. Places and regions mentioned in Chapter Three.   90
3.2. Artefact types mentioned in Chapter Three.   92
3.3. Neolithic house types at Knowth.   95
3.4. A Later Neolithic house at Skara Brae.   97
3.5. A chambered tomb at Carrowmore.   99
3.6. Plans of the megalithic cemeteries at Loughcrew and Knowth.   100
3.7. A passage grave and chambered cairn at Loughcrew.   101
3.8. The principal monument at Newgrange, seen from the River
      Boyne.   103
3.9. The changing location of the decorated surfaces in Irish passage
      tombs.   105
3.10. The relationship between internal and external features at three
      passage graves.   107
3.11. The layout of the Neolithic houses at Barnhouse, compared with
      that of Maeshowe.   109
3.12. Internal view of the chamber of Maeshowe.   111
3.13. The Stones of Stenness.   113
3.14. Plans of the Irish monuments at Newgrange and Ballnahatty.   115
3.15. The development of megalithic art in the Boyne Valley and
      Orkney.   117
3.16. Six circular structures associated with Grooved Ware.   119
3.17. Some major circular structures in southern and central England.   121
3.18. The henge monument at Avebury.   125
3.19. Stone and timber 'avenues'.   127
3.20. Five large henges and associated monuments.   129
3.21. Silbury Hill.   131
3.22. Outline plans of the henges at Mayburgh and Catterick, and their
      location in relation to the Great Langdale quarries.   135
3.23. The main structural elements at Stonehenge.   137
3.24. The outer setting of monoliths at Stonehenge.   139
3.25. The geographical extent of the Bell Beaker phenomenon in
      Europe.   145
3.26. The distribution of decorated gold lunulae.   149
3.27. Three settlement sites associated with Beaker pottery.   151
3.28. The triangular relationship between Wessex, Brittany, and the
      Aunjetitz Culture.   155
3.29. A typical 'single' burial.   159
3.30. Orientation of the inhumation graves in the flat cemetery at
      Keenoge.   163
3.31. The Cursus Barrows.   165
3.32. The development of the Snail Down complex.   167
3.33. Mountaintop cairn of Moel Trigarn.   169
3.34. Field walls and enclosures at Roughan Hill.   171

3.35. Later Neolithic/Earlier Bronze Age monuments at Balnuaran of
       Clava, Island, Loanhead of Daviot, the Brenig, Beaghmore, and
       West Deeping.   173
4.1. Places and regions mentioned in Chapter Four.   180
4.2. Artefact types mentioned in Chapter Four.   182
4.3. A Middle Bronze Age round house at Yarnton.   183
4.4. The distribution of Bronze Age coaxial field systems.   189
4.5. Middle Bronze Age settlements and buildings.   191
4.6. Field systems and settlements on Dartmoor.   194
4.7. Settlement and fields at Barleycroft.   195
4.8. Middle Bronze Age cemeteries in England.   199
4.9. The timber platform at Flag Fen.   205
4.10. Crannogs and nearby deposits in Lough Gara, plus a plan of
       timber structures at Balinderry.   207
4.11. Late Bronze Age ringworks and associated deposits.   209
4.12. Land boundaries and open settlements in the Bourne Valley and
       on the Berkshire Downs.   211
4.13. Late Bronze Age mortuary monuments in Britain and Ireland.   213
4.14. Settlements, fields, and associated deposits at Bradley Fen and
       Reading Business Park.   215
4.15. The distribution of 'weapon zones' in Britain, plus plans of five
       circular monuments in Ireland.   219
4.16. Multivallate hillforts in Ireland and the Isle of Man.   220
4.17. The distribution of pennanular gold bracelets.   221
4.18. The Late Bronze Age stone circle at Drombeg.   221
5.1. Places and regions mentioned in Chapter Five.   228
5.2. Artefact types mentioned in Chapter Five.   231
5.3. The middens at East Chisenbury and Balksbury.   235
5.4. Two circular enclosures at West Harling, plus a model suggesting
       the evolution of landscapes with circular and rectangular
       enclosures.   238
5.5. An Iron Age round house at Yarnton.   239
5.6. Linear ditches and associated settlements on the scarp of the
       Yorkshire Wolds.   243
5.7. An excavated pit alignment at Shorncote.   245
5.8. The hillfort at Herefordshire Beacon.   247
5.9. The hillfort at Moel Y Gaer and the structures inside it.   249
5.10. The Neolithic henges of Devil's Quoits and Ferrybridge and their
       place in the Iron Age landscape.   253
5.11. Three Iron Age enclosed settlements in Wales.   255
5.12. Outline plans of five Iron Age occupation sites in Scotland and
       one in northern England.   257
5.13. Three open settlements in eastern England.   259
5.14. The character of Iron Age settlement in Britain and the
       near-Continent.   261
5.15. Iron Age vehicle burial at Ferrybridge.   263
5.16. The distributions of weapon burials, terrets, and horse bits.   265

5.17. The settlement and cemetery at Garton and Wetwang Slacks.   267
5.18. The timber structure at Navan Fort and the cairn that replaced it.   273
5.19. Plan of the Broch of Gurness.   274
5.20. The Broch of Gurness.   275
5.21. Plans of the coastal sites of Hengistbury Head and Cleavel Point.   276
5.22. The sequence of pre-Roman structures at Silchester.   277

PREFACE

I had been teaching British and Irish prehistory for a long time when I realised that my courses were out of date. The same was true of the museum displays concerned with the prehistoric period and even of the policies enacted by government agencies. Why was this?

On reflection, the reason has become clear. There has been a massive increase in the amount of archaeological fieldwork that has taken place as part of the planning process, and this happened at a time when universities and museums were playing a smaller role in practical archaeology. It would be all too easy to talk of a schism in the discipline, but it is certainly true that the flow of information has diminished. That is hardly surprising because the growth of developer-funded archaeology has put new pressures on those undertaking the work. There have always been problems with excavators who do not publish their results, but in the commercial climate that now prevails, the production of academic papers is often delayed or abandoned. That is especially unfortunate because the number and scale of field projects is undoubtedly increasing.

I suppose that there have been two ways of reacting to this state of affairs. One is to insist that any fieldwork conducted under these conditions must have its limitations. It must have been carried out hurriedly and without sufficient background research. I have heard this complaint from many academics, and in my view it is unjustified. Whatever the merits of commercial archaeology, the amount of good quality fieldwork is on the increase and more funds are available for more detailed analysis of the results than had been available before. The best field units may well be carrying out better quality research than some of the staff in universities. Work is now being undertaken on an unprecedented scale and often in regions where little had been attempted before. The problem is not one of professional competence but of information, for the results of so much activity have undermined received wisdom about the past.

Another way of thinking about the situation is to recognise that the expansion of developer-funded archaeology has also been liberating for prehistorians. It has not been based on the old orthodoxies but on the requirements of the planning process, with the result that unfamiliar kinds of material have been recovered and new areas have been investigated that had been neglected before. At last it may be possible to move beyond the small number of regions in which fieldwork had been concentrated for more than fifty years. And in the process it has become clear how very limited accounts of insular prehistory have been. The material recovered over the last two decades provides some of the material for a new synthesis.

This book makes a first attempt to redress the balance, for it is the result of a prolonged period of research that has involved both the fieldworkers who have produced so much new information and the archives in which their reports are held. This has not been an easy task, and it has been possible only because I was able to employ an excellent research assistant, Tim Phillips. He amassed so much material that I sometimes despaired of bringing this book to completion. At the same time, Dave Yates was undertaking a thematic study of Bronze Age field systems, using many of the same sources. Between them they collected such important information that it is only right that they should be the dedicatees of this book. When entire organisations are still debating the right way forward, Tim and Dave have shown what can be achieved by single-mindedness, energy, efficiency, and sheer hard work.

Of course what follows is not just a synthesis of the results of developer-funded fieldwork, for the book also draws on the standard academic literature, on the results of research excavations and those of field surveys, and on studies of museum collections. What is new is that these traditional sources have been combined with less familiar material. I have attempted to distil what I learned from field archaeologists, but I have not quoted directly from small circulation documents that would not be available to the reader.

If this book has a distinctive approach, it is that it focuses on landscapes, monuments, and settlement patterns rather than artefacts and their chronology. That is not because such studies are unimportant. Rather, they have been conducted and published with such flair that they do not need to be duplicated here. The other novel feature – a somewhat surprising one – is that it treats Britain and Ireland on the same terms.

A word about the maps. As this book is intended for an international audience, there seems little point in locating the individual sites in relation to local government boundaries that are constantly changing. Instead each chapter includes a map indicating the specific regions mentioned in the text. Britain and Ireland have been divided into twenty-six areas, and the captions for those maps locate every site according to those divisions. The divisions themselves sometimes correspond to modern geographical units, but, more importantly, they divide the study area into sub-units of approximately the same size. They are intended simply as a guide to site location, for it would have been impossible to locate each place mentioned in the text without overloading the drawings.

I have been exceptionally fortunate that so many people have helped this project on its way. The staff of regional archives have been very helpful and many of the field archaeologists whose work has influenced the outcome have been generous with their time, information, and ideas. I am only sorry that they are now so numerous that it impossible to list them here. I am certain that the finished work is the better for their help and advice.

Yet there are also some acknowledgements that must be made individually. Aaron Watson is responsible for all the figure drawings and the great majority of the photographs; the others have been supplied by Francis Pryor, the Cambridge Archaeological Unit, the Highways Agency, and Oxford Archaeology. Different aspects of this research have been supported by my university in Reading, and by English Heritage and Historic Scotland. The whole project would have been impossible without a grant from the Arts and Humanities Research Council, which funded a research assistant for three years and underwrote the preparation of the illustrations.

Finally, some people have been especially helpful in the writing of this work, and they must be mentioned here. Chris Evans, Gill Hey, Carleton Jones, Alan Lupton, and Francis Pryor have allowed me to use their material in the illustrations. I have also been able to cite important material in advance of publication thanks to the kindness of Tim Allen, Alistair Barclay, Stefan Bergh, Kenny Brophy, Alex Brown, Murray Cook, Marion Dowd, Roy Entwistle, Mike Fulford, Paul Garwood, Frances Healy, Gill Hey, Elisa Guerra Doce, Carleton Jones, Hugo Landin-Whymark, David Mullin, Andrew Powell, Francis Pryor, and Helen Roche. Elise Fraser did invaluable work on the bibliography and Chloe Brown on the text. Alison Sheridan read the entire text in draft. She suggested many good ideas and has saved me from many mistakes. Every book is a collaboration between the person named on the cover and those who have helped it in its way, and this is no exception. To all of you – field archaeologists, academics, heritage managers, enthusiasts – I owe a debt of gratitude that this book is intended to repay.

Frontispiece: The view of Ireland from the coast of southwest Scotland, emphasising the short sea crossing between them.

CHAPTER I

THE OFFSHORE ISLANDS

THE VIEW FROM AFAR

The existence of Britain and Ireland posed a problem for the geographers of the Classical world. Their experience was limited to the Mediterranean and they had devised a scheme which saw the cosmos as a circular disc with the sea at its centre. For Hecataeus of Miletus, the land extended northwards into what is now Europe, southwards into Africa, and to the east as far as India, but beyond all these regions there was a river, Oceanus, which encircled the earth and marked the outer limit of the world (Fig. 1.1). Only the dead could reach its farther shore. There were two routes communicating directly between the inner sea and the most distant margin of the land. One was by the Arabian Gulf, whilst the second led through the Straits of Gibraltar into the Atlantic (Cunliffe 2001a: 2–6).

Strictly speaking, the two islands studied in this book were beyond the limits of the world and so they could not exist, yet, as often happens, theory came into conflict with practical experience. Long before the expansion of the Roman Empire there were reasons for questioning the traditional cosmology. Although it is no longer believed that Stonehenge was designed by a Mycenaean architect, there seem to have been some connections between Britain and the Aegean during the second millennium BC, although these links are confined to a few portable artefacts and would have been indirect (A. Harding 2000: chapter 13). In the first millennium, contacts between the Mediterranean and these outer islands intensified during what is known as the Atlantic Bronze Age (Ruiz-Gálvez Priego 1998), and, later still, there are ceramic vessels of Greek origin among the finds from the Thames and other English rivers (Harbison and Laing 1974). Since metalwork of local manufacture has been discovered in the same locations, there is no reason to dismiss the exotic items as spoils of the Grand Tour.

The paradoxical status of Britain and Ireland became even more apparent during the mid-first century BC when Julius Caesar twice invaded southern

England, and again after the Roman Conquest which took place a century later. It was a source of political prestige to have travelled to the limits of the land, and still more to have annexed territory on the outermost edges of the world. Perhaps that is why the emperor Agricola was so anxious to subjugate Orkney, the archipelago off the northern tip of Scotland, and even made plans for an invasion of Ireland (Fitzpatrick 1989).

The very existence of Britain and Ireland seemed impossible to conceive, and yet they had actually been known to travellers for some time. Pytheas explored the Atlantic seaways about 320 BC, but his account was not always believed (Cunliffe 2001b). Tacitus says that it was in AD 85 that the Roman fleet circumnavigated the entire coastline of Britain and first established that it was an island (Rivet and Smith 1979: 93). Even then, people were unsure of its location, and a popular view placed Britain somewhere between Spain and Gaul. The Greek geographer Strabo supposed that Ireland was further to the north. Still more distant was Thule, a frozen landmass that had been described by Pytheas. This was probably Iceland. It became identified with the Shetland Islands simply because they seemed to represent the furthest point where human settlement was possible. Again the sheer remoteness of these places was what impressed Roman writers (Cunliffe 2001b).

Many of these confusions were not resolved until Britain and Ireland were mapped by Ptolemy in the middle of the second century AD. This was a scientific project which drew on observations assembled from a variety of existing sources. It was not the result of original exploration, and it formed only a small part of a larger programme of mapping the then-known world. Ptolemy's map revealed the outlines of both the main islands, prominent capes and headlands, the mouths of important rivers, and the positions of certain mountains and forests. It also included a variety of significant places within the interior, but it was never his intention to document the pattern of settlement (Rivet and Smith 1979: chapter 3). Apart from three important features, the map was basically correct. Following earlier practice, Ireland was still positioned too far to the north. Smaller islands were also located inaccurately and were sometimes shown further from the mainland than was actually the case. A more important difficulty was the depiction of part of Scotland which seemed to extend along an east-west axis, where the experience of early sailors showed that it should have run from south to north. Rivet and Smith have suggested that this arose because of confusion between two different locations represented by the same name, Epidium (1979: 111–13). In their view the map can be reorientated to give a better approximation of the coastline (Fig. 1.2).

Such early accounts also provide evidence of the original names of the largest islands. Britain was first known as 'insula Albionum', the island of the Albiones. Later, that was replaced by Pretannia, which soon became Britannia. Ptolemy's

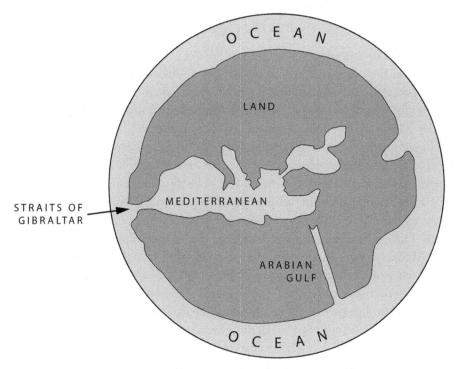

Figure 1.1. The world according to Hecataeus of Miletus.

account distinguishes between Megale Britannia (Great Britain) which refers to the larger island, and Mikra Britannia (Little Britain) which describes Ireland. Elsewhere he refers to them as Alvion and Hivernia, respectively. Ireland was better known by the Greek name Ierne or its Latin equivalent Hibernia (Rivet and Smith 1979: 37–40).

Ptolemy's map of the islands was conceived as a strictly scientific exercise, but accounts of their inhabitants took a different form. Although these texts are sometimes characterised as ethnography, they were conceived within a literary genre which stressed the important differences between the civilised populations of Greece and Rome and the barbarians with whom they came into contact. Indeed, it seems as if geographical distance from these centres of high culture was one way of assessing the features of different populations. Thus those who traded with the Roman world were held in more esteem than other groups; the British were more backward than the Gauls; and the inhabitants of Ireland were more primitive still (J. Taylor 2000). Such accounts were composed according to well-established conventions. Very little of what they said was based on first-hand observation, and many of their contents disagree with the findings of modern archaeology. If Britain and Ireland existed after all, it was important to emphasise that in cultural and geographical terms they remained extremely remote.

THE IMPORTANCE OF BRITISH AND IRISH PREHISTORY

Ireland and Britain were at the limits of the Roman world, but they were also placed on the outer rim of Europe. Much of lowland Britain was eventually incorporated in the Roman Empire, but Ireland remained outside it altogether, and so for significant periods of time did the area that is occupied by Scotland today. Given their marginal position, what can the prehistory of these small islands contribute to a series concerned with world archaeology?

There are several answers to this question, and these will serve to introduce some of the main themes of this book. The first point follows from what has been said already. The inhabitants of Britain and Ireland do not seem to have experienced the drastic changes that characterised other parts of prehistoric Europe, and they remained largely beyond the influence of societies in the Mediterranean. In a recent paper Patrice Brun (2004) has considered the emergence of social stratification over the period from 2500 BC. He follows the conventional distinction between 'chiefdoms', 'complex chiefdoms', and 'early states' and studies a series of regions extending from the Aegean to Scandinavia and from the Balkans to Spain. All these areas underwent major social changes. It was only 'England' that seems to have remained largely unaffected. Here what he calls simple chiefdoms existed continuously from the mid-third millennium BC until the Roman period. Brun acknowledges that there are problems with this kind of scheme, but he also makes an important point. It seems as if the sequence in Britain and Ireland followed a different course from other parts of prehistoric Europe. For that reason their distinctive character deserves to be investigated in detail.

Within that lengthy sequence certain periods and regions have featured in wider discussions of theoretical archaeology. The artefact record has supplied some influential case studies concerned with production and exchange. Ian Hodder (1982a) investigated the distribution of Neolithic axes, and so did Sylvia Chappell (1987) in a study carried out from the United States. The exchange of fine metalwork has also played an important role in archaeological writing. The contents of certain exceptionally rich burials in Wessex are considered in discussions of prehistoric chiefdoms by Colin Renfrew (1973) and Timothy Earle (1991), and during later periods the production and distribution of metalwork provided the basis for Michael Rowlands's influential study of kinship, alliance, and exchange in ancient society (Rowlands 1980).

The early monuments of Britain and Ireland have also inspired some studies with a wider application. These include Colin Renfrew's accounts of monument building and social organisation in southern England and in Orkney (Renfrew 1973; 1979) and Ian Hodder's discussion of the relationship between Neolithic houses and more specialised monuments (1982b: 218–29). Michael Shanks and Christopher Tilley (1982) have investigated Neolithic mortuary

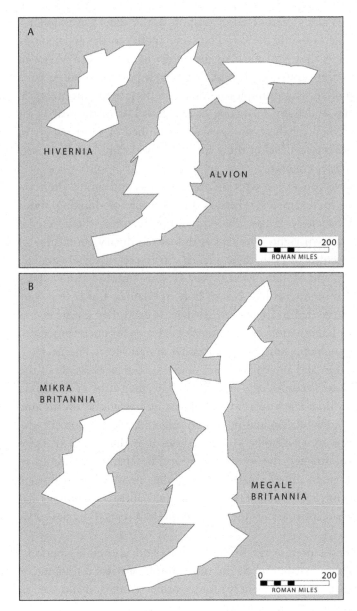

Figure 1.2. A: Ptolemy's map of Britain and Ireland. B: Ptolemy's map as reorientated by Rivet and Smith (1979).

rites in southern Britain, and Tilley himself has published widely quoted interpretations of several prehistoric landscapes in Wales and England (Tilley 1994). The 'royal sites' of Iron Age Ireland have also attracted international attention (Wailes 1982).

These examples are well known, but each of them has been selected to illustrate a particular thesis, and there is a risk of viewing them in isolation. Thus the archaeology of Stonehenge and the surrounding landscape may be very well known, but it is rarely considered in relation to the other developments that happened during the same period. The same applies to the archaeology of megaliths, whether these are the passage tombs of the Boyne Valley in Ireland, the monuments on the Scottish island of Arran, or their counterparts in Orkney. All too often such examples are divorced from their chronological and regional settings and their distinctive character is lost in the search for general principles. Many of these studies were published as short papers in which it was impossible to develop these ideas in any detail. This book sets such research in a wider context.

Those studies were concerned with theoretical issues and simply drew on Britain and Ireland for examples. There is another way of thinking about their distinctive archaeology. It has four outstanding features which deserve investigation in their own right. The first is the extraordinary abundance of monumental architecture in both these islands. Structures like Newgrange, Maeshowe, Avebury, and Stonehenge are very famous, and the same applies to later prehistoric monuments like Navan Fort or Maiden Castle, but they are all too rarely considered in their local settings. Instead they are treated as instances of a wider phenomenon and investigated in terms of general processes. These may involve such apparently practical issues as prehistoric engineering, territorial organisation, and ancient warfare, or more abstract ideas about the importance of ancestors, cosmology, and ritual. The megaliths of Neolithic Ireland have featured in a Darwinian model of mating behaviour, on the one hand, and in discussions of shamanism, on the other (Aranyosi 1999; Lewis-Williams and Pearce 2005: chapter 8). Sometimes it is the details of these structures that have attracted the most attention. The chambered tombs in the Boyne Valley contain roughly half the megalithic art in Western Europe (G. Eogan 1999), and the layout of Stonehenge and allied monuments has been studied by archaeoastronomers for nearly a hundred years (Ruggles 1999: 136–9).

A second feature of prehistoric Britain and Ireland is their exceptional material wealth. This is partly due to the distribution of natural resources – copper is quite widely available, there is tin in southwest England and gold in Ireland – but it also depends on the distinctive manner in which finished arte-facts were deposited (Bradley 1998a). Discoveries of high-quality metalwork do not provide a representative sample of the artefacts that were once available, for their raw material could easily have been recycled. Instead these objects were deposited in graves and in natural locations such as rivers and bogs. That is why they have survived to the present day. Nor were all these objects of local manufacture, for many of them were made from foreign ores and deposited far from their sources. The Thames, for example, is nowhere near any deposits of copper or tin, and yet it includes one of the highest densities of prehistoric weapons anywhere in Europe. Both Britain and Ireland participated in the circulation of metalwork over considerable distances, and they are not alone in containing an exceptional number of votive deposits. It is the range of contacts illustrated by these finds which makes them so remarkable.

A third element is perhaps the product of an exceptionally long history of landscape archaeology in these islands. In Britain, this began with the work of antiquarians like John Aubrey and William Stukeley (Sweet 2004), and, in Ireland, it intensified with the topographical records collected by the Ordnance Survey a hundred and fifty years ago (Herity and Eogan 1977: 7–9, Waddell 2005: 97-103). Both countries shared a tradition of documenting surface remains, especially those of earthworks. This first drew attention to a feature that still distinguishes their archaeology from that of other regions. It seems as if the landscape was subdivided by fields and boundaries at an earlier date, and sometimes on a larger scale, than any other part of prehistoric Europe. In the later years of the nineteenth century the tradition of topographical survey extended to settlement excavation, and the early twentieth century saw the development of aerial survey. In England, this revealed new features of the prehistoric landscape at a time when similar methods were rarely used in other countries.

The final characteristic of Britain and Ireland is the most obvious of all, for both are islands located some distance from Continental Europe. Each is accompanied by a series of much smaller islands with a distinctive archaeology of their own (Fig. 1.3). A number of them provide important evidence of prehistoric activity, such as Rathlin Island and Lambay Island off the Irish coast, both of which include stone axe quarries, or the Isle of Man midway between Ireland and England, with its distinctive chambered tombs. Just as important are the archipelagos where many monuments and settlements survive. These include the Inner and Outer Hebrides to the west of Scotland, and Orkney and Shetland which are usually referred to as the Northern Isles. The list could be much longer, but in each case the archaeological record has some unusual features.

This raises a wider issue, for it is sometimes supposed that island societies develop a peculiar character of their own. They can build extraordinary field monuments. This argument has been influential in the archaeology of the Mediterranean (Broodbank 2000) and has been applied to Polynesia, too (Kirch 2000). It could certainly account for such remarkable phenomena as the megalithic tombs of Neolithic Orkney or the Iron Age towers of the Hebrides and the Northern Isles, but on a larger scale it might also characterise Britain and Ireland as a whole, for they include unusual forms of architecture which are not known in Continental Europe. Perhaps the most distinctive are the henges and cursus monuments of the Neolithic period.

Two of these observations help to set the limits of this account. In a sense this study cannot commence until both these regions were islands. Before that time the area occupied by England, Wales, and Scotland was continuous with Continental Europe and should not be considered in its own terms. This investigation begins when their geography assumed more or less its present form, although the territories of present-day Scotland and Ireland may have been uninhabited. This is also an account of their *prehistory*, and, although it is not an entirely satisfactory term, it helps to define where this account should end. It concludes with their discovery by travellers from the Mediterranean and their incorporation in a wider world.

THE SENSE OF ISOLATION

Britain and Ireland did not assume their present forms simultaneously, and this had serious consequences for their ecology and for the hunter gatherers who lived there. Ireland was cut off by the sea at a time when Britain was still attached to the European mainland. That happened well before Ireland had any inhabitants and certainly before a number of animal species could have become established. They include wild cattle, elk, red deer, and roe deer, none of which formed part of the native fauna. Britain, on the other hand, was continuously settled from the end of the Ice Age and had already been colonised by these species before it was separated from the Continent. Because this happened quite late in the development of postglacial vegetation, it also had thirty percent more plant species than its western neighbour (Bell and Walker 2004: 167–8). The time interval is extremely significant. It seems as if Ireland became detached from southwest Scotland by a narrow channel. This had happened by about 12,000 BC as the polar ice cap melted and sea levels rose. The English Channel had formed by 8000 BC, and the fertile plain that linked what is now eastern England to northern France, the Low Countries, and Denmark was gradually reduced in size between about 10,000 and 6000 BC, when Britain was completely cut off from the Continent (Shennan and Andrews 2000; Fig. 1.4). Finds from the bed of the North Sea show just how important this area had been (B. Coles 1998; Flemming, ed. 2004).

The earliest settlement of Ireland seems to have taken place by boat around 8000 BC (Woodman 2004). By this stage the North Sea plain was already threatened by the rising water, but it was before large areas of territory had been lost. The earliest dates from Scotland are of the same order. They begin around 8500 BC and increase in frequency after a thousand years. They are similar to those from west and north Wales (David and Walker 2004). The Isle of Man was separated from Britain and Ireland by about 8000 BC and may also have been colonised by sea. It appears that this took place sometime before 6500 BC (McCartan 2004). Some of the islands off the west coast of Scotland were also used from an early date. Orkney was eventually settled by hunter gatherers, and there are other early sites in the Shetland Islands (Melton and Nicholson 2004). It is uncertain whether the Outer Hebrides were occupied, although the results of pollen analysis do raise that possibility (Edwards 2004).

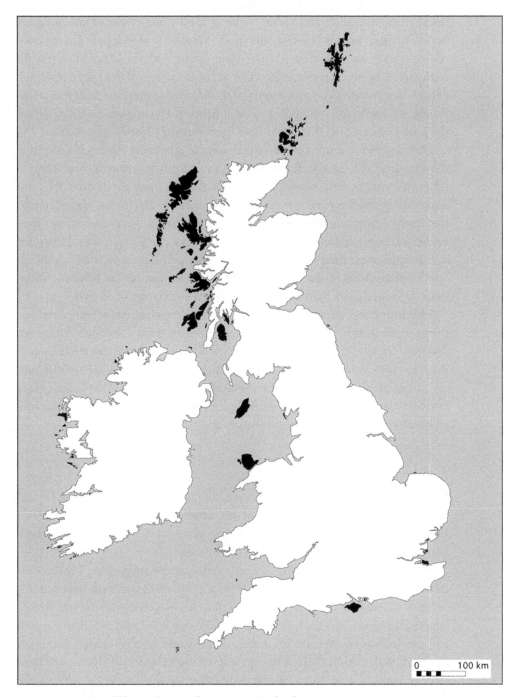

Figure 1.3. The offshore islands of Britain and Ireland.

Ireland was obviously colonised long after any land bridge had been sev-
ered, and there are points in common between the material culture of its first
inhabitants and the artefacts found in Britain. That connection seems to have
been quite short lived, and from about 6000 BC it seems as if their histories

diverged. Significantly, there is no evidence for the movement of raw materials between these islands. In fact, the Irish Mesolithic developed a distinctive character of its own which it shared to some extent with the Isle of Man. It had a distinctive settlement pattern, too. The occupation sites of the later Mesolithic period concentrate along rivers and the shoreline, and there are indications that fishing was particularly important. That is hardly surprising since wild pigs were the only large animals that could have been hunted (Woodman 2004).

The material culture of Mesolithic Ireland gradually diverged from that found in England, Scotland, and Wales. A similar process seems to have affected relations between Britain and Continental Europe from about 7500 BC, and again new artefact types came into use. Roger Jacobi (1976) has suggested that this resulted from the formation of the English Channel and the loss of a land bridge joining Britain to the mainland. This raises chronological problems, for at that stage some links were still possible, although the rising sea made direct communication increasingly difficult. At all events this was the first time when what happened in Britain assumed a distinctive character of its own.

That introduces another theme of this book. To what extent were developments in prehistoric Britain independent from those in Continental Europe, and how far were they simply a continuation of them? How much evidence is there for the establishment of local identities in different parts of both islands, and, in particular, did events in Ireland and Britain follow a different course from one another? One way of defining local practices is to compare the archaeological records on either side of the Irish Sea.

THE LIE OF THE LAND

Such local traditions first emerged during the lengthy period in which Britain and Ireland were separated, first from one another, and then from Continental Europe. They were also influenced by the physical character of both islands and the pattern of communication within them.

At this point it is essential to say more about their geography. That immediately raises the problem of names (Fig. 1.5). It would be easy to write this account in terms of current political boundaries, which divide the two islands between England, Scotland, and Wales, on the one hand, and Northern Ireland and the Irish Republic, on the other. That would be misleading. Although England, Wales, and Scotland occupy almost the same territories as they have since the middle ages, a similar argument does not apply to Ireland. Six of the modern counties form part of the United Kingdom, whilst the remainder comprise a separate nation state. As *Ulaid*, Ulster was one of the ancient kingdoms of Ireland, but it was more extensive than the area that is under British rule and called by that name today. Thus it is best to refer to Ireland as a whole except where the archaeological evidence requires a different procedure. The other geographical unit is the island of Britain which was accepted as a distinct entity from the time of the first explorers. It is no longer accurate to talk of

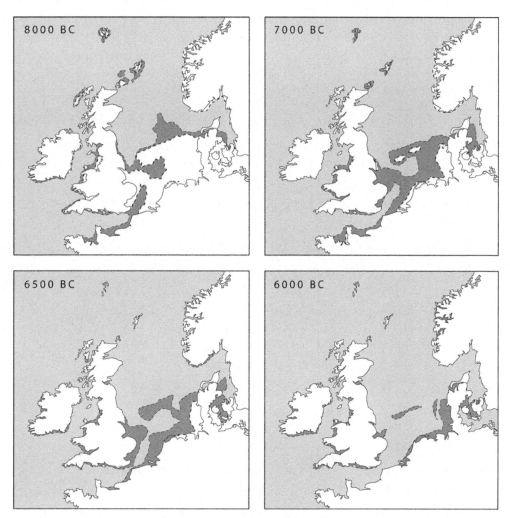

Figure 1.4. Stages in the separation of Britain from the Continent. Information from B. Coles (1998) and Shennan and Andrews, eds. (2000).

the 'British' Isles since most of Ireland is an independent country. In recent years, Scotland and Wales have achieved a measure of political autonomy, and in this account they are treated simply as topographical units. There is nothing to suggest that they possessed any cultural cohesion during the prehistoric period.

These points are important, for scholars have been careless in writing about the two islands. They have sometimes treated Ireland as a dependency of its neighbour, even in periods when this was not the case. They can also use the name England as a synonym for the island of Britain. Quite often this conveys the unconscious idea that certain areas were at the centre of events and that others were largely peripheral. Norman Davies (1999), who devoted many pages to documenting this confusion, eventually called his account of insular history by the neutral title 'The Isles'.

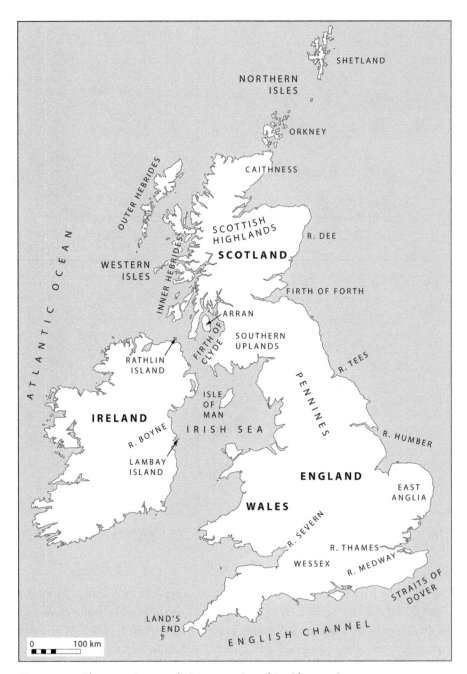

Figure 1.5. Places, regions, and rivers mentioned in Chapter One.

The two main islands have a different physical structure from one another. Britain has been divided by prehistorians into a Highland Zone towards the north and west and a Lowland Zone to the south and east (C. Fox 1932). That does not do justice to the complexity of the situation. Even within the Lowland Zone, there are significant differences of elevation which have

Figure 1.6. Land over 200 metres in Britain and Ireland.

had a major impact on the distribution of settlement; and large tracts of land which form part of the Highland Zone include sheltered, well-drained soils as capable of supporting farmers as regions further to the south (Fig. 1.6). For example, many areas along the east coast of Scotland have the characteristics conventionally associated with southern Britain. In the same way, some of the exposed chalkland along the English Channel coast may have been less hospitable than parts of northern England. Human activity often focused on the valleys of major rivers, extending up the east coast from the Medway to the Dee and along the west coast from the Severn to the Solway. This was not recognised by archaeologists until aerial survey extended into these regions.

That is not to say that the distinction between upland and lowland regions was unimportant, but it could probably be expressed in a better way. England and the southern part of Scotland are bisected by a spine of hills and mountains which run from south to north before they broaden out into larger areas of raised ground, the Southern Uplands and the Scottish Highlands, respectively. These are separated from one another by a system of valleys extending across country between the Forth and the Clyde. There are other regions of high ground along the shores of the Atlantic and the Irish Sea. Western Britain is often more exposed than the land along the North Sea, and this difference may have had a greater influence over the distribution of early settlement than the conventional division between Highland and Lowland Zones.

No such distinction would be appropriate in Ireland, where discontinuous areas of high ground extend around considerable sections of the coast and enclose the Central Lowland, parts of which contain poorly drained raised bogs. Although there are many local exceptions, the best land is found to the south and east, and much of the poorest is towards the north and west. A band of particularly favourable soils follows the coastline of the Irish Sea. The west coast is exposed to the full force of bad weather coming in from the Atlantic. These distinctions are clearly illustrated by the sizes of modern farms, which are generally larger to the east and south. Again there are a number of fertile river valleys (Aalen, Whelan, and Stout 1997).

There are important differences between land use in the two islands. These are largely the result of differences of temperature and rainfall. In Britain, southern England experiences most sunshine; northern and western Scotland have the least. Today the areas with lower precipitation are more suitable for growing crops. The crucial threshold is about 90 cm of rain a year. This permits cereal growing across most lowland regions and allows it to extend up the North Sea coast into Scotland (Coppock 1976a, 1976b). By contrast, rainfall is rather higher to the west of the mountains which divide the island in half, and here there is a greater emphasis on livestock. A similar distinction can be observed in the pattern of settlement, with larger groups towards the east and south, and smaller, more dispersed settlements to the north and west.

To a large extent the same is true in Ireland, where there are similar contrasts in natural conditions. The main areas which are suitable for growing crops are towards the south and east coasts which experience more hours of sunshine than other areas. Dairy farming is important in the north and west of the island. The character of settlement varies from one region to another, but again it is more dispersed towards the west where it is cooler and damper (Aalen, Whelan, and Stout 1997).

Having said this, another observation is important. The Classical authors quoted at the beginning of this chapter made much of the remote position of Britain and Ireland. They even persuaded themselves that Shetland was the most distant place in which human beings could live. They were able to make such claims because the early travellers were able to establish their locations by the position of the sun. It is certainly true that in terms of modern geography, Land's End is on the same latitude as Newfoundland, and Edinburgh is as far north as Moscow, but such observations are deceptive because of the effects of the Gulf Stream. This warms the land from southwest England to the Northern Isles and makes it considerably more hospitable than would otherwise be the case.

The natural environment changed significantly during the postglacial period (Huntley and Birks 1983). A few species were present from the outset, notably hazel, birch, and pine. Oak began to colonise England and Wales by about 8500 BC and was present in Ireland by 8000 BC. The latter period also saw the appearance of elm in England and Wales, and over the next thousand years it established itself in Ireland and then in Scotland. After that, other species assumed an increasing significance. Alder was growing in England around 6300 BC, and over time it spread to Wales and Ireland and finally to Scotland. Lime became important in Wales and England from approximately 5000 BC, and ash appeared roughly simultaneously.

This might give the impression that what had been a rather open landscape was colonised by dense woodland, and this is a stereotype which has been hard to eradicate. In his famous book *The Personality of Britain* Cyril Fox declared:

> Southern Britain presented an illimitable forest of "damp oakwood", ash and thorn and bramble, largely untrodden. The forest was in a sense unbroken, for without emerging from its canopy a squirrel could traverse the country from end to end. (1932: 82)

That may not be true. There are several reasons for believing that the vegetation cover was less uniform than environmentalists once supposed. It is clear that it formed a complex mosaic which was sensitive to the local topography, climate, and soils. There were regional differences in its composition even over quite small areas, and different species predominated from one region to another. For example, by the end of the Scottish Mesolithic only the southern half of the country was actually dominated by oak. Parts of the North Sea littoral and much of the west coast had a significant component of hazel, and this pattern extended as far as the Inner Hebrides. The Outer Hebrides, Caithness, and the Northern Isles were dominated by birch, whilst pine flourished in the mountainous interior (Tipping 1994a).

There are problems in understanding this evidence because certain species produce much more pollen than others. This could mask the evidence for areas of open ground. In any case there were many breaks in the canopy. Perhaps the most obvious were at the coast and beside lakes and rivers, but there were regions which were above the treeline altogether. These included high ground in Wales, northern England, and the north of Scotland. In each case the more open conditions would have attracted concentrations of grazing animals which could have had a further impact on the vegetation. The same was true along the paths which they followed through the landscape. Other breaks in the cover might have formed quite naturally as trees died or as areas of woodland were affected by storms or lightning strikes (T. Brown 1997). Once this had happened, these clearings could have been maintained or even enlarged by herbivores. Naturally created breaks in the forest cover might also be exploited by burning (Simmons 1996), but there is uncertainty whether this was deliberate. Nor can scholars agree on how far Britain and Ireland were covered by closed forest (Vera 2000). Recent work on the English chalk even suggests that some areas were never colonised by woodland in the way that had always been supposed (French and Lewis 2005).

THE WATERWAYS

Grazing animals may have moved along the rivers. The same must surely apply to the paths followed by prehistoric people, and yet this simple idea is seldom taken seriously. There is a long-standing assumption in British archaeology that the main patterns of communication followed what are known as ridgeways: long-distance routes extending across the high ground. It is difficult to appreciate how tenacious such ideas can be. Avebury, for example, is thought to be located at one end of a long-distance path that extends to the flint mines of eastern England. Hillforts of later date were built at roughly equal intervals along this track.

Some of these routes did play a role as drove roads during the historical period, but their relevance to prehistoric archaeology is doubtful. They are cut by ancient boundary ditches which take no account of their existence. The same applies to early field systems and to excavated settlements. There is a simple reason why this idea became so popular. Before very much was known about the natural environment of Britain, archaeologists had assumed that the hills were free of vegetation and that the lowlands were forested and sparsely settled (C. Fox 1932). Nothing could be more misleading, but it was true that many low-lying monuments had been levelled by the plough whilst their counterparts on the higher ground survived. In the end it took the development of aerial photography to redress the balance.

This first raised the possibility that it was the major valleys that saw most prehistoric activity. It also suggested that the rivers would provide a more likely system of communication than a network of upland paths. That was also implied by numerous finds of logboats dating to every period from the

Mesolithic onwards. Andrew Sherratt (1996) has drawn attention to the way in which a number of English rivers share exactly the same names, often ones of considerable antiquity. It had been supposed that this happened because communities were so isolated that they were unaware of the duplication, but there is such striking evidence for the long-distance movement of artefacts that this seems most improbable. Perhaps certain rivers shared the same name because they were connected in people's minds; they formed distinct sections of more extensive routes. In fact Sherratt's argument goes considerably further, for he postulates two major sources of origin for these patterns of communication. One was the Thames Estuary and the other was the south coast of Wessex. By following major rivers, travellers might have been able to avoid some of the most difficult waters along the coast and pass safely from the English Channel to the Irish Sea. A third major focus surely existed in northeast England and linked the Humber Estuary to the midlands and the west coast of Britain. Sherratt did not take his model any further, merely suggesting some points of contact along the Irish Sea. Carleton Jones has taken a similar approach to prehistoric Ireland, although here some of the major rivers may have been less suitable for transport than their counterparts in Britain (C. Jones in press). In this case more use may have been made of higher ground. Figure 1.7 combines both these schemes so that they link eastern England to the Atlantic. Sherratt argues that the nodal points in this system of communication were selected for major monuments, from the first ceremonial centres to late prehistoric hillforts.

These routes were only a part of a wider pattern. Sherratt (1996) observes that one of their sources, the Thames Estuary, was ideally placed for contacts with Continental Europe by the Rhine and the Seine. Similarly, the coast of Wessex was easy to reach from Brittany and Normandy. He calculates the distances between significant parts of the European coastline. Many different areas are within a hundred kilometres of one another. This suggests links not just between western Britain and the east of Ireland, but also between parts of southern England and northern France (Fig. 1.8). Even more areas are within two hundred kilometres of one another, suggesting potential connections between the entire coastline of southern England and the area between Finistère and the Rhine. That zone also extends northwards into East Anglia. Towards the Atlantic, it links western England, Wales, and southwest Ireland. There are other potential connections between the north of Ireland and the west coast of Scotland. The North Sea is the one exception, cutting Britain off from Scandinavia, but even those areas could be linked by following the shoreline by way of Belgium and the Netherlands.

The important point is that different regions of Britain and Ireland could have been in contact with parts of mainland Europe that had few connections with one another. The principal contrast, and one which will be discussed throughout this book, is between an axis based on the English Channel and the North Sea, and another which extended from Britain and Ireland into

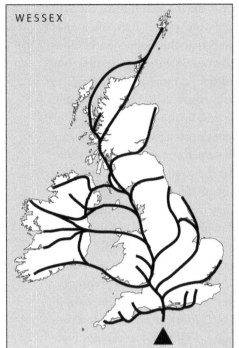
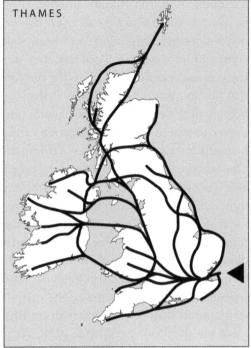
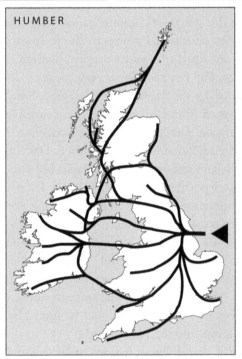

Figure 1.7. Riverine connections extending from the coast of Wessex, the Thames Estuary, and the Humber Estuary. Information from Sherratt (1996) and Jones (in press), with additions.

Figure 1.8. The distance between different parts of the shorelines of Britain, Ireland, and the near-Continent. The figure indicates potential connections between different areas at distances of 100 km and 200 km and does not allow for the practicalities of marine navigation. Information from Sherratt 1996, with additions and modifications.

Atlantic Europe. The first linked England and Scotland to an enormous area extending from France to south Scandinavia. The second joined southwest England, Wales, and Ireland to western France and the Iberian peninsula. Sherratt's scheme does not take into account the practicalities of travelling by water, but there have been important studies of ancient routes across the English Channel (McGrail 1977: 207–22 and 265–88). A little-known paper by Margaret Davies (1946) took a similar approach to navigation in the Irish Sea (Fig. 1.9).

McGrail's research was specifically concerned with the sea routes documented by Classical writers in the immediate pre-Roman period. This is important because it explains some of the premises of his argument. It is concerned with trade in bulky commodities including wine amphorae and tin. It also presupposes that ships were equipped with sails. This is a reasonable proposition and is supported by depictions of late prehistoric vessels, but it is likely that earlier boats were rowed or paddled. He confines his attention to the routes suggested by written accounts and compares their suitability for long-distance voyages in relation to sea conditions, visibility, prevailing winds, and currents.

McGrail concludes that the most dependable sea routes were those crossing the English Channel towards its narrowest point at the Straits of Dover. They were a little more reliable than the passage from the River Rance in northwest France to the mouth of the Hampshire Avon, yet all of them were significantly better than the longer crossing between Finistère and the southwestern peninsula of Britain. The most favourable route had a 'reliability factor' of 100; the least suitable scored 43. McGrail's figures also suggest that a sensible procedure would have been to use one of the easier routes from the Continent to Britain and then to sail along the coast. The coastal route between Wessex and different parts of southwest England scored between 81 and 100.

McGrail's analysis does not extend far beyond the English Channel, nor is it directly concerned with earlier prehistory. Davies's paper does both, although it actually investigates the distribution of megalithic tombs. It is concerned mainly with the Irish Sea, although her study area extends from southwest Wales to the coast of Scotland. She draws attention to a number of important factors, not all of which are relevant to the area considered by McGrail. Like the Mediterranean, the Irish Sea is partly enclosed. It is rather more open to the south, but to the north it is entered through a narrow channel. There are powerful tides which converge on the Isle of Man from both directions. Thus they provide a series of sea routes from northwest and southwest Wales and create potential links between Ireland, southwest Scotland, and Cumbria (Waddell 1992). There is slack water from the southern tip of the Isle of Man westwards towards the Irish coast, and it would have made that region particularly accessible by sea.

There were also certain hazards to avoid. These included whirlpools and eddies in the areas with the strongest tides. On the other hand, in good weather travellers in these waters would never have been out of sight of land, for the Irish Sea is ringed by a series of distinctive peaks which can be recognised from the water (E. Bowen 1972: 40–1). All were more than six hundred metres high, which means even the lowest of them could have been identified under optimum conditions from a distance of ninety kilometres. Further to the north, navigation would have been easier since it was possible to travel from one offshore island to another without venturing far into open water. The same could have been true along the less sheltered northern and western coasts of Ireland and the north of Scotland. People could also have travelled up the North Sea coast of Britain, between estuaries like those of the Humber and the Tees and the drowned valleys known as firths along the Scottish shoreline.

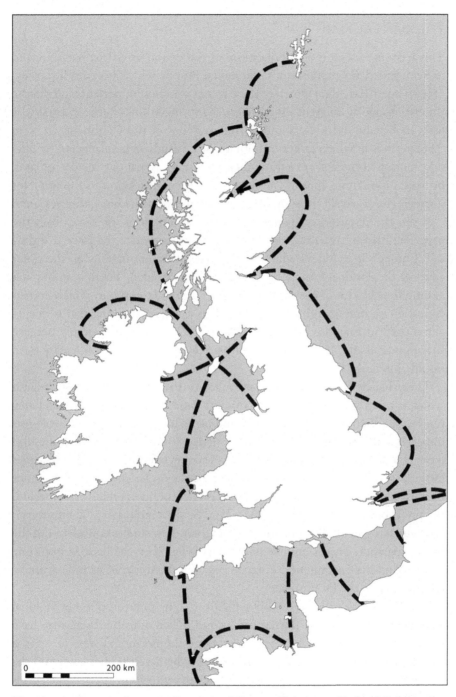

Figure 1.9. Sea route between Continental Europe, Britain, and Ireland. Information from C. Fox (1932), M. Davies (1946), and McGrail (1997).

THE MENTAL MAP

This account raises important questions of perception. Are Britain and Ireland to be regarded as extensions of Continental Europe which were readily accessible by boat? If so, then which of these routes was most important, and did the pattern change at different times? Were the strongest links between particular parts of Britain and Ireland and separate regions of the Continent, or were there periods in which either or both of these islands were unaffected by outside contacts? Is it correct to study their prehistory as that of two areas of land, or would it be more appropriate to think of them in relation to the sea? Not surprisingly, nearly all these options have been investigated in earlier research.

Again the discussion depends on certain assumptions inherited from the past. The British have always had an ambivalent attitude to the place that they call 'Europe'. It is a view which they share with other nations on the outer edges of the continent, including Denmark and Sweden. There is an implicit assumption that Europe is somewhere else: a distinct entity to which certain countries are only marginally attached. It is a way of thinking that is deeply entrenched in English culture and one which is exacerbated simply because Britain is an island. It is supposed to have preserved its cultural integrity from outside influence.

These beliefs have coloured approaches to the prehistory of both islands which is often written in terms of modern political divisions. This tendency can be identified at a variety of scales and has made the work of archaeologists unnecessarily difficult. It is normally done for convenience, but the question is rarely asked whether these distinctions had any relevance to social identities in the past. The main division is between books on Britain and books about Ireland. There are also scholarly and persuasive accounts of prehistoric England, the pre-Roman archaeology of Wales, and Scottish prehistory. There is even one which is specifically concerned with Ulster. Few studies consider both the islands together. That is quite extraordinary when they can be seen from one another and the geographical distance between them can be as little as thirty kilometres (see the Frontispiece).

That procedure makes it doubly difficult to think in terms of other regional alignments. For example, during the second millennium BC there may have been closer connections between Ireland and the north and west of what is now called Scotland than there were between the Scottish Highlands and the southern part of that country. Nor is it necessary to limit these connections exclusively to Britain and Ireland. Between about 1500 and 800 BC southeast England had strong links with what is now northern France (Marcigny and Ghesquière 2003: 164–74), and before the Roman Conquest there were many features in common between Brittany and southwest England.

At the same time prehistorians in both islands have exhibited a sense of cultural insecurity. There are different reasons for this. One is purely methodological. Before the advent of radiocarbon dating, insular archaeologists were almost entirely dependent on chronologies developed on the mainland. Normally these were based on events in the Mediterranean or Egypt. Such schemes could be extended to the outermost margins of Europe only by emphasising connections between these areas. There was no alternative to this procedure, but it raised a problem, for it was necessary to say why those connections were possible and how they had occurred. They were generally explained by the movement of people and ideas from the complex societies of southern and central Europe towards the edges of the Continent. It was a method that had its strengths and weaknesses. Thus Stuart Piggott (1938) could suggest what still seem plausible links between a few artefacts from Bronze Age burials in southern England and the contents of the shaft graves of Mycenae. Richard Atkinson (1956) took the view that Stonehenge had been designed by a Mediterranean architect, a theory which can be rejected in the light of radiocarbon dating.

This procedure had unexpected side effects. One was the assumption that Britain and Ireland occupied such a peripheral position in Europe that artefacts of Continental affinities would have been adopted only after a significant interval of time. That is why so many phenomena have proved to be significantly older than was first supposed; there have been few chronological adjustments in the opposite direction. The other feature was a predilection for naming insular phenomena after well-defined sites or cultural groupings on the Continent. Thus Gordon Childe's *Prehistoric Communities of the British Isles* refers to Mesolithic traditions as 'Tardenoisian', after a site in France, and 'Azilian', after another in Spain. There were 'West Alpine' settlements in lowland England during the Bronze Age, and Iron Age groups were named after places or regions in Austria, Switzerland, and France (Childe 1949). This process seems to have operated in only one direction, and, with the exception of the 'Wessex Culture', British and Irish terminology was rarely employed on the mainland.

The influence of this way of thinking is illustrated by the title of one of the most famous books on insular prehistory, Cyril Fox's monograph *The Personality of Britain*. It subtitle is revealing, for it considers 'Its influence on inhabitant and invader in prehistoric and early historic times'. It concludes with a list of twenty propositions. Among them are these statements:

> The position of Britain adjacent to the Continent renders her liable to invasion from any point on some five hundred miles of the European coast.

> The portion of Britain adjacent to the continent being Lowland, it is easily overrun by invaders and on it new cultures of continental origin tend to be *imposed*. In the Highland, on the other hand, these tend to be *absorbed* (emphasis in the original) (C. Fox 1932: 77).

Although these ideas were first published in 1932, Fox's book was reissued in successive editions until 1959. It blends artefact studies and historical geography

so adroitly that it is difficult to remember why so many migrations were postulated in the first place. That was because arguments about chronology had
become entangled in questions of explanation. Writing in 1966, Grahame
Clark questioned the 'invasion hypothesis'. It was used uncritically and had
been applied to almost every archaeological problem (Clark 1966).

Irish archaeologists had experienced the same difficulties in working out a
chronology, and resorted to similar methods to those of their British colleagues,
but in this case there was another problem This was because of the origin myth
set out in *Lebor Gabála Érren*, the 'Book of the Taking of Ireland' (Waddell
2005a: 18-23). It describes five successive invasions which were responsible for
the settlement of the country. Timothy Champion (1982) has pointed out that
some of their sources seem to come from the Bible and others from universal
histories composed in the late Roman period. The invaders appear to have
originated in Greece and the east Mediterranean. Although this account was
never taken literally, it had an influence on the way in which Irish prehistory
was studied, and it is surely significant that its translator and editor, Robert
Macalister, was the professor of archaeology at University College, Dublin.
Like the British scholars criticised by Grahame Clark, Irish archaeologists were
tempted by the invasion hypothesis, and it was not until 1978 that its usefulness
began to be questioned (Waddell 1978).

There are two ways of resolving this confusion. The more radical is simply
to assert that the present-day notion of Britain and Ireland as self-contained
entities is itself an anachronism. It has no relevance to the prehistoric period,
and the differences between separate communities may have been less clear-
cut in the past. For example, Caesar records that the same kings ruled territories on either side of the English Channel (*Bello Gallico* II 4, 6–7). Ewan
Campbell (2001) has expressed a similar idea in discussing the relationship
between early medieval Ireland and the kingdom of Dalriada on the west
coast of Scotland. The sea may not have been a barrier but a connecting
link.

Another approach is to explain the movement of artefacts and ideas by an
ill-defined notion of 'trade', but again this runs a certain risk of anachronism.
It seems likely that the exchange of artefacts had more to do with diplomacy
than economics (Sahlins 1974: chapters 4 and 5). The movement of goods and
services may actually have been a way of forming and maintaining alliances,
but once that possibility is raised, prehistorians face another problem. They
may be captivated by the diffusion of fine pottery and metalwork, but such
evidence may be only the visible residue of an exchange of personnel. Instead
of long-distance trade in swords and spears, perhaps they might consider the
circulation of marriage partners. People were always on the move. The question
is how frequently this happened and how many of them settled in new places
as a result. Much of the trouble is created by the language of archaeology.
The movement of people overland is seen as settlement or migration; their

relocation by sea is regarded as an invasion. That is hardly appropriate when the island of Britain is nearly a thousand kilometres long and is separated from northern France by a twentieth of that distance.

OBSERVING WHAT HAS VANISHED

There are many ways of writing about the prehistory of these two islands. What does this version have to offer?

The first point to make is that it attempts to cover the prehistory of Britain and Ireland on equal terms, and in each case it is informed by the results of commercial archaeology, many of which have yet to enter the public domain. They represent a vital resource for future scholars, but one which is too little known. At many points they have provided information which is radically different from conventional wisdom about the past. They have identified new kinds of monuments and have extended the work of archaeologists into areas that had hardly been investigated before. They also suggest unexpected links between developments in different regions.

This book is intended as a contribution to social archaeology, and the main approach is to concentrate on settlements, monuments, and landscapes rather than portable artefacts. To some extent this is a matter of personal taste, but it is more than that. For many years the prehistory of Britain and Ireland had been studied through material culture, even though little was known about its original contexts. The work of recent years has helped to redress the balance so that the deposits of valuables which had normally been discovered by chance can be investigated in relation to other less spectacular phenomena. It is an approach that not only builds on the results of field archaeology, but also can take into account research on the prehistoric environment.

Chronology still presents a problem, and is likely to do so until AMS dating becomes a standard feature of any excavation. It is also important to extend current programmes concerned with the analysis of individual objects. The difficulty is exacerbated by questions of terminology. Wherever possible, this account refers to calibrated radiocarbon dates, as the period labels that are in common use were devised during the nineteenth century at a time when the importance of technological innovation was taken for granted. It would be helpful if the terms Neolithic, Bronze Age, and Iron Age could be abandoned altogether, but that might lead to problems of communication. In any case attempts to devise more flexible schemes have not been altogether successful. For example, in his book *The Age of Stonehenge* Colin Burgess (1980) defined a series of periods named after excavated sites, but there were problems with this procedure. Some of those excavations had not been published at the time and one of the sites has since been redated. Burgess admitted this rather ruefully when the book was reprinted twenty years later, but he did not alter its contents (Burgess 2001: 13–14).

The chapter divisions do not follow the conventional framework laid down by the Three Age Model. Thus the end of the Mesolithic period is considered together with the first half of the Neolithic. The Later Neolithic is treated together with the Earlier Bronze Age, for whilst there is a clear distinction between these periods in some areas, in others that does not apply. Major changes happened halfway through the Bronze Age, and this is acknowledged by treating the later part of this period in a chapter on its own. The same applies to the earlier Iron Age.

There has been a tendency to write at length about periods where the available material is plentiful and varied and to devote less space to phases when the archaeological record is more homogeneous. That does not do justice to the realities of prehistoric life where a human generation would have remained the same from the Mesolithic to the Iron Age. To try to provide a more-rounded account of prehistoric Britain and Ireland the length of each chapter is roughly proportional to the length of the period that it studies. It also means that periods that are rarely discussed as a whole are treated on the same terms as those which have textbooks written about them. Within the word limit set by the publisher, this account observes a ratio of roughly two thousand words a century.

Lastly, this book is only one account of a remarkable series of phenomena and is conceived as an interpretation, not a manual. The archaeological literature is overwhelmingly descriptive, whether it consists of accounts of artefacts, field surveys, or excavations, and it is essential that the student master the details of this material. But it is even more important to achieve a sense of perspective, and this has been difficult because so many studies are limited to particular areas and periods of time. There is a need for a bolder treatment, even if it eventually proves to be mistaken. That risk is well worth taking, and it applies not just to this particular version, but to every attempt to come to terms with the past.

CHAPTER 2

A NEW BEGINNING

TWO MODELS

This chapter discusses the beginnings of the Neolithic period in Britain and Ireland and is concerned with the time between approximately 4000 and 3300 BC. That simple statement raises many problems (Figs. 2.1 and 2.2).

In order to work out when the Neolithic started, it is necessary to establish what that term means today. It is a period label which has been inherited from the past and has had rather different connotations from one generation to another. The adjective 'Neolithic' was originally devised to describe a particular kind of technology based on the use of ground and polished stone, although it was soon appreciated that the finished artefacts were often found with ceramics. This definition became less important once it was discovered that these innovations occurred at the same time as the adoption of domesticates. Gordon Childe (1952) even spoke of a 'Neolithic Revolution', a term which he intended to evoke the important social and economic changes associated with the development of farming. Still more recently, attention has shifted to the idea that the Neolithic period also saw profound changes in human attitudes to the world and that these were reflected in the construction of monuments and the use of a more complex material culture (Hodder 1990).

Each of these definitions has a certain validity. The problem is how their different components might be integrated with one another. Thus the oldest characterisation of the Neolithic period works well in England and Scotland, but in Ireland, and possibly in Wales, ground stone artefacts had already been made by hunter gatherers (Costa, Strenke, and Woodman 2005; David and Walker 2004). Monuments do seem to be a new development (Bradley 1998b), but again they cannot characterise the entire Neolithic phenomenon. In most regions they were not built at the very beginning of this period, and there are some areas in which they were never adopted on a significant scale. For example, in southwest Ireland, there is evidence for Neolithic houses, but the conventional range of stone-built tombs is missing and part of the population

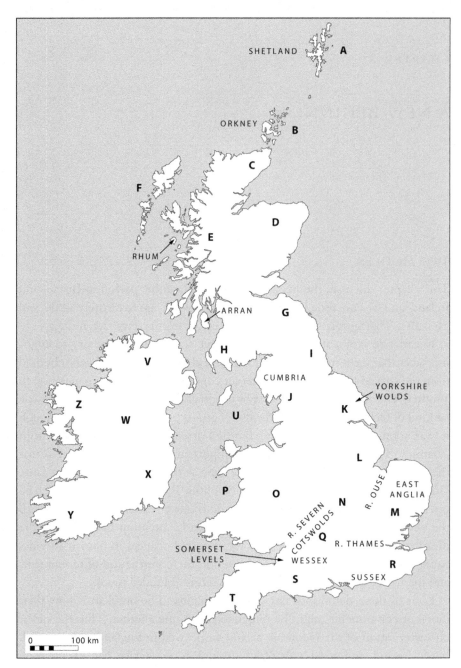

Figure 2.1. Places and regions mentioned in Chapter Two. For the purposes of this
map Britain and Ireland have been divided into 26 areas and the individual sites are
listed according to these divisions. A: Shetland; B: Orkney (*Knap of Howar; Stonehall*);
C: Northern Scotland; D: Northeast and Central Scotland (*Balbridie, Carsie Mains,
Claish; Cleaven Dyke, Littleour, Pitnacree*); E: Western Scotland (*Achnacreebeag*); F: Outer
Hebrides (*Bharpa Carinish, Eilean Domnhuil*); G: Eastern and Central Scotland on either
side of the Firth of Forth (*Balfarg*); H: Southwest Scotland; I: the English/Scottish
borderland; J: Northwest England (*Carrock Fell*); K: Northeast England and the

may have been buried in caves (Ó'Floinn 1992). That also happened in regions like northern England which had a tradition of building mortuary monuments (Barnatt and Edmonds 2002). In the same way, recent fieldwork in Ireland, and to a lesser extent in Scotland and Wales, has produced convincing evidence of houses and cereal growing, but in England this is relatively rare (Grogan 2004a; Darvill 1996). It seems as if different definitions of the Neolithic period apply to each of these islands, and yet their material culture shares many features in common. In particular, the ceramic sequence begins with a series of finely made undecorated vessels which are normally grouped together as Carinated Bowls. They were used until about 3700 BC alongside another ceramic tradition that may first have developed in Brittany (Herne 1986; Cowie 1993; Sheridan 2003a). The development of regional styles of decorated pottery did not happen on a significant scale until later. In much the same way most parts of Britain and Ireland include some of the same kinds of stone artefacts.

A more serious problem involves the question of explanation. How did the insular Neolithic originate? Did it begin among the indigenous hunter gatherers who are described in the conventional terminology as 'Mesolithic'? How was it related to what was happening during the same period in Continental Europe, and to what extent did it develop a distinctive character of its own?

In many ways the evidence from Ireland comes closest to the accepted definition of the Neolithic period (Cooney 2000). Here there were changes in the nature and distribution of settlement and in the character of material culture. Substantial houses are widely distributed and are commonly associated with cereals and domesticated animals. Field systems are known in the west of the country, and over its northern half there is a dense distribution of mortuary monuments. In southern England, on the other hand, the situation is less clear-cut. There are local differences between the distributions of Mesolithic and Neolithic occupation sites, but this is not always the case. In regions like the wetlands of the Somerset Levels (Coles and Coles 1986: chapter 4), wild resources were still exploited, and there may also have been some continuity

Figure 2.1 (*continued*) Peak District (*Duggleby Howe, Rudston, Star Carr*); L: Eastern England between the Humber and East Anglia; M: East Anglia (*Etton, Eynesbury, Fornham All Saints, Haddenham, Springfield*); N: the English Midlands (*Dallington, Husband Bosworth, Raunds, West Cotton*); O: The English/Welsh borderland (*Gwernvale*); P: West Wales from the southwest to Anglesey; Q: the Thames Valley, Cotswolds, and South Midlands (*Abingdon, Ascott under Wychwood, Crickley Hill, Hazleton, Stanwell, Yarnton*); R: Southeast England (*Court Hill, Ramsgate, Whitehorse Stone*); S: Wessex (*Dorset Cursus, Flagstones, Hambledon Hill, Maiden Castle, Robin Hood's Ball, Rybury, Stonehenge*); T: Southwest England (*Aveline's Hole, Carn Brea, Helman Tor, Hembury*); U: the Isle of Man (*Billown*); V: Northern Ireland (*Thornhill*); W: from the Irish Midlands to the east coast (*Knowth*); X: Southeast Ireland; Y: Southwest Ireland (*Ferriter's Cove*); Z: the Irish west coast (*Ballyglass, Carrowmore, Céide*).

in the ways in which stone artefacts were made. In the south the evidence for domestic buildings is very limited indeed (Darvill 1996). Cereals are usually found in small quantities along with evidence of wild plant foods (Moffet, Robinson, and Straker 1989; Robinson 2000), and the material remains of the period are dominated by a series of stone and earthwork monuments which seem to have played a role in public events and in the treatment of the dead (Bradley 1998b).

Such stark contrasts do not extend into every area, but they have given rise to an important debate between the proponents of an 'Irish/Northern British' model which sees the Neolithic period as a radical break with the past (Cooney 2000: chapter 7), and a 'Southern English/Wessex' model which stresses continuity, acculturation, and a mobile pattern of settlement (J. Thomas 1999). Scottish prehistorians have resisted the influence of the English interpretation and have taken exception to the idea that whatever happened in the rich archaeology of the south and east must have established the pattern for both islands (G. Barclay 2001).

These differences extend to the ways in which the archaeological record has been interpreted. Irish prehistorians consider that at the start of the Neolithic period an agricultural economy was introduced by settlement from overseas. Every aspect of the archaeological record seems to have changed quite rapidly, suggesting that the indigenous population soon adopted a new way of life. This model is much the same as that applied to parts of mainland Europe, where it seems as if the northwards spread of farming was accomplished by the settlement of new land (Whittle 1996: chapters 6 and 7). That process had been checked in the early fifth millennium BC, but later it could have resumed. To the west it proceeded without a break, and it may be significant that there is a general resemblance between the first megalithic monuments in Ireland and along the Atlantic façade of Britain and those in northern and western France (Sheridan 2003b). These areas may have been among the sources of a new population. It seems possible that this development began before a Neolithic way of life was established elsewhere.

By contrast, the 'Wessex' model has been influenced by research in Northern Europe, where the Neolithic period began at virtually the same time as it did in Britain (J. Thomas 1988). Again it involved the creation of impressive monuments to the dead, but in this case the remains of houses do seem to have survived. Economic changes took place much more gradually, and in south Scandinavia it seems that at first the settlement pattern was based on domesticated animals. Arable farming on any scale did not appear until later. It seems likely that the early exploitation of domesticates ran in parallel with the continued use of wild resources. The commonest interpretation is that the indigenous people adopted elements of a new way of life through a long period of contacts across the agricultural frontier to the south (Fischer 2002). This is suggested by the presence of pottery and imported axes on Mesolithic sites

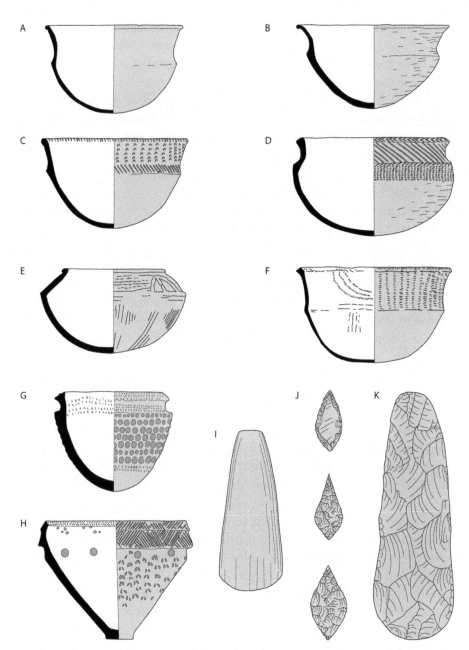

Figure 2.2. Outline drawings of the artefact types mentioned in Chapter Two. A and B: Early Neolithic carinated bowls; C–F: Middle Neolithic decorated styles; G and H: Peterborough Ware; I: ground stone axe; J: leaf-shaped arrowheads; K: unpolished axe.

and may have been related to the development of increased social complexity among the local population. The idea is certainly supported by the evidence of cemeteries. In this case the movement of ideas may have been as important as the movement of farmers.

The southern English model is explicitly based on analogy with the sequence in Scandinavia (J. Thomas 1988), and it is true that the Neolithic of these regions could have had some features in common: an initial emphasis on mobility and the use of domesticated animals; a settlement pattern which in some regions has resulted in the survival of rather insubstantial houses; the formal deposition of elaborate artefacts in pits or similar features; and the construction of various kinds of earthwork monuments including long mounds and, eventually, enclosures. The problem is that these comparisons apply to the Neolithic end of what was a much longer sequence. How does the British and Irish Mesolithic compare with its North European counterpart?

The Scandinavian model depends on several key features: a long period of contact with areas to the south, shown by the movement of nonlocal artefacts and the adoption of an unfamiliar technology; reduced mobility and possibly the year-round occupation of certain favourable locations; increasing evidence of social complexity suggested by the development of cemeteries and votive deposits; and the introduction of small quantities of cereals and domesticated animals to settlements whose economy was otherwise based on hunting, gathering and fishing. These processes seem to have been vital to the adoption of agriculture and to the changes that went with it.

As Peter Rowley-Conwy (2003; 2004) has observed, there are few signs of these features in Mesolithic Britain and Ireland. If anything, the best evidence for social complexity during the Mesolithic comes from the beginning of that phase, and so it can have no bearing on the origins of farming in these countries. The largest domestic buildings all belong to the early Mesolithic, as do the one convincing cemetery at Aveline's Hole and the possible indications of others. The only place with much evidence of ritual activity is the early site at Star Carr (Conneller 2004), and the sole indications of a complex material culture are provided by a series of decorated artefacts which date from the first part of this period. It even seems possible that the settlement pattern in Britain and Ireland became more mobile during the later Mesolithic (Myers 1987; Costa, Strenke, and Woodman 2005). At present there is a single site, at Ferriter's Cove in southwest Ireland, where domesticated animals have been identified in a secure Mesolithic context dating from about 4300 BC (Woodman, Finlay, and Anderson 1999), yet the first unambiguous evidence of cereal pollen on either side of the English Channel dates from between 4050 and 3850 BC (Innes, Rowley-Conwy, and Blackford 2003). The earliest traces of cultivation with the primitive plough known as an ard occurs even later, between about 3500 and 3250 BC (Sherratt 1997: fig. 3.2). Still more important, the settlements which do contain a mixture of Mesolithic and Neolithic material culture are largely found along a restricted section of the Scottish coastline, but there is nothing to prove that both assemblages were in use simultaneously (Wickham-Jones 1990; Armit and Finlayson 1992). Although this could be compared with the evidence from Northern Europe, it seems to be a local phenomenon, and one which may even have happened some time after the beginning of the Neolithic period. It cannot support any model with a wider application.

Indeed, there are signs of discontinuity at the end of the fifth millennium BC and the beginning of the fourth. One of the features that was once supposed to indicate greater control over the environment during the later Mesolithic period was deliberate burning of the natural vegetation (Simmons 1996). This might have increased the food supply and could certainly have helped to concentrate game animals in particularly favourable locations. It is now clear that this was being done from the very beginning of the Mesolithic. If it happened increasingly often, that would be expected as the landscape was invaded by trees. In no sense can this be thought of as a 'pre-adaptation' to farming, and at the beginning of the Neolithic this practice came to an end (Edwards 1998). In the same way, there is new evidence for human diet from the analysis of human bones found near to the sea. This work suggests that during the Mesolithic period coastal communities had made significant use of marine resources, but at the beginning of the Neolithic it was significantly reduced. From that time much greater use was made of terrestrial plants and animals. The sample is limited because few Mesolithic bones survive, but the results of this work can be matched along the Atlantic coastline from Portugal to Brittany and also in south Scandinavia (M. Richards 2003; 2004).

There is another revealing trend in the environmental record. To a large extent the beginning of the Neolithic period corresponds with a dramatic decline in the amount of elm pollen. It no longer seems likely that this is the result of a specific economic practice, like ring-barking growing trees or collecting leaf fodder. It is more likely that the phenomenon results from the rapid spread of a disease which attacked this particular species (Girling and Grieg 1985). It happened over such a restricted period of time that the 'Elm Decline' has been used as a chronological marker, and yet it seems likely that the spread of the disease itself was facilitated by the movement of people on an increasing scale. It may also have been accelerated by the creation of more areas of open ground. According to a recent study this phenomenon has a mean date of 3940 BC (Parker et al. 2002).

The earliest radiocarbon dates for Neolithic artefacts and monuments begin around 4000 BC, and again there seems to have been little or no chronological difference from one end of these islands to the other. These dates raise certain difficulties. This was a period where the calibration of radiocarbon dates is not precise, meaning that the true ages of particular samples have a wide distribution. As a result it is not clear whether the inception of the Neolithic was more like an event than a gradual process. One possibility is that it took place over three centuries or more, starting at about 4000 BC. Another is that the main period of change was rather later and that events moved at a faster

pace. It would certainly be implied by the direct dating of carbonised cereals, which suggests that they appeared around 3800 BC (Alex Brown, pers. comm.). Another difficulty is in deciding when Mesolithic material culture went out of use. There are too few dates to shed much light on that process, but they do show that in Northern England the use of microliths extended into the very beginning of the fourth millennium BC (Spikins 2002: 43).

However this evidence is interpreted, the British and Irish Neolithic apparently draws on two sources. There are a number of obvious links between the insular record and the evidence from Continental Europe. Perhaps this has been obscured because scholars have been looking for a single origin for insular Neolithic artefacts. This has not been found, although there are general links between the undecorated Neolithic pottery of northern France, Belgium, and the southern Netherlands and the earliest pottery in Ireland and Britain (Louwe Koojimans 1976), just as there may have been further connections with northwest France (Sheridan 2003b). It is less clear how the insular flint industries are related to those on the Continent, but in this case some of the variation may result from the use of different raw materials. Far more important are two other elements whose significance is not disputed. The main domesticated animals of the British and Irish Neolithic were cattle, sheep, goats, and pigs. There were no cattle in Ireland during the Mesolithic period, and, in Britain, the native wild cattle were quite distinct from the animals that first appear in the Neolithic period, which have much more in common with those in mainland Europe (Tresset 2003). Pigs could have been domesticated locally, but there are no wild progenitors for sheep or goat in either island. The same applies to wheat and barley. These staples must have been introduced from the Continent, although no traces of seagoing vessels survive.

The second component is monumental architecture, which seems to have become an established feature of the landscape from an early stage of the Neolithic, although this may not have happened immediately (Bradley 1998b). Again it is probably unwise to seek a single source of inspiration for any of these structures, but the tradition of long mounds or 'long barrows' that is so widespread in Britain and Ireland was distributed along the edges of the Continent as far east as Denmark and Poland and as far west as Brittany. Some of the insular structures contained stone chambers of forms that are not unlike those in Atlantic Europe (Sheridan 2003b). In the same way, distinctive earthwork enclosures defined by an interrupted ditch had a very wide distribution on the Continent, reaching from Bornholm to the east to Ireland to the west. It also extends as far south as Spain. They are particularly common in Denmark, northern Germany, Belgium, and the north of France. Many of these monuments are remarkably similar to one another (Bradley 1998b: chapter 5). They also bear a strong resemblance to those in southern Britain and may have been used in the same ways, although in these islands they were first built some time after the earliest long barrows.

Since such connections are widely accepted, why has it been so difficult to define the sources of the British and Irish Neolithic? Perhaps this is because of the islands' distinctive geography, which allowed them to form links with regions of the European mainland that would not have been in regular contact with one another. That may be why the insular Neolithic was so distinctive even when it was obviously influenced by practices in Continental Europe. It drew on many different sources of inspiration. The problem for future research is not to discover *the* source of the insular Neolithic but to explain how so many diverse influences were drawn together in a new synthesis over a short period of time.

Why did Britain and Ireland 'become Neolithic'? It is certainly true, as Julian Thomas (1988) recognised, that this process happened simultaneously across a considerable area. It affected southern Scandinavia at the same time as these two islands. Since there is no evidence for contacts between Britain and Northern Europe during the later Mesolithic period, it suggests that the initial impulse must have begun on the Continent. Four different models have been proposed, and, logically, they should apply not just to Britain and Ireland but to Denmark, Sweden, and The Netherlands as well.

The first is that in each of these areas indigenous hunter-gatherers were well aware of farming communities and their practices but were reluctant to change their way of life. That reluctance might have been because of deep-rooted reservations about Neolithic systems of belief (Bradley 1998b: chapter 2), or it could have been because the local environment was so productive that there was little need to experiment with new ways of producing food. In the first case, their growing exposure to Neolithic customs and material culture might have led to internal tensions and the growth of social inequality. If so, the adoption of farming could have been a social strategy designed to build prestige. The second possibility is that the adoption of domesticates was the result of adverse circumstances as the economic prosperity of local hunter-gatherers was threatened by failures of the food supply (Zvelebil and Rowley-Conwy 1986). Each argument is plausible in itself, but neither seems to have a direct bearing on the prehistory of Britain and Ireland. There is very little evidence for contacts between insular hunter-gatherers and Continental farmers, and there are no signs of social complexity in the insular late Mesolithic. Rather, Ireland became isolated from Britain and Britain became isolated from the European mainland.

Another observation is that Continental farmers had little experience of the sea (Dennell 1985: 174). That is logical since it appears that agriculture spread across the Continent from southeast to northwest. This process was probably accomplished through the movement of people whose only experience would have been of travel overland. That might suggest that the colonisation of Britain and Ireland would have been delayed until the settlers had familiarised themselves with marine navigation. It is a plausible argument, but it fails to account for one important factor, as the insular Neolithic began simultaneously with that in the Netherlands and much of Denmark, both of them regions that could have been settled without the use of boats. Another element may have been involved.

In Northern Europe the territory occupied by early farmers had remained much the same over a long period of time. Why were they so reluctant to settle larger areas? Perhaps the reason that the initial expansion of agriculture seemed to falter was that it had reached the limits of the land where it could produce a dependable supply of food. Beyond it there were regions with unfavourable weather and poorer soils. Recently Clive Bonsall and his colleagues have observed that the expansion of early farmers into just those areas seems to have occurred as the climate changed, so that it would have been possible to practice the same economy over a more extensive territory (Bonsall et al. 2002). This may be a coincidence, but it does suggest an incentive for expansion that had been lacking before. It also seems to be the only model which explains developments in Britain and Ireland as well as those in Scandinavia. Although it is expressed in very general terms, it provides a useful working hypothesis.

Colonisation by sea is currently an unfashionable option, and it certainly does not account for every aspect of the insular Neolithic. There are also a number of features that could be more closely linked to a Mesolithic way of life. The most important may also be the most intangible. Neolithic material culture was adopted remarkably quickly over large parts of Britain and Ireland. Perhaps this was influenced by existing knowledge of insular geography. Extended journeys along the rivers and around the coastline might have depended on the accumulated experience of the indigenous population. That could explain why some of the Neolithic ceremonial monuments were built in places which had already fulfilled an important role in an older pattern of communication. It applies to the location of certain enclosures and tombs on sites that had been used before, but, provided clearings were maintained by grazing animals, it need not presuppose an unbroken sequence of human activity. The same may apply to the use of other places in the landscape, and it is has been observed that Mesolithic occupation sites at strategic places in the uplands often include finds of Neolithic arrowheads (Spratt 1993: 77). These sites may have been used by hunting parties, but it remains to be seen whether the two groups of artefacts were contemporary with one another.

There was also a certain continuity in the use of woodland. The well-preserved timber trackways in the Somerset Levels show that coppicing was important from an early stage (B. Coles and J. Coles 1986: chapter 3), and Tony Brown (1997) has suggested that many of the earliest settlements were located in natural clearings where the tree cover had been reduced by lightning strikes and strong winds. Such places would have attracted animals and light-loving plants on either side of the conventional distinction between the Mesolithic and Neolithic periods. The real change happened only when people made a deliberate decision to increase the area of open ground.

That is less of a problem on those coastal sites where it is clear that shell middens continued to accumulate after 4000 BC, but this was a local phenomenon, confined to western Scotland and the Inner Hebrides (Armit and Finlayson 1992). Another intriguing convergence is represented by the use of raw materials. It seems clear that in a number of regions, including parts of the southern English chalk (Gardiner 1989) and the Scottish islands of Arran and Rhum, stone sources that had first been used in the Mesolithic period were exploited on a more intensive scale during the Neolithic (Wickham-Jones 1990). In the same way, coastal hunter gatherers in northwest England had worked small pieces of a distinctive kind of tuff which they probably collected from stream deposits. During the Neolithic period the parent outcrop was discovered in the Lake District mountains and became one of the largest sources of polished axes (Bradley and Edmonds 1993). It is unlikely that this happened by chance. People may well have traced these pebbles to their point of origin, using the same techniques as mineral prospectors.

There is more to say about the spread of portable artefacts, for here there was not only continuity but change. It seems as if one of the first developments of the Neolithic period was the establishment of flint mines close to the English Channel coast in Sussex and Wessex (Barber, Field, and Topping 1999). It happened in the early fourth millennium BC and suggests that land clearance and the working of timber were important from the start of the Neolithic period. The mines themselves have close counterparts in many parts of mainland Europe, extending from southern Sweden, through Denmark, The Netherlands, and Belgium to northern France (Weisberger ed. 1981). The English mines seem to have been devoted mainly to the production of axes and appear to have been located in isolated positions beyond the limits of the settled land. It is interesting that these mines originated at such an early date since adequate raw material could have been found in surface deposits – as it obviously was during the Mesolithic (Gardiner 1989). Not everyone may have had access to mined flint, and it could be that certain objects took on a special significance. It is not clear how far they travelled across country, but to judge from those examples found in stratified contexts, the earliest products of highland axe quarries like those in the Lake District were distributed over a limited area (Bradley and Edmonds 1993: chapter 8). That contrasts with the movement of jadeite axes across Europe. These had been made in the foothills of the Alps, yet their distribution within Britain extends from the south coast of England to northern Scotland (Pétrequin et al. 2002).

It is always easier to document the movement of objects than the spread of ideas, but there were also certain social practices that may have retained their importance from the Mesolithic to the Neolithic. In southern Ireland one was the use of caves for the deposition of human bones (Marion Dowd, pers. comm.). This is especially interesting since disarticulated human remains are also found in Neolithic chambered tombs. Vicki Cummings and Alasdair Whittle have drawn attention to the close relationship between some of these structures in Wales and features of the natural topography, suggesting that places with a long established significance in the landscape may have been monumentalised (2004: chapter 7). A number of these places are associated with Mesolithic artefacts. Even if the Neolithic period began with settlement from overseas, it is clear that the indigenous population had a part to play. Almost certainly, it would have outnumbered the immigrants.

So far this account has employed two traditional terms, 'Neolithic' and 'Mesolithic', and has considered their connotations. Other terms have a more straightforward chronological significance. For the purposes of this study, the Neolithic period is divided between two largely independent sequences of change, which will be referred to as 'Earlier' and 'Later' Neolithic, respectively. It is the first of these that is studied in this chapter. The Earlier Neolithic can be subdivided according to its pottery styles, and these show a certain correlation with changing forms of monuments. The commonest division is between an 'Early' Neolithic typified by fine undecorated vessels, when such structures were relatively rare, and a 'Middle' Neolithic phase with a more varied ceramic tradition and the development of a variety of mortuary monuments and earthwork enclosures. The division is usually made at about 3600 BC (Gibson 2002: chapter 4). Unfortunately, few settlements or monuments are dated with sufficient precision, and in the sections that follow the Early and Middle phases are treated together unless otherwise stated.

HOUSES AND SETTLEMENT PATTERNS

The Neolithic took different forms in different areas. In England, the number and size of extraordinary field monuments support Julian Thomas's notion that the period is best defined by a particular way of thinking about the world (J. Thomas 1999). In Ireland, it also involves the rapid adoption of agriculture (Cooney 2000).

One of the most striking results of field archaeology in recent years has been the discovery of Neolithic houses in Ireland and to a smaller extent in Scotland and Wales (Fig. 2.3; Grogan 1996; Grogan 2004a; G. Barclay 1996). This contrasts with their remarkable rarity in England (Darvill 1996). This can hardly be a result of differential survival. Many of the structures found in Ireland were in areas that had experienced a long history of cultivation, just as some of the projects carried out in England have examined well-preserved deposits. In fact the expansion of commercial fieldwork has been a more recent development in Irish archaeology, although the number of projects is rapidly increasing. In England, on the other hand, there have been many more excavations on sites

CORBALLY

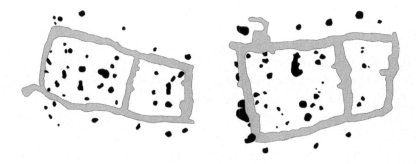

LISMORE FIELDS

0   10 m

Figure 2.3. Plans of the Earlier Neolithic houses at Corbally, in the east of Ireland, and Lismore Fields, northern England. Information from Purcell (2002) and Darvill (1996).

of every period, yet few Neolithic buildings have been found. The contrast is a real one and needs to be explained.

Different kinds of Neolithic archaeology are represented by work in these two countries. In Ireland, a long period of research concerned with megalithic tombs has given way to investigations of occupation sites. In England, on the other hand, attempts to locate substantial settlements have gone out of fashion. Either the most promising candidates proved to be more specialised structures like earthwork enclosures, or the remains of living places were so ephemeral that they encouraged prehistorians to devote more attention to monuments. In Scotland and Wales fieldworkers have been able to study settlements and tombs, but only in Orkney is it possible to treat all these aspects of the Neolithic together on equal terms.

Such variations do appear to reflect certain realities. In Ireland and in northern and western Britain, the house and the individual settlement seem to have provided a focus for domestic life, even when they were complemented by specialised monuments. In England, and especially in the south and east, the sheer scale of certain monuments draws attention to the very limited evidence for everyday activities, and again this may reflect priorities in the past rather than the biases among fieldworkers in the present. On the other hand, such differences have been made all the sharper by a process of 'rethinking the Neolithic' which has drawn attention to the ways in which its archaeology does not conform to established preconceptions.

Those expectations have been drawn from the archaeology of Continental Europe and fail to convince for two reasons. First, they have been influenced by the material remains of a much earlier period than the Neolithic of Britain and Ireland. Such stereotypes grew out of work on the Linearbandkeramik and its immediate successors. They relate to a time up to a thousand years before the period in question. They refer to a remarkably stable pattern of settlement typified by massive domestic buildings, but this was coming to an end in the mid-fifth millennium BC, and by 4000 BC no trace of it remained (Whittle 1996: chapter 6). Around the rim of Continental Europe the evidence is rather like that in Britain and Ireland, and the remains of occupation sites are less apparent. Often they are reduced to scatters of artefacts and pits, and the presence of well preserved dwellings is altogether exceptional. A second stereotype has been even more pervasive. Because the well-known settlements of the Linearbandkeramik were characterised by massive longhouses, there has been a tendency to interpret later timber buildings in the same terms. None of the excavated structures in Britain and Ireland is of the same proportions, nor is there any convincing evidence that people and animals had lived together under the same roof. For that reason it is misleading to talk of Neolithic 'longhouses' in the study area. In fact many of these buildings can only have accommodated a limited number of occupants.

In fact there is a further contrast that needs to be explored. The longhouses of the sixth and earlier fifth millennia BC in Continental Europe had been organised into hamlets or even small villages. At present it seems likely that the first Neolithic dwellings in Britain and Ireland had a more dispersed distribution, although an exception may occur at Stonehall in Orkney (Colin Richards, pers. comm.). Otherwise it seems as if these buildings are quite isolated, although they can be grouped into small clusters and distributed fairly evenly across the landscape. Those in Ireland are often quite near to the coast. To some extent the pattern may be changing as a result of recent fieldwork. For example, the supposedly isolated Neolithic houses at Corbally in the east of Ireland now appear to form part of a wider distribution, with more than one nucleus where several houses occur together (Purcell 2002; Grogan 2004a). There is also evidence that some Neolithic structures were replaced in the same positions. Without a much finer chronology this provides virtually the only evidence of sequence, and at present it is impossible to tell how many other buildings were in use together. It is often suggested that this pattern was established around 4000 BC, but a recent study has shown that much of the dating evidence is based on the structural timbers which were usually of oak. Radiocarbon dates on short-lived samples suggest that 3800 BC provides a better estimate (McSparron 2003). Again this has implications for the rate of change.

There were regional differences in the forms taken by Earlier Neolithic houses, although all the securely dated examples were rectangular, oval, or square. Other distinctions emerged with the passage of time. Most were built out of wood, but rather later stone houses with a similar ground plan have been identified at Eilean Domhnuill in the Outer Hebrides (Armit 2003a) and in the Orkney settlements of Knap of Howar (A. Ritchie 1983) and Stonehall (Colin Richards, pers. comm.).

Despite these distinctions, a number of the structures shared certain features in common. Their contents can be distinctly unusual, for they include signif-icant quantities of fine pottery but few other artefacts. In some cases, objects seem to have been placed in their foundations, and a number of examples have produced significant quantities of carbonised grain. These finds have led to confusion. On the one hand, the exceptional character of such deposits encouraged the view that the buildings were used in ritual and ceremonial (J. Thomas 1996a; Topping 1996). On the other, it suggested that if large quantities of grain are found in these houses, that should have been standard practice at Neolithic settlements (Rowley-Conwy 2004). Both observations may be misleading. The artefacts in the post holes and wall trenches might have been offerings that were made when the building was erected. The exceptional collections of pottery may have been placed there when those structures were abandoned and destroyed, in which case neither group of objects need have been associated with the occupation of the houses themselves. The discovery of carbonised grain can also be confusing, for in common with other Neolithic buildings, some of them were burnt down. A similar process happened on so many sites, from cursus monuments to long barrows, that it seems to have been intentional. These finds may shed light on the domestic rituals associated with the occupation of houses, but they do not transform these dwellings into some kind of specialised monument. It is possible that Neolithic longhouses in parts of Continental Europe were abandoned when one of the occupants died (Bradley 2001). That interpretation may also be relevant here, not least in those cases where the sites of earlier settlements had been buried beneath mounds or cairns.

The idea that certain rituals centred on the domestic buildings may also explain the exceptional structures that were built in Scotland at this time. At first sight these share the attributes of the Irish houses. They were recti-linear with rounded ends, some were divided into small compartments, and again they were associated with fine pottery and with burnt grain. On the other hand, they have certain exceptional features. The artefact assemblage contains significant quantities of ceramics, but very few lithic artefacts (Bar-clay, Brophy, and MacGregor 2002). The buildings are apparently isolated from any dwellings, yet they can be found quite near to specialised earthwork monuments of the kinds described later in this chapter. These structures had been built on a massive scale, and yet the separate rooms were so small that circulation about the interior would have been exceptionally difficult. Still more revealing, they had been burnt down and replaced on at least one occasion. The first to be excavated was selected on the basis of an aerial photograph which suggested that it might have been an early medieval feasting hall (N. Reynolds 1978). That was obviously wrong, but the excavators of another example at Claish have observed that it could have been a public building of a similar kind (Barclay, Brophy, and MacGregor 2002). The features of an ordinary dwelling were apparently reproduced on a monumental scale, but people would still have understood the reference to domestic architecture.

Both the Scottish and Irish buildings have been used to counter the popular idea that the Neolithic settlement pattern was based on mobility and perhaps on the use of wild resources. Although domesticated animals provided food and secondary products, it is the cereals from these sites that have attracted most attention, for discoveries of this kind have been less abundant in southern England, where Neolithic houses are rare (Robinson 2000). These new discoveries certainly call into question some of the tenets of the new interpretation, but it is important to see them in perspective, for buildings of these kinds were quite short lived. They do not represent the normal pattern for the Neolithic period. Many of them were erected during the first few centuries of the fourth millennium BC, and after that time they largely disappear, to be replaced by more ephemeral circular buildings. That is true of most of the well-preserved structures in Ireland, but it does not apply so clearly to the Scottish sites. A similar change is illustrated by the less extensive evidence from England and Wales. From approximately 3500 BC the settlement pattern in different regions of Britain and Ireland seems to have been rather more homogeneous, and almost everywhere houses and settlements are harder to identify. The representation of substantial rectilinear dwellings had varied from one region to another, but in most cases they were built over a limited period of time.

That interpretation is strongly supported by recent work in Ireland. Here it seems as if the first Neolithic settlements made a significant impact on the natural environment. Pollen analysis has identified a series of major clearings at the beginning of this period. These are associated with the appearance of cereal pollen (O'Connell and Molloy 2001). That is not surprising in the light of the excavated evidence, but it is revealing that, after a brief phase of expansion during which substantial houses had been built, some of those clearings regenerated. From then on, there are more indications of pastoral farming than there are of crop cultivation. Rather similar claims have been made at a number of sites in Britain where clearings were either abandoned at an early stage or reverted to less intensive land use (Whittle 1978), but in this case there seems to have been greater regional and chronological variation, and the main impact on the landscape did not come until the Later Neolithic period. It is not clear why these changes happened, but Petra Dark and Henry Gent (2001) have made the interesting observation that the first cereals introduced to these islands would probably have been protected from crop pests. That immunity would have broken down over time, meaning that the earliest crops would have been unusually productive.

Another development in Irish archaeology has been the discovery and dating of systems of stone-walled fields on the west coast (Fig. 2.4). These are associated both with settlements and tombs, but until quite recently it appeared that they had been used during the later part of this period. Now it is clear that they were of a much earlier date (Molloy and O'Connell 1995). An extensive programme of radiocarbon dating shows that Céide Fields were established by about 3700 BC and that they had already been invaded by peat by 3200 BC. Although they were used mainly as pasture, it is clear that cereals were being grown there too. It remains to be seen how many field systems existed at this time, for it is clear that land boundaries of many different periods are buried beneath the Irish blanket bog. There may have been similar developments in other areas. It is possible that fields were established on the Scottish island of Arran during this period (Barber 1997: chapter 11). A rectilinear system of ditches at Billown on the Isle of Man may have formed part of another system of land management during the Earlier Neolithic, but the excavator prefers to regard this as a monument complex (Darvill 2000). Neolithic field systems are found also in the Shetland Islands, but they do not appear to have been established at such an early date (Whittle 1986). Perhaps it is misleading to place too much emphasis on these fields, as soil micromorphology suggests that domestic middens might have been cultivated as garden plots (Guttmann 2005). It would not have been necessary to transport their contents to fertilise arable land.

The environmental record from England does not follow quite the same trajectory as its Irish counterpart, and the evidence for Earlier Neolithic settlement takes a very different form. Here there are few signs of Neolithic buildings. There is no shortage of pit deposits containing the distinctive kinds of material associated with well preserved settlements, and in the Thames Valley there are even the remains of open air middens (Allen, Barclay, and Landin-Whymark 2004). Nor is there much evidence, even from extensive excavations, that several houses existed together on the same sites. There are fewer signs of superimposition than occur with their Irish counterparts, and both in England and Wales massive roofed structures on the scale of the Scottish 'halls' have not been excavated, although one candidate in eastern England has been identified by aerial photography (Oswald, Dyer, and Barber 2001: fig. 3.14). This raises two possibilities. The first is that settlement really was more ephemeral. That might be suggested by the small size and limited contents of most of the artefact scatters and by the restricted number of pits associated with many of these sites. This is reflected by the rarity of carbonised cereals among their contents, compared with the remains of wild plants. That applies even to the large houses recently excavated at Yarnton and Whitehorse Stone (Gill Hey and Alistair Barclay, pers. comm.). On the other hand, it is not inconceivable that large rectilinear houses had originally been more widely distributed and that they were built in a way that did not leave subsoil features behind. Waterlogged wood from the Somerset Levels shows that people were using sophisticated carpentry techniques during this early phase (B. Coles and J. Coles 1986: chapter 3). One indication that such houses may once have existed in England is provided by extensive excavations at settlements along the east coast which are characterised by a number of pits (Garrow, Beadsmoore, and Knight 2005). Traces of structures might not have survived, but there are open areas in between these features which are of roughly the shape and dimensions of the domestic buildings of this date. Other arcs or clusters of pits may have been inside the houses themselves (Fig. 2.5).

A persistent feature of these occupation sites is the presence of pits whose contents were sometimes organised when they were placed in the ground. They can include pottery, lithic artefacts, querns, and animal bones that seem to have been taken from middens, but occasionally they also contain disarticulated human remains (J. Thomas 1999: chapter 4). It was once argued such pits were grain silos, but it seems more likely that some of them were dug specifically to receive these contents. The same kinds of deposits were in the hollows left by fallen trees (Evans, Pollard, and Knight 1999). This practice of burying particular combinations of artefacts and other material is a distinctive feature of the insular Neolithic, and at present it seems to be commoner in Britain than it is in Ireland. It seems possible that this material was carefully buried when occupation sites were abandoned (Healy 1987). That practice has implications for field archaeology. In those parts of England where flint is readily available it can be difficult to recognise concentrations of surface finds dating from this period. In Ireland, the situation is rather different as similar deposits seem to be associated with timber buildings rather than pits.

It is difficult to account for these contrasts. Julian Thomas (2004a) has suggested that one reason why the Irish Neolithic was so different from its British counterpart is that the indigenous population had no large animals apart from pigs. The introduction of domesticated cattle, sheep, and goats might have had a greater impact here than it did in other areas. That seems possible, but it does not explain the emphasis that was evidently placed on cereals, nor can it account for the presence of equally impressive houses and settlements in northern and western Scotland where the native fauna was less impoverished. Perhaps his suggestion accounts for a rather different development, as the Irish pollen evidence suggests an initial emphasis on cereal growing and a greater emphasis on stock raising during a subsequent phase. Maybe that might be explained by a lack of familiarity with cattle before the beginning of the Neolithic period.

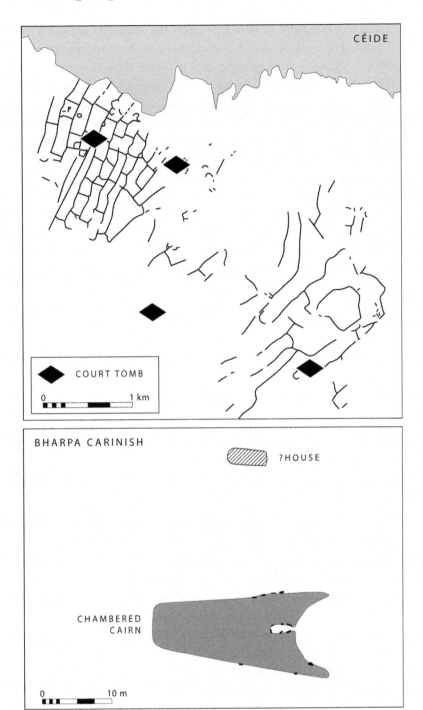

Figure 2.4. (Upper) Earlier Neolithic field system and associated court tombs at Céide, in the west of Ireland. (Lower) Chambered cairn and possible house at Bharpa Carinish, Western Isles. Information from Cooney (2000) and Crone (1993).

It is clear that much has still to be learnt about the Neolithic economy of either island. Studies of carbonised seeds and animal bones have not been particularly informative because of the circumstances in which those materials were deposited. The largest collections of faunal remains come from the excavation of specialised monuments, whilst the main groups of cereals are associated with structures that may have been burnt down deliberately. Perhaps more direct evidence of human diet will be obtained by other methods of analysis, although such work is still in its early stages. Just as the evidence of stable isotopes suggests a drastic change from a marine to a terrestrial diet at the start of the Neolithic (M. Richards 2003; 2004), there seems to be evidence for a major emphasis on animal products during this period. That is not to imply that every community practised the same economy. Human remains from single tombs provide very similar signatures to one another, but there are important contrasts between the samples taken from different sites, suggesting that there was a wide range of variation. In particular, some people seem to have eaten much more meat than others (M. Richards 2000). There is also a little evidence from the chemical analysis of pottery. Some years ago Legge (1981) suggested that Earlier Neolithic people practised a dairy economy. This was because older cows feature so prominently among the animal bones. That suggestion was questioned at the time, but now there is a growing body of evidence that ceramic vessels had indeed held milk or milk products (Copley et al. 2005).

BEYOND THE HOUSE: LONG MOUNDS AND MORTUARY MONUMENTS

What of the earliest monuments? Most accounts of the Neolithic period provide a commentary on a series of separate types. Understandably, those associated with human remains dominate the discussion, not least because so many of these mounds and cairns can still be seen today. This procedure raises a series of problems. First, it suggests that prehistoric people were building these structures according to a series of prescribed templates when excavation has shown that the final forms of such buildings provide little indication of their internal construction. Superficially similar forms of mound or cairn may have developed along radically different lines. Second, there is a tendency to treat all the component parts of such monuments as a unitary conception whereas recent fieldwork suggests that many of them could have had an independent existence and could even be found on their own. A third problem is that closer attention to the sequence at individual monuments suggests that the mound or cairn that had provided the main focus for discussion was sometimes the last element to be built and may even have been intended to bring the use of that site to an end.

In fact it seems as if some of the earliest monuments may have taken a distinctive form in their own right, although the chronological evidence leaves

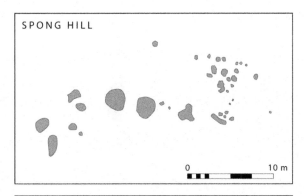

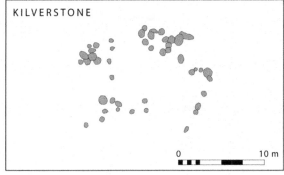

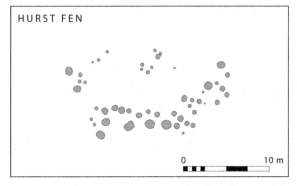

Figure 2.5. Groups of Earlier Neolithic pits at three sites in East Anglia, showing the gaps in their distribution where buildings may have existed. Information from Healy (1988), Clark, Higgs, and Longworth (1960), and Garrow, Beadsmoore, and Knight (2005).

much to be desired. Two elements are particularly important here and in some ways relate to rather similar ways of utilising components of the natural landscape. For the most part they have different distributions from one another. Along the coastline of the North Sea and the English Channel timber 'mortuary houses' are quite common, although this term does not do justice either to their distinctive form or to the material associated with them. Their distribution hardly overlaps with that of 'portal dolmens' which are found in both islands but usually occur in areas further to the west.

LOCHHILL

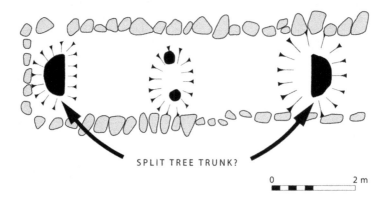

CARREG SAMSON

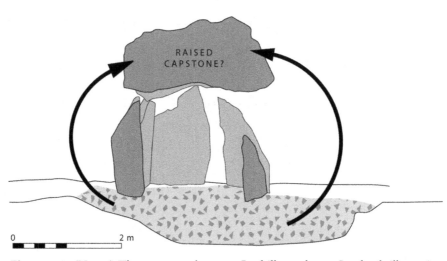

Figure 2.6. (Upper) The mortuary house at Lochill, southwest Scotland, illustrating the use of a split tree trunk. (Lower) The chambered tomb at Carreg Samson, southwest Wales, illustrating the raising of a massive rock for use as its capstone. Information from Masters (1983) and C. Richards (2004a).

Excavation of the 'mortuary houses' has identified settings of D-shaped post holes of considerable proportions (Kinnes 1992). Usually these occur in pairs (Fig. 2.6), although other configurations are found. Work at the well-preserved site of Haddenham in eastern England has confirmed what was long suspected, that these are the remains of tree trunks which had been split in half (Evans and Hodder 2005). Many of these sites are associated with human remains. There are many examples which are buried beneath barrows or cairns, but they were usually built after these posts had been set in place, and there are even sites at which such structures were never covered by a monument. They are particularly interesting since there is evidence that at the beginning of the Neolithic period the holes left by fallen trees could be marked by offerings of

Figure 2.7. The portal tomb at Poulnabrone, in the west of Ireland.

cultural material (Evans, Pollard, and Knight 1999). Perhaps these components of the native woodland were thought to be especially significant.

In upland areas, especially in Ireland and western Britain, a comparable process may be evidenced by portal dolmens. These are usually classified as megalithic 'tombs', although it is not certain that they were originally associated with human remains. Nor is there any satisfactory evidence that they were buried beneath cairns. In fact they seem to have been intended as closed stone 'boxes' covered by a disproportionately massive capstone which could be higher at one end than the other. A number of these monuments resemble natural rock formations (Bradley 1998c), but in certain cases it seems as if the massive covering slab had been obtained on the site itself. Some of the chambers were raised above shallow pits, which may have been the quarries from which the capstone was taken (C. Richards 2004a). The ground surface was split open by this process (Fig. 2.6), just as in other regions trees were divided in half and transformed into wooden monuments. Alasdair Whittle (2004) refers to portal dolmens as 'stones that float to the sky', and that description seems entirely appropriate (Fig. 2.7).

Closed chambers of other kinds may belong to the beginning of the Neolithic sequence in Britain and Ireland, just as they do in western France, where a number of sites were originally associated with monumental cists (Sheridan 2003b). The interior did not become accessible until a later phase. There are a number of indications that a similar process took place in Britain and Ireland. Among the more convincing examples are the 'rotunda graves' of the Cotswolds which were incorporated into later long cairns (Darvill 2004:

60–2), and a remarkable site at Achnacreebeag in the west of Scotland which was associated with pottery in a similar style to that found at monuments in western France (Sheridan 2003a). The Carrowmore cemetery on the west coast of Ireland provides another example of this development, for here a number of massive stone chambers seem to have formed a freestanding element set within a circle of boulders. Such structures are associated with radiocarbon dates beginning around 4000 BC (Burenhult 1980; Sheridan 2003b). The boulder circles may also have parallels in Brittany, but in the Irish case the cemetery developed into a group of passage tombs associated with a purely insular material culture. That development is discussed in Chapter Three.

There are other ways in which the Irish Neolithic is distinctive, for here the remains of houses seem to have been closely associated with mortuary monuments, which most often take the form of elongated mounds or cairns. At Ballyglass in the west of the country two of these overlie the remains of wooden structures (Fig. 2.8; Ó'Nualláin 1972; 1998). One of the cairns was superimposed on the site of an earlier house, but in such a way that its layout acknowledged the position of the demolished building. The same happened at the neighbouring monument, but in this case excavation exposed the plans of three separate structures, two of which overlapped. It seems as if only parts of them survived, but again it is clear that the layout of the tomb was influenced by the organisation of the older settlement. Not far away at Céide it is possible to observe how similar monuments had been integrated into a Neolithic field system (Cooney 2000: 25–9). In such cases it seems clear that mortuary monuments and settlements were closely associated with one another. These are not the only instances in which such a close connection has been suggested, but they are perhaps the most convincing.

Similar links have been inferred in other areas. At Bharpa Carinish in the Outer Hebrides the exiguous traces of another dwelling were found only thirty metres from a chambered tomb and may have shared the same alignment as that monument (Fig. 2.4; Crone 1993). In England and Wales, there are further cases in which a chambered tomb overlay the remains of earlier dwellings. This was clearly demonstrated at Gwernvale (Britnell and Savory 1984: 42–150), but slighter domestic structures also seem to have preceded the well-excavated cairns at Ascott-under-Wychwood (Alistair Barclay, pers. comm.) and Hazleton North (Saville 1990). In the latter case the relationship between these features is especially striking. The building of the cairn proceeded gradually as separate masses of rubble were packed inside a series of bays, each of them defined by dry stone walls. It is clear that the position of an earlier midden was left exposed until the late stage of the project, then the burial chambers were built alongside it.

The connection between houses and monuments perhaps goes further. The stone houses at the island site of Eilean Domnhuill were approached through an impressive stone setting which the excavator compares with the forecourt of a megalithic tomb (Armit 2003a). In Orkney, the comparison even extends

BALLYGLASS

BALLYGLASS

EDENMORE

COHAW

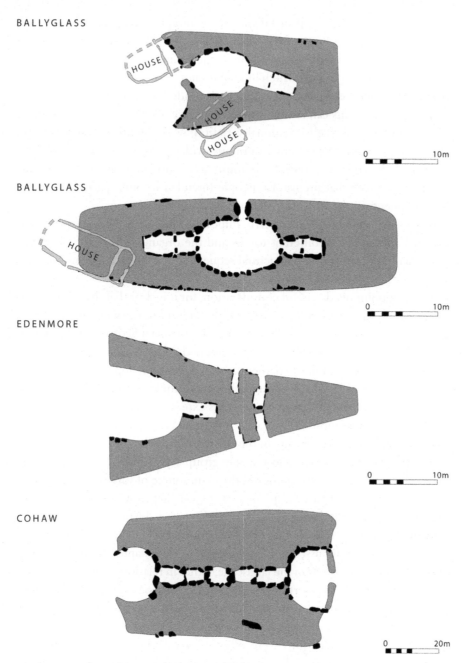

Figure 2.8. Plans of four Irish court tombs, illustrating the variety of court and chamber plans. Two of these monuments, at Ballyglass, in the west of Ireland, overlie the sites of houses. Information from Ó'Nualláin (1972) and (1986) and de Valera (1960).

to the internal structure of the earlier chambered cairns which are divided into a series of separate compartments, linked by a central corridor and separated from one another by screens. Colin Richards has argued that the architecture of these tombs refers to the characteristic form and organisation of the domestic dwellings at sites like Knap of Howar. It seems appropriate to consider such monuments as the houses of the dead (Fig. 2.9; C. Richards 1992). That is certainly suggested by the organisation of the fittings inside structures of both kinds. The stone shelves on which human bodies were placed within the tombs occupy the equivalent positions to the beds inside the domestic buildings.

These monuments can also be studied on a larger scale, but this work often focuses on the evidence for regional variation. Minor architectural details can easily assume a life of their own until any wider patterns are obscured. This is particularly true when megalithic tombs are considered one class at a time, for it presupposes that prehistoric people intended to build particular 'styles' of monuments in the first place. That is by no means obvious.

Two issues seem to be particularly important: the relationship between the external appearance of different tombs and the organisation of the chambers found within them; and the structural sequences that led to these monuments assuming their present forms.

The first point needs careful consideration, for it is clear that there is no consistent relationship between the shape of the mound or cairn and the layout of any structures that were concealed inside it. In northern Scotland, for instance, rectangular or oval cairns were usually positioned so that their long axis was visible on the skyline from the settlement area. That did not apply to all the round cairns built during the same period, but this simple distinction is obscured when the classification of these monuments extends to the burial chambers (T. Phillips 2002). The most likely reason is that the external appearance of these cairns was apparent to everyone in the course of daily life. Access to their interiors may have been restricted to a smaller group. By conflating the internal and external features of such monuments, the main source of variation is obscured.

At the same time that example makes it clear that more than one form of mortuary monument might have been constructed during this period. The simplest distinction is that between long mounds or cairns and the round barrows which are discussed in a later section of this chapter. Sometimes they occupy different positions in the landscape, either in relation to the local topography, as happens in the north of Scotland (T. Phillips 2002), or in relation to different areas, for instance on the Yorkshire Wolds (J. Harding 1996). On the other hand, the distinction is not clear-cut, for excavation has shown that smaller circular constructions were often encapsulated within more massive long mounds. In other words, the outward appearance of these monuments disguises the fact they might have achieved the same form by quite different means. That is sometimes overlooked in categorising their outward appearance.

Apart from portal tombs and those at Carrowmore, the earliest style of monument in Ireland was probably the 'court cairn' (de Valera 1960). They have this name because the internal chambers are generally approached though a curvilinear walled enclosure or 'court' which remained open to the elements (Figs. 2.8 and 2.10). Although many monuments have been damaged, these

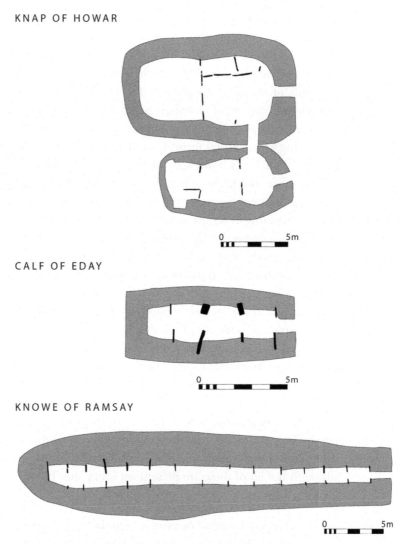

KNAP OF HOWAR

0 ___ 5m

CALF OF EDAY

0 ___ 5m

KNOWE OF RAMSAY

0 ___ 5m

Figure 2.9. Plan of two Earlier Neolithic houses at Knap of Howar, Orkney, compared with the plans of two chambered cairns. At Calf of Eday the chamber is divided into four compartments, whilst Knowe of Ramsay is a stalled cairn with fourteen subdivisions. Information from A. Ritchie (1983) and Davidson and Henshall (1989).

features were normally associated with long mounds like the two examples at Ballyglass. The most obvious characteristic of these sites is their sheer diversity, and yet it seems that many of them had been constructed in a single operation or developed over a restricted period of time. The mound or cairn normally took the same form, but there is considerable variation in every other element. This concerns the nature of the court itself – it can occur singly or in pairs, and individual examples can be more or less enclosed; it may concern the number of chambers or their relationship to one another; or it may be related to differences of scale or accessibility between the separate parts of these tombs.

These distinctions have led to many subdivisions among the plans of Irish court cairns, but the reasons for their creation are very rarely discussed.

Andrew Powell makes the interesting suggestion that these different configurations reflect the complex patterns of kinship and alliance between different segments of the local population (Powell 2005). The tomb plans with their bewildering variety of chambers acted like a genealogy, expressing the connections between different groups of people and enshrining those arrangements in a lasting architectural form. If so, then a single tomb might represent more than the individual household. Rather, the combinations of different courts and chambers might provide an idealised image of social organisation across a wider landscape. Of course, this will be impossible to prove, but the very fact that the remains of so many people are found at these sites would certainly support the notion that the monuments stood for a wider community. Hardly any grave goods were associated with individual bodies, so it seems as if the differences that were apparent in life were not expressed in the structures of these tombs.

In Britain, there are other problems in approaching megalithic tombs, or their equivalents built out of less durable materials. It has been easy to suppose that mounds and cairns were always built to contain burial chambers in the way that seems to have happened in the Irish court tombs. That is not always the case, for there is so much diversity that it is difficult to identify any overarching scheme.

There is a paradox here, for it is true that many of these monuments look very much alike, but in this case they reached their final forms by different means. The classic long barrow or long cairn has certain clearly defined elements, although not all of these are present on every site. In theory, each monument includes most of the following (Kinnes 1992):

- an elongated mound or cairn which should be rectangular, oval, or trapezoidal and higher towards the eastern end;
- a monumental forecourt or facade in front of the entrance, normally facing to the east;
- 'porches', or even avenues, of spaced posts which approach the entrance to the monument;
- stone walls or wooden revetments to support the edges of the mound;
- ditches or quarries which extend along the sides of those monuments and occasionally around the ends;
- a 'burial chamber' or chambers which are approached through the forecourt or may be located in the flanks of the mound or cairn;
- and a blocking of timber or stone introduced when the monument was closed.

Stone chambers could assume many different configurations, but at non-megalithic long barrows the 'mortuary house' took the form considered earlier.

Figure 2.10. The court tomb at Creevykeel, in the west of Ireland.

It usually consisted of two or more split tree trunks which could be bounded by banks or low walls. These structures were sometimes contained within free-standing ditched or fenced enclosures, and there are even sites that contained more than one of them. The precise forms taken by all these features vary from one region to another, and this has led to the recognition of a series of local styles (Masters 1983; Kinnes 1992). Although they do have some validity, the process of classification obscures a large amount of variation.

Put simply, nearly all the elements listed above can be found in isolation, and they occur in various combinations which do not equate with any of the 'classic' forms of monument (Fig. 2.11). Thus mortuary houses are recorded as isolated structures, or they may be recognised inside open enclosures. There are wooden forecourts which have no barrows or burials at all, and there are mounds which never seem to have contained any human remains. The classic form of the monument may encapsulate the positions of smaller structures, including older round barrows or round cairns (Fig. 2.12), and the entire scheme may have been conceived on a modest scale, or it might have required a much greater amount of labour. In the south these monuments were usually sealed or allowed to decay, whilst those in northern England and eastern Scotland were sometimes set on fire.

It seems as if these separate elements should be understood in terms of a process or series of processes which was more or less extended at different sites. Perhaps there never was an ideal conception of how that sequence should end. Rather, there were many local variations which may have been influenced by the status of particular individuals and the ways in which they were to be

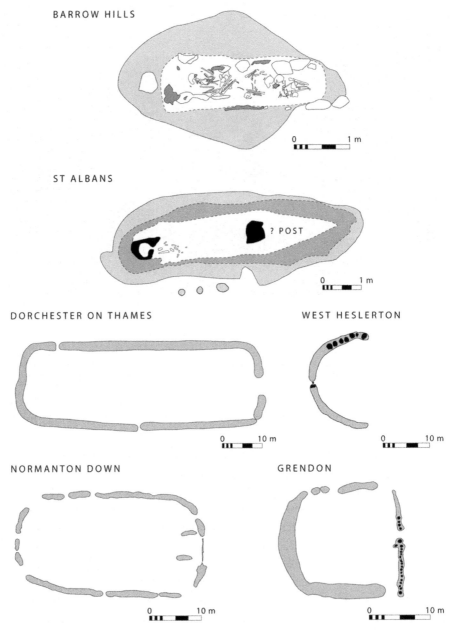

Figure 2.11. Mortuary structures and related features which are traditionally associated with long barrows but in these cases occur in isolation. Barrow Hills (Thames Valley) and St. Albans (eastern England) are versions of the 'mortuary house', and Dorchester on Thames (Thames Valley) and Normanton Down (Wessex) are 'mortuary enclosures' (the latter containing a possible mortuary house). Grendon (East Midlands) and West Heslerton (northwest England) might be compared with the forecourts of long mounds, although the latter example is undated. Information from Niblett (2001), Barclay and Halpin (1999), Whittle et al. (1992), Vatcher (1961), Gibson and McCormick (1985) and Haughton and Powelsland (1999).

STREET HOUSE

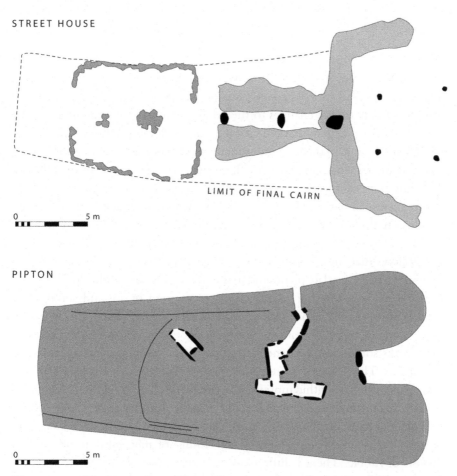

PIPTON

Figure 2.12. The long cairns at Street House, northeast England, and Pipton, south Wales. The cairn at Street House overlay three older structures, here shown in outline: a square enclosure, a 'mortuary house' and a timber forecourt. The long cairn at Pipton seems to have covered a variety of older structures with their own burial chambers. Information from Vyner (1984) and Savory (1956).

remembered. There is another complication. The results of recent fieldwork suggest that the massive monuments which have dominated the literature so far were altogether exceptional and that it is the smaller structures which may really represent the norm. On the chalk of Lincolnshire, for instance, eleven long barrows can be identified as earthworks, but aerial photography has revealed the sites of more than fifty other mounds and enclosures which may have been their less monumental counterparts (D. Jones 1998). Some of these were located in different positions in the landscape, and because they were so much slighter they have been levelled by the plough. On many sites in Britain the structural sequence did not end with the creation of a classic long barrow, and, more often than not, it may never have been intended to do so.

With these qualifications, there is a dominant pattern in Britain which contrasts with what has been said about the monuments in Ireland. Whereas Irish court tombs exhibit a wide variety of ground plans, their architecture makes use of a few recurrent features that were combined in many different ways. This process seems to have taken place over a limited time, or at least it did not involve any drastic changes to the configuration of the monuments. The British evidence suggests that individual examples developed from many different starting points. In this case monuments were modified, extended, and even changed their shapes, and parts of these structures may have been replaced. The only consistent feature of the larger sites was that in the end many of them assumed a similar outward form. When these structural sequences reached their conclusion, the sites were sometimes covered by an elongated mound or cairn (Fig. 2.12).

It follows that these constructions were not necessarily an integral part of such sites until a very late phase, and in the case of non-megalithic long barrows it seems unlikely that the 'chambers' were covered by mounds until those sites went out of use. That mound sealed the features created during earlier phases and cut them off from the living. It may be why the building of these earthworks sometimes happened during a phase when such structures were set on fire. This was not a cremation rite in the way that is often claimed. Like many other Neolithic monuments, the use of these places was brought to an end by burning them down and burying them under a mantle of rubble. It happened particularly often in northeast England and eastern Scotland. In western Britain the equivalent was the closing of megalithic tombs with a deposit of rubble. There is little to suggest that most of these were used for more than a few generations.

If that is true, then other possibilities come to mind. In both countries there are circumstantial links between long mounds and the rectilinear houses of the Earlier Neolithic period (Bradley 1998b: chapter 3), but the distinction between the character of Irish court cairns and most of their British counterparts may correspond to a broader division in the settlement pattern. In Ireland, houses are widely distributed and sometimes occur in small groups on, or close to, the sites of chambered tombs. These tombs have a variety of ground plans, but they are built out of segments which could be arranged in many different configurations from one monument to the next. Even when this happened, the structure retained its distinctive form. There were few radical changes in the evolution of individual sites, and it often seems as if the formation of these particular cairns happened over a fairly short period.

In Britain, on the other hand, it seems possible that the settlement pattern was much less uniform, and in the south and east it may have been characterised by significantly greater fluidity. Here a bewildering variety of structures was associated with the celebration of the dead; indeed, their number and diversity are still increasing as a result of modern fieldwork. Some of these monuments remained unchanged, including a series of round barrows which will be discussed later in this chapter, but where larger mounds and cairns were built over them, they would have been among the few fixed elements in the Neolithic landscape.

BEYOND THE HOUSE: SETTLEMENTS, BODIES, AND TOMBS

Why was it that domestic buildings suggested the appearance of the tombs? A useful starting point is the work of Lévi-Strauss (1983) on what he calls 'house societies'. He is most concerned with kinship organisation and the emergence of hierarchies, but his work is particularly important because it shows how the idea of the 'house' extends to the occupants for the building and the members of a wider community.

It is in this sense that the term is used in a recent paper by Mary Helms (2004), who discusses the different worldviews of mobile hunter-gatherers and the first farmers. One might almost say that it is by the construction of houses, both real and metaphorical, that particular groups distinguish themselves from others and define their membership. Their composition is less fluid than that of hunter-gatherer communities, and it is maintained over a longer period of time. Such concerns are particularly relevant when people are exploiting an unfamiliar environment, and the new arrangement may also reflect the labour requirements of early agriculture. Perhaps that is one reason why houses are such a conspicuous feature at the beginning of the Neolithic period.

A pertinent observation comes from a paper by Janet Carsten and Stephen Hugh-Jones introducing an edited volume devoted to Lévi-Strauss's ideas. They observe how common it is for houses to be regarded as living creatures and to be thought of in the same terms as human beings, who are born, grow old, and die. Like people, houses have biographies of their own.

> Houses are far from being static material structures. They have animate qualities; they are endowed with spirits or souls, and are imagined in terms of the human body.... Given its living qualities... it comes as no surprise that natural processes associated with people, animals or plants may also apply to the house (Carsten and Hugh-Jones 1995: 37).

Perhaps the reason why the British and Irish evidence poses so many problems is that the histories of the buildings in which people had lived were reflected by the ways in which their bodies were treated when they died.

The most obvious contrast is between the regions with houses and those in which they are rare. In lowland Britain, where pit deposits are particularly common, the artefact assemblage occasionally contains human bones. It seems possible that relics had circulated in the same manner as the objects with which they were found. That is consistent with the evidence from mortuary monuments which not only include the remains of complete corpses but can also feature certain body parts to the exclusion of others (Whittle and Wysocki 1998: 151–8). This suggests that the dead were reduced to disarticulated bones and that their remains were distributed in the same manner as domestic arte-facts (Pollard 2004). Although deposits of pottery are associated with some of these monuments, many excavated sites in the south provide little evidence of portable material culture.

Compare this with the situation in Ireland where houses are much more common and isolated pit deposits are rare. Considerable numbers of artefacts are associated with court tombs which also contain charcoal-rich soil similar to that in settlements. Humphrey Case (1973) has shown that this material was usually placed on top of a deliberately laid floor, meaning that it must have been introduced after the tombs had been built. Not surprisingly, such deposits are associated with human remains. Other regions in which stone-built tombs are associated with significant quantities of artefacts, especially pottery, include the north and west of Scotland, both of them regions where the remains of houses have been found.

That contrast is interesting, but it says little about the treatment of the dead. There is an important difference in the principal mortuary rite. In some regions bodies were cremated and in others they were allowed to decay. Certain of the burnt bones might result from the combustion of an entire body; others might have been placed in a fire after they had lost their flesh. The important point is that the unburnt bones could circulate as relics. That would be less likely in the case of cremated bone, and there is little evidence for its deposition in other places.

The distributions of these two ways of treating the body are rather revealing. The burial of corpses is most often found in Britain, where it is commonest in the southern half of the country, although isolated cremations associated with decorated pots are occasionally found in eastern England. Unburnt bones occur on domestic sites over a much larger area. There is evidence for the burning of wooden mortuary structures along the North Sea coast, and in the megalithic tombs of northern Scotland human bones were exposed to fire but were not reduced to ashes. Along the west coast of Scotland, on the other hand, cremation was often employed. That is not surprising as it was one of the main ways of treating the body in Irish court tombs.

Thus the preservation and circulation of human bones was a particular feature of southern England, but seems to have extended across a wider area. The use of cremation characterises many of the Irish sites, but it also extended to parts of northern Britain, where it is more difficult to identify one prevailing rite. That is not to deny that some monuments are associated with cremation and interment. There are a few cremations on southern English sites, but these are generally secondary to deposits of unburnt bone (Darvill 2004: 145). Simi-larly, Irish court tombs show evidence for both these practices, but in this case cremations are more common than inhumations (Cooney and Grogan 1994: fig. 4.14).

The most striking contrast in ways of dealing with the dead is between the areas that show the greatest divergence in the evidence for settlement sites. In southern England houses are rare and pit deposits are more common, including those which combine a selection of domestic artefacts with fragments of human bone. It is here that there is most evidence for the deployment of unburnt corpses in long barrows and megalithic tombs where they might be arranged according to age, gender, or different parts of the body (Whittle and Wysocki 1998). Artefacts are not common at most of these monuments, and it seems possible that the residues of older settlements were allowed to decay and were dispersed in the same manner as human remains. In Ireland, on the other hand, houses are commonly found and isolated pit deposits are unusual. The residues of domestic occupation might have been deposited in tombs together with the remains of the dead (Pollard 2004). In this case the bodies were often burnt and there is little to suggest that bone fragments circulated in the same manner as artefacts.

One last contrast is important. Dermot Moore (2004) has shown that a high proportion of the Irish houses had been destroyed by fire. Although this might have been a result of warfare, the evidence is rather ambiguous, and it seems much more than a coincidence that human corpses should have been treated in exactly the same way as these buildings. Perhaps that is because the careers of particular people and the histories of their houses were in one sense the same. The house was a living creature and its life had to be extinguished in a similar manner to the human body. That may be why, in Ireland, what are apparently domestic assemblages accompanied the dead person to the tomb – they might even have been the contents of the settlement. By contrast, in southern England, the remains of settlement sites were dispersed along with the human bones, some of which were eventually deposited in tombs at which finds of artefacts are uncommon.

The Irish houses could be more substantial than their English counterparts. That may be because they were to play a spectacular role at the end of their lives and those of their occupants. By contrast, the dwellings inhabited in England did not need to do this, and so they might have been quite ephemeral structures. That could be why they have been difficult to find by excavation. These buildings were more than shelters from the elements: they were animated by their involvement in human lives, and, when their inhabitants died, their treatment followed the same principles as that of human bodies. In England, they decayed and their contents were dispersed. In Ireland, they were burnt down and their contents were concentrated in tombs (Fig. 2.13). That may be why there was a close relationship between such monuments and domestic dwellings.

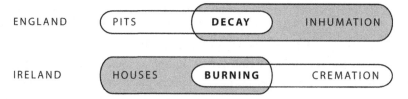

Figure 2.13. Processes connecting the treatment of houses and human bodies in England and Ireland.

BEYOND THE HOUSE: CURSUS MONUMENTS AND BANK BARROWS

Some of the largest structures to employ the idea of the house were neither mounds nor cairns. These were the wooden halls that have recently been found in northern Britain. It is difficult to assess their claims as residential buildings, but their characteristic architecture was obviously based on that of the domestic dwelling (Fig. 2.14). Their siting is important, too. Recently excavated examples at Claish, Littleour, and Carsie Mains are located within a short distance of enormous earthwork mounds (Barclay and Maxwell 1998; Barclay, Brophy, and MacGregor 2002; Brophy and Barclay 2004).

These wider connections raise problems. The rectangular buildings are of several forms, and only the earlier of them could have been roofed (K. Brophy, pers. comm.). Certain connections are very important here. Such structures were erected over the same period of time as one another; they were frequently burnt to the ground and replaced in exactly the same positions; and yet they are usually assigned to different categories. The smaller examples are thought of as halls or monumental houses, and the larger ones are sometimes described as 'long enclosures'; they have even been called 'mortuary' enclosures because they have a similar ground plan to long barrows. The problem does not end there, as many of those enclosures were associated with still more elaborate timber alignments of the kind known as 'cursuses' (Barclay and Harding eds. 1999). There is no consistent method of distinguishing between these three types, and the halls, the long enclosures, and the cursus monuments actually form a continuum. That suggests one way of thinking about these features, for it is possible that individual examples might have grown incrementally, although that process would have been interrupted by episodes of burning and rebuilding.

The excavated structures at Claish and Littleour suggest another dimension to the problem, for each is located close to an exceptionally long mound of a kind which is sometimes described as a 'bank barrow'. In each case that earthwork seems to have developed out of one or more burial mounds of conventional proportions. The Auchenlaich long mound, which is close to the hall at Claish, certainly contained a megalithic chamber (Barclay, Brophy, and MacGregor 2002: 114–19), whilst detailed survey at Cleaven Dyke near to Littleour strongly suggests that it began as a conventional burial mound that

CLEAVEN DYKE

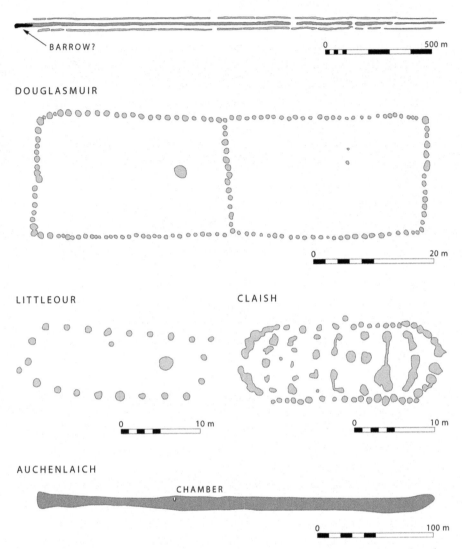

Figure 2.14. The bank barrows at Cleaven Dyke and Auchenlaich, the oval timber structures at Littleour and Claish and the rectangular enclosure at Douglasmuir. All these sites are in east or central Scotland. Information from Barclay and Maxwell (1998), Barclay, Brophy, and MacGregor (2002), and Kendrick (1995).

was gradually extended until it ran for two kilometres. Excavation suggests that a developed stage in the sequence can be dated to the early or mid-fourth millennium BC (Barclay and Maxwell 1998).

The surviving earthwork at Cleaven Dyke poses another problem. For most of its length it consists of a central mound in between two widely spaced ditches, but towards one end those ditches may have defined the limits of an open avenue or enclosure. That raises the question of definition, for elongated mounds of this kind are usually classified as bank barrows, whilst extended rectilinear enclosures are known as cursuses. Cleaven Dyke is not the only composite monument of this kind, and field survey in other regions of Britain has shown that these two classes of field monument are closely associated with one another (Bradley 1983). They are based on the same principle of extending a rectangular or oval monument on a significant scale.

The relationship between the conventional categories can be expressed in this following way (Table 2.1):

TABLE 2.1. *Possible relationships among linear timber and earthwork monuments.*

	Short		Long
Timber monuments	Hall	Long enclosure / 'Mortuary' enclosure	Cursus
Earthwork monuments	Barrow	Long enclosure/ 'Mortuary' enclosure	Cursus Bank barrow

This scheme seems to suggest that in Scotland Earlier Neolithic halls, cursuses, and bank barrows were closely related to one another (Fig. 2.14). Cleaven Dyke is particularly important because of the proximity of the timber building at Littleour, but it has other links with the tradition of long barrows and long cairns. The western end of the monument seems to have originated as a barrow, and a cairn of massive proportions is aligned on its eastern terminal. In the Later Neolithic period the chain of connections extended to a further Scottish site at Balfarg where a structure which has been compared with a timber hall was buried beneath a mound. In time its position was emphasised by the construction of a ditched enclosure. This building dates from about 3000 BC (Barclay and Russell-White 1993).

Are there similar indications from other areas? With the possible exception of the bank barrow at Stanwell (Barrett, Lewis, and Welsh 2000), none of the monuments in England seems to have had a timber precursor, nor have any post-defined monuments been identified there. Other bank barrows are found along the east coast and extend into the southern Pennines, the Thames Valley, and Wessex, but none attains the remarkable length of the principal Scottish examples. No timber hall has been excavated in England or Wales, and, like the cursus monuments, the features that have been described as 'mortuary enclosures' are usually defined by a bank and ditch. The Irish evidence is still more limited. Although a few candidates have now been recognised, the cursuses in that country have not been firmly dated (Condit 1995; Newman 1999). This is significant as their characteristics overlap with those of the ditched roadways leading to high-status sites of the Iron Age.

Chronology is very important, as it seems as if the idea of elongated timber and earthwork monuments originated in the north of Britain during the currency of the Earlier Neolithic timber halls with which they are sometimes associated. They experienced a similar cycle of deliberate burning and rebuilding. This is a feature which they share with some of the domestic dwellings in Ireland. Major earthwork cursuses seem to be later in date. A recent review concluded that they were probably constructed between about 3650 and 3350 BC (Barclay and Bayliss 1999).

Although the English cursuses may have originated after those in the north, they eventually grew to enormous proportions. In their final form they consisted of considerable elongated enclosures with an internal bank and an external ditch. These earthworks were occasionally breached by causeways, but they were rarely provided with formal entrances at the terminals. Individual examples included existing structures in their paths – long barrows, round barrows, or ditched enclosures of various sizes – and sometimes they were also aligned on an earlier earthwork. It was relatively common for a cursus to lead towards (or extend from) an older rectilinear enclosure or even a long barrow, but other arrangements have also been recognised. At Springfield there was a timber circle in this position (Buckley, Hedges, and Brown 2001). The Scottish hall at Carsie Mains was aligned on a similar feature which dates to between 3350 and 3000 BC (Brophy and Barclay 2004).

Some cursuses were built in comparative isolation, but there are also instances in which they seem to have been constructed incrementally, as one of these enclosures was added on to the end of another. Alternatively, they can run side by side, they may converge on certain focal points, or they may overlap. The two largest cursus complexes illustrate some of these patterns (Fig. 2.15). At Rudston in northeast England no fewer than five of these converge on the tallest monolith in Britain (Stoertz 1997: 25–30). Two of the earthworks meet at right angles, and two of them intersect. Long barrows can be seen on the horizon from these sites (H. Chapman 2005), and the terminal of one of the monuments was enlarged to resemble another burial mound of this type. Taken together, the cursuses run for about ten kilometres.

The other major complex is known as the Dorset Cursus, although, properly speaking, it consists of two, and possibly three, such monuments built end to end (Barrett, Bradley and Green 1991: chapters 2 and 3). Again their combined length is ten kilometres. It would have taken half a million worker hours to complete the entire structure. They incorporate burial mounds in their path, and further monuments of the same kind were aligned on the ends of these earthworks. As at Rudston, one of the terminals was built on a massive scale, as if to echo the characteristic form of two adjacent long barrows. At its northern limit, the Dorset Cursus runs up to another mound which was subsequently lengthened to form a bank barrow. The earliest section of this composite monument was orientated on the midwinter sunset. According to radiocarbon dates, it was one of the last examples to be built, most probably between about 3360 and 3030 BC.

Such monuments are generally interpreted as avenues or processional ways, although it is not known whether the construction of the earthworks monumentalised existing paths or represented a new development in the

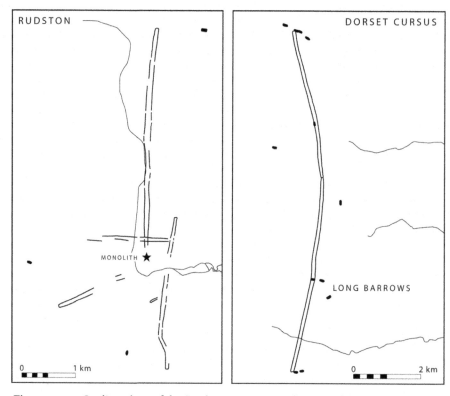

Figure 2.15. Outline plans of the Rudston cursus, northeast England, and the Dorset Cursus, Wessex, showing their relationship to long barrows and watercourses. Information from Stoertz (1997) and Barrett, Bradley, and Green (1991).

landscape. In the same way, because certain examples led between mortuary mounds, it may be that such routes were for the use of the dead rather than the living. Human bones have been found in the excavation of cursuses, and the idea that they were intended primarily for the deceased might also account for the interplay between cursuses, which are entirely open structures, and bank barrows, which are solid mounds. It would certainly help to explain why there were so few points of access to the interior of these monuments. In fact there has been little discussion of the fact that these putative paths were blocked at both ends. That would surely have impeded access to the interior, and yet it was only from there that anyone could have seen the alignments created by these monuments. One possibility is that these structures were originally open and that, like many of the long barrows and long cairns described in this chapter, they were closed during a subsequent phase (I must thank Roy Entwistle for this idea). This has not been established by excavation, although there are occasional sites where no terminals have ever been found.

    Recent fieldwork has shown that most cursus monuments and bank barrows are closely integrated with the features of the local topography (Fig. 2.16). Two particular arrangements are widely recognised. The first is where they extend across valleys so that their terminals are visible from one another and command

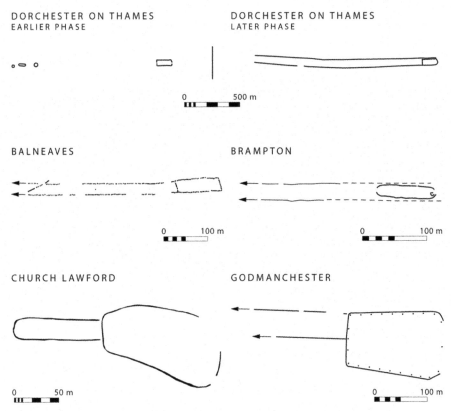

DORCHESTER ON THAMES
EARLIER PHASE

DORCHESTER ON THAMES
LATER PHASE

0   500 m

BALNEAVES

BRAMPTON

0   100 m

0   100 m

CHURCH LAWFORD

GODMANCHESTER

0   50 m

0   100 m

Figure 2.16. Outline plans of five cursus monuments and the enclosures associated with their terminals. The plan of Dorchester on Thames summarises its sequence of construction. The arrows indicate that a cursus is known to extend beyond the area illustrated here. Balneaves is in eastern Scotland, and the other sites in the English midlands. Information from Bradley and Chambers (1988), Brophy (2000), Malim (1999), Palmer (1999a), and McAvoy (2000).

an extensive view over the lower ground. Alternatively, they cut across the contours so that any people travelling along them would have experienced a sequence of changing vistas at different points in their journey (Tilley 1994: chapter 5; Barclay and Hey 1999). It is not always obvious how much of the surrounding landscape would have been clear of trees, but pollen analysis undertaken close to the two largest monuments, the Dorset Cursus and the Rudston complex, has produced unexpected evidence of an open landscape (French et al. 2003; French and Lewis 2005; Bush 1988).

The second situation is perhaps more common. This is where the configuration of cursuses or related monuments seems to follow the course of nearby rivers (Brophy 2000). Sometimes the same principle extends to the siting of several monuments within the same small area. Since people may have followed watercourses as they travelled across country, it is tempting to suggest that these earthworks monumentalised sections of their route, but this hardly accounts for the distinctive forms and associations of these structures. Perhaps they really commemorated the paths that had been taken by the dead or by previous generations as they first settled the land. The flow of the river might even have provided a metaphor for life itself. It is an association that is found in many different societies (C. Richards 1996a), but the only evidence for a connection of this kind comes from the material, primarily ceramics, axeheads, and human bones, that seems to have been deposited in the River Thames (A. Barclay 2002: 88–93). Along its banks there are a number of cursuses. Sometimes they run up to other monuments, usually enclosures or mounds located towards one of the terminals. In relation to the course of the Thames, anyone approaching those structures would have been moving 'downstream'. The same relationship can be recognised in other regions of England, such as the Great Ouse valley (Malim 1999).

Until the fieldwork of the last few years, cursuses had been dated to the Later Neolithic period, and even now it is difficult to appreciate the implications of the new chronology. Three points are of fundamental importance. The first is that linear monuments of the kind considered here may have originated in northern Britain, where the earliest examples were probably wooden structures, rather than the earthwork monuments that are more familiar in the south. The sites which attracted most attention until recently were among the last ones to be built. It is small wonder that they have been so difficult to interpret. In lowland England they are associated with long barrows and allied monuments, but their northern prototypes seem to form part of a still broader pattern which had extended to a variety of large timber buildings.

The second point is that the main distribution of these structures is in exactly the regions where little evidence of domestic buildings can be found. This may be because they had been constructed in a different technique from Earlier Neolithic dwellings in Ireland, but the character of excavated occupation sites in Britain suggests that there were real contrasts in the pattern of settlement between the different parts of the study area. In that respect it may be revealing that major linear monuments are rarely found on the west coast of Scotland and do not occur in the Northern Isles where the remains of houses survive. The situation in Ireland is different again, for there may be some monuments of this type, but they were never substantial features and it is uncertain whether they are of the same date as their British counterparts (Newman 1999). Although the situation could change as a result of fieldwork, it seems as if linear monuments were uncommon in those regions where rectangular houses played a prominent role. Conversely, such monuments are widely distributed in areas where Neolithic settlements have left little trace. Here the domestic buildings could have been more ephemeral, yet it was in such areas that the idea of the house gave rise to an extraordinary public architecture.

The third point is even more important. Cursus monuments and bank barrows may be much more common in Britain than they are in Ireland, but they are unlike other Earlier Neolithic monuments in being an insular development.

Long mounds were built in Continental Europe, but they did not take this specific form, nor did it happen during this particular phase. They are well known in Poland and the north of France, but that phenomenon had no connection with developments in these islands. In fact the closest structural parallels to the British cursuses are found in the Netherlands, north Germany, Belgium, and northern France, but they date from the first millennium BC (Roymans and Kortelag 1999). In this respect it seems as if the insular Neolithic diverged from developments in Continental Europe. The fact that this happened first in northern Britain prefigures the development of henges considered in Chapter Three.

In fact it is necessary to consider the monuments of this period in relation to at least two different axes. This section has been concerned with the importance of specifically local developments, which probably began in Scotland. The other axis connected these islands with the Continent and is represented by the emergence of yet another class of earthwork, the 'causewayed' enclosure. The contrast is all the more striking because this particular kind of monument is so widely distributed. Not only does it take a remarkably stereotyped form, but individual examples seem to have been used in similar ways.

CAUSEWAYED ENCLOSURES

It is an accident of history that the characteristics of the British Neolithic were first defined by the excavation of a causewayed enclosure, so that the earlier part of this period took its name from Windmill Hill, an earthwork on the Wessex chalk (Whittle, Pollard, and Grigson 1999). Now it is apparent that monuments of this form have a limited distribution across the two islands and that they were not among the first monuments to be built. Rather, their use commenced between about 3700 and 3600 BC. They are often found in southern and midland England, but they are rare in the north, in Scotland, and in Wales (Oswald, Dyer, and Barber 2001). Similar enclosures have only recently been identified in Ireland, but some may have taken rather different forms from the other sites. It also seems likely that they were widely adopted in these islands after the first cursus monuments had been constructed in the north, so that for a while the distributions of the two kinds of monuments may have complemented one another.

Causewayed enclosures are so called because they are defined by interrupted ditches (Fig. 2.17). It is not always clear whether the positions of the causeways correspond to gaps in the bank, but it is obvious that this was more than a constructional technique. On the Continent, palisaded enclosures are known whose perimeters were broken in a similar manner. The same may have happened at Knowth (G. Eogan 1984) and perhaps at other sites in Ireland. Some of the enclosures are approximately circular or oval, but this is not always the case.

A recent study draws together much of the research on earthworks of this kind (Oswald, Dyer, and Barber 2001). Two points need making at the outset.

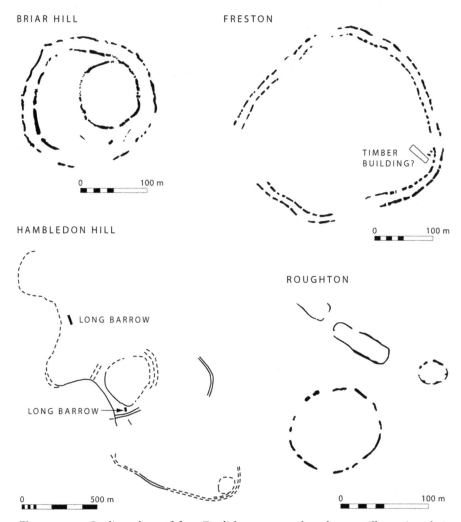

Figure 2.17. Outline plans of four English causewayed enclosures, illustrating their relationship to other earthworks. Information from Oswald, Dyer, and Barber (2001).

These monuments were first identified from surface remains and were subsequently recognised on air photographs, but there are other structures which may have been closely related to them. These are found in western Britain and are typified by the excavated enclosures at Carn Brea and Helman Tor in Cornwall (Mercer 1981a; 1997). They were built on granite and were defined by drystone walls as well as earthworks. They are of the same date as the more conventional sites, but took a rather different form. Often the perimeter extended between a series of prominent natural outcrops, and at Carn Brea the enclosure banks were interrupted at intervals. Similar monuments have been claimed in northwest England (Fig. 2.18; Pearson and Topping 2002) and the west of Ireland (C. Jones 2004: 42–3) but remain unexcavated.

Figure 2.18. The possible Neolithic enclosure on Carrock Fell, northwest England.

The second observation concerns the roles played by these monuments. It has always been supposed that they had a single function which could be established by careful fieldwork. There is some reason to doubt this view. Their Continental counterparts had a lengthy history extending from the late Linearbandkeramik to the Copper Age. Whilst the earthwork perimeter retained its characteristic form, the sites seem to have been used in quite different ways from one period to another. There is also evidence for considerable regional variation. Individual examples extend along a continuum from enclosed settlements or even hillforts to ceremonial centres. Some of these sites were associated with buildings, pits, and specialised deposits of artefacts; others were almost empty (Bradley 1998: Chapter 5). It comes as no surprise that the same should be true in Britain. Thus a walled enclosure like Carn Brea is associated with wooden houses, defences, and areas of cultivated ground (Mercer 1981a), whilst the earthwork monument at Etton in eastern England contained placed deposits of artefacts, animal bones, and human remains. Although it was especially well preserved, it did not include any buildings (Pryor 1998a). The site was liable to flood and would probably have been inaccessible for part of the year.

This does not imply that individual enclosures in Britain and Ireland were either ceremonial centres or settlements, although opinion has certainly oscillated between these two extremes. There are several grounds for caution. Even at carefully excavated monuments from which houses seem to have been absent, the material that was deposited has a similar composition to the finds from domestic sites. It seems as if the pottery is in the same styles, and a recent study of the worked flint from the extensively excavated enclosure complex at

Hambledon Hill failed to identify any features which distinguished it from the assemblages found in settlements (Saville 2002). In the same way, both settlements and enclosures can be associated with pits containing carefully selected groups of cultural material. Both can provide abundant evidence of burning, and human bones are recorded from enclosures as well as the places where people lived. There are some exotic items from the earthwork monuments, but they can be found elsewhere. The main distinction between causewayed enclosures and open settlements is simply the greater formality with which artefacts and other items were deployed (Edmonds 1999).

This has several aspects. There was the formality that was inherent in the very design of these earthworks. They comprised one or more circuits of bank and ditch interrupted at regular intervals by causeways and sometimes by more formal entrances. The perimeter was entirely permeable. There are individual monuments with several concentric earthworks where different activities may have taken place in different areas, but this has only been demonstrated at Windmill Hill where the character of the deposits seems to have changed as one moved towards the innermost enclosure. Here it appears that the outer part of the monument was associated with deposits of cultural material and human remains, mainly those of infants. Craft production, butchery, and the deposition of meat joints were associated with the next sector of the enclosure, whilst it was the innermost space that was most obviously linked with the domestic world (Whittle, Pollard, and Grigson 1999). At Etton, which had only one ditch, the internal space was divided in half (Pryor 1998a). One part included a series of deposits associated with the activities of the living, whilst the other contained imported artefacts and burnt human and animal bones. Again there is no uniformity beyond the basic point that such material had been deposited according to certain conventions.

The extensively excavated enclosure at Etton is revealing in another way, for the excavator has questioned the conventional assumption that this monument was ever conceived as an enclosure in the way that archaeologists had supposed. He suggests that it is better thought of as an arrangement of separate pits, not all of which were dug or maintained simultaneously. Rather than forming a continuous (or discontinuous) bank, the excavated soil was spread around the rims of these features to create a platform from which people could view their contents. The separate pits or ditch segments contained a wide variety of deposits which had been carefully placed there, including human skulls, meat joints, axeheads, and complete pots. These were often laid out in formal patterns then covered over. The individual sections of the perimeter were repeatedly recut, allowing the original offerings to be inspected and further material to be added. A similar process has been identified at most extensively excavated sites. Although there is little evidence, there is no reason to suppose that material culture was deployed with any less formality at the walled enclosures of western Britain.

Having stressed the ways in which these deposits had been treated, it is important to add that certain monuments changed their form and character over time. They may have been rebuilt with continuous earthworks at a late stage in their development, and it was then that most of the causeways in their ditches were removed, creating a continuous barrier. It seems possible that the banks were rebuilt with vertical outer walls or timber revetments, and formal entrances may also have been established. This has not been observed at many sites, but it does raise the possibility that some of the earthworks were gradually changed into defensible enclosures. It may be no accident that among them were Hambledon Hill and Crickley Hill, both of which occupied conspicuous positions that were reused as Iron Age hillforts (Oswald, Dyer, and Barber 2001: 127–30). Other examples may include Carn Brea and Hembury, again in western England. It is particularly interesting that several of these sites include unusual concentrations of arrowheads, suggesting that they had been attacked. The bodies of two men who had clearly been killed by arrows were found in the ditch of the Stepleton enclosure at Hambledon Hill (Healy 2004: 32). There may have been a high level of violence during this period, but the evidence has often been overlooked. It is certainly consistent with the injuries shown by human bones found in other contexts in Britain (Schulting and Wysocki 2005).

Just as causewayed ditches could be rebuilt as defensive earthworks, entire enclosures could be duplicated. Thus there are a number of sites where at least two of these monuments were built close to one another or even side by side. Examples include Hambledon Hill and Rybury, where they are located some distance apart, and Hembury, Court Hill, Fornham All Saints, and Etton, where the two structures were adjacent to one another (Oswald, Dyer, and Barber 2001: 112–13). Only at Hambledon Hill is there evidence that they were built at different times and had different contents (Healy 2004). Enclosures could also extend their area, and Oswald, Dyer, and Barber have suggested that a number of examples with several concentric circuits may have developed over a significant period of time (2001: 75–7). In most cases they seem to have been enlarged, and, as this happened, they might assume a more regular ground plan. These authors comment on a number of examples which would have appeared to be approximately circular to anyone inside them or encountering them from a distance.

Early fieldwork at causewayed enclosures was concerned with investigating their credentials as the elusive Earlier Neolithic settlements of lowland England. Although they produced what seemed to be 'domestic' assemblages, from an early stage it became apparent that there were too many anomalies for this interpretation to be warranted. Instead of the general scatter of animal bones that might have been found at a living site, substantial meat joints had been committed to the ground and sometimes entire animals had been buried there. As well as the remains of animals there were human bones, sometimes burials but more often disarticulated fragments similar to those associated with long barrows. All this material had been placed in the ground with some deliberation, and normally it had been carefully covered over. It seemed more likely that these deposits resulted from specialised events which may have included episodes of feasting, the sacrifice of animals, offerings of food, and the celebration of the dead (Edmonds 1999). There is even evidence of opium poppy from the enclosure at Etton (Pryor 1998a: chapter 10). These ideas received powerful support from excavation at Hambledon Hill which showed that in the enclosure ditches there had been a large quantity of human skulls (Healy 2004).

Similar anomalies soon became apparent among the artefacts from these monuments. On a site like Etton there was a strong representation of decorated pottery, but perhaps more important was the observation that at Windmill Hill there were few large vessels suitable for storage and many small bowls that could be used for serving food and drink (Howard 1981: 11–20). Similarly, the presence of nonlocal artefacts raised an interesting problem. From the early years of the excavation of Windmill Hill it had been apparent that stone axes from distant regions of Britain were distributed on and around the site, and for that reason the enclosure, and others like it, were identified as nodal points in the Neolithic 'axe trade' (Bradley and Edmonds 1993: 50–2). This was illogical since these objects has clearly been brought to these sites but had never left them again. Closer attention to their contexts showed that many of them had been deposited there together with the other material discussed in this section. At Etton, it even seems as if they were destroyed by working them down and placing the resulting fragments in pits together with burnt human bone (Pryor 1998a: 260–8). The walled enclosure at Carn Brea may have been linked with the production of pottery and axeheads in the surrounding area (Mercer 1981a: 189), and what may be a similar site on Carrock Fell in northwest England was located on a mountain top close to a Neolithic axe quarry (Fell and Davis 1988; Pearson and Topping 2002). Such connections made it even less likely that these monuments had been ordinary settlements. Perhaps they were aggregation sites where public events took place.

There are good reasons for accepting this view. The development of causewayed enclosures happened during a period which saw significant changes in the nature of material culture. After an initial phase in which pots had taken a similar form throughout most parts of Britain and Ireland, there are the first signs of regional diversity, reflected by the first adoption of more local styles of decoration (Gibson 2002a: chapter 4). At the same time, there is evidence for a marked increase in the production and exchange of stone axes. The products of individual sources seem to have been distributed over larger areas, and fieldwork at the Cumbrian quarries even suggests that now they were being made in larger numbers and with greater skill (Bradley and Edmonds 1993: chapters 6 and 7). Both these new developments are evidenced at causewayed enclosures, although there is a danger of circularity as these sites provide so many stratified contexts. If the artefact assemblage seems to have been more diverse, so was the human population associated with these monuments. Michael Richards has shown that the bones from different tombs show quite separate dietary signatures from one site to another (2000: 125–35). Those found in the enclosure complex at Hambledon Hill suggest that the people whose remains were deposited there had lived in a whole range of different environments or had engaged in different methods of food production. Further work on a sample of skeletal remains from England suggests that Neolithic people also had a wide variety of lifestyles (Wysocki and Whittle 2000).

In recent years more attention has been paid to the setting of these monuments, and that tendency has only increased with the expansion of field archaeology. It soon became clear that whilst some of the enclosures included enormous collections of Earlier Neolithic artefacts, they were actually set apart from the ordinary settlements of the same period. They might be located in isolated positions towards the margins of the settled landscape and could often be seen from a distance. Some of the sites commanded an extensive view, and others were intervisible with the stone sources where flint axes were made, yet environmental evidence suggests that a number of them had been located within woodland clearings (K. Thomas 1982). Far from being the 'central places' of this period, certain sites were located in peripheral positions and may have been built in neutral locations in between the main concentrations of population. That even applies to an enormous monument complex like Hambledon Hill (Healy 2004).

It has long been accepted that some causewayed enclosures are closely linked to the positions of long barrows, but this statement needs some qualification. They were first built after the earliest mortuary monuments, and while a few examples are located close to burial mounds of the orthodox type, they are also paired with more specialised earthworks. These are usually smaller oval or round barrows of a type that is often associated with a distinctive burial rite. Instead of containing the disarticulated bones of a number of different individuals, they cover the graves of a small number of people and sometimes only one person. They also depart from normal practice because they are associated with grave goods, usually decorated pottery, an arrowhead, or a flint knife. This was demonstrated at Abingdon in the Thames Valley where the ditch enclosing a burial mound of this type contained the same series of deposits as the adjacent causewayed enclosure (Bradley 1992).

One result of the recent expansion of developer-funded archaeology is that more is known about the areas outside causewayed enclosures. Close to the oval barrow at Abingdon there seems to have been a flat cemetery of similar age to the principal monument. The graves were not covered by any kind of mound, and their chronology was only established by radiocarbon dating.

In the same area was what is best described as a 'mortuary house' of the kind associated with long barrows (Barclay and Halpin 1999: 27–31)). This contained the disarticulated bones of a number of individuals which had been placed there during the period in which the enclosure was in use. Again there was no evidence of any barrow. What may have been a similar feature has been observed outside a causewayed enclosure at Husbands Bosworth in the English midlands (Buckley and George 2003: 138–40). At Thornhill in the north of Ireland a group of houses enclosed by a number of discontinuous palisades was associated with further structures which may have been of this type (Logue 2003: 151–3).

Another result of fieldwork in the vicinity of causewayed enclosures has been the recognition that the distribution of pits and artefact scatters may extend beyond the limits of these earthworks. This is most obvious at Etton in eastern England where a large number of pits have been found (French and Pryor 2005: 167). They have the same range of contents as the deposits associated with the enclosures. There is similar evidence from Robin Hood's Ball in Wessex (J. Richards 1990: 61) and Husbands Bosworth in the East Midlands (Buckley and George 2003: 138–40). At Eton in the Thames Valley extensive and well-preserved midden deposits have been discovered in between the sites of two causewayed enclosures (Allen, Barclay, and Landin-Whymark 2004).

The relationship between causewayed enclosures and cursus monuments raises further problems (Fig. 2.19). The dates of the early timber cursuses in northern Britain should overlap with those from causewayed enclosures during the second quarter of the fourth millennium BC. To a large extent their distributions did not coincide. The later cursuses, however, were considerable structures and are found across virtually the entire distribution of causewayed enclosures in the south. Here there seem to be two principal relationships between these very different traditions of earthwork building. In some areas, for example the Thames Valley, the cursus monuments seem to avoid the places where causewayed enclosures had been built, so that it is perfectly possible for both to have been used simultaneously. In other cases it is clear that a cursus or related monument cuts across the position of an existing causewayed enclosure, suggesting that it had fallen out of use.

The clearest examples of this relationship are at Ramsgate in Kent (Dyson, Shand, and Stevens 2000), Etton in eastern England (Pryor 1998a), and Maiden Castle in the south (Sharples 1991: 255–7). The excavation at Ramsgate is not yet published, but at Etton, two cursuses were constructed running more or less parallel to one another following the former course of the River Welland. The Maxey cursus ended alongside the enclosure, whilst the Etton Cursus, which may have continued the axis established by its neighbour, crossed the position of that enclosure, cutting it in half. In principle, that should have involved a

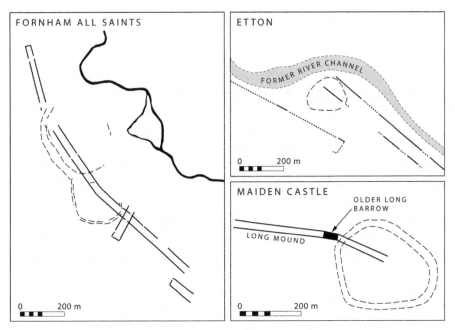

Figure 2.19. The relationship between causewayed enclosures, cursuses, and bank barrows. At Fornham All Saints, East Anglia, a cursus cuts across two of these enclosures and runs parallel to a river. At Etton, East Anglia, two cursuses follow the course of another river and one of them cuts across a causewayed enclosure. At Maiden Castle, Wessex, a long barrow built just outside a similar enclosure was lengthened at both ends. Information from Oswald, Dyer, and Barber (2001) and Bradley (1983).

drastic transformation, but it is intriguing that the older earthwork had already been divided into two parts, one associated with deposits connected with daily life and the other containing human and animal remains (Pryor 1998a: chapter 16). The new division followed a different course but may have maintained the same concept. This is less likely to have happened at Maiden Castle, where it seems likely that a long barrow had been built just outside the perimeter of another causewayed enclosure. That is not an uncommon pattern, but in this case the mound was extended at both ends so that in one direction it ran straight across the existing monument and, in the other, continued for a considerable distance outside it (Sharples 1991: fig. 33). Something rather similar may have happened at Fornham All Saints in eastern England. Here two causewayed enclosures seem to have been built side by side, one of them as an annexe to the original monument. The same axis was followed by a cursus which seems to have cut across both earthworks following a path which runs parallel to the River Lark. There were two other monuments of the same kind nearby, one of them running past an older enclosure and perhaps extending to the river bank (Oswald, Dyer, and Barber 2001: 75–6 and 134–5). It seems clear that an important transformation of the landscape was under way.

THE FUTURE: CURSUSES, ROUND BARROWS,
AND CIRCULAR ENCLOSURES

Although cursuses and causewayed enclosures may have coexisted for a time, it
was the linear monuments that retained their significance for a longer period.
That is not to say that the sites of older enclosures were necessarily deserted,
for many of them do produce finds of artefacts of Later Neolithic and Earlier
Bronze Age date. Nor were these places entirely without later monuments,
generally burial mounds, but it was rare for the original structure to be refurbished during these episodes of reuse. It seems more likely that attention shifted
towards the positions of the newly established cursuses.

In fact one reason why such structures were originally dated to the Later
Neolithic period was simply the fact that they remained the focus for deposits of
distinctive artefacts. These might be placed in and around their earthworks, and
there even seem to be cases in which their ditches were recut. The problem was
made even worse by the character of some of the pottery associated with these
monuments, or with the smaller structures that seem to have been built around
them. This belongs to a loosely defined tradition of lavishly decorated ceramics
collectively known as Peterborough Ware, although it can be subdivided into
a number of regional styles. Although decorated pottery came into use during
the currency of long mounds and causewayed enclosures, the greater part of the
Peterborough tradition had been assigned to the Later Neolithic period, and
it was usually supposed that it did not go out of fashion completely until the
Earlier Bronze Age. Radiocarbon dating suggests that this scheme was incorrect
and that pottery of this type may have been current at a significantly earlier date
than was once supposed; it may have originated about 3400 BC and have gone
out of use during the Later Neolithic period (Gibson and Kinnes 1997). The
implications of this work have not been properly assimilated, for this means
that a number of traditions of monument building could have originated by
the later fourth millennium BC and may have ended much sooner than was
originally believed.

These rather technical arguments affect a series of earthworks which are
commonly associated with cursus monuments, although it cannot be established that they were of exactly the same dates as one another. They also raise
questions of terminology and interpretation.

The problem of terminology needs to be considered first. Here it is necessary
to consider two problematical categories that appear in the current literature:
round barrows and 'hengiform' enclosures (Fig. 2.20). Round barrows are
simply circular mounds, which are generally delimited by a ditch. Although it
is often thought that they are associated with individual burials, that is not always
the case, and particularly along the North Sea coast individual examples may
cover the remains of 'mortuary houses' formed by split tree trunks exactly like
those associated with long barrows. They may also include the disarticulated

RADLEY

PITNACREE

ETTON

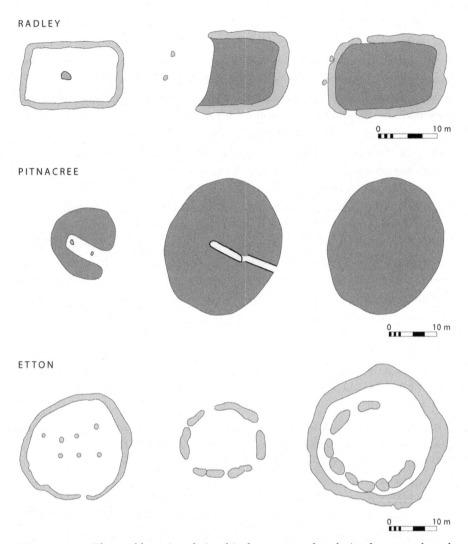

Figure 2.20. The problematic relationship between oval and circular mounds and enclosures. This drawing illustrates three sequences. At Barrow Hills, Upper Thames Valley, an open enclosure containing a grave was replaced by an oval mound with a forecourt and then by a larger earthwork. At Pitnacree (central Scotland), an oval mound enclosing a mortuary structure was replaced in stone and approached by a narrow passage providing access through a larger circular mound. Finally, the entire structure was closed. At Etton, East Anglia, three circular enclosures, two of them incorporating causewayed ditches, were built in succession. Information from Bradley (1992), Coles and Simpson (1965), and French and Pryor (2005).

remains of a number of people (Kinnes 1979). The same applies to some of the small circular cairns in western Britain, which can be associated with simple stone-built chambers (Darvill 2004: 60–2). Both types can also be found buried beneath more impressive long mounds.

There are two reasons for the confusion. The first results from the chronological problems mentioned earlier. So long as Peterborough Ware was considered to be a Later Neolithic tradition, it was very tempting to compare these monuments with the round barrows associated with Bell Beaker pottery and early metalwork in the later third millennium BC. Rather than viewing them as a new tradition that had been introduced from the Continent, it seemed likely that these monuments were built in a long-established local style, in which case only the artefacts selected for burial would have been a novel development (Kinnes 1979). That idea is no longer tenable, and there is little or no evidence for a continuous tradition of round barrows extending through the Later Neolithic, although it is uncertain quite when their construction lapsed.

The second source of confusion was that a number of circular mounds really did contain individual burials with grave goods, although some of these monuments may actually have included a succession of such deposits. The mounds were of various sizes, from the 'great barrows' of northern England to the smaller examples recorded in East Anglia, Wessex, or the Thames Valley. They are sometimes claimed to be a particular feature of northeast England, but the results of commercial fieldwork have shown that this is not the case. Moreover, some of the Neolithic 'round barrows' on the Yorkshire Wolds excavated in the nineteenth century have proved to be only the most prominent parts of denuded long barrows. This has been established by recent fieldwork and is also apparent from the results of air photography (Stoertz 1997: 23–4). That is not to deny that individual burials were important in this area, but one reason why they have played such a prominent role is that northeast England saw a major campaign of fieldwork during the Victorian era. The excavations of the last twenty years have shown that similar graves can be found in most parts of Britain.

In Ireland, there have been similar problems, but in this case they have been resolved by radiocarbon dating. These concern what are called Linkardstown cists (Raftery 1974). They are individual inhumation burials placed within massive stone coffins and buried beneath a substantial round cairn. These burials are quite distinct from the main classes of megalithic tomb, and were inaccessible once the monument had been built. Again there was the same temptation to interpret these single burials in the light of superficially similar practices during the Earlier Bronze Age, but radiocarbon dating has shown that in fact they belong to the period between about 3600 and 3300 BC (Brindley and Lanting 1990). They occur in a restricted zone crossing the middle part of the island from east to west, but may be of similar date to their British counterparts.

'Hengiform enclosures' raise a similar problem, for the term implies that they are related to the enclosures known as 'henges' which were built in the Later Neolithic period. They are supposed to be miniature versions of these monuments (Wainwright 1969), but the morphological argument is far from convincing, for in some cases they are simply circular earthworks with one or more entrances; others were defined by causewayed ditches. The chronological argument is on even weaker ground, for the link with henges was postulated at a time when it was believed that the currency of Peterborough Ware extended well into the third millennium BC. Now that seems unlikely, meaning that in lowland England at any rate the currency of these two forms of monument need not have overlapped. Again the conventional terminology conceals some dangerous assumptions about the chronology of different earthworks.

In this case there are even more problems to consider. Most of the hengiform enclosures have been identified from crop marks or by excavations on sites which had been levelled by cultivation. For that reason it is often uncertain whether these were the remains of circular enclosures that were open at the centre or were ploughed-out round barrows of the kind described already. Moreover, one of the defining characteristics of a henge monument is the presence of an external bank and an internal ditch. In many cases it is impossible to reconstruct the form of the original earthwork with any confidence (Bradley and Chambers 1988). All that is clear is that the ditch was repeatedly recut. Sometimes the monument also increased in area as the perimeter was rebuilt. If broader comparisons are needed, it would be more consistent with the evidence to suggest that these were miniature versions of causewayed enclosures. That would account for the interrupted ditches which define a number of these monuments and for the structured deposits of artefacts, human bones, and food remains that are occasionally found there. It may be that these represent the end of a long tradition. It is certainly true that they are commonly associated with cursuses rather than large curvilinear enclosures.

There is another problem, too. In their desire to fit excavated monuments into well established 'types', fieldworkers have exercised some latitude in their identification of *round* barrows and *ring* ditches, for a number of these monuments are not actually circular. That provides an important clue, for it is already apparent that Earlier Neolithic mortuary monuments included a number of oval mounds which are unhelpfully described as 'short long barrows'. Until recently these seemed to represent the end of the tradition of building elongated mounds, but there is reason to doubt this now. Although certain examples are associated with individual burials with grave goods, others include more complex arrangements of human bones. Earthworks of this kind can be associated with settings of split tree trunks exactly like those associated with more orthodox monuments, and the radiocarbon dates from the two groups of earthwork overlap. A few of these mounds were even rebuilt to a circular ground plan during a secondary phase. As so often, an unnecessarily rigid typology conceals what was probably a continuum. The point is illustrated by the excavation of a valley-bottom site at Raunds in the east midlands which revealed a whole series of 'non-standard' Neolithic monuments (Healy and Harding in press).

Oval mounds were built on various scales, from the substantial structures that are found at the southern terminal of the Dorset Cursus (Barrett, Bradley, and Green 1991: chapter 2) to much smaller and lower mounds like the example associated with the Abingdon causewayed enclosure (Fig. 2.20; Bradley 1992). Even so, they share one important characteristic, for the earthwork was commonly flanked by a ditch on three sides, leaving one end of the structure open. That space was usually filled during a subsequent phase, so that the completed structure had a continuous perimeter, although it was often broken by narrow causeways. Such monuments are commonly found close to cursuses and may even share the same axis as those monuments. Cursuses can extend up to earthworks of this kind and may even incorporate them in their terminals. A good example of these relationships may be found at Eynesbury in eastern England where a U-ditched long barrow seems to have been built on the same alignment as a nearby cursus (Ellis 2004). An even shorter mound of similar type was located beside that earthwork with its long axis at right angles to it. At some stage (the dating evidence is not altogether satisfactory) the larger barrow seems to have been lengthened and contained within a second cursus monument. The smaller mound was closed by excavating a narrow ditch across its open end (Fig. 2.21)

Again the evidence is rather ambiguous. On most sites the excavated remains are reduced to features cut into the bedrock, and it is not always clear whether they enclosed a mound or whether some monuments were open at the centre. Oval mounds certainly survive as earthworks, but low platforms and open enclosures have also been recorded by field survey. This may reflect the amount of human labour that could be invested in the creation of individual structures, but it is just as likely that any mounds might have been composed largely of topsoil and turf. In that case nothing would survive a long period of ploughing. The argument is especially troubling as it is known that some of the surviving long mounds, among them examples of considerable size, were built in exactly this way. Despite all these uncertainties, it seems likely that oval mounds or enclosures were used during the same period as Neolithic round barrows and long barrows and were associated with similar mortuary rituals. What is not so clear is when they went out of use.

Lastly, it seems as if a few large circular enclosures were built during the currency of cursus monuments, and sometimes in their vicinity. Again there are problems of terminology, for they have been described as early henges. At present two groups of enclosures pose particular problems. In Wessex, the earliest enclosure at Stonehenge is precisely circular and is defined by a causewayed ditch with three main entrances and an internal bank (Cleal, Walker, and Montague 1995: chapter 5). Another enclosure at Flagstones, closer to the south coast, takes the same form, and both are associated with a series of placed deposits of human and animal bone very similar to those from conventional causewayed enclosures (R. Smith et al. 1997: 27–47). The only problem is that they are unusually late in date and may belong to the very end of that tradition. In the same way, several larger enclosures in northeast England

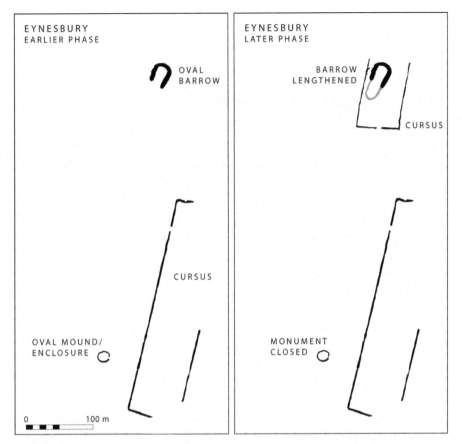

Figure 2.21. The possible sequence at Eynesbury, East Anglia, where two cursuses are associated with oval or circular mounds, each of which was modified in the course of its history. Information from Ellis (2004).

are characterised by a circular ground plan and an interrupted ditch. One of these monuments encloses the enormous Neolithic round barrow of Duggleby Howe (Fig. 2.22; Kinnes et al. 1983), and the same relationship can be suggested between monuments at Maxey in East Anglia (Pryor et al. 1985) and perhaps at West Cotton (Healy and Harding in press) and Dallington in the East Midlands (Oswald, Dyer, and Barber 2001: fig. 3.4). Yet another circular enclosure of this kind lies astride the Thornborough cursus. These earthworks are especially confusing, for in northeast England they seem to have been replaced by henge monuments of conventional type (J. Harding 2000: 90–5), in the same way as may have happened at Stonehenge. This evidence is discussed in Chapter Three.

Those developments were still in the future, and it seems unlikely that they had a significant impact on the course of events during the Later Neolithic period. They are better thought of as representing the last expressions of a whole range of ideas that had been present in Britain, and sometimes Ireland, from the first introduction of agriculture. A different kind of sequence will be considered in Chapter Three, but first it is necessary to sum up the main themes so far.

THE PAST: ANCESTORS AND ORIGINS

Gabriel Cooney called one chapter in his influential study of Neolithic Ireland 'The dead are everywhere' (2000: 86–126). It could not be more appropriate. Many of the settlements and monuments considered in this chapter have been associated with human remains, often incomplete bodies or isolated bones. It seems as if what have been described as burial mounds were really more specialised monuments to which the dead could be brought and from which relics might be taken away. Although there are intact bodies at long mounds and megalithic tombs just as there are a small number of flat graves during this period, it seems as if individual bones could also be treated like artefacts and passed from one location to another before their final deposition.

Why should people have shown so much concern with the dead, particularly when finds of Mesolithic burials in Britain and Ireland are very rare? On one level it is easy to argue that this is a general characteristic of agricultural societies. The adoption of farming required forward planning, and necessitated a new sense of time quite different from the annual cycles that dominate the lives of foragers. Land clearance was a lengthy process which extended from one generation to another, so that the success of food production was partly due to the efforts of earlier generations. Strategic decisions had to be made which also influenced activities in the future. A certain proportion of the domesticated animals had to be maintained over the winter months if people were to have sufficient breeding stock. Some of the harvest needed to be stored so that it could be sown in the following year, and areas of land might have to remain fallow in order to regain their fertility. In that sense one could argue that early agriculturists place more emphasis on ancestry than mobile hunter gatherers (Meillassoux 1972). Moreover, they feel a sense of obligation to their ancestors, to whom they owe their prosperity.

The problem with this model is its wide application. James Whitley (2002) has complained that British prehistorians invoke the importance of ancestry in virtually everything they write, so that the significance of these ideas is asserted rather than argued. There is some justification for this view: ancestors are certainly fashionable in contemporary archaeology. Are there other ways in which to explain the distinctive character of the Earlier Neolithic period in these islands?

This chapter began by discussing the origins of the insular Neolithic, contrasting the arguments for acculturation and continuity with those which favour a more radical disruption. To what extent were changes brought about by settlement from overseas? The conventional approach to this question is remarkably

DUGGLEBY HOWE

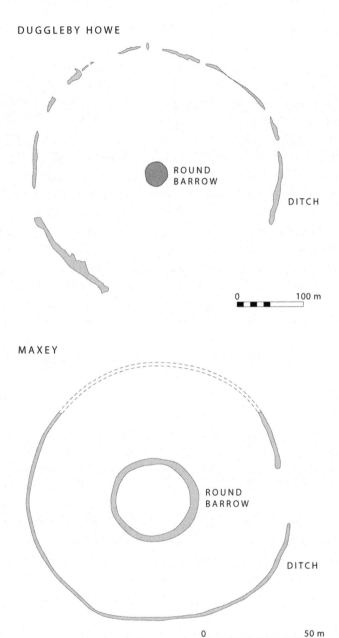

ROUND
BARROW

DITCH

0   100 m

MAXEY

ROUND
BARROW

DITCH

0   50 m

Figure 2.22. (Upper) Outline plan of the Neolithic round barrow surrounded by an interrupted ditch at Duggleby Howe, northeast England. (Lower) A similar relationship at Maxey, East Anglia, where the mound is not closely dated and the outer enclosure has been interpreted as a henge monument. Information from Kinnes et al. (1983) and Pryor et al. (1985).

unhelpful. In principle, it should be possible to define the source, or sources, of any migrants through a close comparison between the material culture of Neolithic Britain and Ireland and its counterparts on the European mainland. Although there are a number of general similarities, particularly among the undecorated ceramics which were the earliest in these islands, attempts to define more exact links have so far failed. That is probably because the study area would have been accessible from so many different areas of Continental Europe. These included parts of the mainland whose inhabitants may have had few contacts with one another. Indeed, it is ironic that it has been easier to suggest the sources of the cattle introduced from overseas than it has been to trace closely related artefacts. Not surprisingly, they connect northern France and southern England (Tresset 2003).

That leaves the question of monumental architecture. This was an entirely new phenomenon at the beginning of the British and Irish Neolithic. There were no precedents apart from a setting of massive timbers on the site which was later to become Stonehenge and a few post holes of similar date, and even these were thousands of years earlier than the time considered here (Allen and Gardiner 2002). Again it is important to emphasise that the only signs of social complexity in the insular Mesolithic come from the first part of that period. The new developments were of three main kinds: long mounds, causewayed enclosures, and cursuses.

The first two of these traditions originated in Continental Europe, whilst the third was possibly inspired by the building of monumental 'houses' in Scotland and was considered in the previous section. There has been considerable discussion of the mounds and enclosures and it is not necessary to repeat all the arguments here. Nonetheless there is a strong case that long barrows first developed as representations of domestic buildings. A common objection is that these types are not contemporary with one another; long barrows originated when long houses were going out of use. That is probably true, but this very observation helps to account for the relationship between them. On a site like Balloy in north-central France where such barrows were constructed over the sites of older domestic buildings, it seems clear that people had intended to commemorate the characteristic form of a kind of dwelling that was no longer being built (Mordant 1998). Rather than confining their attention to classifying these physical structures, prehistorians should consider the wider importance of the house among early farmers. It was a metaphor for a certain way of living, and it may have been this concept that was celebrated as the pattern of settlement changed. It seems possible that the houses of the dead referred back to a past when buildings of similar proportions had been inhabited by the living. If so, their construction was also a statement of origins.

The same could apply to Continental causewayed enclosures, for they seem to have had a similar history. The first were simply the earthwork perimeters around settlements containing long houses, but soon the relationship between these features became more complicated. Empty enclosures might be built at some distance from groups of domestic buildings, or they might enclose the positions of settlements that had recently been abandoned. In a parallel process to the development of long barrows, these earthworks assumed a life of their own as the tradition of building massive dwellings lapsed. By this time the earthworks had assumed a greater formality and their characteristic ground plan was well established, but most of them were no longer used as settlements. Rather, they seem to have been aggregation sites for a wider population: places where feasts took place, dead bodies were exposed, artefacts were made and exchanged, and where increasing numbers of objects, animal bones, and human remains were deposited in pits and ditches. Whilst these were very different from the practices that took place in older settlements, the way in which the perimeter maintained its traditional form suggests that some links were still maintained. Perhaps these enclosures evoked a tradition of communal living that had existed in the past but which was no longer considered feasible or even appropriate (Bradley 1998b: chapter 5). Again it seems as if the architecture of these monuments made a direct reference to the past.

Why is this so relevant to Britain and Ireland, where there had never been a tradition of long houses or enclosed settlements? Perhaps it is because these monuments were still considered to refer to a distant past. Maybe their construction and use evoked an origin myth, as it may have done in Continental Europe. That could account for the continuous recycling of the remains of the dead and would suggest that the Earlier Neolithic population showed an almost obsessive concern with its own history. If so, it seems difficult to argue for complete continuity with the Mesolithic period. If the inhabitants of both islands celebrated a distant origin in other times and places, who is to say that they were wrong?

CHAPTER 3

NORTH AND SOUTH

TIME AND SPACE

If Chapter Two was really about time, Chapter Three is more concerned with space. The earlier part of the Neolithic period was interpreted in terms of origins and ideas about origins. If people introduced farming from the Continent, they also seem to have acknowledged their past by the kinds of monuments that they built. The construction of long mounds may have commemorated the houses of their ancestors, and causewayed enclosures the settlements in which earlier generations had lived. Chapter Two juxtaposed archaeological arguments about the character and chronology of the Earlier Neolithic period with an interpretation of the ways in which prehistoric people might have thought about their own histories (Figs. 3.1 and 3.2).

Chapter Three takes a different turn. It considers an even longer sequence, from the years preceding 3000 BC up to 1500 BC, but for part of that time communities in these two islands seem to have closed in on themselves, and links with Continental Europe may have lapsed. In their place there were stronger connections between different parts of Britain and Ireland. Those new alignments are summed up by the title 'North and South'. The situation did not change significantly until the adoption of metals in the late third millennium BC.

In another way, the processes described in both chapters do have something in common. Chapter Two was mainly concerned with the ways in which unfamiliar practices were adopted in both islands. They included new ways of living, new methods of food production, novel attitudes to the dead, and, most of all, the creation of a distinctive range of monuments. These buildings provided the clearest indication of a fresh way of thinking about the world. There were certain changes during the crucial period between 4000 and 3300 BC, and yet these local differences seemed less important than more general trends. But there is another way of interpreting some of the evidence. It is an approach that can also be taken to the archaeology of the following period.

If the contents of long barrows and long cairns suggest that personal differences were played down, this may not have gone unopposed. During the mid-fourth millennium BC there were individual burials in Britain, most of them in round barrows (Kinnes 1979). Such monuments were widely distributed, and by 3000 BC they were associated with a distinctive range of grave goods (Kinnes 2004). The idea that they were a special feature of northern England has been discredited by the results of contract archaeology. The importance of individual burials seems to have increased as the process of monument building intensified and reached its limits. At the same time, these graves are often found close to earthworks of long-established forms, including causewayed enclosures and cursuses, or were even added to existing mortuary monuments like those at Whitegrounds (Brewster 1984) or Biggar Common (D. Johnston 1997). One way of thinking about this sequence is to suppose that the very process of organising and executing the building of these enormous structures emphasised the roles played by particular individuals. The creation and use of these monuments may have helped to highlight the importance of certain members of society (J. Barrett 1994: chapters 3 and 4). Perhaps it was these people whose influence was signified by a new burial rite.

That sequence is widely accepted in British archaeology. Unfortunately, these developments have also been misunderstood, for it has been claimed that the adoption of individual burials in round barrows was something that happened only once: it seemed as if it was established by 3500 BC and that the tradition continued uninterrupted until the introduction of metalwork a thousand years later (Kinnes 1979). To some extent the argument was based on the chronology of Peterborough Ware which was associated with certain of these sites, for it was thought to have been used throughout the Later Neolithic period. The argument is no longer sustainable (Gibson and Kinnes 1997), and in fact there is very little evidence of single graves between about 3000 and 2400 BC. Although a new burial rite may have been established during the currency of causewayed enclosures, cursuses, and even long barrows, it seems to have lapsed not long afterwards.

This has important implications. Individual burials were again deposited in round barrows from the late third millennium BC, but they cannot have conformed to an established insular tradition. Rather, they seem to have resulted from contacts with mainland Europe which resumed at about this time. It may be no accident that they occurred during and just after another peak in the construction of monuments. This was a process that had happened once before. When it took place in the middle of the Neolithic period, its effects had been quite short lived, but when a similar development occurred between 2500 and 2000 BC it had a lasting impact (Barrett 1994: chapters 3 and 4).

The details of these changes are obscured by the terminology used in Britain and Ireland. The major phase of monument building is normally treated as a 'Neolithic' phenomenon, whilst the development of mortuary monuments can

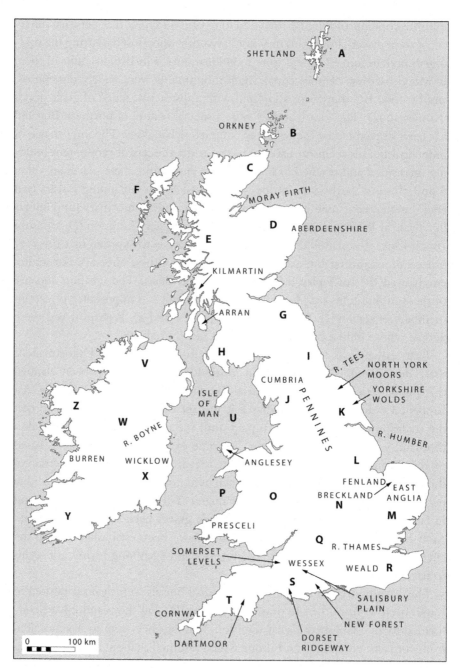

Figure 3.1. Places and regions mentioned in Chapter Three. For the purposes of this map Britain and Ireland have been divided into twenty-six areas, and the individual sites are listed according to these divisions. A: Shetland; B: Orkney *(Barnhouse, Crossiecrown, Cuween, the Howe, Isbister, Maeshowe, Midhowe, Pierowall, Quanterness, Ring of Bookan, Ring of Brodgar, Skara Brae, Stonehall, Stones of Stenness, Taversoe Tuick, Wideford)*; C: Northern Scotland *(Balnuaran of Clava)*; D: Northeast Scotland *(Broomend of Crichie)*; E: Western Scotland *(Temple Wood)*; F: Outer Hebrides *(Calanais)*; G: Eastern and Central Scotland on either side of the Firth of Forth *(Balfarg, Biggar Common, Blackshouse*

be assigned to an *Early* or *Earlier Bronze Age* because they are associated with the first metalwork (the term *Earlier* Bronze Age is preferred here because the *Later* Bronze Age is discussed in Chapter Four). It is clear that these different elements overlap in time, even within the same region. Thus in the small area close to Stonehenge, large structures built out of timber and stone date from the same period as the first graves with metal artefacts (Cleal, Walker, and Montague 1995). It would be wrong to organise this account around a period framework which distinguishes between phenomena that were contemporary with one another. In any case the character of early metallurgy differed between the two islands, although gold and copper may have been worked in both areas before the production of bronze. For that reason Stuart Needham (1996) refers to a 'metal-using Neolithic' which continued until the end of the third millennium BC.

Such differences of terminology reveal a deeper unease. Some of the burial practices that were to be important in the second millennium were clearly established during a time of change which is difficult to characterise by a period label, and yet these developments ran in parallel with others of great antiquity. There is no obvious point at which to interrupt the narrative, and to do so would obscure an important trend, for it was also between 2500 and 2000 BC that a major phase of monument building was followed by the deposition of burials with grave goods. Rather than seeking to keep those different elements apart, this chapter considers them together, for both were vital components in a more general sequence of change.

If this chapter cuts across conventional period boundaries, it also eschews established regional divisions in order to identify the long distance networks that

←——

Figure 3.1 (*continued*) *Burn, Cairnpapple, Meldon Bridge, North Mains*); H: Southwest Scotland (*Dunragit*); I: the English/Scottish borderland (*Milfield*); J: Northwest England (*Langdale, Long Meg, Mayburgh, Pike o' Stickle, Shap*); K: Northeast England and the Peak District (*Arbor Low, Catterick, Duggleby Howe, Ferrybridge, Fylingdales Moor, Thornborough, West Heslerton, Whiteground*); L: Eastern England between the Humber and East Anglia; M: East Anglia (*Arminghall, Grimes Graves, Lawford, Mildenhall, Seahenge, Sutton Hoo, West Whittlesey*); N: the English Midlands (*Barnack, Catholme, Gayhurst, Raunds*); O: the English/Welsh borderland (*Hindwell, Walton*); P: West Wales from the southwest to Anglesey (*Barclodiad Y Gawres, Bedd Branwen, Brenig, Great Orme, Llandegai*); Q: the Thames Valley, Cotswolds, and South Midlands (*Devil's Quoits, Dorchester on Thames, Radley*); R: Southeast England (*Belle Tout, Monkton, Ringlemere*); S: Wessex (*Amesbury, Avebury, Crouch Hill, Durrington Walls, Greyhound Yard, Maumbury Rings, Mount Pleasant, Silbury Hill, Snail Down, Stonehenge, West Kennet, Woodhenge, Wyke Down*); T: Southwest England (*Stanton Drew*); U: the Isle of Man; V: Northern Ireland (*Ballynahatty; Beaghmore, Kiltierney, Rathlin Island, Tievebulliagh*); W: from the Irish Midlands to the east coast (*Balgatheran, Dowth, Fourknocks, Keenoge, Knowth, Lambay Island, Loughcrew, Monknewtown, Newgrange, Tara*); X: Southeast Ireland (*Knockroe*); Y: Southwest Ireland (*Grange 'stone circle', Lough Gur, Ross Island*); Z: the Irish west coast (*Carrowkeel, Carrowmore, Knocknarea, Roughan Hill*).

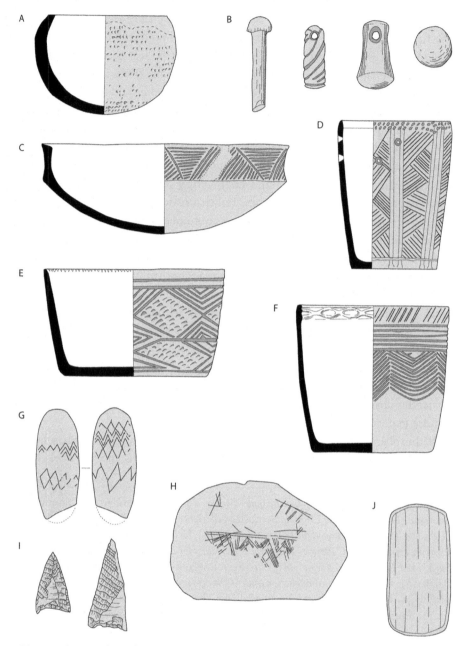

Figure 3.2. Outline drawings of the artefact types mentioned in Chapter Three. Fig. 3.2a shows artefacts ascribed to the Later Neolithic and Fig. 3.2b those of the Earlier Bronze Age. Fig. 3.2a. A: Carrowkeel Ware; B: bone pin, two pendants, and a stone ball of the kind found in passage tombs; C: Unstan bowl; D–F: Grooved Ware; G and H; decorated stone plaques; I: oblique arrowheads; J: polished flint knife. Fig. 3.2b. A–C: Bell Beakers; D: gold earring or hair ornament; E: decorated gold disc; F: barbed and tanged arrowheads; G: battle axe; H and I: axeheads; J and K: daggers; L: halberd (shown as hafted); M and N: Food Vessels; O: Collared Urn; P and Q: spacer plate necklaces of jet (P) and amber (Q).

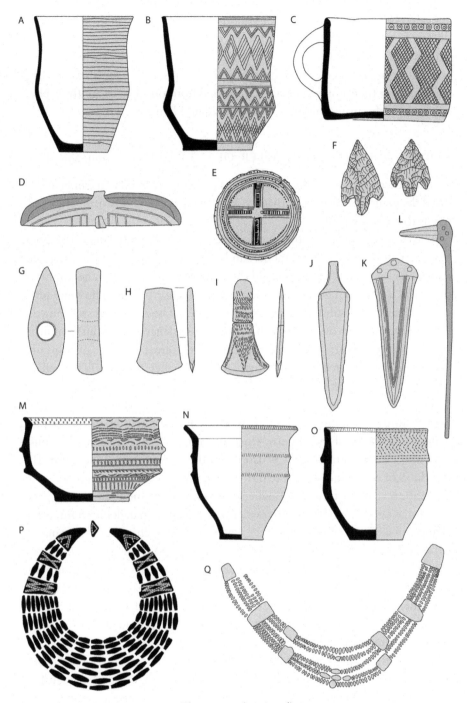

Figure 3.2 (*continued*)

appeared and disappeared between 3300 and 1500 BC. Some of these concerned different parts of Britain and Ireland and did not involve any contact with the European mainland. Others linked some of these areas into an international arena. The importance of such changing alignments is most apparent at a large scale, and yet their impacts would have varied from one area to another. These are some of the issues that have to be considered here.

HOUSES AND THE CHARACTER OF SETTLEMENT, 3300–2000 BC

Despite these regional alignments, there is one general trend that can be recognised throughout Ireland and Britain. The character of prehistoric settlements seems to have changed.

The clearest evidence of this transformation comes from Ireland, for it is here that the nature of these settlements can be compared directly with the pollen record. As noted in Chapter Two, in the first half of the fourth millennium BC there was a peak of clearances associated with cereal pollen. The same phase saw the building of substantial rectangular houses, whose remains are being discovered increasingly often. After that time the evidence takes a different form. New clearings are certainly known but there is less direct evidence of crop cultivation and in some areas human activity made a smaller impact. O'Connell and Molloy (2001) suggest that there may have been more emphasis on stock raising.

The character of domestic dwellings changed too, for by the Later Neolithic period sturdy rectangular buildings were often superseded by ephemeral and generally smaller oval and circular structures, although slight rectangular houses have also been identified which date from the earlier third millennium BC. Buildings of both kinds are more difficult to recognise than their predecessors. Excavation at Knowth in the Boyne Valley has shed some light on this problem. It has defined a structural sequence which runs in parallel with important changes in material culture (Fig. 3.3). The first phase is characterised by undecorated pottery of the kind which is found throughout these islands during the earlier fourth millennium BC. It is associated with a series of rectilinear buildings and two discontinuous palisades which can be compared with causewayed enclosures found on the Continent. Some of these structures had been disturbed by later land use, but others were preserved beneath a series of tombs (G. Eogan 1984; Eogan and Roche 1997).

The main passage tomb at Knowth also sealed the remains of stake-built round houses associated with decorated pottery which was probably an Irish counterpart of Peterborough Ware. The circular buildings overlapped one another and not all of them survived intact, but they were so much slighter than their predecessors that no trace of these structures remained beyond the limits of the mound. Since that earthwork reached its final form about 3000 BC, it follows that this kind of domestic architecture must have been established before then.

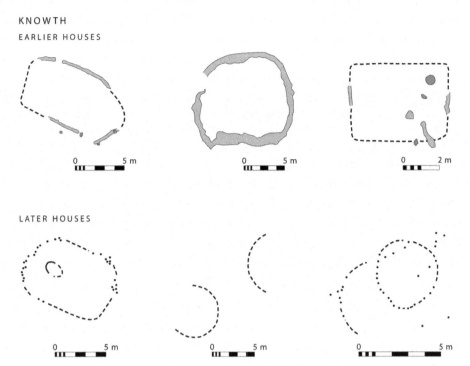

Figure 3.3. Successive house types predating the building of the passage tombs at Knowth in the Boyne Valley, Ireland. Information from Eogan and Roche (1997).

It seems possible that the structures identified at Knowth formed only part of a more extensive settlement. That is certainly suggested by the remains of circular buildings associated with two of the other concentrations of passage tombs in Ireland. A series of rather ephemeral round houses has been identified close to those on Knocknarea (Bergh 1995), and well over a hundred round houses or stone enclosures have also been identified just below the cemetery at Carrowkeel. It is not known how many of the structures were used at the same time, nor is it certain how they were related to the tombs, but these buildings seem to date from the late fourth and earliest third millennia BC (Stefan Bergh, pers. comm.). They may have been used by visitors to these cemeteries, but the best comparison could be with settlements in Orkney where a similar change from rectangular to circular houses took place in the late fourth millennium BC. Here there were small villages of round or oval houses. The best known is Skara Brae (Clarke and Sharples 1990), but the excavated settlement of Barnhouse is perhaps more relevant to the argument. It was established by 3100 BC and was located only a short distance away from the passage tomb of Maeshowe (C. Richards 2004b).

Neolithic houses are preserved in Orkney because they were built of stone (Fig. 3.4). Others are difficult to identify because they were constructed of wood, yet examples have now been recognised on the Scottish mainland and also in England and Wales. The earliest circular dwellings are associated with Peterborough Ware and others are found with Grooved Ware, the ceramic tradition that replaced it during the earlier third millennium BC (Darvill 1996). Although there were still some oval and rectangular structures, circular buildings are being discovered in increasing numbers by excavations in both islands.

Such houses were used throughout the period considered in this chapter, and their forms did not change significantly with the introduction of metals. Some were defined by rings of post sockets, but a few examples were so small that they may have played a specialised role. The surviving evidence usually consists of hearths and circles or arcs of stake holes. There are also pairs of isolated post holes which face southeast. They may be all that remains of the porches of insubstantial buildings which, like so many others, had been aligned on the sunrise. All these structures are accompanied by pits. The clearest indication of a wider settlement pattern comes from the extreme north. In Shetland oval stone-built houses dating from the late fourth millennium BC are found in small groups associated with irregular field plots and clearance cairns. Chambered tombs were located in between these groups of dwellings but were sometimes connected to longer land boundaries. Again that pattern continued unchanged into the Earlier Bronze Age (Whittle 1986).

It is difficult to consider more than a small sample of well-preserved settlements because the structural evidence is so easily destroyed, but in areas with an abundant supply of raw material another source of information is provided by the results of field walking. This has been a particular feature of southern England where flint is widely available. This method can define occupation areas only in the broadest terms, but again there is a striking contrast with the period discussed in Chapter Two. The occupation sites of the Earlier Neolithic period have not been easy to define by field walking because little material remains on the surface. That is probably because the contents of individual settlements were deliberately buried when a site was abandoned (Healy 1987). Although later settlements do include some pits, their positions are generally marked by extensive spreads of artefacts. These cover very large areas, and it is sometimes difficult to decide where one concentration ends and another begins. The inhabitants seem to have made profligate use of the available flint and generated large quantities of debitage during the course of occupation. They also employed a much wider range of separate types than their predecessors, who had favoured a small number of lightweight multipurpose tools (Bradley 1987). That may suggest that certain areas were used more intensively and perhaps for longer periods of time. The largest lithic scatters may have been the sites of settlements as extensive as any of those found in Ireland.

Such observations have not been made in isolation, for in Britain, pollen analysis reveals a continuous expansion in the areas that were occupied (Bradley 1978: 107–9). The same pattern is indicated by the distribution of artefacts,

Figure 3.4. The interior of a well preserved Later Neolithic house at Skara Brae, Orkney.

and it suggests that a wider range of environments were being used than at the beginning of the fourth millennium BC. Some of the clearings may have been quite short lived, but it seems as if activity increased in the uplands, beside natural wetlands, and along the coast. Indeed, by 2000 BC. the occupied area shows a stronger resemblance to the Mesolithic pattern than it does to that during the Earlier Neolithic period. Recent work around two of the major ceremonial centres in England indicates that they had been built in open grassland (Bush 1988; French and Lewis 2005).

Similar evidence is provided by a series of rock carvings made between about 3000 and 2000 BC. They were a feature of Northern Britain and Ireland, and their distribution is revealing (Bradley 1997: chapters 5–10; Beckensall 1999). Although they can cluster around the ceremonial monuments of the Later Neolithic, they may be as closely related to the wider pattern of settlement. They can be found in the vicinity of lithic scatters, as well as on higher ground which overlooks the occupied area. They are associated with passes providing routes across the uplands; they are around springs and waterholes; and they are found by sheltered harbours on the coast. In northern England, western Scotland, and southwest Ireland, rock art may be associated with valleys leading through the wider landscape. Although such places must have been visited during the Earlier Neolithic period, this evidence suggests that larger areas were being used than before. It also raises the possibility that travel between different regions became increasingly important.

The previous chapter drew attention to different interpretations of the Earlier Neolithic settlement pattern. Archaeologists working in lowland England took a quite different view from their colleagues in Ireland. That was hardly surprising since the remains of rectilinear houses were regularly discovered in some regions and were virtually absent in others. There were various possible explanations, extending from the differential destruction of field evidence to a genuine contrast in the character of Neolithic activity, or even the nature of the rituals involving the houses of the dead. After 3000 BC, many of these differences disappeared, and in both countries settlements may have had rather more in common.

It is with the expansion of contract archaeology that insubstantial circular buildings have come to light. It is not clear whether these structures were adopted because settlement was organised in a different way. It is obvious that crop cultivation continued, but little is known about methods of food production, as nearly all the excavated evidence comes from ceremonial sites. It seems possible that the subsistence economy did become more diverse, but there is little reason to suppose that the increase in pastoralism documented by pollen analysis in Ireland extended to Britain as well. In any case it seems unlikely that Later Neolithic houses were organised according to purely practical considerations. Just as the shapes of dwellings changed, so did those of monuments.

HOUSES, TOMBS, AND ARENAS: IRELAND, ORKNEY, AND NORTHERN BRITAIN

Again the initial development began beyond these islands. Chapter Two considered one of the main styles of mortuary monuments and its origins. It seems to have been based on the model of the long house and had obvious prototypes extending along the coastline of the Continent from Denmark and Poland, at one extreme, to Brittany and Normandy, at the other. Such monuments might be formed of several different materials, and some were constructed of earth and timber, whilst others contained stone chambers.

Another tradition of mortuary monuments developed first along the western coastline of Europe, and in this case practically all the structures were built of stone (Scarre 1992). These are the megaliths known as passage tombs. They are so called because they have two distinct elements. An entrance passage leads to a chamber which is generally situated at the centre of the covering mound. Most sites observe a clear distinction between these two components; the passage restricts access to the interior and may be low and narrow; the chamber, on the other hand, can be unexpectedly large and is sometimes spanned by a high corbelled roof. A number of these sites were decorated by abstract pecked designs (Shee Twohig 1981). Passage tombs in Britain and Ireland are usually associated with circular cairns.

Although there are many variations among these monuments, two points seem to be established. These structures have so many features in common that they can be regarded as a single architectural tradition. It is no longer possible to argue that different regional groups developed entirely independently of one

Figure 3.5. A stone chamber located inside a circle of boulders at Carrowmore in the west of Ireland. The mountain of Knocknarea can be seen in the background.

another (Renfrew 1973b: 125–9). At the same time, it is clear that the oldest of these monuments are found in Continental Europe. Among the areas in which they developed was the Iberian peninsula. This is important for it lay well outside the areas colonised by the first farmers (Arias 1999). Although it may have experienced some settlement from other regions, there seems little doubt that the native population remained largely unaffected. For that reason it is likely that passage tombs were an indigenous invention, and throughout Atlantic Europe there seem to be precedents for the building of small mortuary monuments during the Mesolithic period (Scarre 1992).

There is some evidence for the chronology of passage tombs from the north of Scotland. Those on the mainland are among the structures associated with round cairns noted in Chapter Two, but they were considered together with other forms of monument because some of them were incorporated into long cairns during the earlier fourth millennium BC. The distribution of passage tombs extends as far as the Northern Isles, and it was in Orkney that the largest examples – those of the Maeshowe type – were built in the years around 3000 BC (C. Richards 2004b). That would suggest that such structures had an extended history.

The Irish evidence is even more striking. It seems as if the first passage tombs are those at Carrowmore in the west of the country which are associated with radiocarbon dates extending back to the very beginning of the Neolithic period (Burenhult 1980 and 1984; Sheridan 2003b). The monuments in question consist of above-ground megalithic chambers, enclosed by a ring of boulders, and may not have been covered by a cairn (Fig. 3.5). Comparable structures are known from other areas around and near the coast of the northern half

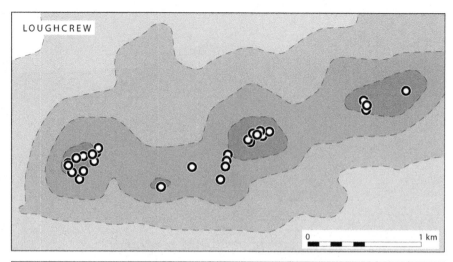

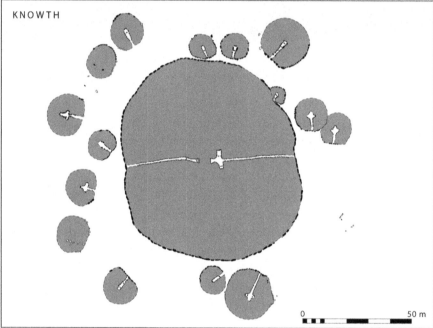

Figure 3.6. (Upper) Plan of the clusters of passage tombs on the high ground at Loughcrew in the east of Ireland. (Lower) Outline plan of the cemetery at Knowth, Boyne Valley. Information from G. Eogan (1986) and Cooney (2000).

of Ireland and along the Atlantic façade of Britain, with structural echoes in northwest France. In some cases there are signs of a rudimentary entrance passage, and the tombs may have been open to the elements. The chambers at Carrowmore were revisited at various times after their construction, especially during the Iron Age.

The radiocarbon dates from Carrowmore extend between about 4000 and 3000 BC (Sheridan 2003b), but only one of the dated structures may have been

Figure 3.7. A denuded passage tomb and a chambered cairn at Loughcrew.

covered by a cairn. This is Tomb 51, which is the focal point of the complex. It is the largest monument and occupies the highest ground. It is also the only one to have been decorated with pecked designs. It was not built until about 3550 BC. Most of the other dates for Irish passage tombs come from the Boyne Valley, near to the east coast where much larger monuments were constructed around 3000 BC (ApSimon 1986). The Mound of the Hostages at Tara was built and used between 3350 and 2900 BC (O'Sullivan 2005). It is possible that passage tombs were adopted through a gradual process of competitive emulation: successive monuments increased in size and in the labour needed to build them. That is the view of Alison Sheridan (1986), who interprets their plans according to this hypothesis.

The sequence proposed by Sheridan would mean that during the fourth millennium the earlier passage tombs were used in parallel with the court cairns discussed in Chapter Two; the earliest examples were built as a result of contacts along the Atlantic seaboard of Europe, whilst court tombs reflect a different axis with its emphasis on areas further to the east. What seems important is that by the later fourth millennium BC, passage tombs became the dominant element in the Irish landscape, and that is why they are considered here.

They are mainly found in the north and centre of the country where their distribution focuses on a zone extending between Drogheda to the east and Sligo to the west. The main concentrations of these monuments form a series of cemeteries, of which Carrowkeel, Loughcrew (Figs. 3.6 and 3.7), and the concentration of monuments in the Boyne Valley (Fig. 3.8) are perhaps the best known examples (G. Eogan 1986). In each case one massive monument is surrounded by a series of smaller tombs, but that configuration may be repeated several times. Thus it applies to at least three different clusters of chambered tombs at Loughcrew; there were distinct concentrations of monuments at Carrowmore and on the nearby mountain of Knocknarea; and a similar arrangement may once have existed with each of the large tombs in the Boyne Valley: Newgrange, Knowth, and Dowth. Within any one cemetery the tombs were carefully located in relation to one another: at Knowth they surrounded the space that was eventually occupied by the largest monument, and here the entrances of the satellite tombs were directed towards that focal point (G. Eogan 1986). Such cemeteries could even incorporate tombs of other kinds. On a still larger scale it seems as if groups of monuments in different places might have been aligned on one another. Thus those on the mountaintop at Carrowkeel acknowledge the position of a similar cemetery on the summit of Knocknarea (Bergh 1995). Those sites are intervisible, yet some of the passage tombs at Loughcrew seem to be orientated on similar sites in the Boyne Valley, although they cannot be seen (Patrick 1975).

It has been difficult to work out a chronology for these monuments because they were permeable structures. They could be entered and their contents supplemented or removed over a considerable period of time. That raises a problem, yet the contents of Irish passage graves were strikingly consistent, and so were the practices associated with them. Most of the remains were of adults whose bodies had been cremated. There were smaller numbers of children, and a higher proportion was represented by unburnt bones. Some of the cremations might be placed in stone basins inside the main chamber or a series of side chambers, where other finds include a specialised group of bone artefacts such as pendants and pins, stone balls, and a style of profusely decorated pottery which takes its name from the cemetery at Carrowkeel. At Fourknocks, the unburnt bones were mainly in the entrance passage (Cooney 2000: 103–12).

There is some evidence that Irish tombs were rebuilt or refurbished during their period of use. Palle Eriksen (2004) suggests that the great mound at Newgrange was modified on at least two occasions. Other monuments were treated in a more drastic manner. Recent work on the main passage tomb at Knowth has established that many of the orthostats were reused from another structure; they had been taken down and moved, and much of the original decoration was discovered on the backs of the stones (G. Eogan 1998). At Newgrange and Knowth it is clear that the carved designs had been renewed and changed on more than one occasion. George Eogan (1997) has identified several overlays on some of the uprights at Knowth, leading him to suggest that the earliest designs were incised linear motifs and that the pecked circles and spirals that are often associated with the Boyne Valley may have been a later development.

In fact the decoration of such tombs could have had two distinct aspects. Those people who were permitted to enter the chamber and passage would have viewed a particular selection of carved motifs, but the very structure of

Figure 3.8. Distant view of the principal monument at Newgrange, seen from the River Boyne, with another, smaller mound in the foreground.

the monument must have meant that they had to inspect them in sequence. At the same time, those who were not allowed to go further than the perimeter of the cairns would have been aware of a different selection of images. Once again they would have seen them in a prescribed order as they moved round the kerb.

These conventions may have changed over time, for most Irish passage tombs do not have decorated kerbstones (Fig. 3.9). They are a special feature of those in the Boyne Valley, and even here there may be evidence of a complex sequence. It seems as if the decorated kerb of the principal mound at Knowth was the last part of that structure to be built (G. Eogan 1997). The distribution of quartz may follow a similar pattern, for Stefan Bergh has suggested that it was originally deposited inside the chambers of Irish passage tombs. Only in the latest of these sites did it embellish the exterior (Bergh 1995: 156). Again it seems as if different features may have been directed towards different audiences. That is especially important in the Boyne Valley where the raw materials used around the exterior of the largest monuments seem to have been introduced to the site from an enormous area extending from the Wicklow Mountains sixty kilometres to the south, to the coastline about fifty kilometres to the north. They seem to provide a model of the wider landscape, yet many were simply pieces of distinctively coloured stone. This practice may show how far people travelled to visit the tombs (Mitchell 1992).

Certain individuals may have been allowed to observe phenomena that were denied to others. This is most apparent from the celestial alignments associated with Irish tombs. Their full extent is uncertain because some of the monuments are poorly preserved or were restored without adequate record. It is accepted that the entrance passage at Newgrange is aligned on the midwinter sunrise, although the light actually travels down a specially constructed channel which was built above the entrance of the tomb (O'Kelly 1982). The passages at Knockroe were aligned on the midwinter sunrise and sunset, respectively (M. O'Sullivan 2004), and at Knowth and Loughcrew they may have marked the positions of the equinoxes (Brennan 1983). Two points are most important here. All the convincing alignments are concerned with the movements of the sun. There does not seem to have been the same interest in the moon. Second, these effects could have been seen only from the interior of these monuments and would have been lost on spectators who were excluded from the chamber. Few people could have watched them, for if too many were present they would have obscured the only source of light.

It seems possible that the use of passage tombs involved other experiences that were restricted to a small number of participants. Jeremy Dronfield has argued that some of the abstract designs associated with Irish megalithic art refer to the visual images associated with altered states of consciousness (1995 and 1996). A similar interpretation has been applied to Upper Paleolithic cave paintings and is supported by research in neuropsychology (Lewis-Williams and Dowson 1993; Lewis-Williams and Pearce 2005). The problem is that such ideas explain why certain designs assumed so much importance; but there was nothing to prevent them being copied from one decorated surface to another until they lost their original associations. There is also some experimental evidence that the peculiar form of the passage tomb, with its narrow entrance passage and high central chamber, creates unusual acoustic effects (Watson and Keating 1999). They may even have helped to generate the mental and physical conditions described by Dronfield.

It is quite possible that mounds covering Irish passage tombs were modelled on the layout of the circular house, as they were in Atlantic Europe. That is especially likely since the cemetery at Knowth overlay the remains of a series of such dwellings. That is not the only link between them, for the circular ground plan of the houses and the tombs is echoed in other media, in particular the curvilinear decoration with which some structures were embellished. This may have had an even wider significance as certain of those monuments were laid out according to the arc traced by the sun across the sky (Bradley 1998b: chapter 7).

The adoption of the largest passage tombs created restrictions of access that may have been less apparent before. Space was very restricted within the chambers and side chambers, and here there were rather different designs from those on the exterior of the monuments. In the same way, only a small number of people would have been able to appreciate the solar alignments that had been built into the architecture of these buildings. More people would have been excluded. Perhaps the monuments were associated with a smaller section of

LOUGHCREW CAIRN L

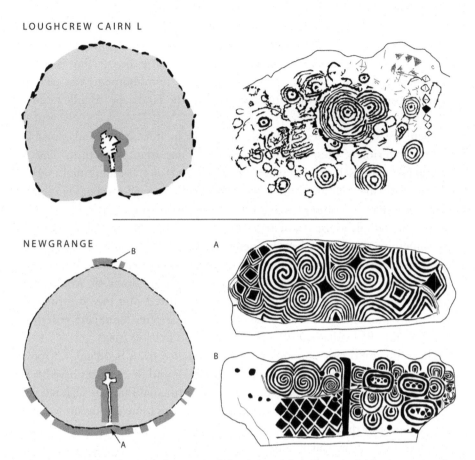

NEWGRANGE

Figure 3.9. The changing location of the decorated surfaces in Irish passage tombs. At Loughcrew in the east of Ireland, most of the designs are confined to the chamber. At Newgrange, Boyne Valley, they extend to the outer kerb (Information from Shee Twohig (1981) and O'Kelly (1982).

society than the court tombs that preceded them. It seems as if the knowledge and ability necessary to plan these buildings may not have been generally available, even though their actual construction would have required an enormous workforce. Alison Sheridan (1986) is surely right to suggest that the construction of passage tombs was a source of prestige. Different communities attempted to outdo one another in mounting these ambitious projects. The same should apply to the separate clusters of passage graves within the larger cemeteries.

There were few burials inside these monuments, and there is little to suggest that particular individuals were provided with grave goods, although this evidence may have been affected by later disturbance to the sites. Even so, there are signs that social divisions were acknowledged in architectural form, as the tombs within the individual cemeteries varied greatly in size. The passage tombs in the Boyne Valley also had decorated kerbs that would have been accessible to larger audiences than the chambers concealed behind them. That marks the beginning of a new development. The closed spaces of the chambers eventually lost some of their importance, and the surrounding area was occupied by new forms of architecture. At the same time the curvilinear decoration which is such a feature of the exterior of these monuments was echoed by rather similar designs on natural surfaces in the landscape (Bradley 1997: 62–5).

There are various clues to this development in Ireland. It seems possible that the exterior of these tombs became more important with time. This is most apparent on Knocknarea where Stefan Bergh (1995) has identified a series of low platforms built around the flanks of several passage tombs (Fig. 3.10). They could have accommodated a larger audience than the chambers. There is another example at the decorated tomb of Knockroe (M. O'Sullivan 2004), and something similar may have happened outside the kerbs at Newgrange and Knowth where excavation has found many artefacts (O'Kelly 1982; Eogan and Roche 1997). They have been interpreted as evidence of domestic activity, but that seems unlikely. Much of this material accumulated after the construction of these monuments and, in the case of Newgrange, after the quartz covering of the mound had collapsed (O'Kelly, Cleary, and Lehane 1983).

There are important contrasts with the evidence from Scotland. Chapter Two made the point that some of the long cairns found there might have been based on a domestic prototype, albeit one in Continental Europe. That related to the outward appearance of these structures. Perhaps more important was the private aspect of the monuments. There is little relation between the appearance and siting of the cairns and the layout of the chambers concealed within them, and yet some of these evoked the internal organisation of the house. That applied to the chambered tombs found on the mainland of northern Scotland and to those in Orkney. Their characteristic ground plan resembled the rectangular dwellings of the Earlier Neolithic period, which were arranged as a series of 'rooms' on either side of a central passage.

Most of these monuments were fairly simple, and their chambers were generally divided into three sections, but in Orkney this principle seems to have assumed a life of its own. Here the most complex of these structures was Midhowe which was separated into many more compartments, which is why they have been described as 'stalled cairns' (Davidson and Henshall 1989). There are some variations, but for the most part the chamber was entered at one end of the building. This was not a major feature of these sites, but again its position follows the organisation of the excavated dwellings. Both the houses and tombs are associated with decorated Unstan bowls as well as plainware. It seems as if the chambers contained the remains of a considerable number of people, although individual body parts were later removed or rearranged (C. Richards 1988).

It seems as if new kinds of monument emerged in the latter area towards the end of the fourth millennium BC. These were passage tombs with structural

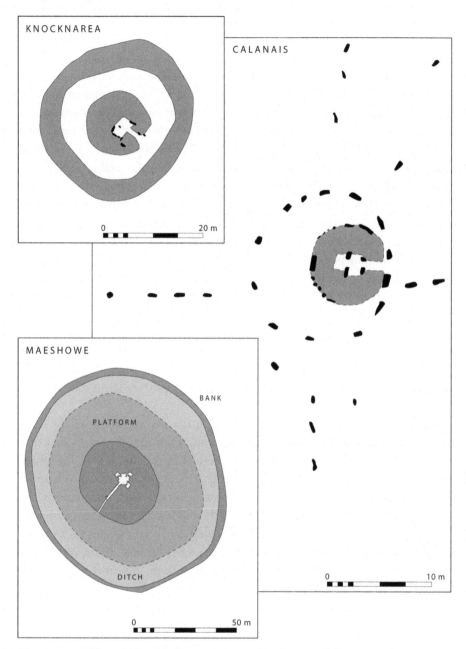

Figure 3.10. The relationship between internal and external features at three passage tombs. One example at Knocknarea in the west of Ireland is surrounded by a bank. Calanais, Outer Hebrides, is located within a stone circle approached by rows of monoliths, and the monument at Maeshowe, Orkney, is situated on an earthwork platform bounded by a ditch and bank. Information from Bergh (2000), Burl (2000) and Davidson and Henshall (1989).

features in common with those in Ireland, yet they were also transformations of the domestic dwellings of the same period. On one level the houses of Later Neolithic Orkney form part of the general tradition of circular dwellings considered at the beginning of this chapter. On another, they are quite idiosyncratic. This may be because they are exceptionally well preserved, but they also have a number of unusual features which are echoed in monumental architecture. Among these are their entrance passages, the presence of intramural compartments and the use of decorated stones (C. Richards 1991; A. Shepherd 2000). They changed their internal organisation over time, and it is the earlier of these buildings that have the closest connection with passage tombs.

The first of these houses have a roughly cruciform interior and a circular external wall, so that they combine elements of older and newer ways of organising space. The circular structures have one entrance facing a central hearth. There may be recesses set into the thickness of the walls, but the main focal point was at the back of the dwelling (Fig. 3.11). Such buildings could be grouped together into small villages. At Barnhouse, the separate dwellings seem to have formed two concentric rings around an open area (C. Richards 2004b: chapter 3), whilst those at Skara Brae were connected by a series of low passageways. In this case important thresholds were marked by incised motifs (A. Shepherd 2000). Similar designs are also found on the portable artefacts associated with these sites, including the decorated pottery known as Grooved Ware (Saville 1994).

Many of these elements are represented in the passage tombs of the same period. The main difference between them and their predecessors is that they were increasingly subdivided. Whereas the earlier monuments had a simple linear ground plan approached by a short entrance passage, now the chamber had a more complex layout. It utilised some of the same elements as the domestic dwellings, but it also exaggerated them (Figs. 3.11 and 3.12). Someone entering even the most complex of the stalled cairns would still have moved along the central axis between the successive compartments. In the Maeshowe tombs, however, the main chamber was further from the exterior, and each of the side chambers had to be accessed separately. Indeed, there are cases in which the side chambers led to still further cells, each with a narrow passage of its own. These subdivisions are similar to the recesses that were built into the houses at Skara Brae. The importance of the thresholds inside these tombs is emphasised by panels of incised decoration very like those in the dwellings (Bradley et al. 2001). This comparison is important, for such images resemble the earliest motifs found in the Boyne Valley (G. Eogan 1997), but they are different from the pecked designs in the Irish tombs which may have referred to altered states of consciousness.

How were these monuments used? Excavation at Quanterness suggests that the chambers and side chambers contained large amounts of unburnt human bone. The excavator, Colin Renfrew, argues that these monuments housed the

BARNHOUSE

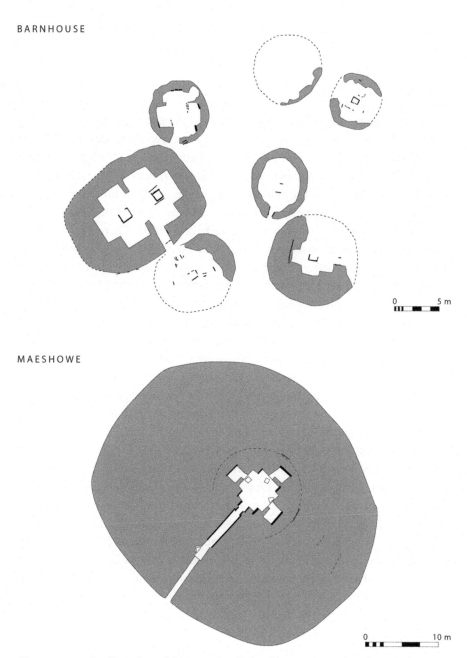

MAESHOWE

Figure 3.11. Outline plan of the Later Neolithic houses at Barnhouse, Orkney, compared with that of the nearby chambered tomb of Maeshowe. Information from C. Richards (2004b).

bodies of entire communities (1979: chapter 12). Many of these corpses had lost their flesh elsewhere. Colin Richards, however, suggests that the Maeshowe tombs also included some of the body parts that had been removed from earlier stalled cairns (Richards 1988). This is suggested by radiocarbon dates for individual bones, but it is difficult to interpret this evidence when so many deposits had been disturbed by animals (A. Ritchie 2004).

Maeshowe tombs are not only elaborations of the basic plan of a dwelling, they are located close to the living sites themselves. In some cases these tombs seem to be paired with individual settlements. This applies to the relationship between the passage grave on Cuween Hill and the excavated houses at Stonehall, but the same pattern connects the passage grave on Wideford Hill to a nearby living site, and the famous tomb at Quanterness to another settlement at Crossiecrown (Colin Richards, pers. comm.). In other cases the monuments may have been built over the sites of older dwellings. This certainly happened at the Howe (Ballin-Smith 1994: chapter 2), and the same relationship has been postulated at Maeshowe (C. Richards 2004b: chapter 9). There may also have been a link between that tomb and the Later Neolithic village at Barnhouse. The settlement included a stone decorated with a complex pattern. Fieldwork in 1999 showed that a piece with exactly the same motif had been built into the foundations of the chamber at Maeshowe (Bradley et al. 2001).

In another way the sequence in Orkney is similar to that in Ireland. Niall Sharples (1985) has made the point that the earlier Orcadian tombs were entirely focused on the interior space: that is where the human remains are found, and there are few artefacts anywhere else. The later tombs have a different character. Whilst they include even more bones, there are further deposits outside them. In a few instances it seems as if special structures were created for the purpose. Maeshowe is particularly relevant here, for the chambered tomb is built on an earthwork platform enclosed by a ditch and possibly a wall. This seems to have been contemporary with the tomb (C. Richards 2004b: chapter 9). At two other Orkney monuments, Quoyness and Taversoe Tuick, a platform was built around the perimeter of an existing passage tomb, restricting access to the interior (Davidson and Henshall 1989: 154–8 and 160–3). The platform at Quoyness included pottery and animal bones. At Isbister and Midhowe walled enclosures may have been built on to the original construction (ibid., 125–30 and 146–8) and at Sharples's own site at Pierowall a platform was constructed against the collapsed perimeter of the cairn (Sharples 1984). In each case it is as if the monument was turned inside out so that the exterior assumed more importance than the interior. That is similar to the sequence that Audrey Henshall (2004) describes on the Scottish mainland and in the Western Isles. It also recalls the evidence from Ireland where platforms were constructed outside the perimeter of the tombs on Knocknarea and where the edge of the ruined mound at Newgrange became the focus for deposits of cultural material.

Maeshowe contributes to this discussion in other ways. The tomb is most unusual because the corners of the burial chamber are defined by four tall pillars, whilst another four frame the entrance passage. Although they are undoubtedly impressive, they do not contribute to its stability. Since they had been quarried some distance away, why were they there at all? A possible answer is provided

Figure 3.12. Internal view of the chamber of Maeshowe, Orkney, showing one of the pillars defining the limits of the structure and the entrance to a side cell.

by a substantial socket cut into the earthwork platform. Is it possible that these stones had been taken from another monument on the same site (C. Richards 2004b: 242–4)? If so, they could have been reused, like the decorated orthostats incorporated in the passage at Knowth.

A possible model for such a setting exists not far away at the Stones of Stenness, a ring of enormous uprights encircled by a ditch (Fig. 3.13; G. Ritchie 1976). Nearby there are two more monuments: an even larger stone circle, the Ring of Brodgar, which is inside a similar earthwork (G. Ritchie 1998); and the Ring of Bookan which may be the site of a second passage tomb set within an enclosure (Henshall 1963: 232–3). Most of these sites are undated, but it is generally agreed that Maeshowe must have assumed its present form around 3000 BC. The base of the ditch surrounding the Stones of Stenness is associated with radiocarbon dates of 3100–3000 BC.

At the same time the plan of the chambered tomb at Maeshowe resembles that of the latest structure in the nearby settlement of Barnhouse, which is of similar age. This building was the largest on the site, but again its exterior was supplemented by a platform (C. Richards 2004b: chapter 5). One of the characteristics of this building is that it contained two massive stone-lined hearths. There is a similar hearth in the centre of the Stones of Stenness, and it is possible that there had been a structure of the same kind there. Both the sites exhibit virtually the same organisation of space.

Colin Richards (1996b) argues that all three of these constructions – the house, the tomb, and the stone circle – refer to one another at the same time as this complex provides a microcosm of the surrounding landscape. There are also contrasts between these sites. Whatever its origins, the preserved structure at Maeshowe is a tomb. It may be augmented by an earthwork platform and enclosed by a ditch, but it lacks the impressive facade of a monument like Newgrange. The monument is closed to the wider world. Both are orientated on the midwinter sun, but that could have been observed only from the chamber. A stone circle, on the other hand, is a largely permeable structure, and Richards himself emphasises the visual relationships between the monoliths and more distant areas of high ground. It was essentially an open arena of the kind that is known as a henge and could certainly have accommodated a large number of people. The nearby stone circle of the Ring of Brodgar provides some indication of the wider significance of such monuments, for recent work suggests that, like Newgrange, it had been built out of raw material introduced from several different sources (C. Richards 2004c).

Some of the same issues arise with the Irish monuments. Newgrange presents problems of its own. The great passage tomb is enclosed by a series of monoliths. They are not concentric with the kerb but emphasise the position of the entrance and the section of the perimeter which had been enhanced by blocks of quartz. The original excavators took the view that the chambered tomb and the stone setting were contemporary with one another (O'Kelly 1982), but a more recent investigation suggests that the monoliths were not erected

Figure 3.13. The Stones of Stenness, Orkney.

until the mound had collapsed (Sweetman 1985). The evidence is ambiguous, but the published section drawings suggest that the stone sockets might have been dug from a ground surface associated with Grooved Ware and Beakers. Stone circles are associated with chambered tombs at other sites in Ireland, and the Mound of the Hostages is surrounded by a series of 'fire pits' dated between 2030 and 1690 BC. These might have been the sockets for upright stones that have since been removed (O'Sullivan 2005: 228–33). In northern Scotland, monuments of superficially similar character were enclosed by stone circles during the Earlier Bronze Age (Bradley 2005a: 100–6).

The stone circle is not the only structure to be built outside the principal monument at Newgrange, for adjacent to the great mound there was a massive oval enclosure made up of concentric rings of pits delimited by an outer circuit of posts (Fig. 3.14). This occupied virtually the same amount of space as the passage tomb and was associated with fragments of burnt animal bone (Sweetman 1985). Its chronological relationship to the stone circle is unclear, but this structure was built long after the tomb. It dates from the later third millennium BC. Like the Stones of Stenness, this monument has been described as a henge.

The term also describes several circular enclosures in the Boyne Valley which had been built by excavating soil from the interior and using it to construct a bank (G. Stout 1991). These earthworks are usually found close to passage tombs, and an example not far from Newgrange contained one of these monuments. Another of these sites, at Monknewtown, included a cremation associated with Carrowkeel Ware (Sweetman 1976). The most informative example is the Giant's Ring at Ballynahatty near Belfast (Fig. 3.14), which may have been laid out around the position of an existing passage tomb (Hartwell 1998). Such earthworks are usually compared with Later Neolithic monuments in Britain, and the link with megaliths certainly suggests that their histories might have overlapped, but a note of caution is necessary here as Helen Roche (2004) has demonstrated that the only extensively excavated monument related to this kind, The Grange 'stone circle' at Lough Gur, was built during the Later Bronze Age.

It is usual to distinguish between 'Irish' henges, which are embanked enclosures (Condit and Simpson 1998), and a 'British' form in which the material for the bank came from an internal ditch (Wainwright 1969). In fact a few earthworks of the latter type have been identified in Ireland, although there is room for some uncertainty as very similar monuments date from the Later Bronze Age and Iron Age; there may have been no connection between them. On the other hand, one of these enclosures at Dun Ruadh certainly originated in the Later Neolithic or Earlier Bronze Age periods (Simpson, Weir, and Wilkinson 1992), whilst another on the west coast has a radiocarbon date in the late third millennium BC (MacDonagh 2005: 12–13). The putative henge of Longstone Rath has produced pottery of similar date although the excavation has never been published (Sheridan 2004a: 29–30).

The Irish henge monuments are defined by their characteristic earthworks, but enclosures of other kinds were built of wood. One was immediately outside the principal passage tomb at Newgrange, but the details of its structure have still to be defined. Another enclosure, apparently defined by two parallel palisades, has been identified by geophysical survey on the Hill of Tara (Fenwick and Newman 2002). Again it includes a passage tomb within its area. A better preserved monument is found not far from the Giant's Ring and, like its counterparts at Newgrange and Tara, it seems to have formed only one component of a more extensive monument complex, including a series of 'megalithic cists' (Hartwell 1998). These were miniature passage tombs which were built inside shallow pits, and, like their full-size prototypes, they were associated with Carrowkeel Ware. Again the principal enclosure was defined by two parallel circuits of posts (Fig. 3.14). They enclosed the position of a timber circle with a massive square setting at its centre. The wooden structures at Ballynahatty are associated with Later Neolithic Grooved Ware and with a quantity of animal bones which are perhaps the remains of feasts. The enclosure and the timber circle were both burnt to the ground. Afterwards the positions of the posts in the circular building were marked by cairns.

The evidence from Ballynahatty is particularly relevant to the argument, as a similar circle was constructed outside the eastern entrance to the principal tomb at Knowth (Eogan and Roche 1997). Again this was associated with placed deposits of cultural material, including sherds of Grooved Ware. They should be contemporary with at least some of the features in front of the

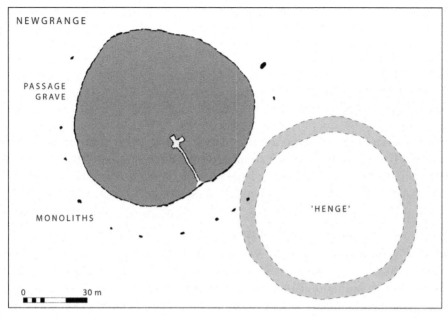

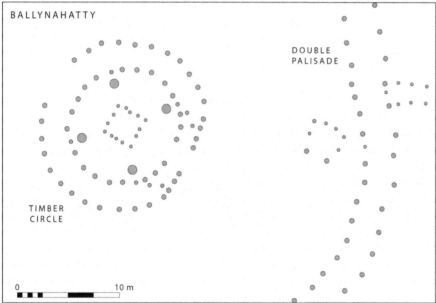

Figure 3.14. (Upper) The relationship between the main passage tomb at Newgrange, Boyne Valley, the setting of monoliths that encloses it, and the adjacent pit and post circle which has been interpreted as a henge. (Lower) The excavated area of the palisaded enclosure at Ballynahatty, northern Ireland, and the timber circle inside it. Information from Bradley (1998) and Hartwell (1998).

entrance to Newgrange, and not far away from them were the sockets of another ring of posts (Sweetman 1987). Further examples, again associated with Grooved Ware, have been found in the course of commercial excavations in Ireland.

ACROSS THE SEA

If the archaeological sequence in Ireland took a similar form to that in northern Scotland, were there any direct connections between those processes?

Alison Sheridan (2004a) has recently discussed this question. She emphasises two important points. The megalithic tombs on either side of the Irish Sea seem to have developed through a process of competitive emulation among different communities until these monuments grew to enormous proportions. That is as true of the stalled cairns of Orkney as it is of Maeshowe, and the same argument applies to the largest passage tombs in Ireland and, perhaps, to the largest and most elaborate court tombs as well. Eventually that process may have involved the emulation of exotic artefacts, practices, and beliefs. It is illustrated by the latest monuments in Orkney, whose extraordinary architecture drew on the Boyne passage tombs as one source of inspiration (G. Eogan 1992). It may also explain the adoption of the first henges in Britain and Ireland.

At the same time, both these sequences shared another feature which could have developed independently. This was a gradual change in the audiences who used the monuments. Space would always have been restricted inside the passage tomb, but it seems as if the areas outside these buildings may have assumed a growing significance. The building of external platforms, timber settings, or earthwork enclosures continued a process that was already well advanced, and as these structures came to overshadow the original importance of the tombs, it seems likely that social relations were transformed. There may still have been the same emphasis on the supernatural, but the significance of mortuary rites might have been reduced.

One connection is especially important. Grooved Ware apparently originated in Orkney, where it may have developed from the kind of pottery associated with Unstan bowls (Hunter and MacSween 1991). It could have been introduced to Ireland some time before Carrowkeel Ware went out of use (Sheridan 2004a). The earliest Grooved Ware in Orkney had incised decoration, and similar material has now been identified on the other side of the Irish Sea. The same kind of decoration is found in other media and can be used to illustrate a wider network of contacts at the turn of the fourth and third millennia BC. Some of the main divisions of space inside the Maeshowe tombs were indicated by incised motifs (Bradley et al. 2001). They are entirely absent from the earlier tombs in Orkney, but have an exact counterpart in the

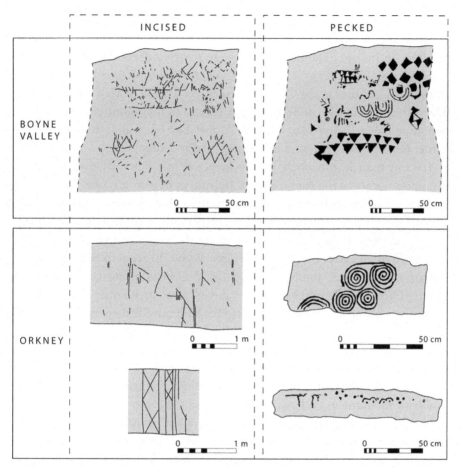

Figure 3.15. The development of megalithic art in the Boyne Valley and Orkney. In Ireland incised decoration precedes the creation of pecked designs on the same surfaces. Both techniques were used in Orkney, but here the sequence is conjectural. Information from G. Eogan (1997) and Bradley et al. (2001).

first phase of decoration in the passage graves of the Boyne Valley (Fig. 3.15; G. Eogan 1997). Similar designs were added to stone artefacts in Later Neolithic Orkney (Saville 1994), and again these have their counterparts in other regions. The most obvious are several stone plaques found on the Isle of Man (Burrow 1997: fig. 6.3). There is a similar object from an axe quarry in north Wales (Warren 1921) and a decorated antler from a small henge monument in East Anglia (G. Simpson 1981: 44–7). In fact such connections extend to a recently discovered panel of rock art on Fylingdales Moor in northeast England (Brown and Chappell 2005: 64–9).

There are other connections between the monuments on either side of the water. It has long been argued that the characteristic form of Maeshowe makes a direct reference to the passage tombs of the Boyne Valley (G. Eogan 1992).

This would certainly explain why the history of Orkney changed its course so drastically. There are other monuments in Britain which are closely related to those in Ireland. The most obvious are the two decorated passage tombs on Anglesey (Hemp 1930; Lynch 1967), but further links have been suggested with individual sites in the Outer Hebrides and the Isle of Man (Henley 2004; Darvill 2000). Similar connections may extend to megalithic cists of the kind found at Ballynahatty (Hartwell 1998), for they bear some resemblance to rather larger structures found in Orkney (Dalland 1999).

It is easy to make too much of the evidence of megalithic art, for whilst it is a common feature of the later tombs in Ireland, in Britain it is rare. The incised decoration of the Maeshowe tombs may have close affinities with the early designs found in the Boyne Valley, but the pecked motifs that are also known in Orkney have their closest parallels along the west coast of Britain. They extend from an early stone circle, Temple Wood, in western Scotland (Scott 1989), to the passage tomb of Barclodiad Y Gawres in north Wales (Lynch 1967). There are other links between distant areas. A number of chambered tombs in Scotland and Ireland had platforms built outside them during, or even after, their main phase of use. Similarly, Newgrange, Maeshowe, and Knockroe are all aligned on the midwinter sun.

Henges and stone circles are also shared between regions on either side of the sea, and sometimes their structures suggest a direct connection between British and Irish monuments. Whatever the origin of the stone circle at Newgrange, it seems possible that a monument of the same kind at Kiltierney in the north of Ireland was used around 3000 BC (Sheridan 2004a: 30). That would be consistent with the dates for the Stones of Stenness (G. Ritchie 1976), and both these sites are associated with Grooved Ware. At Llandegai on Anglesey, a henge monument may be of similar age. This is associated with Peterborough Ware and dates from about 3200–3100 BC. The enclosure is unusual because its bank is placed inside the ditch; a second henge at Llandegai, built around 2700 BC, shares the same alignment, but in this case the earthwork adopts the conventional form (Lynch and Musson 2001: 36–77). A number of other monuments could have been built at the beginning of the third millennium BC. A stone setting at Temple Wood in western Scotland (Scott 1989) is decorated with the same design as two of the passage graves in Orkney. The large stone circle at Long Meg and her Daughters in northwest England illustrates the same relationship, for here an outlying monolith is embellished with the characteristic repertoire of Irish megalithic art. It also establishes an alignment on the midwinter sunset (Burl 1994).

A key site is Calanais on the island of Lewis in the Outer Hebrides (Henley 2005). Here a stone circle with unusually tall monoliths is approached by no fewer than four avenues or alignments which are laid out at right angles to one another and converge on the centre of the circle. It is not clear when they were built, but inside that circle is a tiny passage tomb. Its entrance is

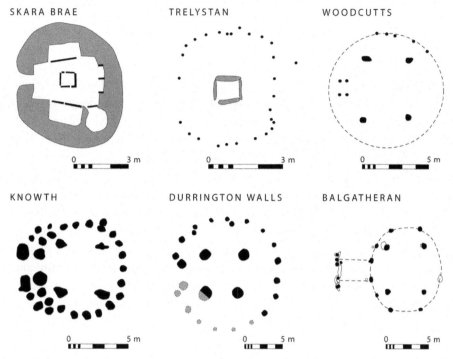

SKARA BRAE   TRELYSTAN   WOODCUTTS

0   3 m   0   3 m   0   5 m

KNOWTH   DURRINGTON WALLS   BALGATHERAN

0   5 m   0   5 m   0   5 m

Figure 3.16. Six circular structures associated with Grooved Ware. The structures at Skara Brae (Orkney), Trelystan (north Wales), and Woodcutts (Wessex) are interpreted as houses, whilst those at Knowth (Boyne Valley), Durrington Walls (Wessex), and Balgatheran, in the east of Ireland, are thought to have played a more specialised role. In each case the basic design seems to be similar: a square within a circle. Information from Richards (2004b), Britnell (1982), Eogan and Roche (1997), Wainwright and Longworth (1971), M. Green (2000), and O'Driscoil (2001).

orientated on one of the rows of uprights. These structures date from the early third millennium BC and were associated with Grooved Ware (Ashmore 1999). They are of particular interest as the layout of the ring of monoliths resembles that of a cruciform passage tomb, but in this case it has been opened out to form a monumental enclosure. There are a few other sites where such tombs are juxtaposed with stone circles, but again their chronology is not clear.

Whilst the stone circle at Calanais is unique, henges generally take standard forms. There are some connections between the Later Neolithic monuments on either side of the Irish Sea. The earthwork monuments in Ireland were generally embanked circular enclosures. Two of these occur in northern England, at either end of a land route crossing the Pennines (Topping 1992; Moloney et al. 2003), and there may have been other examples in southwest Wales, although this needs to be confirmed by excavation (G. Williams 1984; Darvill and Wainwright 2003).

The timber circles come in a variety of sizes, from small post settings indistinguishable from ordinary houses (Fig. 3.16) to more grandiose structures that were probably specialised buildings (Fig. 3.17; Gibson 2005). The smaller could easily be roofed; this would have been difficult with the largest examples. The important point is that these buildings form a continuum and that structures of quite different sizes observe the same organisation of space. A particularly striking pattern is exemplified by the circle at Ballynahatty which encloses a central square of large posts (Hartwell 1998). That design is found quite widely and extends from Ireland to southern England (Sheridan 2004a). It occurs outside the passage grave at Knowth (Eogan and Roche 1997), whilst the same arrangement was followed on the island of Arran off the Scottish coast (Haggarty 1991) and at Durrington Walls on the Wessex chalk (Wainwright and Longworth 1971: 41–4). All these sites were associated with Grooved Ware. In some ways these structures raise the same problems as the halls discussed in Chapter Two. Perhaps they were public buildings whose form was modelled on that of the domestic dwelling. They come in a variety of sizes just like enclosures and tombs, and it may be that, like those monuments, the escalating scale of construction was one way in which different groups of people competed in a process of conspicuous consumption. That term seems especially appropriate since some of these places provide evidence of feasts.

Finally, there is a more general relationship to observe between Later Neolithic Ireland and the same period in Britain. For the most part local communities drew on distant areas as a source of ideas which they employed in idiosyncratic ways. In certain cases these geographical connections may have focused on quite small regions at the expense of their wider hinterland. To some extent that was true of Orkney, and it was certainly true in Cumbria in northwest England and Kilmartin Glen on the west coast of Scotland. The same idea might apply to Anglesey, with its decorated passage graves and the early henge monument at Llandegai. All these places have a number of features in common with Neolithic Ireland. Perhaps that is not surprising, for they were on the coast and yet were generally cut off from inland areas. Cumbria and Anglesey were isolated by mountains, Orkney and Kilmartin by water. The Isle of Man, on the other hand, shares elements with Ireland and Scotland and has distinctive features of its own, in particular a series of cremation cemeteries (Burrow 1997: 191–2).

The evidence for such connections takes many forms: particular types of field monuments, unusual portable artefacts, decorated tombs, and open-air rock art. What matters is that these bear a stronger resemblance to features of Irish archaeology than they do to the repertoire of the British Later Neolithic. Perhaps the best example is Cumbria (Watson and Bradley in press). The Langdale quarries provided some of the stone axes used in Ireland. One of the major henges in northwest England, Mayburgh, lacks the customary ditch and is an embanked enclosure of Irish type. As mentioned earlier, the large stone circle, Long Meg and her Daughters, includes an isolated monolith decorated

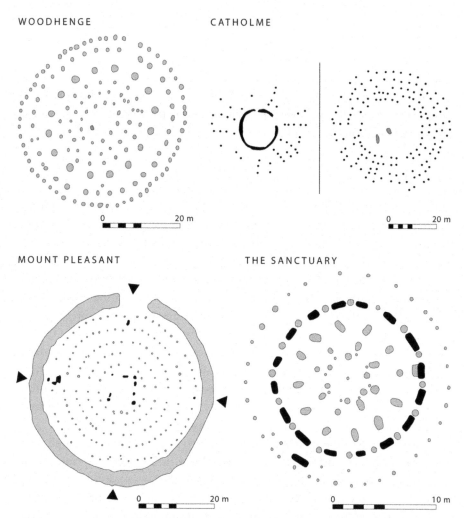

WOODHENGE CATHOLME

0   20 m

0   20 m

MOUNT PLEASANT THE SANCTUARY

0   20 m

0   10 m

Figure 3.17. Some major circular structures in southern and central England. The examples at Woodhenge, Mount Pleasant, and The Sanctuary, all in Wessex, have been excavated, whilst those at Catholme in the English Midlands are drawn from air photographs. On the excavated sites the positions of posts are shaded and stones are shown in black. Information from Pollard (1992, 2001) and A. Harding (1987). The arrows indicate the positions of the four 'corridors' leading towards the centre of the monument at Mount Pleasant.

in the same style as the passage tombs of the Boyne Valley. The same is true of a number of decorated outcrops and smaller monuments. It seems as if communities living in this area developed stronger links with their neighbours to the west than they did with communities across the Pennines.

Such connections may be acknowledged by two exceptional monuments: the passage tombs of Maeshowe (Davidson and Henshall 1989: 142–6) and Barclodiad Y Gawres (Lynch 1967). Both are particularly similar to monuments in Ireland. That applies to their architecture and to their characteristic decoration. At the same time, they diverge from the predominantly eastern orientation of such sites. Maeshowe faces southwest and is aligned on the mid-winter sunset. Barclodiad Y Gawres faces north–northwest and could not be aligned on either the sun or the moon. What they do have in common is that both are directed towards Ireland. It is impossible to be sure that this was originally intended, but, given the evidence that Irish Neolithic cemeteries were orientated on one another, the idea should be taken seriously.

THE LATER HISTORY OF HENGES

It may seem unusual to devote so much space of the archaeology of Ireland and Scotland, when some of the most famous monuments of the Later Neolithic are in southern Britain, but it seems impossible to understand them in terms of local developments.

There is a problem which is not always acknowledged when studying these monuments. In the absence of excavation, virtually all the attention has been paid to their earthwork perimeters, with the result that the sites are classified according to their size and the number of entrances. That procedure cannot take account of any internal features. Moreover the timber circles and stone circles that are sometimes inside them are also found in isolation, suggesting that the earthwork perimeter was not an essential component of these sites.

For that reason it seems wise to begin this discussion with freestanding rings of posts and stones. That has one advantage, for ditches can be cleaned or recut and banks can be rebuilt. It may be difficult to find material associated with their original construction. On the other hand, the wooden uprights were sometimes charred when they were set in the ground. As a result, they provide a reliable source of dating evidence, although individual posts could have been replaced. Alex Gibson (2005) has studied their chronology in relation to the scale on which these monuments were built. The earliest were of modest proportions; they became much larger in the period around 2500 BC, when some of them adopted a more complex layout, and during the second millennium BC their size diminished. Much less is known about stone circles, but to a limited extent they may have followed a similar pattern (Barnatt 1989; Burl 2000). Some of the largest examples date from the mid to late third millennium BC, and after that time they decreased in size. Since stone structures often replaced those of timber, it is not surprising that these trends should overlap.

A growing number of post settings have been found in isolation. Others have been located outside the earthworks of major monuments, as they have at Ferrybridge in northeast England (Roberts 2005: 37–41 and 197–9). This has important implications, for the distribution of Later Neolithic ceremonial sites is essentially a distribution of earthworks, which sometimes occur together in small groups. Certain regions have always stood out because such features are rare. The results of developer-funded excavation raise the possibility that timber circles are more widely distributed. It was the practice of bounding these structures by a bank and ditch that varied from one region to another. Again a comparison with stone settings may be helpful. It is known that certain of them replaced timber monuments, but many of the most impressive examples are completely unenclosed. That cannot be explained by the problems of constructing earthworks in places with an intractable bedrock, for the same areas often contain cairns (Burl 2000: fig. 2).

Two features of these sites are especially revealing: their spatial organisation and their development over time.

The timber circles were not necessarily isolated. More than one example could be built on the same site, and some of them were approached by wooden avenues, comprising two rows of posts; similar alignments have been found in isolation in northeast England and are generally associated with Later Neolithic ceramics (Tavener 1996). The Northern Circle inside the earthwork henge of Durrington Walls illustrates this point. It takes the characteristic form of a square within a circle, and is approached by two rows of close-set timbers which provide access through a wooden screen just outside the monument (Wainwright and Longworth 1971: fig. 17). A similar phenomenon is recorded with stone circles. For example, two of those at Stanton Drew in southwest England are approached by short alignments of paired stones. Geophysical survey suggests that they were built on the sites of timber buildings (David et al. 2004).

Although the wooden monuments are described as circles, that was not always the case as some are ovals or ellipses. This is important as it creates a long axis. That orientation could also be emphasised by a formal entrance. A good example is the timber setting at Woodhenge where a combination of these techniques meant that the site was orientated on the midsummer sunrise (Cunnington 1929). It was possible to vary the lengths of the upright posts so that the structure was graded in height from one side to the other. This is difficult to demonstrate when nothing remains but post holes, yet there should have been a consistent relationship between the depths to which the uprights were buried and the extent to which they stood above the ground. On that basis Roger Mercer has argued that a timber circle at Balfarg in eastern Scotland was higher towards the west (1981b). That is not improbable as many stone circles illustrate the same phenomenon. The well-preserved timber setting known as Seahenge in eastern England provides evidence of a similar arrangement around 2000 BC. Here the tallest uprights were towards the southwest, facing the setting sun (Brennand and Taylor 2003). It is not clear how common this alignment might have been, but it was first used at chambered tombs like Maeshowe.

The internal organisation of timber circles varies from single rings of posts to more complex patterns (Gibson 2005). The largest monuments involve the erection of as many as six concentric rings, and the setting revealed by geophysical survey beneath a stone circle at Stanton Drew may have had nine (David et al. 2004). A visitor to such monuments might have expected to pass through the entrance and to proceed to the centre of the circle, but this was not always possible as the posts may have been linked by screens. The distribution of the artefacts deposited inside Woodhenge certainly suggests that people had to move around the perimeter of the building, approaching the innermost space along a curving path that has been likened to a maze (J. Harding 2003: 74–81). Another monument, identified by air photography at Catholme in the English midlands, was associated with radial lines of posts, extending out from the centre like the spokes of a wheel (A. Harding 1987: 268–71).

Different parts of these buildings were associated with different kinds of archaeological material. For example, at Durrington Walls the distributions of pottery and flint artefacts in the Southern Circle avoided one another (Richards and Thomas 1984). Sometimes it seems as if such deposits could have been placed there in sequence. At Woodhenge, the groups of wild animal bones were closer to the entrance than those of domesticates. A similar contrast has been recognised between deposits of pig bones and those of cattle. Such conventions also extended to portable artefacts, so that stone axes were associated with the outside of the monument. Fragments of these tools occurred in the outer part of the building, but, apart from one example made of chalk, none was found towards its centre (Bradley 2000b: 124–7).

It is not clear how these deposits were related to the individual posts. Had they been placed around them whilst they were still intact, and were they preserved in the hollows left behind when the timbers decayed? Were they placed in pits when those uprights had already rotted, like the cairns built over the postholes in the circle at Ballynahatty? Recent excavation at the Sanctuary at Avebury even suggests that on some sites the individual timbers were replaced soon after they were erected, implying that the act of setting them up was more significant than the overall design (Pitts 2001). The same is true at Durrington Walls (Parker Pearson et al 2006: 235).

It is commonly supposed that timber circles were replaced by settings of stones, but there may have been composite monuments in which both materials were used together (Fig. 3.17). For example, the post setting at Mount Pleasant was structured around four corridors laid out at right angles to one another. To the north and south, the passages were of even width; the other two became narrower as they approached the centre of the circle. Although the excavator suggested that this building was replaced by a series of standing stones, it seems more likely that these features were contemporary with one another and that the monoliths functioned as barriers screening the centre from view (Pollard 1992). Something similar may have happened in the Sanctuary, close to Avebury, where the innermost part of a timber circle was hidden by placing upright stones in between adjacent pairs of posts. This was executed so precisely that it seems likely that those posts were erected at the same time. The stone circle closed off the innermost part of the building.

Figure 3.18. The henge monument at Avebury, Wessex, showing the position of the ditch, a section of the Outer Circle, and, in the background, the position of the Southern Circle.

At other sites the replacement of timber monuments in stone might have fossilised their characteristic form and protected them from decay. This seems to have happened throughout most parts of England and Scotland (Fig. 3.18; Wainwright 1969); it is suggested by the results of geophysical survey in south-west Wales (Darvill and Wainwright 2003); and it is one way of understanding the sequence of structures outside Newgrange (Sweetman 1985). The successive monuments occupy the same area of ground, and sometimes they may be exactly the same size as one another. The stone circles also take up details that were present in the wooden buildings. They respect their orientations, and even the timber avenues may have been replaced by monoliths. Quite often the circles are graded in height towards the south or west. The connections with wooden monuments may be emphasised in other ways, as several of the uprights at Avebury had been used for grinding stone axes (Gillings and Pollard 1999).

Just as timber circles might be replaced in a more durable medium, the rarer wooden avenues had their equivalents in stone (Fig. 3.19). In this case there is no evidence that post settings were removed, but the routes leading to a number of major henges are certainly lined by monoliths. The best known example is the West Kennet Avenue at Avebury which links the henge to the Sanctuary, but recent fieldwork shows that another avenue extended from the western entrance of the monument and cut across the remains of an older enclosure (Pollard and Reynolds 2002: 100–5). The same could have happened at Broomend of Crichie in northeast Scotland (J. Ritchie 1920), and there may

have been an alignment of standing stones linking the Stones of Stenness and the Ring of Brodgar on Orkney (C. Richards 2004b: chapter 8). Another large stone circle which once possessed a long stone avenue was at Shap in Cumbria (Clare 1978). These are not the only examples, yet little is known about how these structures were used. If one avenue at Avebury communicated between two different stone circles, its counterpart seems to have been decommissioned, and at one stage it was apparently closed by a row of standing stones (Pollard and Reynolds 2002: fig. 39).

Some of the monuments are enormous and their construction would have involved much more labour than the timber settings that preceded them. That is particularly true when the source or sources of the stone were some distance away. It was obviously important to use materials taken from particular places, and the Ring of Brodgar may have been built out of materials from different parts of Orkney (C. Richards 2004c). That may have been the case at Stanton Drew (Lloyd Morgan 1887), and it even seems possible that stones were taken from older buildings in the way that had happened at Knowth (G. Eogan 1998).

Parker Pearson and Ramilsonina (1998) draw attention to the physical properties of the raw materials used on these sites. Wood is an organic substance and comes from living trees. Stone, on the other hand, stays the same for ever. They compare this evidence with contemporary practice in Madagascar, where wood is associated with the living, and stone monuments with the dead. Commentators have taken exception to this use of ethnographic analogy (Barrett and Fewster 1998), but that interpretation is consistent with the archaeological evidence from Britain. The timber structures found in henges are often associated with a rich material culture, including deposits of pig bones which may result from feasting (Albarella and Serjeantson 2002). The stone monuments, on the other hand, have few associated artefacts. They are found with human remains and with little else. It seems as though places which had once been connected with the living were now devoted to the dead.

A similar development can be recognised at another group of monuments. Not all the sites described as henges were above-ground structures. Another way of defining a circular space was by a ring of pits. The smallest were the same size as the simpler timber circles, whilst the largest was at Maumbury Rings in southern England. This was an enclosure with an external bank, but instead of the usual post settings a ring of deep shafts was excavated. There were approximately forty-five of them, each dug about ten metres into the chalk. It is clear that the shafts had been filled in deliberately. It is known that the process took place in stages, and that each episode had been accompanied by the deposition of artefacts and bones (Bradley 1975: 34–6). A similar sequence was identified at a smaller monument forty kilometres away on Wyke Down, where the earliest deposits included carved chalk objects and antler. There followed a series of flint implements and animal bones, whilst the latest material also included sherds of Grooved Ware, human cremations, and part of an unburnt skull (Barrett, Bradley, and Green 1991: 92–106). A similar pattern

CALANAIS   STANTON DREW

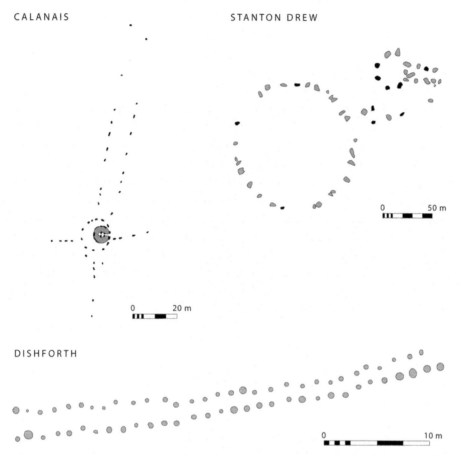

DISHFORTH

Figure 3.19. Stone and timber 'avenues'. Those at Calanais, Outer Hebrides, run up to a stone circle inside which a small passage grave was constructed. At Stanton Drew, southwest England, two short avenues approach stone circles which are suspected to overlie timber monuments. The timber avenue at Dishforth, northeast England, is associated with Later Neolithic pottery and radiocarbon dates. Information from Burl (2000), David et al. (2004), and Tavener (1996).

was identified at Maumbury Rings, where carved chalk objects and deer skulls were in the middle filling of the shafts and finds of human bones were towards the surface (Bradley 1975: 18–22).

Human bone is so common in pit circles that their presence has been misunderstood. This was particularly true during excavations at Dorchester on Thames in southern England, where these monuments were interpreted as cremation cemeteries (Kinnes 1979). This approach was based on a misunderstanding. It is clear that the deposits of human remains were secondary to the monuments at which they were found, so those structures cannot have been built for the disposal of the dead. The point is particularly obvious at Dorchester on Thames, where a series of cremations had been placed in the hollows left after posts had rotted or had been removed from the ground. Rather than associating the remains of the dead with the creation of these structures, they may have registered a change in how such places were used. They may have become more closely associated with the dead. Similar evidence has been recognised on other sites, including the upper levels of the Neolithic round barrow at Duggleby Howe, but in this case the monument was associated with burials from the outset (Kinnes et al. 1983).

It has never been easy to account for the earthworks of henges, especially since it would have needed so many people to build them. To construct the perimeter of Avebury would have taken about a million worker hours (Startin and Bradley 1981). They might have acted like amphitheatres, allowing a large number of people to watch the events taking place inside them. The banks would provide an excellent view, and yet on the British sites they were separated from the interior by a ditch. The basic format was the same whatever the extent of the enclosure and whether or not there were any structures within it. In principle, this would suggest that large numbers of people participated in the use of these places, but the architecture of the monuments might also have emphasised the distinction between those who were allowed into the enclosures and the audience on the bank.

Another way of looking at this evidence is to suggest that the banks of henge monuments were intended as barriers or screens. They actually concealed events from the greater part of the population. That may be why they were sometimes higher at the entrance. Until recently that idea would not have found much support, but it is becoming apparent that similar structures were enclosed by massive palisades (Gibson 1998). They are relevant to this discussion because they would have hidden the interior of these monuments from view. They could not have accommodated any spectators, and the people inside these enclosures would have been cut off from the wider community.

There are a few sites at which it is possible to compare the timber enclosures with earthwork monuments (Fig. 3.20). At Mount Pleasant a large construction was built inside an already existing earthwork (Wainwright 1979). Not far away, at Greyhound Yard in Dorchester, there was a freestanding palisaded enclosure of similar proportions (Woodward, Davies, and Graham 1993: chapter 2). It seems unlikely that the banks were intended to provide vantage points and that timber structures acted as screens, for their roles seem to be interchangeable. Durrington Walls and Greyhound Yard enclose dry valleys which might be regarded as natural amphitheatres, but one was ringed by an earthwork and the other by a wooden stockade (ibid; Wainwright and Longworth 1971). Mount Pleasant occupies a domed hilltop which would not have allowed as much visibility over the interior, yet here an earthwork was replaced by a timber enclosure. All those sites are in central southern England, but at Blackshouse Burn in southern Scotland a bank was constructed on the line of the two palisades. Here there was no evidence of an internal ditch (Lelong and Pollard 1998).

Other palisades were equally extensive, but in this case they were not accompanied by any earthworks. Some of them contained the sites of pit or post

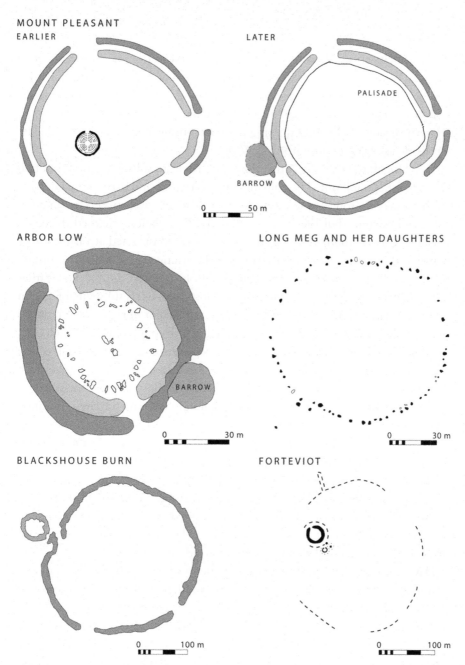

Figure 3.20. Five large Later Neolithic henges and associated monuments. At Mount Pleasant, Wessex, a barrow was built over the enclosure bank and a palisade was erected inside the enclosure during a secondary phase. Another barrow may have been superimposed on the bank at Arbor Low, northern England, although the sequence is uncertain. The stone circle of Long Meg and her Daughters, northwest England, was built over one edge of an older earthwork enclosure. At Blackshouse Burn, southern Scotland, a timber enclosure was overlain by a rubble bank. A smaller enclosure was built outside one of its entrances. At Forteviot, central Scotland, another small henge monument was built within a large palisaded enclosure approached by a short 'avenue'. Information from Wainwright (1979), Burl (2000), Lelong and Pollard (1998), and Driscoll (1998).

circles. Such settings have been identified by excavation at West Kennet in Wessex (Whittle 1997) and at Dunragit (J. Thomas 2004b) and Meldon Bridge (Speak and Burgess 1999) in southern Scotland. They have also been identified by geophysical survey and air photography at other sites in northern and western Britain. At Dunragit, a ring of enormous uprights was surrounded by a palisade associated with Grooved Ware.

It is difficult to reconstruct these monuments from subsoil features, but two characteristics stand out. The palisades were very high and their entrances were exceptionally narrow. These monuments were generally between five and ten hectares in extent, but the largest, at Hindwell in Wales, enclosed thirty-six hectares (Gibson 1999). They seem to have been constructed at various times between about 3000 and 2000 BC and may be arranged in sequence according to the few radiocarbon dates that are available (Gibson 1998). The earlier monuments were defined by wide-spaced posts with a less substantial fence in between them. In time, the intervals between the major uprights were reduced until, finally, contiguous posts were bedded in a deep foundation trench. It is clear from this that increasing amounts of wood were employed in constructing these barriers. There are also hints that the scale of these projects changed in the way that happened with timber circles. The first enclosures were the smallest. They increased in size in the mid-third millennium BC, and the latest examples were conceived on a less ambitious scale.

The individual posts seem to have been between five and nine metres high. Thus they would have hidden whatever was happening behind them. The entrances add to this effect, for they are very narrow, and in certain cases people would have passed through them in single file. At Dunragit, Forteviot, Walton, and Meldon Bridge they are approached by short avenues of paired uprights not unlike that at Durrington Walls. They do not share a common orientation (Speak and Burgess 1999: 24–6 and 110–14).

Having considered the different components of a series of Later Neolithic monuments, how were they related to one another? It is clear that these sites saw a complex sequence of activity, and Alex Gibson (2004a) has argued that in certain cases the earthwork perimeter was the last feature to be built. It might have been impossible to erect the circles inside it because of the presence of the ditch; sometimes it is poorly aligned with the internal structures; and at Milfield North a post circle must have been buried by the bank. He suggests that this sequence was followed at a number of monuments, including Woodhenge, Arminghall, Arbor Low, Balfarg, and Cairnpapple. His argument is supported by work on the Scottish henge at North Mains, for here a timber circle was associated with radiocarbon dates in the Later Neolithic, but a cremation burial sealed beneath its bank dates from the Earlier Bronze Age (Sheridan 2003c: 167); the interval may have been as much as five hundred years. Gibson suggests that far from providing a monumental setting for the buildings inside them, the construction of the earthwork brought their use to an end.

Figure 3.21. Silbury Hill, Wessex.

It is still more difficult to relate the palisaded enclosures to the structures that were built within them. At present the only satisfactory evidence comes from Mount Pleasant, where a substantial earthwork seems to have been supplemented by a circuit of posts. There is no way of relating the bank and ditch to the timber circle on the site, but it is clear that the palisade was a later development. This is shown by the radiocarbon dates and also by their ceramic associations. The palisade was constructed at a late stage in the development of the site, and in time it was burnt down (Wainwright 1979).

A few earthwork or palisaded enclosures were also associated with mounds. Whilst these are often thought of as barrows, that may not have been their purpose, and excavation at the largest of these, Silbury Hill in Wessex, showed that it had not covered a burial (Fig. 3.21; Whittle 1997). Although they are poorly dated, they might be considered as raised platforms which would provide a vantage point from which a small number of people could observe activities that were otherwise concealed. It is certainly true that Silbury Hill commands a view into the West Kennet palisaded enclosures, just as the building of Conquer Barrow on the edge of the henge at Mount Pleasant might have allowed people to see over the palisade into the interior of the monument (Wainwright 1979). The same could have happened at other sites, although it is not clear whether the principal function of these platforms was to raise certain people above the level of those inside the monuments or to allow them privileged access to events that were hidden from view. It is usually supposed that these practices were peculiar to southern England, but that need not be true. There seems to have been a mound on the axis of the entrance at Dunragit (J. Thomas 2004b), and viewers could have seen into the Later Neolithic enclosure at Newgrange from the raised area on top of the largest chambered tomb.

MAKING CONNECTIONS

Although this account has dealt separately with timber circles and stone circles, earthworks and palisaded enclosures, it is clear that these elements overlap and were to some extent interchangeable. There seems no point in regarding them as separate 'types', for not only do the categories overlap, structures of ostensibly different forms are often found together within the same complexes. These might juxtapose open sites and enclosures, large monuments and much smaller ones. In the same way, certain sites are associated with considerable numbers of artefacts, whereas others have very few. This cross-cuts any classification based on their architecture and implies that some places were used in very different ways from others. Certain structures may have been visited infrequently; others may even have been inhabited, whatever their more specialised roles (Wainwright 1978).

Nonetheless certain tendencies can be identified amidst so much variety. In some cases these monuments increased in size until they reached a peak in the middle and late third millennium BC, after which they were usually constructed on a smaller scale. Wooden structures that were subject to decay were sometimes replaced in stone, and when this happened the activities associated with them seem to have changed their character so that a site which had originally been used for feasting became a place for the dead. Even when this did not happen it seems that at a late stage in their history, some of these monuments were screened off – and possibly closed – by an earthwork or a palisade.

That did not happen in every area. Many timber and stone circles were never conceived on an elaborate scale. Nor were their positions emphasised by the construction of enclosures. Some of the regions in which henge monuments are apparently rare include Neolithic post circles which are not associated with any earthworks. That was particularly true along the North Sea coast where their place was sometimes taken by small palisaded enclosures. That contrast between larger and smaller monuments is found in many parts of Britain and may reflect important differences in the ways in which societies were organised or in their capacity to mobilise workforces for the building of monuments (J. Harding 1995: 127–32). In Wessex, the Thames Valley, northeast England, central Scotland, Orkney, and the Boyne Valley large monuments were the norm, but In East Anglia, the English midlands, and northern Scotland smaller structures may have played the same roles.

A striking feature of the larger sites is the way in which individual monuments or groups of monuments increased in scale in parallel with one another. Within the limits of radiocarbon dating this happened over a restricted period of time, and some of these developments could have taken place simultaneously in different regions. The consumption of human labour was associated with consumption of other kinds, as these sites were used for lavish feasts and for deposits of special artefacts (Richards and Thomas 1984; Albarella and Serjeantson 2002). Neither process was confined to the interior of these monuments, and similar material was buried in pits in the areas around them. Not all these pit deposits were distinct from those on settlements, but they were created with greater formality and had a wider range of contents. The position of one of those outside Durrington Walls was marked by a cairn (Stone and Young 1948), and at Lawford and Crouch Hill middens with similar contents seem to have been enclosed by a ditch (Shennan, Healy, and Smith 1985; Gardiner 1987). Artefacts were deposited also in water. In Ireland ard shares were placed in rivers together with stone axes (D. Simpson 1993).

Sometimes the closest connections seem to be between regions that were long distances apart. For example, the oval stone settings described as 'coves' are found inside a small number of stone circles, but these are distributed from Scotland to Wessex (Burl 2000: 31–3). Similarly, the double-ditched henges of northeast England are closely paralleled in the upper Thames Valley (Bradley and Holgate 1984). If communities were seeking to emulate each others' achievements, that process was geographically extensive. It seems to have extended from Orkney to southern Britain and drew in people on either side of the Irish Sea. What is quite remarkable is that after the demise of passage tombs, it does not seem to have involved any reference to Continental Europe.

Monuments are the embodiment of particular ideas and there will always be room for doubt over the strength of such connections. Fortunately, they are evidenced in other media, among them artefacts which had moved a long way from their sources. This is most obvious in the case of ground stone axes, which were made in increasing numbers at quarries in Britain and Ireland. Some of them had been established during the Earlier Neolithic period, but petrological analysis suggests that their distribution was most extensive during the currency of henges (I. Smith 1979). That is very striking, for much of the stone had been obtained in remote and inaccessible locations, on mountains like Tievebulliagh and Pike O' Stickle. They were produced also on offshore islands like Lambay Island and Rathlin Island which seem to have been inhabited at the time. A high proportion of their products are found in distant areas which had adequate raw materials of their own (Bradley and Edmonds 1993: chapter 9; Cooney 1998). Moreover, the contexts of these finds suggest that when their use-life was at an end, some of them were deposited with some formality. Similar considerations apply to the use of high quality flint. Some of the most elaborate artefacts – polished knives and finely flaked arrowheads – were made in workshops near to the northeast coast of England (Durden 1995), whilst similar raw material was extracted by mining at Grimes Graves close to the Fen Edge (Mercer 1981c). It seems likely that the finest of their products were distributed along the North Sea littoral from northeast Scotland to the Thames Estuary.

Such connections are equally apparent from the distribution of Grooved Ware. This ceramic tradition seems to have developed in Orkney, where it has features in common with the designs on houses, passage graves, and stone artefacts, but it was soon adopted in other parts of Britain and Ireland. The Grooved Ware tradition is peculiar to these two islands, and yet it is widely distributed within them. In that respect it contrasts with the kinds of decorated ceramics that developed from the mid-fourth millennium BC. British and Irish Grooved Ware can be divided into a series of substyles, but the main source of variation seems to be chronological rather than geographical (Garwood 1999). Their styles vary according to the contexts in which these vessels are found. Grooved Ware is a particular feature of Later Neolithic ceremonial centres, and it may be no accident that occasional vessels found at these sites are decorated with motifs that occur in megalithic art. These vessels might have been made locally, but such designs link them to widely distributed traditions of monumental architecture.

One way of explaining such connections is by studying where the main monuments are found. A number of writers have expressed surprise that they should be situated so near to Roman roads or forts, or even close to the royal centres of Early Medieval Scotland (Loveday 1998; Driscoll 1998). The probable explanation is that such places were especially accessible and that they were located on obvious routes across the landscape. Some of these areas may have included Later Neolithic settlements, but that is not always apparent, and many of the places with most surface finds of the same period lack such monuments entirely. Henges and related structures can be found along the valleys leading through the uplands, near to navigable rivers and the places where they were easiest to cross, and also near to the sea. These would have been the ideal routes for later roads to follow and would have been well placed as power bases from which to oversee the local population.

Sometimes it is possible to connect this evidence with the movement of portable artefacts. The stone axes mentioned earlier provide the best example. Some of these were made in the Cumbrian mountains throughout the Neolithic period and were brought down to the surrounding lowlands, where they were ground and polished (Bradley and Edmonds 1993: 144–53). There are a number of major monuments in this area, each of them located on one of the routes leading towards the quarries. There was one group of major monuments near to Carlisle on the route leading north into Scotland (McCarthy 2000). To the north east of the high ground there is also the unusual henge monument of Mayburgh, an embanked enclosure of Irish type (Topping 1992). It is located beside one of the principal routes across the Pennine mountains. On the opposite side of the high ground there was another henge at Catterick which was built in exactly the same way (Moloney et al. 2003): the two sites seem to be paired (Fig. 3.22). A ground stone axe was deposited in the entrance of Mayburgh, whilst the lowlands between the Pennines and the North Sea

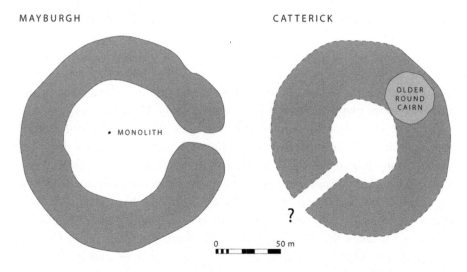

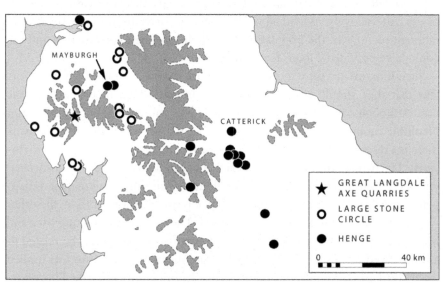

Figure 3.22. Outline plans of two henge monuments, Mayburgh (northwest England) and Catterick (northeast England), each of which was built of cobbles and lacked the usual ditch. The map shows their positions in relation to other monuments of similar date and the site of the Great Langdale axe quarries. Information from Bradley and Edmonds (1993), Topping (1992), and Moloney et al. (2003).

contain an unusual concentration of artefacts from Cumbria (Manby 1988). Other monument complexes are found to the south of Catterick, each of them at the entrance to a similar route leading through the high ground towards the west coast of Britain.

The strategic siting of such monuments is apparent at a more general level. Deposits of unusual or exotic artefacts are commonly found near to them. Good examples are the cluster of such finds around the monument at Arbor

Low (Bradley and Hart 1983) or the concentration of broken mace heads close to the Ring of Brodgar (C. Richards 2004b: 223–6). The same happens in Wessex, where special artefacts were deposited in pits and were accompanied by a selection of animal bones and decorated pottery (J. Thomas 1999: chapter 4). A similar pattern is found in northeast England, although there some of the imported items may have been deposited in water (J. Harding 2003: 97).

Other artefacts from the vicinity of these sites provide a different kind of information. These are the less elaborate flint tools that were used and discarded in the surrounding area. Around the Thornborough complex they included raw materials which could not have been obtained in the vicinity. It seems likely that they provide one indication of the distances that people had travelled to these places. Jan Harding (2000) has compared their visits to a pilgrimage, and Colin Renfrew has taken the same approach to the henge monuments of Orkney (2000: 16–17). Often such structures were built in groups, and people may have needed to move between them, performing particular rituals in particular places. Alternatively, individual monuments may have been the prerogative of different sections of the population, in which case their construction and use could have provided a focus for competition.

Such monuments were located not only for their accessibility. It was important that they should also acknowledge what had been inherited from the past. Although some henges are located close to causewayed enclosures, Later Neolithic monuments are more often associated with cursuses. Occasionally there is a direct connection between the new construction and an older earthwork. The bank of the henge at Catterick incorporated a round cairn associated with Peterborough Ware (Moloney et al. 2003), and the same may have happened at Arbor Low, although the sequence is usually thought to be the other way round (Barnatt and Collis 1996: 133–4). The stone circle of Long Meg and her Daughters was built beside an existing earthwork which may be related to a causewayed enclosure. Some of the monoliths had slumped into its infilled ditch (Burl 1994). Similar earthworks have been identified in the Thornborough complex, and here it seems as if the henges had been superimposed on these older structures: an interpretation which is supported by recent fieldwork (J. Harding 2000).

It was still more important to create these monuments in places with the right natural setting, for many of the henges used the surrounding topography in the same ways. From Avebury to Orkney, circular monuments were purposefully built at the centre of circular landscapes: places that were surrounded by a ring of hills (Bradley 1998b: chapter 8). Sometimes the horizon merged with the enclosure bank, but in other cases it was concealed from view. Aaron Watson's fieldwork has demonstrated that such effects had been carefully contrived so that a particular monument might appear to occupy the centre of the world. Had it been sited anywhere else, those visual effects would have been lost

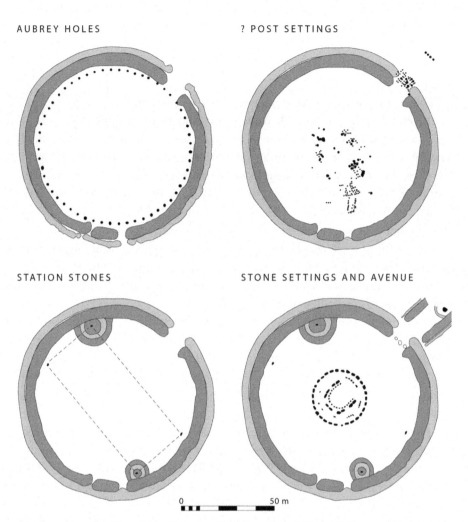

AUBREY HOLES ? POST SETTINGS

STATION STONES STONE SETTINGS AND AVENUE

0   50 m

Figure 3.23. Outline plan of the earthwork at Stonehenge, Wessex, and the main structural elements on the site. Information from Cleal, Walker, and Montague (1995).

(Watson 2001 and 2004). If such a site were to provide a microcosm of the surrounding country, it was vital that it should have an unimpeded view of the horizon. A number of enclosures were also aligned on prominent hills or valleys, and others on the position of the sun (Parker Pearson et al 2006: 238–40).

A good way of summarising these points is to consider the best known of all the prehistoric monuments in Britain, for it epitomises many of the processes that have been described so far.

In some respects Stonehenge is unique. It has an unusual structural sequence; its architecture makes use of techniques that are not found anywhere else; some of its raw materials were introduced from a great distance; and its scale is unprecedented. At the same time, each of these characteristics is related to more general trends during the Later Neolithic period and helps to define the issues that need discussing here (Cleal, Walker, and Montague 1995).

The first enclosure at Stonehenge is one of a distinctive group discussed at the end of Chapter Two. It dates from 3000 BC or a little after, and its form seems to be related to that of the last causewayed enclosures. Its ditch was interrupted at many points and had been deliberately refilled to cover a number of placed deposits, mainly of animal bones (ibid., chapter 5). This earthwork was probably contemporary with a nearby cursus, although only small parts of those sites are visible from one another (J. Richards 1990: 93–6). The segmented enclosure at Stonehenge was precisely circular and was located in the centre of a circular landscape formed by a horizon of higher ground, but that effect was limited to the area around the monument. The Stonehenge Cursus was aligned on a long barrow and on the equinoctial sunrise. It also pointed towards the valley of the River Avon.

It is ironic that the enclosure at Stonehenge should have given its name to an entire class of sites, for it is a class to which it does not belong. In contrast to the earthwork of a henge, its bank is inside the ditch, and those elements that do have affinities with monuments of that kind belong to a later period. Although there are no absolute dates for the second phase at Stonehenge, the existing enclosure was probably associated with two structures, as well as an enigmatic setting of timber uprights in its northern entrance. At the centre of the monument there may have been a timber building, although its plan can no longer be recovered (Cleal, Walker, and Montague 1995: chapter 6). That is because its position is still occupied by standing stones, but also because it formed the principal focus for antiquarian excavations. Even so, it is known that post sockets existed in this area and that some of them were earlier than the monoliths. The distribution of these post holes is confined to the zone occupied by the later stone circles, suggesting that one kind of structure replaced another, as so often happened at these sites.

The second structure is undated. It consists of two parallel rows of posts extending between another entrance to the monument and the central area just described. These seem to have formed a narrow avenue. Close to the centre of the site it was interrupted by a wooden screen (ibid., chapter 6). Exactly the same arrangement is found at Durrington Walls, where its prehistoric context is well established. At Durrington, it led to the Northern Circle, a ring of uprights associated with Grooved Ware (Wainwright and Longworth 1971: fig. 17).

The third component of this phase at Stonehenge is a series of pits concentric with the inner edge of the bank. They contain deposits of artefacts and cremated bone in their secondary filling. One reason for suggesting that they are later in date than the earthwork enclosure is that more cremation burials were found

Figure 3.24. The outer setting of monoliths and lintels at Stonehenge.

in features dug into the top of the bank and the upper levels of the ditch. Richard Atkinson (1956 and 1979) interpreted this as evidence of a cremation cemetery, but that idea is untenable, for these features had obviously been refilled before such deposits were made. It is better to follow the ideas of the original excavator, Colonel Hawley, who regarded the Aubrey Holes as post sockets. He observed signs of friction on the edges of these features where uprights had been manoeuvred into place (Cleal, Walker, and Montague 1995, 102). They are likely to be the remains of a palisaded enclosure of the early form defined by Alex Gibson (1998).

By this stage an earthwork which was probably related to a causewayed enclosure had been reconstructed as some kind of henge. This was not a unique occurrence, as a similar sequence has been postulated at a series of monuments in northeast England, the best known of them at Thornborough (J. Harding 2000). The interior of Stonehenge was screened off from the surrounding area not by one palisade but by two, and the positions of older structures were marked by deposits of human bone. This may have marked the closure of the original monument. It also prefigured an increasing concern with the dead.

The next development at Stonehenge typifies a wider development in the late third millennium BC. This was the translation of the timber monument into stone. It is not quite clear when this happened, and it may have been a complex process. There seem to have been two main elements which were not necessarily built simultaneously. There are the four Station Stones (Cleal, Walker, and Montague 1995: 26). These are located just inside the enclosure bank where they form a precise rectangle. This has never been adequately explained, and yet the basic configuration seems familiar. A circular earthwork perimeter enclosed a rectilinear arrangement of uprights. This resembles the layout of several timber monuments, including the North Circle at Durrington Walls (Wainwright and Longworth 1971: 41–4). It may be that the first setting of monoliths at Stonehenge conformed to the same organisation of space. It is more difficult to reconstruct the arcs of monoliths in the middle of the site. There appear to have been two circles of uprights, arranged in pairs, although they may never have been completed (Cleal, Walker, and Montague 1995: chapter 7).

The form of the innermost stone setting raises problems, for the uprights were later removed and erected in other positions. Nevertheless some of the reused monoliths had been shaped so that they could support lintels. It is a moot point whether that plan was abandoned before the project was complete, or whether these stones had been brought from somewhere else. At all events it suggests that a deliberate attempt was being made to copy the characteristics of a timber building in a more durable medium (Gibson 2005: 143–51). Such a scheme was executed during a later phase in the history of Stonehenge, but using a different raw material.

The original project had made use of the distinctive types of rock which are generally called 'bluestones'. They originated in southwest Wales, in another landscape with stone and earthwork monuments. They also came from a small area where stone axes were made (Thorpe et al. 1991). It is not clear how they were transported, but enough is known to reject the idea that they had been carried to southern England by melting ice. It would have taken a huge effort to obtain them and to bring them to the site. This must be the ultimate example of the links between such monuments and materials from distant locations.

By 2400 BC the abandoned scheme seems to have been reinstated using a different raw material. Two massive structures were built, using local sarsens instead of imported bluestones. Although some of its elements were rearranged, that really represents the final form of the monument. It consisted of a massive circle of sarsens joined together by lintels enclosing a second horseshoe-shaped setting in which pairs of uprights were linked in a similar fashion. Inside each of these circuits there were low pillars of Welsh rock which seem to have been reused from an earlier structure (Cleal, Walker, and Montague 1995: chapter 7). Each stone must have had its own history, for nearly all those making up the inner setting of bluestones came from the same source. By contrast, the outer settings made use of material from a variety of different places in the Presceli Mountains. The finished structure was not only a striking monument in itself; it referenced a landscape over two hundred kilometres away (Bradley 2000b: 92–6).

During the same phase the perimeter of Stonehenge was modified, and now an earthwork avenue extended from the northern entrance of the enclosure to the Avon where there were timber circles close to the river at Woodhenge and

Durrington Walls (Cleal, Walker, and Montague 1995: 291–329). There must have been a link between these different sites, for Stonehenge was very much a copy of a wooden monument. The sarsens had been shaped, and the lintels were secured in place using joints that would have been more appropriate in timber carpentry. The surfaces of some stones were treated so that they resembled carved wood, and one of them had probably been used to polish axes. Much later, in the sixteenth century BC, bronze axeheads were depicted by carvings on three of the monoliths (ibid., 30–4). In many ways this structure epitomises tendencies that have already been identified at other monuments. For example, the sarsen horseshoe is tallest on the southwest side of the circle, and the bluestone pillars are paired with the sarsen uprights in a similar fashion to the composite structures at Mount Pleasant and the Sanctuary. Still more striking, the finished structure is obviously aligned on the sun. Looking northeastwards, it rises at midsummer over the course of the avenue. To the southwest, it sets at midwinter behind the tallest pair of stones. The rising ground along the final section of the Avenue enhances this effect. From this position the horizon is hidden from view, and behind the circle there is nothing but the sky. The whole layout of the monument can also be understood as a series of barriers screening an area in its centre which few people could have ever have seen.

That hypothesis applies to many of the larger monuments constructed during the later third millennium BC, but the building and use of Stonehenge introduce some new elements. Although many of these finds are poorly documented, it seems clear that the monument was associated with an unusually large quantity of human bones. Few of them have any contexts and none has been accurately dated, but if this observation is correct it adds weight to Parker Pearson's and Ramilsonina's interpretation (Parker Pearson and Ramilsonina 1998). Their case is all the stronger since radiocarbon dates suggests that the sarsen structure at Stonehenge would have been contemporary with the timber buildings at Durrington Walls and Woodhenge (Parker Pearson et al 2006: 233). Not only were the stone structures a more durable version of those timber monuments, their associations were completely different from one another. The timber circles were associated with many portable artefacts and a considerable quantity of animal bones. Stonehenge contained very few objects. In their place were finds of human remains.

As the associations of such monuments changed, so did the scale on which they were built. Stonehenge must have made greater demands on human labour than any other building of the time, and yet it is comparatively small. Even the final sarsen circle is not much over thirty metres in diameter. This chapter has considered the ways in which access to particular monuments was restricted. This structure took that process to its limits. A building that would have required more labour than ever before was impossible for large numbers of people to visit.

The crucial transition from a timber monument, less impressive than its neighbours at Durrington and Woodhenge, to a uniquely complex piece of architecture came at a special time in the archaeology of southern England, for this was when the first metalwork appears and when a new ceramic style, the Bell Beaker, is found in graves. Both these developments would have been impossible without renewed contacts with Continental Europe, and yet these novel media surely expressed some of the same social divisions as more traditional monuments like Stonehenge. This chapter began by suggesting that monument building was one of the processes by which an elite might distinguish itself from other members of society, and the growing scale of these structures during the later third millennium BC suggests that competition within and between different communities must have intensified at this time (Barrett 1994: chapters 1, 2, and 4). How appropriate that Beaker pottery should be associated with the transformation of Stonehenge and that it should be at Amesbury, only a short distance away, that one of the earliest burials associated with these new forms of material culture should be found (Fitzpatrick 2003). This was not only one of the first of a new tradition of individual graves, it was one of the richest. A Beaker mass grave was found nearby, and close to it there was another enclosure containing sherds of Grooved Ware (Fitzpatrick 2005). The growth of Later Neolithic monuments was sometimes associated with the promotion of long distance relationships. Now that process extended beyond Britain and Ireland, and both these regions were drawn into an international network.

A WORLD ELSEWHERE

The first appearance of Beaker pottery at Stonehenge forms a logical part of a sequence in which the successive buildings on the site became more elaborate but less accessible. The stone structures make sense only in terms of insular developments. That applies even to the deposition of human remains, as that had started when the timber monument went out of use. On the other hand, it no longer seems possible to argue that individual burials or the building of round barrows formed part of a current tradition in southern England. The first Beakers were associated with a new development and one which must have resulted from contacts with mainland Europe. Exactly the same applies to the earliest metalwork.

If Grooved Ware was an insular ceramic tradition, originating in the north but ultimately adopted in most parts of these islands, Bell Beakers represent a very different phenomenon. Their distribution is truly international and extends from Denmark to North Africa. They are found as far east as Hungary and as far west as Portugal (Salanova 2002). That has raised problems of interpretation, for they are often associated with early metalwork as well as new burial practices. It would be easy to argue that they represent a class of prestigious artefacts employed in social transactions, but that cannot supply the entire answer. Like Grooved Ware, Bell Beakers can be found in special contexts, but they occur also in settlements.

One important influence was the practice of individual burial with grave goods associated with Corded Ware in Northern and Central Europe (Case 2004a). Scholars have discussed its relationship with Bell Beakers, and for a long time it seemed most likely that these two ceramic styles were used in succession, so that the earliest Bell Beakers might have been in the north where they could have developed out of the Corded Ware tradition (Lanting, Mook, and Van der Waals 1976). Now that is uncertain. The oldest radiocarbon dates for Bell Beakers come from Portugal (Kunst 2001), and it seems as if the earliest vessels have a distribution extending up the Atlantic coastline from the Iberian Peninsula (Salanova 2002). These finds are commonly associated with human remains, some of them in megalithic tombs, and with the earliest use of metal. The first Bell Beakers in Northern Europe are contemporary with the vessels that were once taken as their prototypes.

That realignment poses a further problem. If Bell Beakers and Corded Ware were independent developments, how and why were elements of both these two traditions combined? Bell Beakers are closely associated with metalwork, including weapons and personal ornaments, and with archery equipment. Corded Ware was also associated with burials, but these contained a rather different assemblage in which stone battle axes and flint knives played a more prominent part (Harrison 1980: chapters 2 and 3). Both groups were dominated by fine decorated pots which could have contained liquids, and some of those found in the Iberian Peninsula certainly seem to have held fermented drinks (E. Guerra Doce, pers. comm.). Humphrey Case (2004a, 2004b) suggests that these sets of objects were employed to display social position.

Those two groups were first linked together through a well-established exchange network based on the long distance movement of Grand Pressigny flint from western France (Fig. 3.25; Salanova 2002). This distinctive honey-coloured material bore some resemblance to metal and was distributed over an enormous area extending along the Atlantic and Channel coasts as far as The Netherlands and reaching inland until it connected the distribution of early Bell Beakers to that of Corded Ware. In time the two traditions lost their separate identities, and it was during this second stage that further artefact types were introduced to Britain and Ireland.

Despite this complex process, the new forms of material culture adopted in these islands were part of an international phenomenon. That development presents some problems of its own.

Chapter One discussed the 'invasion hypothesis' which had played such an important role in prehistoric archaeology during the mid-twentieth century, and the reaction that followed Grahame Clark's review of this concept in 1966. He took a minimal view of migrations during prehistory and attacked what he saw as an uncritical approach to the subject. He believed that there were only two cases in which significant numbers of people had settled distant areas. One was the introduction of agriculture discussed in Chapter Two, and the other was the invasion, or invasions, of the 'Beaker Folk'. This was so much part of the framework accepted at the time that his pupil David Clarke (1970) actually suggested a greater number of episodes of Beaker settlement from Continent than previous scholars in this field. Only recently has it been possible to devise a more scientific method for studying migration. This is based on the analysis of human bone. The first results certainly suggest a certain amount of mobility, but it is too soon to discuss its extent or significance (Fitzpatrick 2003).

Clarke took an increasingly flexible approach in a later publication (Clarke 1976). That was because studies of the Bell Beaker phenomenon in Continental Europe were meeting with a problem. Although this style of pottery might be associated with early metalwork and with a restricted range of funeral gifts, it was hard to identify the other elements that were necessary to define an archaeological 'culture'. There was no Beaker economy, these artefacts could be found with a variety of monument types and, most important of all, Beaker settlements and houses assumed many different forms. More often than not, this distinctive material assemblage was associated with kinds of buildings that were already well established (Besse and Desideri 2005). Faced with such anomalies, Clarke (1976) talked of the Beaker 'network'. Other researchers referred to a Beaker 'package' (Burgess and Shennan 1976).

Again there are both empirical and theoretical problems to address. A practical difficulty concerns Beaker chronology in Britain and Ireland. David Clarke (1970) had postulated a series of migrations linking specific parts of Continental Europe to particular parts of these islands, identifying such links on the basis of pottery types and their associations. Once the colonists had settled here, they made their pottery in more local styles which gradually changed their character over time. Continental scholars disputed some of the long-distance connections on which his interpretation was based and proposed a simpler scheme. The British and Irish sequence had apparently moved in parallel with well-documented developments in The Netherlands (Lanting and Van der Waals 1972).

It remained to test these ideas by a programme of radiocarbon dating. This was undertaken by the British Museum in the late 1980s (Kinnes et al. 1991). The results were unexpected, for they did not support any of the existing schemes. They suggested that there was little evidence for a succession of different types, even when it was indicated by artefact associations. Some of the dates were exceptionally late. This left students of the period in a quandary. Most executed the difficult manoeuvre of rejecting the validity of any Beaker chronology yet ascribing their material to styles which presuppose such a sequence.

Since the Beaker dating programme was published in 1991, more radiocarbon dates have been obtained and a clearer pattern has begun to emerge (Needham 2005). The overall date range has been narrowed to between 2,400

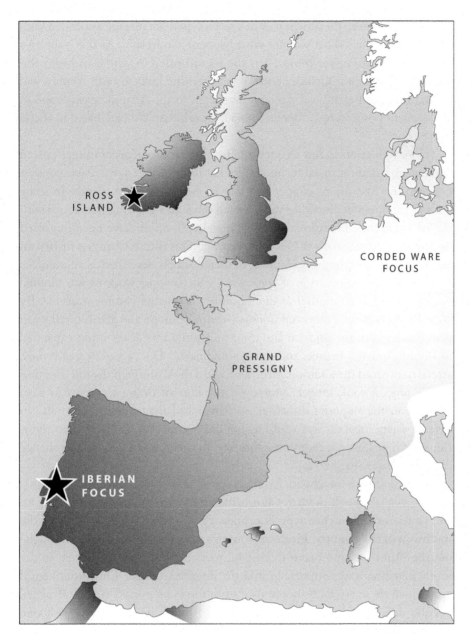

Figure 3.25. The geographical extent of the Bell Beaker phenomenon in Europe, emphasising its Atlantic origins in relation to the flint source at Grand Pressigny and the copper mines at Ross Island. Beaker distribution from Salanova (2002).

and 1800 BC, and now it does seem as if the earliest Beakers are especially close to those found on the Continent; most later types represent insular developments. It is only with the earlier styles that human migration can be postulated.

What were the contexts of Beaker material in Britain and Ireland? They differ so fundamentally that the contrasts between them help to identify the issues that need discussion. It is commonly supposed that fine Beakers are associated with burials, where they form part of a stereotyped assemblage associated with specific individuals. That was not what happened in Ireland. As this is the area with the earliest copper mines, it is the logical place in which to begin this account. Although it includes pottery with stylistic links to both western and central Europe, Ireland was directly connected to the Atlantic seaways and in an excellent position to be drawn into a network that had originated in Iberia (Case 1995).

The introduction to this chapter touched on the problems of using a period framework based on metal technology. That is important as there is a contrast between the first use of copper and that of bronze in these islands. In some parts of Europe metalworking was adopted through a growing familiarity with the raw materials. Occasional items of metalwork might have been imported into what was essentially a Neolithic setting. This did not happen in Britain and Ireland where the first adoption of metals is best described as an event.

It marked the culmination of a process by which copper working was adopted in one society after another as the requisite knowledge became available. By 3000 BC, it had been taken up in north-central Europe and across the Iberian peninsula, and in the mid- to late third millennium its distribution expanded to Britain, Ireland, France, and south Scandinavia. The production of bronze artefacts involved the addition of tin, and across the Continent the full adoption of this process took longer. Moreover, the idea of doing so seems to have travelled in the opposite direction, so that it had happened by 2200 BC in Britain where local tin was available, but did not reach Central and Northern Europe for at least another two centuries. In Spain and Portugal the change came even later (Pare 2000).

The earliest Irish metalwork has always presented problems. It consists mainly of axeheads, although there are also halberds and knives or dagger blades. All were made of a distinctive type of copper whose most likely origin was in the southwest of the country. Products from this source were distributed throughout the island and also occur in Britain, particularly towards the west; in the south, metalwork was imported across the English Channel. On chronological grounds all these artefacts should date from the same period as early Beakers, but the different kinds of material were not found in association with one another. The problem was summed up by Humphrey Case in an article entitled 'Were the Beaker-people the first metallurgists in Ireland?' (1966). Whether or not metalworkers had used Beaker pottery, where had they acquired such a specialised technology? Despite the reaction against prehistoric migrations, it was clear that such complex technological processes as metallurgy had not developed spontaneously. They had to be taught and learnt.

Both these problems are closer to resolution with excavations at Ross Island, near Killarney in southwest Ireland (O'Brien 2004a). This site had always been suggested as the source of the earliest copper extraction, but until fieldwork took place there in the 1990s it was assumed that any archaeological evidence had been destroyed. Fortunately that was not the case and it was possible to investigate not only some of the mines where the raw material was extracted but also a work camp in which the ore was processed. That specialised settlement included a number of circular buildings and was associated almost exclusively with Beaker pottery. At last the beginnings of Irish metallurgy could be set in a wider context.

The project shed some light on the processes followed at the mines. This permitted a tentative comparison between the technology employed at Ross Island and early metallurgy in other parts of Europe. O'Brien suggests that the closest links were with the procedures followed along the Atlantic coastline between Spain and Normandy. The dates from Ross Island show that mining there commenced around 2400 BC and continued until about 1900 BC. Metalwork of similar composition and character is found in western France.

Apart from the settlement of Lough Gur, also in southwest Ireland, there are no other sites where early metal is associated with Beaker pottery. That is probably because they were deposited according to different conventions. As O'Brien observes, the earliest metalwork is dominated by axeheads. They may have replaced their stone equivalents, and, like them, they are sometimes found in hoards or votive deposits. In contrast, Beaker pottery may have taken on the existing roles of Grooved Ware. In some cases it has been quite difficult to tell the difference between these two styles.

Irish Beakers are associated mainly with settlements and monuments, although there can be problems in distinguishing between these kinds of site. The best known settlements are those at Newgrange and Knowth (O'Kelly, Cleary, and Lehane 1983; Eogan and Roche 1997). In both cases there seems to be the same link with an important structure from the past, and a small tomb at Knowth actually includes one of the few Beaker burials in Ireland. The supposed settlement at Newgrange was located in front of the entrance to the tomb and overlay a deposit of rubble which had fallen from its mound. Although it has been claimed that the settlement includes the remains of houses, its main features were stone-lined hearths. The Beakers were apparently found together with Grooved Ware, and it seems possible that both were deposited in the course of feasts (Mount 1994). At the neighbouring monument of Knowth, Beaker ceramics were stratified above the levels containing Grooved Ware, but even here the excavated assemblage presents some problems. It was associated with concentrations of ceramics, flint artefacts, and hearths. The Beaker pottery is unusual, for some of these groups include a high proportion of finely decorated vessels (Eogan and Roche 1997: chapter 5).

Beaker pottery is associated with another distinctive class of monument. This is the wedge tomb which has a wider distribution than any other type of megalith in Ireland (O'Brien 1999). These monuments will be considered later in this chapter, but at this point it is worth saying that similar associations are found in Atlantic Europe, where many of the Beaker burials were associated with the reuse of chambered tombs. In Ireland the decorated vessels are generally found with cremations and are not accompanied by other grave goods. Radiocarbon dates suggest that wedge tombs were built between about 2400 and 2100 BC (Brindley and Lanting 1992). After their construction they remained in use for a considerable time. During their later history the wedge tombs in the west of Ireland provided an alternative to the cist cemeteries in the eastern part of the country.

One reason for stressing this contrast is that the very artefacts that were used as grave goods in Britain are found in different contexts in Ireland. That obviously applies to the Beakers themselves, but it is also true of the objects that one might expect to find with them (Waddell 1998: 199–223). The characteristic arrowheads of this period do occur in wedge tombs, but they were also deposited in a hoard. The stone wrist guards that are associated with Beakers in British burials have sometimes been found in bogs. The tanged copper knife is another type that can occur in graves, but this did not happen in Ireland, where again some of these artefacts may be associated with hoards and votive deposits. When a tradition of individual burial first developed in Ireland, as it did about 2200 BC, it was associated not with Beakers but with a different style of pottery, the Food Vessel (Sheridan 2004b).

Other kinds of metalwork are rarely associated with the dead either in Britain or Ireland. This is particularly true of axes, which seem to have been the main products of the Irish smiths. These are generally found in isolation or with other metal artefacts. Some were deposited in dry land hoards and occasionally marked by a stone, but often they were associated with water and placed in bogs, rivers, and lakes. In some cases it is clear that they had been laid down with a certain formality. Even the single finds carried a special significance. Stuart Needham (1988) has shown that they changed their associations during the Earlier Bronze Age. The first examples were placed in bogs and the later ones in rivers.

The early beginning of copper working in Ireland should not overshadow the use of native gold, for this also began in the later third millennium BC. Three kinds of artefact are important (G. Eogan 1994: chapter 2). There are gold discs which were produced from about 2300 BC, as well as the distinctive artefacts which are often described as ear rings, although they were probably hair ornaments. Beaker-associated gold trinkets are known from various parts of Europe, but these ones are relevant because they were probably produced in Ireland. They are associated with the earliest Beaker burials in Britain and date from approximately 2350 to 2150 BC. The other form is the lunula, which is often interpreted as a decorated collar. A few come from Britain and northwest France, but again the design appears to be Irish (Fig. 3.26). They are usually single finds, and none is clearly associated with a burial. They were made during the currency of Beakers and share their characteristic decoration (J. Taylor 1970). It shows the special significance of this style of pottery.

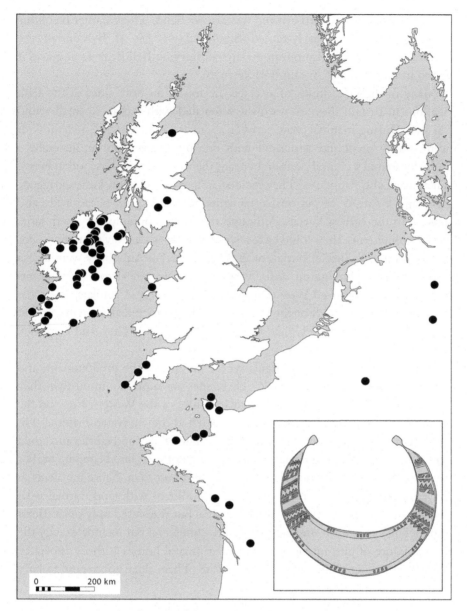

Figure 3.26. The distribution of decorated gold lunulae. Information from G. Eogan (1994).

That contrasts with the situation in Britain. To some extent it may be due to its geography, for the closest connections were probably those across the English Channel and between the east coast and The Netherlands. They may account for the differences between the burials in Britain. Some of them include the classic components of the Bell Beaker repertoire. Others contain battle axes whose forms refer back to the Corded Ware tradition, and yet their distributions overlap completely. The Irish practice of placing bodies in chambered tombs is represented only in northern and western Scotland, where Earlier Neolithic monuments were selectively reused (Bradley 2000a: 221–4). By contrast, the Central and Northern European practice of burying Bell Beakers in graves is found in most parts of Britain (Clarke 1970).

Many of the same kinds of artefacts are found on both sides of the Irish Sea, but in Britain they are normally associated with burials in small round barrows. During an initial phase between about 2500 and 2150 BC such mounds were usually small and associated with one inhumation burial, generally a male, located in a central position beneath the monument (Garwood in press). There were also flat graves. They include archery equipment, knives, daggers, awls, and a variety of personal ornaments. Gold is found occasionally and appears in the earliest burials. Although they were contemporary with large henge monuments, they could be located a short distance away from them. For instance, the rich Beaker burials recently excavated at Amesbury were over a kilometre from Durrington Walls, although they were near to a circle of pits associated with Grooved Ware (Fitzpatrick 2003, 2005). A similar pattern has been identified around Stonehenge (Exon et al. 2000) and also occurs around the Devil's Quoits in the Upper Thames Valley (Barclay, Gray, and Lambrick 1995).

Beakers are found in settlements where they form the predominant, and sometimes the only, ceramic style. These sites are more common than they are in Ireland and seem to be a particular feature of the Western Isles and the North Sea coast. Alex Gibson (1982) has studied the excavated material. His work shows that the vessels occur in a wide range of sizes and fabrics and could represent a complete assemblage rather than a set of specialised equipment. For the most part the domestic ceramics are more robust than their equivalents in graves, suggesting that certain vessels were meant to withstand normal wear and tear whilst others might be finely finished but were used only once (Boast 1995). The occupation sites are often quite ephemeral but include exactly the same mixture of pits, middens, and circular or oval houses as those associated with Peterborough Ware and Grooved Ware. There does not appear to have been a separate type of 'Beaker' house.

In southern England, some of the best preserved evidence is sealed by deposits of hill wash in valley bottoms (M. Allen 2005). Here there are traces of ard cultivation. Similar evidence is found on sand banks and gravel bars beside the River Thames in London (Sidell et al. 2002: 30–5). On the edge of the Fenland near Peterborough, Beaker pottery has been found together with groups of stake holes (F. Pryor, pers. comm.). Some may mark the positions of settlement sites, and there seem to be fence lines suggesting the existence of small plots or fields. This is especially interesting in view of Pryor's suggestion that important land divisions were marked by the deposition of Beaker artefacts in pits (2001: 70–2). These could well have been integrated into a network of lightly built fences that would leave little trace behind. Perhaps

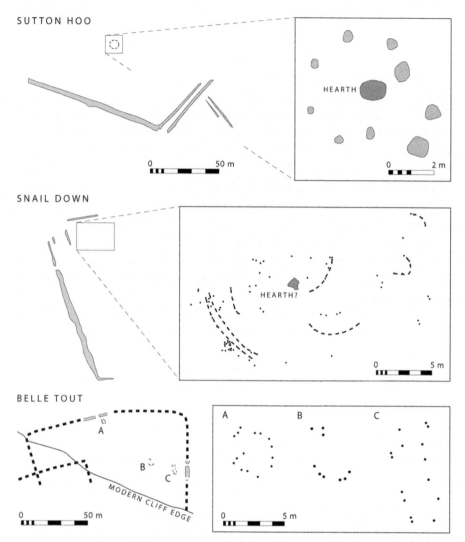

Figure 3.27. Outline plans of three settlement sites associated with Beaker pottery: Sutton Hoo (East Anglia), Snail Down (Wessex), and Belle Tout (southeast England). The site plans indicate the course of low banks or ditches, and the insets show settings of post holes, hearths, and arcs of stake holes. Information from Carver (1998), N. Thomas (2005), and Bradley (1970).

they can be compared with the shallow gullies associated with Beaker and later pottery found beneath the early medieval cemetery at Sutton Hoo in eastern England (Fig. 3.27; Carver 2005: chapter 11). There may be similar evidence from Snail Down in Wessex, where the earthworks of two field boundaries seem to underlie a group of round barrows (N. Thomas 2005: 73–6). A circular house was associated with the settlement at Sutton Hoo, but at Snail Down arcs of stake holes provide the only evidence of domestic buildings. Something similar may have happened at Belle Tout on the coast of southeast England where an ephemeral earthwork enclosed an occupation site associated with Beakers and Food Vessels (Bradley 1970).

An important link with traditional practice is found at some of the henges. For the most part, Beaker pottery is associated with the stone phases of these monuments, although this association is not always clear-cut. One way of viewing the connection is to suggest that the adoption of Beakers happened once those structures became more directly associated with the dead. The same idea might be expressed by graves in the vicinity. At the same time, it seems likely that the distribution of cultural material at these sites was governed by strict conventions: certain items had to be deposited in certain places. That was obvious during the Grooved Ware phase, but now it seems as if some of the same protocols determined the ways in which Beakers were to be deployed. That is especially obvious with the excavated material from Mount Pleasant, where there were continuities in the distribution of artefacts and animal bones (J. Thomas 1996b: 212–22). Again the adoption of Beaker pottery did not involve a radical change.

A more obvious development affected some of the megalithic tombs in Scotland, as they were selectively reused for Beaker burials. There is little sign that their structures were modified, although certain architectural details may have been copied in building a new series of monuments (Bradley 2000a: 220–31). The reused tombs contain human remains and pottery, but there are few other artefacts, and some were blocked during this phase. Other monuments may have been 'closed' in a different way. This could have happened to some of the timber and stone circles which were surrounded by ditches or palisades at a late stage in their history. In northern Scotland earlier monuments might also be closed by the erection of a ring of monoliths (Bradley 2005a, 100–6).

If the first deposits of metalwork were in Ireland, by 2000 BC they were common in Scotland, although there were few in England and Wales. That change is significant as it spans the period in which bronze working developed in Britain (Rohl and Needham 1998). Some of the raw material was imported from Ireland, but now this was probably alloyed with Cornish tin. The British metalwork was more varied than its Irish counterpart which was dominated by large numbers of axes and halberds. These are the kinds of material that are found in hoards and in natural places like bogs and rivers. It emphasises the point that during the Beaker ceramic phase one group of artefacts might be associated with the dead, whilst another was employed in a quite different sphere. Stuart Needham (1988) suggests that the deposits in graves were connected with the individual, and those in hoards with the wider community.

These new developments articulate with the practices discussed in the first part of this chapter. Irish copper axes were deployed in the same fashion as the stone axes that they replaced, and Beaker pottery took on many of the roles of Grooved Ware. There was no change in the pattern of settlement, and people still lived in insubstantial round houses, as they had done for over five hundred years. In the same way, Beakers were associated with structural changes at British henges which perpetuate, and even enhance, their traditional architecture. They were deposited according to the same conventions as Grooved Ware, and so was the material associated with them. It was only the development of a new tradition of individual burial that marks a radical departure, and even this can be explained as the visible outcome of the social divisions promoted by the building and use of large monuments (J. Barrett 1994: chapter 1). People formed new alliances to highlight their own positions, and in doing so they also adopted a new technology. No doubt that process involved the movement and exchange of personnel, but its roots were in local developments that extended far into the past.

DISTANCE AND ENCHANTMENT

These questions have been considered in some detail because the same issues are important in the Earlier Bronze Age. How was British and Irish material culture related to that in Continental Europe? What is the significance of the types of artefacts shared between these islands and the mainland, and does the evidence of burials and metalwork hoards provide an accurate picture of life during this period?

There can be little doubt that approaches to these problems have been influenced by the archaeology of a few areas and, in particular, Wessex. They have also placed an undue emphasis on the objects found in graves (Annable and Simpson 1964). That was understandable in the early development of Bronze Age studies, for it was only by identifying those objects with the widest distributions that there was any prospect of relating insular material culture to the historical chronology established in the Mediterranean. At the same time, a small selection of exceptional artefacts has come to dominate the discussion for reasons which are explained by the history of fieldwork. Long before settlement excavation was considered possible or useful, well-preserved barrows were investigated for grave goods. The work focused on the deposits beneath the centres of these earthworks and rarely extended to the monuments as a whole. That was because antiquarians believed that it was where the richest material would be found. Since they did very little to record the structures of the mounds, the contents of a biased sample of graves provided the material available for study.

Those early excavations were devoted to standing monuments which survived in great numbers on the chalk of southern and northeastern England because both regions had been used as grazing land. In the nineteenth century, there were people with the financial means and social connections to conduct large numbers of investigations. For a long time research focused on the contents of their collections (Annable and Simpson 1964; Kinnes and Longworth 1985), and even now the results of their fieldwork provide a misleading impression of the Earlier Bronze Age.

Such biases in the record can be remedied in several ways. More sophisticated excavations have treated individual mounds, and even the areas outside them, as cemeteries that might contain a whole range of burials of different ages and types. The development of aerial photography, and more recently of contract excavation, redresses another imbalance in the record. It no longer seems as if the main concentrations of Bronze Age barrows were located on high ground, as was once supposed. Rather, they are only the surviving part of a wider distribution of monuments associated with major valleys. The remainder of this distribution has been obliterated by cultivation. Such work also shows that the great concentrations of burials long recognised in areas like Salisbury Plain, the Dorset Ridgeway, or the Yorkshire Wolds have their counterparts in areas where few earthworks survive. For example, many round barrows are located along the rivers discharging into the Fenland (Evans and Knight 2000), whilst the density of round barrows on the island of Thanet in southeast England is similar to that in most parts of Wessex (Field 1998).

In both the Beaker period and the Earlier Bronze Age finds of high quality metalwork are known well outside the areas which have usually been studied. Among recent discoveries in England are a group of gold ornaments associated with a barrow at Lockington in the East Midlands (Hughes 2000). There is a gold vessel from an enigmatic monument at Ringlemere and a number of other finds from Kent (Varndell and Needham 2002; Champion 2004). Elsewhere, in the Midlands, two barrows, at Raunds and Gayhurst, are associated with enormous collections of bones, suggesting that hundreds of animals had been slaughtered and consumed in the course of feasts (Davis and Payne 1993; A. Chapman 2004). There is little to distinguish the most complex grave assemblages at lowland monuments like those at West Heslerton in northeast England from the burials in the better known cemeteries on the chalk (Powelsland, Haughton, and Hanson 1986; Haughton and Powelsland 1999). The real difference is that these monuments did not survive above ground and had been protected from antiquarian activity.

There have perhaps been fewer new developments in Irish archaeology, but this is because some areas are poorly suited to air photography. There has been a marked increase in discoveries as large areas of topsoil are stripped in the course of developer-funded excavations. Like the east coast of Scotland, Ireland contained many flat cemeteries in which the dead were buried in stone cists (Waddell 1990). Here barrows or cairns were less often built and the sites of cremation pyres are occasionally identified in fieldwork. Some of the graves recently discovered in Scotland are just as noteworthy as the better known examples in the south of England. Indeed, one result of contract archaeology

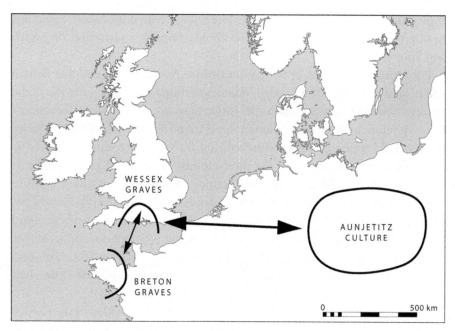

Figure 3.28. The triangular relationship between the Earlier Bronze Age burials of Wessex and those in Brittany and the Aunjetitz Culture.

has been the recognition of burials in pits and flat graves even in barrow-dominated landscapes.

The contents of Earlier Bronze Age burials pose problems. It is obvious that unusual artefacts were obtained from a distance and that local products imitated exotic types. In the past this was explained in two ways. The first has proved especially tenacious. True to the intellectual climate of the time, Stuart Piggott's classic account of the rich graves of the 'Wessex Culture' drew on Continental parallels to postulate an invasion of southern England by an elite from Brittany (Piggott 1938). This was based on the close similarities between the grave goods in these two areas (Fig. 3.28). Although Piggott took a cautious line in later life, Sabine Gerloff followed the same interpretation nearly forty years afterwards (Gerloff 1975: 235–46). However, most of the pottery found in association with exotic grave goods in Britain and Ireland is of insular forms, suggesting that this approach may be misleading.

A similar relationship was proposed with the burials of the Aunjetitz Culture with its focus on what is now central Germany (Gerloff 1975). It is true that, like Wessex, this region contains some exceptionally rich burials. They were associated with round barrows, but in fact most of the graves in this tradition are found in flat cemeteries, and even more artefacts were deposited in hoards. There are stylistic links between the metalwork from this region and Britain, but these are equally apparent from the distribution of other objects. Amber beads are distributed from Britain and Scandinavia as far as the Mediterranean, and those made of faience are found even more widely, with distinct concentrations in Greece, Central Europe, southwest France, Britain, and Ireland (Sheridan and Shortland 2004).

For a long time studies of the Earlier Bronze Age also supposed that Britain and Ireland were on the outer edge of ancient Europe and that its core was in the Mediterranean. This was taken as the ultimate source of inspiration for a number of developments, from monument types to the design of Stonehenge. Some of these links were implausible – British and Irish passage tombs are Neolithic and cannot be compared with the tholos tombs of Greece; Stonehenge bears no resemblance to Mycenaean architecture – but it may be that the entire approach was wrong. Why should these islands have been dependencies of the European mainland? It is ironic that the closest link between the study area and the wider world should involve movement in the opposite direction. Amber which had probably been imported from Scandinavia was used to make jewellery in Wessex, and a few of the finished artefacts were deposited in the shaft graves at Mycenae (Sheridan, Kochman, and Aranauskas 2003).

A useful perspective on such long-distance contacts is provided by the faience beads which were in use in Britain and Ireland between about 1900 and 1500 BC (ibid.). Might they provide more convincing evidence of international trade? It was once considered that the Mycenaeans were exchanging southern faience for northern amber. It is true that these finds were linked by a similar technology, but now it is obvious that it was the technology that was adopted in these different areas: the beads were not exported from a single source, and the British examples made use of tin from southwest England. At the same time, there must have been contacts from one end of the island to the other, for a number of the artefacts with this distinctive composition were made in the north of Scotland.

The same applies to the adoption of metallurgy, and here a core–periphery model is equally inappropriate. Ireland contains gold, and some of the objects produced there were exported to the Continent. Copper mining was established in the southwest of the country from 2400 BC, and new sources were exploited when Ross Island went out of use. Around 1900 BC other mines were established in Wales and parts of northern England and remained in operation for about three hundred years, and in one case for even longer (Rohl and Needham 1998). It is clear from metal analysis that Cornish tin was also being exploited from an early stage. In Britain, bronze was used before it was adopted in neighbouring regions of the European mainland.

It seems more consistent with the evidence to suggest that the concentrations of richer burials in Europe are closely related to the proximity of metal sources. That would explain the prominent position played by Britain, Ireland, and northwest France, with communities in Wessex well placed to control the cross-Channel movement of tin from southwest England and its distribution across both these islands (Sherratt 1996). Similarly, the growth of the Aunjetitz

Culture is surely related to the mining of Alpine copper and the growth of fortified settlements whose inhabitants could have controlled the movement of the metal (Shennan 1995). In each case similar processes seem to have been at work, and so it is hardly surprising that communities in these different areas formed alliances with one another.

A new study by Stuart Needham (2000) suggests an even more satisfactory way of thinking about this evidence. Although he was specifically concerned with relations between southern England and Brittany, his ideas have a wider application. He accepts that there were close connections between individual artefacts on either side of the Channel and that objects might have moved in both directions. They were particularly important because they referred to links with distant areas. They could also be made out of materials with unusual physical properties, like amber, gold, and jet. The work of the anthropologist Mary Helms (1998) is relevant here. She discusses the role played by knowledge of distant places and unfamiliar practices. Travel may be a source of social power, and the acquisition of exotic items can assume a cosmological significance. The very fact that some of those connections were with remote places lends them their special power. That may be why drawings of axeheads and daggers feature on a number of stone monuments in Britain, including a series of burial cists in the west of Scotland (Simpson and Thawley 1972).

There were significant changes over time. These are illustrated by the movement of portable artefacts, but metal analysis provides a still more general picture (Rohl and Needham 1998). After the discovery of Cornish tin the inhabitants of southern Britain may have exported raw materials, both as native ores and in the form of bronze, but by about 1650 BC the occupants of these islands were making less use of local metals and the European mainland was becoming an increasingly significant source of raw material. That was especially true in the south. The sequence is consistent with studies of ancient seafaring. Before the first exploitation of copper and tin, travel across open water may have been dangerous and infrequent, and it is surely significant that it was then that the earliest sewn-plank vessels seem to have developed. They remained important from that time onwards, but they may not have been limited to a purely practical role, for their remains have been found in the Humber Estuary not far from a number of the richest burials in northern England (van de Noort 2003). Sea travel may been a way of obtaining foreign valuables but could also have been a method of winning prestige.

Not all the links were between these islands and the European mainland. The best illustration of this point is the abundance of metalwork deposits in northeast Scotland, a region which also includes the moulds for making axes. What is extraordinary is that the copper seems to have been introduced from a part of Ireland 750 km away, and tin from equally distant sources in western England. Needham (2004) suggests that the two regions may have been linked to one another, not just in economic terms but by the distinctive orientation of the local Scottish stone circles which are often directed towards the southwest or south-southwest. These are the directions of the copper and tin sources, respectively. The monuments may also have been aligned on the positions of the moon or the sunset (Bradley 2005a: 109–11), but Needham's argument emphasises as well as anything else the peculiar character of such long distance connections.

RELATIONS WITH THE DEAD

At various points in this chapter the text has referred to 'single' or 'individual' burials. The terms have been used interchangeably, but now it is necessary to consider them in detail. They are imprecise, and yet they are impossible to eliminate from archaeological writing.

On one level the idea of single burials was an artefact of early fieldwork (Fig. 3.29). Antiquarians thought that round barrows were memorials to important individuals. Each mound would cover a grave containing their remains, accompanied by a variety of artefacts (Ashbee 1960). The first excavators targeted what was sometimes the earliest of a whole series of burials. If their finds were to be studied as a coherent assemblage, it was important that they had been deposited at the same time, and yet one grave might actually include the remains of several people. They could have been buried simultaneously, some bodies might be incomplete, or the grave might have been reopened for the reception of other corpses or groups of bones. Renewed excavation of these monuments shows that such features were often overlooked. In any case there are too few graves to represent the entire population and it is clear that isolated body parts continued to circulate, as they had during the Neolithic period.

The term 'single' burial cannot refer to the deposition of one body per barrow, as more recent excavations demonstrate that this was an important feature in some phases and less significant in others, but not every grave contained a mixture of human remains in the manner of an earlier long barrow. Most intact bodies were accompanied by some selection of artefacts. That is why those objects seemed to be associated with specific 'individuals'.

There are problems with using that term. In modern Western thought the 'individual' carries specific connotations relating to identity and agency (Brück 2004). Those ideas developed during the Enlightenment, and there are societies in which this approach is not appropriate: people are not thought of as autonomous entities but are defined in terms of their relationships with others. The idea of an individual burial might be equally misleading because the portrayal of the deceased created during the funeral was composed by the mourners who placed particular objects in the grave. It is not clear whether these had been the property of the dead person, and certain items, including gold ornaments, may have been made for the occasion (Coles and Taylor 1971).

Figure 3.29. A typical 'single' burial as depicted in Canon Greenwell's *British Barrows* (Greenwell 1877).

Some artefacts were so fragmentary that they might have circulated over several generations (Woodward 2002), yet the presence of flowers in Scottish graves must be explained as gifts (Tipping 1994b). The corpse could not determine how it was displayed in death; the image encountered by the modern archaeologist reflects the relationships between the deceased and those who undertook the burial.

Perhaps the grave was an arena for negotiating relationships between the living and the dead, but that is not how the evidence has been understood until now, for more emphasis has been placed on the contrast between 'richer' and 'poorer' graves (Pierpoint 1980: chapter 9). The distinction between adult and child burials has been studied and so has that between men and women, although gender distinctions were inferred on the basis of grave goods as barrow diggers rarely retained the excavated bones. In each case the objective has been the same: to use the contents of the burials to reconstruct social organisation. From the work of William Stukeley in the eighteenth century, there have been two main trends. Archaeologists have employed the grave assemblage to infer social status and to identify the activities associated with particular people in the past. Just as Stukeley identified Kings' Barrows and Druids' Barrows on Salisbury Plain, recent writers discussed the graves of warriors, archers, leather workers, smiths, and shamans (Case 1977; Woodward 2000: 119–22). This approach makes many assumptions. The dead were equipped by those who survived them, and the deceased might be accompanied by the material associated with more than one of these roles. Thus the man who has become known as the 'Amesbury Archer' might have been a hunter, but he was portrayed also as a warrior, a flint worker, and a smith, for his grave contained several sets of objects that might otherwise have been distributed between different burials (Fitzpatrick 2003).

Of course there were contrasts between the contents of these graves, but the British and Irish evidence seems surprisingly uniform. There are a few exceptional deposits, but the range of variation is comparatively limited considering how many burials have been excavated. The quantity of metal items is hardly impressive compared with the contents of Aunjetitz hoards like those at Dieskau (von Brunn 1959), and it is overshadowed by the large number of objects consigned to rivers during the Later Bronze Age (Bradley 1998a). Some burials are accompanied by a locally made pottery vessel, and even the necklaces of jet, faience, and amber might be composites made out of material which was already worn and broken (Woodward 2002). There were episodes of lavish consumption and display, but these were mainly concerned with the building of cremation pyres and with funeral feasts (J. Barrett 1994: chapter 5; Davis and Payne 1993). Few burial mounds attained the proportions of the larger Neolithic monuments, and some Bronze Age barrows developed incrementally over a long period of time. The presence of exotic items in the graves illustrates the importance of connections with distant areas, but the portable wealth of this period seems rather insignificant compared with what is known from Central Europe. There seems little justification for postulating a rigid social hierarchy.

The same point is illustrated by the distribution of mortuary monuments. Passage tomb cemeteries and the largest henges had been widely spaced across the landscape, as if they provided focal points for a large area around them. Earlier Bronze Age cemeteries occur at much smaller intervals, although they are sometimes close to ceremonial monuments. They are so common, and their contents are so consistent, that they are best regarded as the burial places of local communities (H. S. Green 1974). If higher-status monuments are to be identified, then they are more likely to be those associated with long-established sites like Stonehenge (Exon et al. 2000). Indeed, Rosamund Cleal (2005) has pointed out that the burials close to that monument are significantly richer than those near the equally impressive henge at Avebury.

In any case burial rites changed over time. They have been studied by Paul Garwood, whose work makes use of a large number of radiocarbon dates (Garwood in press). These are mainly from England and Wales, but it is possible to suggest some points of comparison with Scotland and Ireland.

The first Beaker round barrows were quite simple and have already been discussed. Between about 2150 and 1850 BC burial mounds became much more diverse, and many structures underwent a sequence of transformations. In particular, barrows might be associated with a larger number of deposits and with a wider variety of people. They included a greater proportion of women's graves and those of children. There was also a wider range of variation in the treatment of the body, and cremation became more important at this time.

This contrasts with the period between about 1850 and 1500 BC. It saw the development of the major cemeteries that are often supposed to characterise the whole of the Earlier Bronze Age. Although the mounds were often large and might assume specialised forms, they were frequently constructed in a single phase, and the central graves may contain only one body. The linear barrow cemeteries of the Wessex downland seem to date from this period and are unusual in being organised in such a formal manner. This is not found widely in other areas, although it is sometimes considered as the norm. Cremation was widely practised, and certain of the individual mounds contain the richest grave groups of this period.

A basic distinction is between the use of an individual mound for a whole series of burials (such as a cemetery barrow/cairn), and the development of barrow cemeteries, which are groups of barrows, each containing one or more interments. Both have to be considered here. A good starting point is with the mortuary monuments of northeast England, where any mound may include several graves and where each grave could contain more than one body (Petersen 1972). Such cemetery mounds occur very widely. In the south, for instance, well-excavated and well-preserved monuments in Wessex contain the remains of roughly fifteen people, while the cairn at Bedd Branwen on Anglesey included a similar number (Lynch 1971). Mounds in Ireland include as many as nineteen, (O'Sullivan 2005: 169–70), although the median is six (Waddell 1990). There was considerable variation from one region to another. The round barrows of central southern England contain an unusual variety of artefacts, but these sites cannot typify the range of mortuary practices found in these islands. English barrows are commonly organised into small groups, but in other regions, most obviously in North Wales and Ireland, such mounds are often isolated (Lynch, Aldhouse-Green, and Davies 2000: 121–8; Waddell 1990; J. Eogan 2004).

There were other ways of commemorating people without constructing a monument. In the East Anglian fens bodies might be placed in bogs or pools together with Earlier Bronze Age artefacts (Healy and Housley 1992). Their remains are also found in caves in northern England (Barnatt and Edmonds 2002), and across large parts of Ireland, areas of western Scotland, and along the coast from the River Tees to Aberdeenshire there were cemeteries of flat graves, most of which lacked any mound or cairn (Waddell 1990; Cowie and Shepherd 2003). In the west of Ireland they are much less common, and here wedge tombs were used instead. Like Neolithic monuments, they include a mixture of burnt and unburnt bones (O'Brien 1999). Such variation is by no means unusual. Apart from the many people whose remains have left no trace, the deposits found in graves include inhumations, cremations, and smaller groups of disarticulated bones. Although inhumation was favoured at an earlier stage than cremation, the use of both rites overlapped and deposits of each kind can even be found in the same grave.

There is a way of thinking about such evidence which combines several of the points made so far. Not all the graves that were once described as 'individual' burials contain the remains of one person, although this is frequently the case. Male burials adopt a different body position from those of women (Tuckwell 1975; Greig et al. 1989: 79–80), but within these deposits artefacts are associated with particular people and are often placed in specific locations in relation to the corpse. At the same time, other burials are found on the same sites. This discussion has highlighted the way in which the image of the dead was manipulated by those conducting the funeral, for they were responsible for the selection of the artefacts that were to be buried. Perhaps the organisation of the cemeteries also expressed the relationships amongst the dead themselves.

In 1972 Petersen criticised the idea that Earlier Bronze Age burials were organised around single graves. He studied the records of a large number of excavations, mostly in northern England. It was clear that many graves contained the remains of several people. Following the chronology that was accepted at the time, this could be compared with the Neolithic practice of collective burial. It was less obvious how this evidence was related to other regional traditions during the same period. That subject was taken up by Koji Mizoguchi nearly twenty years later (Mizoguchi 1993). Like Petersen, he paid particular attention to the round barrows of northeast England. He observed that there were certain consistent relationships between successive burials in the same graves. Often the original excavation had been reopened. That means that its precise position was known, but when it happened other features of the original burial were taken into account. Where the first burial was that of an adult man, the next interment was generally that of a woman or a young person who would be laid out either on the same alignment as the previous burial or at right angles to it. That process might be repeated. At the same time where inhumations and cremations were found together, the unburnt corpse was the first one committed to the ground, and the cremation was generally placed in the grave either in a subsidiary position or at a higher level in its filling. At times it is clear that relics were removed. Not all the earlier skeletons are complete, and it is possible that artefacts were also taken away. For example, careful excavation showed that the central grave at Gayhurst Quarry had been recut on five occasions (A. Chapman 2004).

The same processes apply to the siting of different graves. They may be juxtaposed, they can be aligned on one another, or their positions may respect one another with such accuracy that this must have been intended. It would have required detailed knowledge, and such information even extended to the configuration of the corpse. This is clear from Jonathan Last's analysis of the burials from a round barrow at Barnack in eastern England (Last 1998). Another example of these patterns is the cemetery at Keenoge in the east of Ireland which includes a series of graves, most of them in pits or cists; the inhumations were

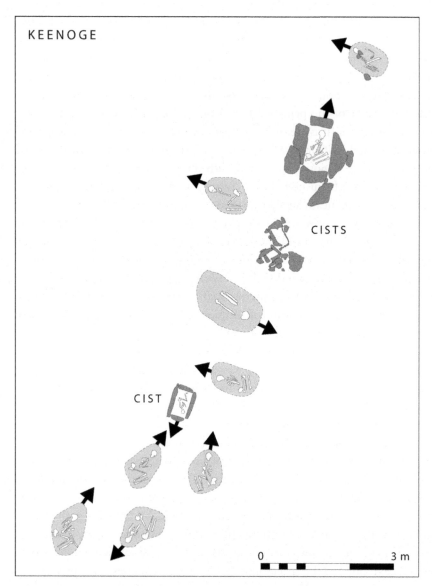

Figure 3.30. The Earlier Bronze Age flat cemetery at Keenoge in the east of Ireland, emphasising the orientation of the inhumation graves. Information from Mount (1997).

often accompanied by cremations (Mount 1997). With few exceptions, the burials followed approximately the same alignment, but the bodies in adjacent graves tended to be organised in pairs, one with its head to the east and the other laid out in exactly the opposite direction. The only divergence from this pattern concerned a few graves with a northsouth axis, but the inhumations were paired in a similar manner (Fig. 3.30). It resembles the process described by Last, but this time the principle extended to a flat cemetery.

Those relationships were expressed on an intimate scale and were presumably played out over a short period of time, so that newer burials might be related to those of the recently dead. The same principle applies to people who had died long before, but it is more difficult to see it at work. Perhaps the best evidence comes from earthwork monuments. For a long time it was assumed that these could be reduced to a few distinctive forms, so that there would be a consistent relationship between the appearance of any particular barrow and the character of the principal burial or burials (Ashbee 1960). That was unduly optimistic as it is clear that, except in the late group of single-period barrows discussed by Garwood (in press), the shape of any individual mound is no guide to the deposits associated with it. Impressive earthworks may be found with sparsely furnished graves – or with none at all – and more elaborate graves may occur beneath smaller mounds or outside them altogether. That is because monuments were rebuilt or extended over time, so that in principle they might begin with an unmarked grave and pass through a series of structural stages during which they changed from one 'type' of monument to another (J. Barrett 1994: chapters 2 and 5). It is misleading to pay too much attention to their outward appearance, for it merely marks the point at which that process stopped. Sometimes the remains of simpler constructions are buried beneath the outer mantle of a larger earthwork.

A similar process extended to the relationships between the mounds in the same group, although Paul Garwood's study suggests that the complex linear cemeteries which are so common in Wessex date from the end of this period and include some barrows with only one grave. They show a number of relationships. Although the separate monuments could be some distance apart, it is quite common for them to be orientated on certain focal points or for the monuments to be arranged in lines so that every barrow had its neighbour or neighbours (Fig. 3.31). In that way one earthwork might refer to the position of another, and sometimes they were even combined as formerly discrete structures coalesced. Just as mounds could be linked together, they could also be kept separate, and some of the larger cemeteries can be subdivided into several clusters or rows of mounds. Recent excavation suggests that such principles extended to the spaces in between these structures. This process was followed at Monkton in Kent, where the cemetery includes a post alignment (Bennett and Williams 1997). At Radley in the Thames Valley, there were two parallel lines of round barrows, but there were also some flat graves, including a row of urned cremations which followed the long axis of the cemetery (Barclay and Halpin 1999: 128–33). This is one of the barrow groups whose siting was influenced by the presence of a Neolithic monument, and it reinforces the suggestion that the organisation of these complexes was one way of relating those who had recently died to the dead of earlier generations. Garwood (in press) suggests that some of the linear cemeteries were also directed towards the setting sun, thus linking the fortunes of the dead to the annual cycle of the seasons. That may have been the case at Snail Down on the Wessex chalk, where two lines of barrows were established between about 1800 and

Figure 3.31. The Cursus Barrows near to Stonehenge, Wessex – part of an Earlier Bronze Age linear cemetery.

1500 BC (Fig. 3.32; N. Thomas 2005). One may have been directed towards the sunrise, and the other towards the sunset. This formal pattern seems to have been imposed on a scattered distribution of older mounds, two of which had been built over the remains of a settlement.

This discussion began with the suggestion that the identities of the dead were constituted by their relationships with the living and that these were expressed through the choice of materials placed in the grave. That may well have been true, but it seems at least as important to recognise that not all the Earlier Bronze Age cemeteries contain the burials of 'individuals'. Rather, they are organised around the relationships between the dead themselves: not only those who had just died but also the burials of their forbears. The same idea is expressed by the circulation of heirlooms or even human bones, and their eventual deposition in the grave. The result is rather like a genealogy in which the placing of the grave, its orientation, and its contents locate any particular person within a wider network of social relationships extending into the past. That might be expressed quite informally in the organisation of a flat cemetery or a single mound, but it could also be set out on a massive scale through the development of a large barrow cemetery.

That is where Garwood's analysis is so helpful, for it draws attention to important changes in the ways in which these processes operated over time. Between 2150 and 1850 BC round barrows were built and reconstructed on a large scale. These monuments were often located in relation to existing features of the landscape, including Beaker mounds, but the most important way of signifying relationships between the past and the present was by reopening older graves and adding new deposits. In the same way, where the first barrows might have covered only one grave, now such monuments included a wider variety of burials whose positions within the mound seems to have been determined by real or imagined relationships with the dead (Barrett 1994: chapter 5).

The same concerns were important in the last major phase of barrow building, between 1850 and 1500 BC, but it was the spatial relationship between different monuments that assumed more importance. That is particularly obvious in Wessex where linear cemeteries developed, many of them built out of specialised forms of mound that were constructed in a single phase. They include the burials of individual corpses associated with a rich array of grave goods, but this time they are located in relation to a more complex history in which the placing of any one mound was related to the positions of all the others. As Garwood (in press) points out, these lines of monuments could be read as a sequence of individual graves, and the same argument has been pursued by Mizoguchi (1992). Now those relationships were displayed to everyone, and the mounds had even greater authority because they were orientated not only on the remains of the past but occasionally on the position of the sun.

Genealogies provide one way of codifying relationships, but there were other, less tangible connections that were displayed through the use of artefacts. One is the relationship with previous generations epitomised by the transmission of relics. The other is the pattern of long-distance alliances that linked people in Britain and Ireland with those in Continental Europe. This was shown by the use of unusual or exotic artefacts, and it may be no accident that they played a particularly prominent part in Earlier Bronze Age Wessex, the very region in which formal barrow cemeteries found their fullest expression towards the end of this period. Rather different practices were followed in other areas, and it remains a priority for future research to explore the wider significance of these distinctions.

This account has been concerned with relationships, but there is one which has not been considered so far. That is the relationship between the dead and the places in the landscape where they were buried. There are three points to make here. The first is that the distribution of standing monuments is incomplete. It is all too easy to suppose that round barrows were a major feature of the uplands, but even the surviving monuments overlook lower ground, and aerial photography has shown that they are often located in valleys and beside watercourses (Field 1998). The impressive earthwork barrows on the hills of Wessex and the Yorkshire Wolds have created a misleading impression for they were accompanied by similar monuments that have been ploughed out. There is no real difference between these regions and the river terraces where many other burials are found.

Having said that, it is probably true that the basic pattern was influenced by the continuing attraction of a variety of monuments, particularly henges and

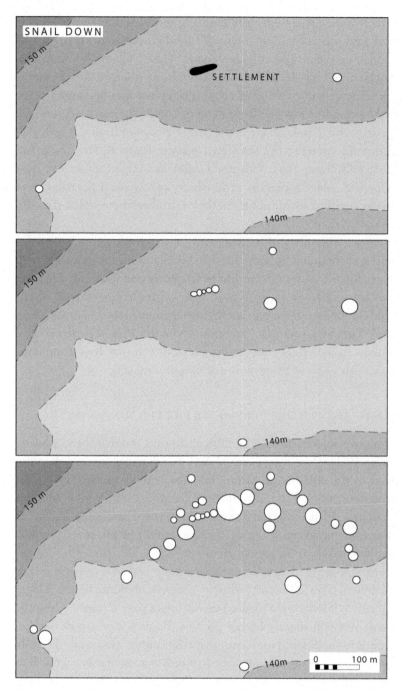

Figure 3.32. Three successive phases in the development of the Snail Down complex, Wessex. The sequence begins with the Beaker domestic site shown in detail in Fig. 3.27 and ends with two lines of Earlier Bronze Age round barrows. Information from N. Thomas (2005).

cursuses, which were already established during the Neolithic period. These
are associated with mortuary monuments of later date, some of which include
particularly striking collections of grave goods. This is obviously the case in
southern England, but it is equally obvious around the stone circles of Orkney
(Sheridan, Kochman, and Aranauskas 2003). Flat cemeteries developed in the
vicinity of henge monuments like Broomend of Crichie in northeast Scotland
(J. Ritchie 1920), and in Ireland one of the largest groups of Bronze Age burials
was in the mound covering the decorated passage tomb at Tara (Newman
1997a: 147–8; O'Sullivan 2005: Chapter 4). Just as wedge tombs were used
during this period, older megaliths in northern and western Scotland were
selected for the burial of the dead before their chambers were sealed (Bradley
2000a: 221–4).

Lastly, there are a number of barrows and cairns which fall outside these
trends. These are prominent monuments that were built on exceptionally high
ground, especially hills and mountains in north Wales and northeast England.
They are not always easy to identify from below, but they command extensive views and can be seen from one another (Pierpoint 1980: 266–70; Gibson
2004b: 156–9). They raise important questions about the place of Earlier Bronze
Age monuments in the wider pattern of settlement and may have commemorated people with a special position in the community (Fig. 3.33).

MONUMENTS AND THE SETTLEMENT PATTERN 2000–1500 BC

It is frustrating that settlements can be difficult to find and that the candidates
which are suggested are not always easy to date. For that reason more attention
has been paid to the distribution of monuments, as this can shed some light
on where and how people lived. But much of the difficulty arises because it is
commonly supposed that certain areas were used as 'ritual landscapes' and given
over to the commemoration of the dead. That cannot be taken for granted,
and the argument needs to be substantiated.

In fact there is some evidence for the relationship between cemeteries and
living areas, but it takes different forms in different regions. In the Upper
Thames, it seems as if settlement focused on the lower river terraces, whilst the
largest barrows were on slightly higher ground (Bradley et al. 1996: 18–19).
Around Raunds in the English midlands, that relationship was reversed (Healy
and Harding in press), but in each case the two zones were not far apart. Close to
Stonehenge a third pattern can be identified (Peters 2000). Here the smallest
barrows, which were associated with poorly furnished graves, were usually
located on the lower ground and occur in areas where there is evidence for the
clearance of surface stones – presumably such regions were being ploughed.
The larger barrows were located in more prominent positions on the higher
ground. These were associated with a more complex series of graves and with
a wider range of funeral gifts. Just as important, these monuments made use of
turf, suggesting that they had been built on grazing land. In northern Scotland

Figure 3.33. The mountaintop cairn of Moel Trigarn, southwest Wales.

the evidence takes yet another form. Here it has been shown by field walking that the artefact scatters left by occupation sites were set apart from Neolithic chambered tombs but located near to the Earlier Bronze Age Clava Cairns (Phillips and Watson 2000).

In other cases barrows were directly superimposed on settlements. This was particularly common in East Anglia (Gibson 1982: 27–48), but it is found widely. Indeed, at a few sites, including the Brenig in North Wales, mortuary monuments were built over the remains of older dwellings (Lynch 1993: chapter 13). That may have happened in other cases, although the structural evidence is not always convincing. On Dartmoor, it has been suggested that collapsed round houses were reused as mortuary cairns (Butler 1997: 137–8), but this idea needs to be checked by excavation.

Where barrows and settlement areas were further apart there might still be a direct connection between them. At Roughan Hill in the west of Ireland a series of wedge tombs were constructed in between a number of enclosed settlements (Fig. 3.34). These were interspersed with an irregular system of field walls. Excavation has shown that they were associated with round houses and with Beaker pottery. It seems likely that activity continued into the second millennium BC (C. Jones 1998). In northeast England the main areas with evidence of Earlier Bronze Age land use are overlooked by chains of barrows and cairns running across the higher ground. These enclose the valleys which were suitable for settlement, and Don Spratt argued that they marked the outer limits of small estates or territories (1993: 116–20).

There are many reasons why domestic sites are so difficult to find. Excavation on the Scottish island of Arran showed that the sites of Earlier Bronze

Age houses had been ploughed when they went out of use (Barber 1997). Another problem arises in field survey, for in upland areas the remains of stone-built houses resemble the enclosures known as ring cairns which were built in increasing numbers during this phase. They played various roles as ceremonial sites, cremation cemeteries, and pyres, but on the ground they can be hard to distinguish from the remains of houses or settlements. The link may have been intended, for there are indications that abandoned buildings were enclosed within a mantle of rubble so that they resembled monuments of this type (Barnatt, Bevan, and Edmonds 2002). A similar problem applies to many of the small cairns found in the uplands, a number of which certainly date from this period. They seem to have accumulated around prominent boulders or outcrops which would have been difficult to move when the land was tilled. For that reason such features are interpreted as clearance cairns and have been taken as evidence of agricultural settlement. On the other hand, excavation has demonstrated that a number of them covered human burials or formal deposits of artefacts. Does this mean that they had been misinterpreted? An interesting way of thinking about the problem was suggested by Robert Johnston (2000), who argues that the resemblance between mortuary monuments and field cairns was no accident, because the dead were integrated into the working of the land.

Timber monuments illustrate a similar problem. Just as the timber circles inside henges look like enlarged versions of ordinary domestic dwellings, a number of graves were ringed by circles of posts or stakes before barrows were built on the same sites. They raise similar problems to the ring cairns, for a few examples could be construed as the remains of dwellings, especially where such structures are associated with hearths or concentrations of artefacts (Gibson 1982: 27–48). Perhaps these features were considered as the houses of the dead, and their forms referred to those of domestic buildings. Again there is a significant overlap. Nowhere is this more obvious than at West Whittlesey in the English Fenland, where a row of three circular structures was identified in excavation (Knight 2000). Two of them were round barrows, whilst the third was an Earlier Bronze Age henge enclosing a circle of posts. Fifty metres away there was a settlement of the same date which included the remains of a small round house. In such cases the cross-reference between these different types must have been intentional.

As in the Beaker phase, some occupation sites survive because they are deeply buried. Well-preserved dwellings have certainly been found among the coastal dunes in the Western Isles, for example on South Uist (Parker Pearson, Sharples, and Symonds 2004: 43–52). These are exceptionally fertile areas, and prehistoric ard marks are often recorded there. Earlier Bronze Age settlements have also been found on the edge of the English Fenland, notably at West Row Fen, Mildenhall (Martin and Murphy 1988), and others are identified in areas that had not been settled before. In some cases their remains have been preserved because such areas were not occupied for long. The distribution

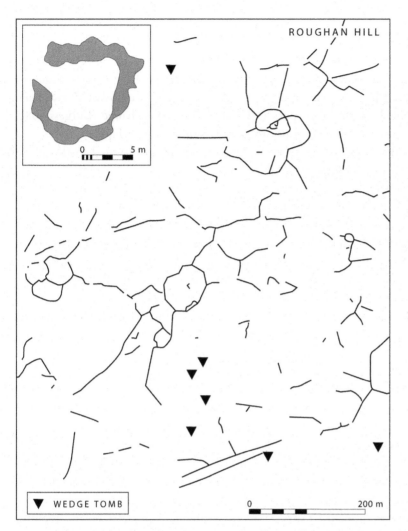

Figure 3.34. Field walls and enclosures at Roughan Hill in the west of Ireland, with an inset showing the plan of an excavated house. Information from C. Jones (1998, 2004).

of barrows, cairns, and other monuments suggests that the Later Neolithic expansion of settlement accelerated during this phase. That is certainly supported by pollen analysis. The distribution of such monuments is much more extensive than that of their predecessors and includes large areas of lowland England which are currently covered by heathland, as well as tracts of moorland in upland regions. Among these areas were the New Forest, the Weald, the Breckland, the Pennines, and the North York Moors. Human activity extended into a wider range of environments, but clearance and exploitation caused significant changes to the soils which often became acidic and poorly drained (Bradley 1978: 113–14). These examples have been taken from English archaeology, but similar trends have been identified by field survey in other areas. The difficulty is that certain types of monument have been investigated at the expense of others, so that it is obvious that barrows, cairns, and stone circles were being built there during this period, whilst the evidence from domestic sites has attracted less attention. That is not to deny that certain excavated settlements do date from this phase, but others have been assigned to the Earlier Bronze Age on the premise that the high ground would have been uninhabitable during later periods because of climate change (Burgess 1985, 1992). That is controversial (Young and Simmons 1997; Tipping 2002), and some of the field evidence that had been confidently assigned to this phase dates from a later period.

The settlement evidence from the uplands often shows the same sequence. The stone-built houses which are visible on the surface were not necessarily the first to be built, and excavation has demonstrated that before the landscape was cleared and surface rock was exposed domestic buildings might have been made of wood (Fleming 1988: chapter 6). Not many have been excavated, but they do seem to have been more substantial than the Beaker dwellings considered earlier in this chapter. Unfortunately, where such structures were not replaced in stone they have been difficult to find, although their positions can be located where their floors were levelled into sloping ground, leaving a distinctive circular platform behind. Otherwise they may be detected by open patches within a wider distribution of boulders and small monuments. A number of the houses and cairns were linked by low walls or banks of rubble which define a series of irregular areas suitable for cultivation. Sometimes small enclosures have been tacked onto one another as increasingly large areas were cleared. They can incorporate clearance cairns, whilst others seem to be scattered across the surrounding area. There are excavated fields in the Burren in the west of Ireland (C. Jones 1998), in Shetland (Whittle 1986), in the Scottish Highlands (McCullagh and Tipping 1998), and on the island of Arran (Barber 1997), but they seem to survive as surface remains in most upland regions. Apart from the remarkable evidence from Dartmoor, which is discussed in Chapter Four, there is little sign of more extensive or regular systems.

In a recent article Simon Timberlake (2001) suggests that the land use in the uplands provides the context for early copper mining in Wales and the west of Ireland. This was sometimes undertaken in remote areas that were perhaps being visited for the first time. These sites were not obviously related to nearby settlements or monuments and may have been used by small numbers of people on a seasonal basis. The output of the mines was very limited and for the most part their period of use was restricted to the Earlier Bronze Age. Like comparable sites in northern England, they seem to have operated between approximately 1800 and 1500 BC, after which they were abandoned. The one exception was at Great Orme Head in North Wales (Dutton and Fasham 1994; Lewis 1998; Timberlake 2002). This was the site of the largest group of mines in Britain or Ireland, and here activity continued into the Later Bronze Age.

Upland areas also contain some specialised monuments (Fig. 3.35). Space does not permit the enumeration of all these separate types, and in any case

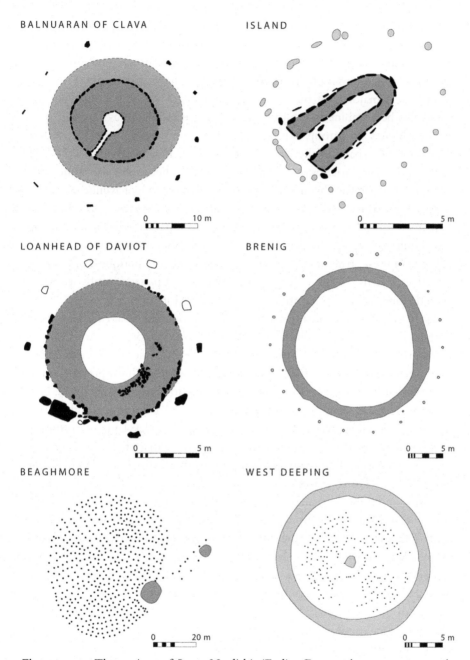

Figure 3.35. The variety of Later Neolithic/Earlier Bronze Age monuments. At Balnuaran of Clava, northern Scotland, a stone circle encloses a passage grave. At Island, southwest Ireland, a setting perhaps of posts encloses a wedge tomb. At Loanhead of Daviot, northeast Scotland, a recumbent stone circle is added to an existing ring cairn, and at Brenig, north Wales, another ring cairn is enclosed by a setting of posts. At Beaghmore, northern Ireland, a setting of boulders is approached by a small stone row, and at West Deeping, East Anglia, a round barrow overlies concentric rings of stakes. Information from Bradley (2000a), O'Kelly (1958), Bradley (2005a), Lynch (1993), Pilcher (1969), and French (1994).

they underwent constant modification. Like the round barrows considered earlier, they could change their outward appearance from one phase to the next, so that their surface remains provide little indication of how individual monuments had developed over time (Bradley 1998b: chapter 9).

The great majority of these are arrangements of standing stones, but they could also be combined with the walled enclosures known as ring cairns and even with the Clava group of passage tombs which were perhaps the northern Scottish counterparts of the late wedge tombs in Ireland (Bradley 2000a). In addition to these varieties of circular monuments, there were also stone alignments which may have been miniature versions of the longer avenues associated with henges (Burl 1993). Most of these forms could appear in combination, so that stone circles might enclose ring cairns and passage tombs, whilst stone rows could run up to round barrows, cairns, or other settings of monoliths.

Some of these structures have well-defined local distributions. For example, the Clava Cairns, which consist of ring cairns and passage tombs set within graded stone circles, are confined to the inner Moray Firth (Bradley 2000a), whilst in the neighbouring region of northeast Scotland similar rings of uprights contain cairns but also include a massive horizontal block; these are known as 'recumbent' stone circles (Bradley 2005a). In the same way, in eastern and central Scotland there are small rectangular stone settings ('four posters') which seem to include low cairns associated with cremation burials (Burl 1988). Local traditions can be identified in other areas, too. At a site like Beaghmore in northern Ireland there are circular settings of small boulders laid out in complex geometrical patterns. They include numerous concentric rings but also feature a series of straight alignments radiating out from a central cist (Pilcher 1969; Foley and MacDonagh 1998). Again they can be found with other kinds of structure, and these particular monuments are sometimes linked to stone rows.

It is easy to lose direction amidst so many specialised constructions, but many of them can be interpreted as local manifestations of a series of quite simple ideas that were widely shared across the two islands. Like their Neolithic predecessors, the circles were often graded in height towards the south or west, and sometimes they made effective use of differently coloured stones. At Balnuaran of Clava, for example, two of the passage tombs were aligned on the midwinter sunset (Bradley 2000a: 122–9). The stones employed on that side of the monuments were often red and absorbed the light. In the opposite direction, towards the rising sun at midsummer, the rocks were grey and white and frequently contained inclusions of quartz which would reflect the light.

How were these monuments related to the mortuary rituals considered earlier? They are often found near to Earlier Bronze Age barrows and cairns, and in some cases they contain human cremations, which are presumably those of people who could not be buried in a more formal manner. Other monuments include the remains of pyres, but in this case the bones were usually removed and deposited somewhere else. This may have happened during a secondary phase, and a common sequence is for an open enclosure, defined by a ring of monoliths, to provide the site for a later mound or cairn (Bradley 1998b: chapter 9). That might impede access to the interior, and on some sites the earlier building was almost completely buried beneath the new construction (G. Ritchie 1974). In such cases it is tempting to suggest that monuments which could have been used by a large number of people were taken over as the burial places of selected individuals. On the other hand, recent fieldwork shows that was not the only way in which such sites developed. In north and northeast Scotland it is clear that cairns, enclosures, and platforms might all be built before the stone circles on the same sites. In that case it seems likely that the erection of the ring of monoliths enclosed the older monument and brought its use to an end (Bradley 2005a: 105–6, 112–16). That is similar to what had happened with the earthworks of henges.

The relationship between such monuments and settlements changes from one region to another. The Clava Cairns, for example, were built over, or near to, occupation sites, and yet the stone circles of northeast Scotland, with which they have much in common, were often placed in more conspicuous positions on the outer edge of the settled land (Bradley 2005a: 108–9). The stone settings at Beaghmore in the north of Ireland may even have been built amidst the remains of an older field system (Pilcher 1969). The distinctive stone rows of southwest England introduce another variation, for they seem to run upslope from the areas with evidence of habitation towards mortuary monuments located on the higher ground (Barnatt 1998: 99–102).

The monuments are sometimes embellished with the pecked motifs known as cup marks, and many of them contain significant quantities of quartz (Burl 1981). Often they provide evidence of burning in the form of pits that had been filled with charcoal (Lynch 1979). Some of these structures could have been orientated towards the setting sun, but others may have been more directly associated with the moon (Ruggles 1999). Such associations connect a series of monuments of very different forms: the stone circles of northeast Scotland, the Clava Cairns, four-posters, wedge tombs, and some of the stone alignments found on the west coast of Scotland and in northern Ireland. These geographical links are reinforced by the movement of copper and, to some extent, by pottery styles.

Nearly all these elements refer back to Neolithic practice, although they are often associated with Beakers and with Earlier Bronze Age ceramics. The resemblance is not limited to their distinctive forms, as they illustrate the association between stone monuments and the remains of the dead that was highlighted by Parker Pearson and Ramilsonina (1998). They add some new elements, but the structures themselves are smaller and occupy less conspicuous positions in the landscape. They also illustrate an increasing concern with the moon rather than the sun. Many provide evidence for the use of fire, and it is possible that certain of these places were used at night (Bradley 2005a: 111–12).

AT THE LIMITS

A number of separate issues have been discussed here and need to be brought together now. They will be treated in greater detail in Chapter Four. Each concerns the distinctive developments of the Earlier Bronze Age and suggests that they were reaching their limits towards the middle of the second millennium BC.

This period between 2000 and 1500 BC is usually thought of in terms of its distinctive burials and the long-distance connections that they seem to illustrate, but in some ways both were changing by this time. It has been customary to think of Britain and Ireland as the periphery of Europe, but as long as local materials were being used that was quite untrue – bronze was produced in Britain at an unusually early date and Irish gold was exported. By 1500 BC, however, it appears that most of the British and Irish copper mines had gone out of use, although activity continued at Great Orme Head (Northover 1982; Timberlake 2002). These developments have never been explained, but they form part of a more general crisis in the distribution of metalwork which saw quite rapid oscillations between the use of insular copper and a greater dependence on Continental sources of supply. Those changes will be discussed in the chapter which follows, but they suggest that access to metal artefacts perhaps became more difficult.

There were also changes in the forms of barrow cemeteries. It has long been recognised that great concentrations of mounds were built close to the monuments of the Neolithic period and that a few of the burials associated with them contain elaborate or exotic objects. What has not been so clear is that great linear cemeteries, such as those around Stonehenge, were a late development (Garwood in press). A landscape that was already permeated with images from the past took on yet another layer of significance (Exon et al. 2000). It may be no accident that these formal arrangements of monuments were among the last to be built. The growing importance of cremation may be important too, for it required a greater consumption of human energy than inhumation burial. The barrow cemeteries that were built towards the end of the Earlier Bronze Age seem almost excessively elaborate, and the sheer complexity of references enshrined in these mounds and graves may no longer have had the desired effect. Perhaps they stopped being an effective method of signally social relationships. The same is true of the layout of Stonehenge, which may have been modified at this time (Cleal, Walker, and Montague 1995: 256–65). Those ideas might have been better expressed in a different medium. Chapter Four documents that transformation.

It is easier to identify another way in which the existing system approached its limits. Many monuments were built during the Later Neolithic and Earlier Bronze Age periods, but there is little to suggest that their construction depended on a major intensification of land use. Instead food production took place over an increasingly large area (Bradley 1991). That is indicated by the distribution of artefacts, settlements, and monuments, and it is shown also by pollen analysis. The problem is that the expansion took in regions that could not sustain a long period of settlement. They were adversely affected by changes to the status of the soils, and some of them became increasingly waterlogged. Although there are certain exceptions, large parts of lowland Britain which were first colonised during the earlier second millennium BC had been abandoned by the Later Bronze Age. The same was probably true in the uplands, and in each case its consequence was the same. A system which had been maintained by a process of continuous expansion was becoming increasingly vulnerable. Long before the first signs of climatic change, that process came to a halt.

Those separate factors – the over-exploitation of marginal land, the excessive elaboration of mortuary rituals, and changes in the supply of metals – are not directly linked to one another, yet all three are tendencies that have been identified in earlier parts of this account. In every case matters were reaching a crisis at about the same time. Taken in combination, they resulted in the single greatest change in these islands since the adoption of agriculture. That striking transformation is the subject of Chapter Four.

CHAPTER 4

PLOUGHSHARES INTO SWORDS

PERIOD DETAILS

Anyone writing an account of prehistory must decide how to shape the narrative. Which were the major periods of change? How are they represented in the archaeological record, and what is the right way of distinguishing between local phenomena and more general developments? The previous chapter considered an 'Earlier' Bronze Age. That raises the question of how the 'Later' Bronze Age should be characterised (Figs. 4.1 and 4.2).

One might suppose that the problem was solved forty years ago, for the term has been used in Irish archaeology since the 1960s. In 1979, it was employed to organise a major synthesis of *The Bronze Age in Europe* (Coles and Harding 1979), and at about the same time an entire conference was devoted to the *British Later Bronze Age* (Barrett and Bradley eds. 1980). There seems to be a consensus that the period should be divided in half, but there any agreement ends.

The different schemes are superficially similar, but they are based on different criteria, and it is not possible to harmonise them. That is understandable, for classification is never a neutral exercise. It depends on the priorities of individual authors and on the questions that they ask. Thus the two-fold division of the Irish Bronze Age favoured by George Eogan (1964) depended on a study of the metalwork. Eogan was unhappy with the existing framework, which split the period into three, and wished to consider the artefacts of the 'Middle' Bronze Age Bishopsland phase alongside those dating from the 'Late' Bronze Age. Stuart Needham (1992) has taken a similar approach to the metalwork from Britain, combining the long-accepted Early and Middle Bronze Ages and separating them from what came afterwards.

Coles and Harding (1979) followed a different procedure, for they saw the major period of change as separating two Continental traditions, each of which exerted an influence outside its area of origin in Central Europe. In the thirteenth century BC, the Tumulus Culture was replaced by the Urnfield Culture.

Although these terms describe two burial rites, they also correspond to important developments in other spheres, including changes in the settlement pattern and in the production and distribution of metalwork. Successive chapters considered the evidence from the remaining parts of Europe.

In 1980 Colin Burgess took yet another approach to the British sequence, although his scheme is like that devised by Coles and Harding in combining studies of metalwork with broader changes in the landscape. In this case these two elements seem to be in conflict. His metalwork chronology has been widely accepted and is supported by radiocarbon dating, but he is less conversant with the results of fieldwork. That was understandable when his ideas were published twenty-five years ago, but he has repeated them in virtually the same form in a recent article (Burgess 2004). He postulates a 'catastrophe' in the twelfth century BC, a situation that he infers from the disappearance of settlements over much of Britain (Burgess 1992). There is no reason to believe that this happened, and domestic sites of this phase are often found by excavation. Burgess postulates a crisis brought about by climatic change, and, in the original version of his interpretation, he connected it with an eruption of the Icelandic volcano Hekla which is registered by Irish tree rings between 1159 and 1141 BC. This interpretation is extremely controversial (Young and Simmons 1997; Tipping 2002), and yet it colours his entire approach to the Bronze Age. Only the metalwork seems to have been unaffected.

There is no doubt that these artefacts can be arranged in sequence and that their distributions and associations may be investigated on a large scale, but such research will always raise some problems. They were deposited according to certain conventions, with the result that only a small fraction of the surviving material is associated with settlements or with the remains of the dead (Bradley 1998a). Most of it exists in isolation. The fact that metal artefacts can be analysed in so much detail does not say anything about their original significance. That must be demonstrated and not assumed. There is no doubt that metalwork has been important for one group of Bronze Age scholars, but did it really dominate the lives of prehistoric people?

As a reaction against this trend John Barrett and the present writer suggested that a more appropriate period division might be based on changes in the settlement pattern (Barrett and Bradley 1980). These were not exactly synchronous from one region to another, but they did share many features. Such developments were less apparent in Continental Europe, and even where they did occur they took a different form. This raised some important questions. Which were more important: the affinities between metal types on either side of the English Channel and the North Sea, or the contrasts between the houses, cemeteries, and domestic landscapes in these different regions? Was it better to emphasise such distinctions or to disregard them? It seemed important to consider what was both distinctive and new.

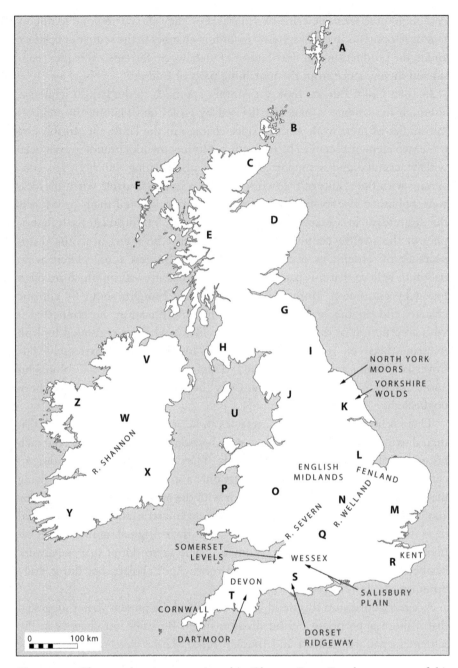

Figure 4.1. Places and regions mentioned in Chapter Four. For the purposes of this map Britain and Ireland have been divided into twenty-six areas, and the individual sites are listed according to these divisions. A: Shetland; B: Orkney; C: Northern Scotland; D: Northeast Scotland (*Covesea, Kintore*); E: Western Scotland; F: Outer Hebrides (*Cladh Hallan*); G: Eastern and Central Scotland on either side of the Firth of Forth (*Duddingston Loch, Edinburgh Castle Rock, Eildon Hill, Traprain Law*); H: Southwest Scotland; I: the English/Scottish borderland; J: Northwest England; K: Northeast England and the Peak District (*Thwing*); L: Eastern England between

Major changes are apparent in several spheres: in the organisation of settlements and land divisions, and in the treatment of the dead. Even the role of metalwork was changing. It is clear that these features were not evenly distributed across Britain and Ireland, but they do encapsulate two fundamental contrasts. There was a contrast with the practices that were discussed in Chapter Three, and there were obvious differences between developments in parts of the British landscape and those in neighbouring areas of Continental Europe. They cannot be dated accurately, but all these processes began in the middle of the second millennium BC. For the purposes of this account the 'Later Bronze Age' combines the Middle and Late divisions defined by metalwork studies and extends from 1500 BC until approximately 800 BC (Needham 1996; Needham et al. 1998). During that time there was a continuous process of change, but it was a process which had its roots in the past.

Table 4.1 sets out the terminology used in this book and compares it with the chronological schemes employed by other writers. The term 'Later Bronze Age' will be used where it applies to the entire period from 1500 BC, but the text refers to the Middle and Late Bronzes Ages, respectively, where it is concerned with specific developments.

CHARACTERISING A LATER BRONZE AGE

None of the features that characterise the Later Bronze Age in these islands was completely new. Rather, they grew out of those of the previous period. Each will be considered later in this chapter, but it is important to trace their sources now.

Perhaps the most striking trend is a marked increase in the frequency of settlement sites. They are widely distributed but often contain more substantial structures than those of earlier periods (Fig. 4.3). They are characterised by considerable stone or timber buildings, they are sometimes enclosed by ditches,

---

Figure 4.1 (*continued*) the Humber and East Anglia; M: East Anglia (*Barleycroft, Bradley, Fen, Ely, Flag Fen, Great Baddow, South Hornchurch, Mucking, Springfield Lyons*); N: the English Midlands (*Bancroft*); O: The English/Welsh borderland (*Beeston Castle, Breiddin, Bromfield, Dinorben, Worcester*); P: West Wales from the southwest to Anglesey (*Great Orme*); Q: the Thames Valley, Cotswolds, and South Midlands (*Carshalton, Eton, Hartshill Quarry, Runneymede, Taplow, Vauxhall, Wallingford, Wittenham Clumps*); R: Southeast England (*Dover, Harting Beacon, Itford Hill, Langton Bay, Shinewater*); S: Wessex (*Bestwall, Down Farm, Dunch Hill, Kimpton, Rams Hill, South Lodge Camp, Testwood, Twyford Down*); T: Southwest England (*Callestick, Greylake, Gwithian, Salcombe, South Cadbury*); U: the Isle of Man (*Billown, South Barrule*); V: Northern Ireland (*Corrstown, Downpatrick, Haughey's Fort, Lough Eskragh, Navan Fort*); W: from the Irish Midlands to the east coast (*Ballinderry*); X: Southeast Ireland (*Lugg, Johnstown South, Rathgall*): Y: Southwest Ireland (*Drombeg, Grange 'stone circle', Lough Gur*); Z: the Irish west coast (*Dun Aonghasa, Rathtinaun*).

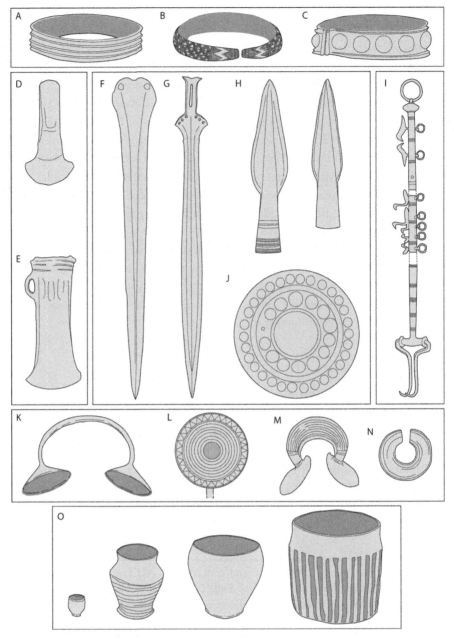

Figure 4.2. Outline drawings of the artefact types mentioned in Chapter Four. A–C: decorated bronze bracelets; D and E: axeheads; F: rapier; G: sword; H: spearheads; I: flesh hook; J: shield; K–N: Irish gold ornaments; O: a Late Bronze Age ceramic 'set'.

fences or walls, and they are associated with substantial collections of artefacts. Moreover they commonly occur together with field systems or longer land boundaries. Such evidence usually occurs on the more productive soils, and settlements of later phases are often located nearby.

TABLE 4.1. *Chronology and terminology for the period between 1500 and 800 BC*

	Burgess	Needham	Barrett & Bradley	This chapter
Early Bronze Age (2000–1500 BC)	Early BA	Early BA	Early BA	EARLIER BA
			Period of change	———
Middle Bronze Age (1500–1100 BC)	Middle BA	Middle BA		
Period of change	———	———	Later BA	LATER BA
Late Bronze Age (1100–800 BC)	Late/ Later BA	Late /Later BA		

To a large extent their distribution contrasts with that of the sites discussed in the closing section of Chapter Three. That is because Earlier Bronze Age examples were quite ephemeral and left little trace behind, but it is also because the newer settlements are less frequent in the marginal areas where remains of the previous phase survive. Those different observations may be linked, for the reorganisation of the lowland landscape that is so much a feature of the Later Bronze Age may have been a response to deteriorating conditions in areas which could not sustain a lengthy occupation. Upland soils were increasingly acidic and poorly drained (Bradley 1978, 1991), and in the lowlands ground conditions were becoming wetter as a result of soil erosion in the river valleys

Figure 4.3. The post holes of an excavated Middle Bronze Age round house at Yarnton in the Upper Thames Valley. Photograph courtesy of Gill Hey and Oxford Archaeology.

(French 2003: chapters 6–10). This process was under way three hundred years before the eruption of Hekla 3 and is best explained as a response to local conditions.

There were two areas in which events took a different turn, and this is important for it seems to mark the start of a process which eventually extended to many parts of lowland England. The first involved some of the more marginal areas which were increasingly used on a seasonal basis. As a result specialised forms of land use assumed a much greater significance. Wooden paths were constructed across many areas of damp ground, including the Somerset Levels (Coles and Coles 1986: chapter 6) and parts of the East Anglian Fens (Hall and Coles 1994: chapter 5). A similar process happened along the banks of the Thames, where brushwood trackways, timber platforms, and even a metalled causeway were created to provide access to the rich grazing land beside the river (Sidell et al. 2002: 34). The earliest bridges may also date from this phase.

There was a greater emphasis on the soils that retained their productivity. In most cases the poorer land first settled during the Earlier Bronze Age was less often used after the mid-second millennium BC, as occupation focused on more productive areas. It was here that regular field systems were established. On Dartmoor, however, there seems to have been an attempt to maintain activity on the higher land by creating an extensive system of fields and longer boundaries. It is not clear how this process was organised and whether it was achieved by compulsion or cooperation (Fleming 1988; R. Johnston 2005). Nor is it clear whether it happened over a short period or was a piecemeal development, but in the end it probably did lead to an equitable division of the resources that were coming under pressure. Those systems extended onto the lower ground beyond the limits of the moor, where fewer traces survive. For present purposes it is significant that these changes began towards the end of the Earlier Bronze Age. At present there is little to suggest developments on this scale in other parts of Britain and Ireland. There may have been field systems of similar date in Cornwall (Nowakowski 2006) and southern Wessex (Ladle and Woodward in press). Otherwise, they belong to later phases.

The second major change concerns the relationship of the living and the dead. Here it is easy to be misled by the Continental terminology. In lowland Britain it is clear that round barrows – 'tumuli' – were supplemented and eventually replaced by the cremation cemeteries known as 'urnfields', but this process was well established before it took place in Central Europe, and developments in these two areas were probably unconnected. Moreover, some of the elements of the new system had their origins in the Earlier Bronze Age. Again the detailed evidence will be considered in due course, but three observations are important at this stage.

The first is that burials seem to have been located close to settlement sites (Bradley 1981). This may well have applied to a number of the mounds built during the previous period, and, in Wessex, it certainly seems to be true of the miniature round barrows found in low-lying positions which are associated with many of the poorest burials. Normally they contain a cremation and a ceramic vessel, and few are associated with any metalwork. Such monuments were sometimes in small groups and continued to attract burials during the later second millennium BC. What had formed only part of the earlier system now became the norm (Peters 2000).

Secondly, cremation cemeteries were not a new development. They were already important in the uplands of Britain and Ireland where they could be associated with ring cairns and small stone circles. In the lowlands a few examples were known in isolation and others were established outside the burial mounds of the same period. The novel development of the Later Bronze Age is that in most parts of Britain such barrows became much smaller until eventually their construction lapsed. In Ireland, they had a longer currency, but again they were never built on an impressive scale (Waddell 1990; Grogan 2004b).

Lastly, as these changes happened, metalwork is found less often with the dead. Occasional metal items have been identified in the excavation of cremation cemeteries, but they are rather rare and are not always associated with one particular burial (Ellison 1980). They are usually small and fragmentary and may consist of a personal item such as a ring. This contrasts with the more elaborate graves of the previous period in which the dead might be accompanied by a wider range of weapons and ornaments. That is not because such types went out of use. Instead their contexts changed so that they are more likely to be discovered in isolation, whether in the collections of metalwork known as hoards, or as deposits in rivers and similar environments (Bradley 1998a: chapter 3). Again such practices were not entirely new. The burial of hoards began with stone axes and other artefacts during the Neolithic period and continued during the Earlier Bronze Age. In the same way, some of the last daggers produced during the previous phase are not only found in graves, they also occur in the River Thames (Gerloff 1975). That development prefigures a more dramatic change during the Later Bronze Age.

Of course this did not take place in isolation. The deposition of metalwork in rivers was well established on the Continent, although it appeared in different manifestations at different times and in different places (Bradley 1998a). For the most part it alternated with the deposition of similar artefacts in graves. Relations with the European mainland were important in another way. Chapter Three ended by discussing how access to metal may have changed. After a period of stability in which southwest Ireland provided a major source of copper, there was more diversity, with mines in mainland Europe supplying some of the raw material, whilst more came from a series of sites in Ireland, Wales, and northern England. By 1500 BC, the exploitation of insular ores appears to have been reorganised, and most of those mines went out of use. This did not apply to the large complex at Great Orme which achieved a brief ascendancy, but from about 1400 BC it seems as if the inhabitants of both islands depended on more distant sources as metalwork was increasingly imported across the English Channel and along the Atlantic coast (Northover 1982; Rohl and Needham 1998). This was only the last stage in a series of fluctuations in the supply of bronze, but it was certainly the most lasting. It is another feature that helps to establish the distinctiveness of the Later Bronze Age.

How significant were these developments? For many years studies of this period were divided between groups of specialists, all with interests of their own. As a result they developed completely different interpretations from one another. At its simplest the contrast was between those researchers who postulated a social collapse around 1500 BC, and those who envisaged a more radical transformation. The evidence of mortuary rites was critical in this regard. Considered in isolation, it suggested that two processes were taking place during the later second millennium BC. Older round barrows were being reused, while newly constructed mounds made fewer demands on human labour. During this period isolated 'single' burials were rare and cemeteries were often organised around groups of cremations which were usually accompanied by pottery vessels. The rich graves that had been such a feature of the earlier period virtually disappeared (Bradley 1998a: 99–100). It was easy to suggest that this reflected a wider change in which the differences of wealth and status expressed by the burial rite lost their original importance. Rather than expressing social distinctions, there was a new ethic of equality. Perhaps the power of a traditional elite was diminishing. Proponents of this view could draw attention to the limited range of variation among the excavated settlements of this phase.

Bronze Age metalwork had often been studied for its own sake, as a self-contained field of research that had little contact with the results of field archaeology. That is not surprising, for, apart from the grave goods of the Earlier Bronze Age, little of this material came from excavated contexts. Even so, it is clear that bronze artefacts give a different impression of the transition. Such items are less often associated with the dead, but their overall frequency increases. It is simply that their contexts change from an emphasis on round barrows to deposits in liminal locations. Although there are many exceptions, tools were generally deposited in hoards on dry land, ornament hoards might also occur in bogs, whilst weapons were most often deposited in rivers (Bradley 1998a: chapter 3). Many of these types are the direct successors of those associated with Earlier Bronze Age burials, but the shift of location meant that they were not always compared with one another. In fact a greater amount of metalwork entered the archaeological record. That seems inconsistent with the idea of a social collapse. The burials and the portable artefacts supported very different interpretations.

In fact the significance of metalworking may have been changing at this time. It has been all too easy to suppose that collections of bronze artefacts were buried for practical reasons and that it was a matter of chance that they were never recovered. Some collections include newly made objects which had yet to be finished, some contain worn or broken objects that could have been melted down, whilst others incorporate the residues of metalworking itself: casting jets, ingots, moulds, droplets, and slag. The connection with metallurgy is clear; the problem is to determine whether the transformation of the metal should be viewed as a purely mechanical process. That is inconsistent with ethnographic accounts of the social position of the smith (Budd and Taylor 1995), and certainly does not account for some of the anomalies illustrated by the hoards: the occasional finds of human or animal bones in these deposits; the discovery of certain of these collections in remote and inaccessible places (Bradley 2000b: chapter 4); the representation of broken objects, parts of which are missing (Bradley 2005b: chapter 5); even the violence with which some of these items had been fractured (Nebelsick 2000). It may be wiser to suppose that the process of working the metal was attended by special protocols. It was ritualised, and some of the material associated with the transformation of the raw material appears to have been buried as a votive offering (Bradley 2005b: 163–4). Although many of these elements can be recognised during the Earlier Bronze Age, they assumed an even greater significance after that time.

THE INITIAL TRANSFORMATION: THE MIDDLE BRONZE AGE (1500–1100 BC)

For many years the remains of field systems had been recognised as earthworks in southern England, and from as early as 1925 there was evidence that the first of them must have been established during the Bronze Age (Toms 1925). On the other hand, archaeologists were so sure that the majority were of Iron Age or Romano–British date that they became known as 'Celtic' fields to distinguish them from the 'English' fields attributed to the Anglo-Saxons (H. C. Bowen 1970). This term soon took on a life of its own, making it hard to accept that many of these land divisions predated the Celtic invasions described by Classical writers in the later first millennium BC. The term was also adopted in The Netherlands, North Germany, and South Scandinavia which, it is generally agreed, were beyond the area occupied by any 'Celts'.

Now a new problem arises. Regular systems of square or rectangular fields obviously developed during more than one period of prehistory. They were present in the west of Ireland at an early stage of the Neolithic, and they were established on Dartmoor and perhaps on the southern margin of Wessex towards the end of the Earlier Bronze Age. Recent research, much of it a by-product of developer-funded excavations, shows that such systems were widely distributed in lowland England and extend into areas in which no earthworks survive (Fig. 4.4). These were established at various times during the Later Bronze Age, but nearly all of them went out of use after that phase (Yates 1999, 2001). The only Celtic fields that can definitely be attributed to the Iron Age belong to the later part of that period and remained important during the Roman occupation (Fulford 1992). Some are in the same places as the Bronze Age systems, but others have a much more extensive distribution, reaching into northern Britain.

There are several reasons for beginning with this evidence. The first is to make the point that the establishment of the larger field systems, especially those on Dartmoor, took a considerable effort. It is easy to be misled by the evidence of burial mounds which became much smaller during this phase, for the amount of labour invested in the subdivision of the land was probably equivalent to that devoted to monument building during earlier periods. It would be quite wrong to suppose that workforces could no longer be mobilised for large-scale projects – it is the nature of those tasks that had changed. This is most apparent from the sheer scale of some of these projects, which might involve the organisation of entire landscapes around a series of parallel boundaries. Some of the dominant axes travel a considerable distance, and, as if to echo older concerns, they could be orientated on the winter or summer solstice (McOmish, Field, and Brown 2002: fig. 3.4 and 153). That is particularly revealing where they cut across the grain of the local topography, with the result that certain plots were left in shadow. Another connection with established practice is the way that some of the field boundaries run up to older mounds, cairns, or the remains of houses. It is usually supposed that this was done for practical reasons, that the barrows provided landmarks on which they might be aligned, but a number of these features cannot be seen from far away, suggesting that it was the associations of such monuments that were more significant (Bradley, Entwistle, and Raymond 1994: 141).

That connection is particularly plausible since the first field systems seem to have been established whilst large round mounds were still being built. That was obviously the case on Dartmoor where the landscape was reorganised during the Earlier Bronze Age, but it may also apply to the information from other areas, including Wessex. There is a small overlap between the radiocarbon dates associated with fields and settlements on the southern English chalk and those from the last rich burials of that period. Although the evidence is unsatisfactory, it seems quite possible that these two elements were linked with one another and that the first stages in the enclosure of the landscape were overseen by the people commemorated in these graves. If so, the process certainly continued after mortuary practices had changed.

One reason for suggesting that these developments played a part in the polit-ical process is that the newly created field systems are so poorly integrated with

Figure 4.4. The distribution of Bronze Age coaxial field systems. Information from Yates and Bradley and Yates (in press).

the settlements; it is difficult to regard them as a unified design (Evans and Knight 2000: 83–6). Although the rectilinear field systems may have grown over a significant period, the houses and enclosures found within them do not conform to the overall layout. Rather, they are scattered at irregular intervals across their area, and the evidence of excavation suggests that they were sometimes a secondary development. That is fascinating, for it raises the possibility (which has still to be tested by fieldwork) that the earliest dwellings in these places may have been ephemeral structures of the kind already identified in the Earlier Bronze Age. Another possibility, first raised by David Field (2001), is that these changes were implemented from settlements which lay outside the areas with coaxial fields. The land divisions were clearly of special significance, for at Gwithian in Cornwall they were associated with cremation burials (C. Thomas 1958; Nowakowski 2006: 16), and at Twyford Down on the chalk of Wessex one was marked by a line of pits, some of them containing human remains (Walker and Farwell 2000: 21). The sequence needs more investigation, for there are even cases in which the enclosed settlements associated with field systems may have been created at a time when some of these landscapes were already going out of use (Barrett, Bradley, and Green 1991: 151–3).

There is also a mismatch between the extent of the larger enclosed landscapes and the small size of the first settlements that have been identified within them

(Fleming 1988: chapter 5; Evans and Knight 2001). In some cases the houses form a dispersed pattern, with different buildings inside individual plots or attached to their boundaries. In other instances, a single field has been occupied by a settlement, but even here the number of houses is limited (Barrett, Bradley, and Green 1991: 153–6). Indeed, the dwellings of the Middle Bronze Age seem to have shifted their locations, giving the illusion of a larger unit than was actually the case (Brück 1999). For instance, the well known 'village' at Itford Hill in southern England was nothing of the kind. It was a small cluster of houses defined by an embanked enclosure which changed its position on three separate occasions (Ellison 1978). What was really new is that the sites of the older buildings were not removed by the plough.

In lowland Britain the domestic buildings were usually round houses (Fig. 4.5). There are few signs of specialised facilities such as stables or byres, and the only ancillary structures may have been small granaries or storehouses. This suggests that the circular buildings played a variety of roles, and it is certainly true that they often occur in pairs, one of them a more substantial structure than the other (Ellison 1981). It often included a series of storage pits beneath its eaves, whilst its neighbour may have been associated with craft production, particularly weaving. There can be several of these modules within a single settlement. Whether or not individual sites were enclosed, the domestic dwellings seem to have been accompanied by a variety of other features. Often the area around them was defined by a fence, a low earthwork or perhaps a hedge, and they can be associated with carefully constructed ponds or waterholes. These appear to be a new development in the Later Bronze Age. The same probably applies to wells, and in each case this would suggest that people were living in the same place for a significant period of time. They would also have been able to occupy locations that could not have been settled before (Chris Evans, pers. comm.).

The evidence for sustained occupation contrasts with that from the individual dwellings, which may have been abandoned every generation. Those dated to the Middle Bronze Age tended to be replaced in a different position, and, when this happened, the site of the older building was often marked by an animal burial, a deposit of pottery, human bones, or perhaps a metal artefact (Brück 1999). Sometimes the remains of earlier houses were covered over, and in south west England the hollows left by their floors were carefully refilled (Nowakowski 2001). At Callestick, the outline of an abandoned house was marked by pieces of quartz (A. Jones 1999), and at South Lodge Camp in Wessex the site of a similar building was commemorated by a low mound (Barrett, Bradley, and Green 1991, 158). At Bestwall Quarry in the same region an abandoned house was formally closed by a heap of burnt stone that was probably connected with cooking food. A bronze bracelet was deposited just outside the building, and another in the middle of its floor (Ladle and Woodward 2003). Such practices were not peculiar to England. In the Outer Hebrides the

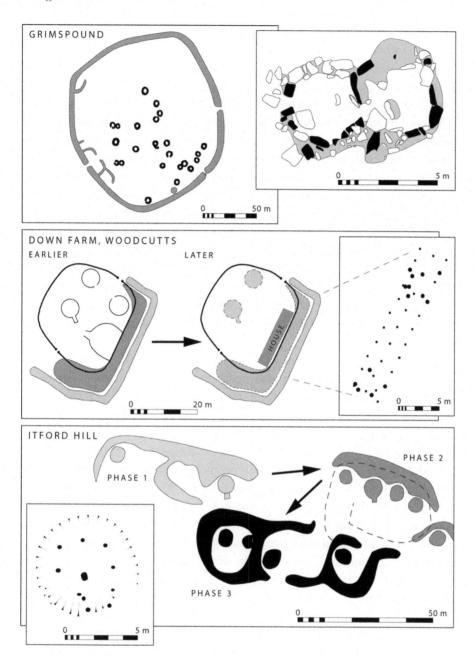

Figure 4.5. Middle Bronze Age settlements and buildings. Grimspound, southwest England, illustrates a large domestic enclosure; the inset shows two conjoined houses on the site. Down Farm, Wessex, is shown in two successive phases, during the later of which a long house was constructed. This is shown as a detail. The open settlement at Itford Hill, southeast England, is sometimes described as a village, but it seems to have been a smaller group of dwellings which were relocated on two occasions. An inset illustrates one of the post-built houses. Information from Butler (1991), Barrett, Bradley, and Green (1991), and Ellison (1978).

successive house floors at Cladh Hallan were associated with groups of metal artefacts and the burial of mummified corpses (Parker Pearson, Sharples, and Symonds 2004: 60–79). Metalwork has been found in houses in Northern Ireland (Suddaby 2003). In Orkney domestic buildings are often associated with deposits of stone ard shares (Downes and Lamb 2000: 126).

It is not uncommon for several groups of dwellings to occur within the same field system, and that also applies to the insubstantial enclosures connected with some of the settlements. This evidence is not easy to interpret. On the one hand, the regular replacement of houses means that certain of the sites may have been used in succession over a relatively short period; the intervals between these occupations may be too short to measure by radiocarbon dating. On the other hand, the small scale of these different units is occasionally at odds with the extent of the surrounding fields, suggesting that a single block of land may have been worked by several communities. That makes it still more difficult to decide how the field systems had been established, but there is another problem as well. There is nothing to show how many individual plots were in use simultaneously, and in theory large parts of landscape may have lain fallow at any one time.

There is evidence for cereal cultivation, with barley as the main crop, but it is only possible to find direct evidence of cultivation where fields survive as earthworks or where they have been deeply buried. A good example of the latter process is at Gwithian in southwest England where large areas of plough marks had been preserved beneath blown sand, together with a series of field boundaries and some evidence of spade cultivation (C. Thomas 1958). On the other hand, many of the field systems recently identified in lowland river valleys may have been used for raising livestock. There are many arguments for this. They often include paired ditches which can be interpreted as droveways communicating between different parts of the landscape; such features are normally integrated with ponds and water holes, and the environmental evidence recovered from those features often suggests that they were located in pasture. These landscapes were best suited to cattle raising, but the only direct evidence is provided by animal bones, although hoof prints have been identified by excavation alongside one of the Bronze Age land boundaries on Dartmoor (K. Smith et al. 1981: 214). The increasing importance of livestock may account for the earliest evidence of salt production at a number of places on the coast.

In fact the evidence is likely to introduce certain biases. By their very nature the waterholes will be associated with areas of pasture rather than cultivated land. Most excavated settlements produce carbonised grain, and there is little to suggest that it had been brought there after it was processed. Moreover, some of the chalkland settlements show a stronger emphasis on sheep than other animals. This is a largely new feature at this time. It may be connected with the discovery of artefacts associated with textile production, principally spindle whorls and loom weights. They raise further problems as they are not uniformly distributed around the landscape, so that entire groups of settlements, like those on the Sussex chalk or their counterparts in the Middle Thames, provide large numbers of these finds, whilst there are other areas, like the downland of southern Wessex, in which they are unusual. It is clear that some settlements had a more specialised economy than others.

There is also a possibility that larger settlements existed at the same time, although the clearest indication of this comes from Dartmoor where the dating evidence is meagre (Fig. 4.6). The edges of the high ground were divided into a series of separate territories by the continuous boundaries known as reaves (Fleming 1988). They may have originated as fences, but today they can be recognised as low walls. They occur in the areas which are more sheltered and have the most productive soils. The larger settlements are usually found beyond their limits, but it is not clear how this is to be interpreted (A. Fox 1973: 100–12). They may represent the surviving fraction of what was once a wider distribution of houses and irregular enclosures that had been established during the Earlier Bronze Age. If so, further examples may have been removed when more regular field systems were established. Alternatively, they may have been located in areas of pasture beyond the regions in which crops were grown. They could have been occupied seasonally and by only part of the population. That might explain why the associated houses are unusually small. On the other hand, there are cases in which irregular enclosures of this kind were respected when the reaves were established, and there may even be instances in which similar structures were tacked on to the newly constructed boundaries.

A few enclosures were built on such a large scale that they might have been high-status settlements. At present, they seem to be peculiar to southwest England, but other sites were defined by an unusually substantial perimeter. At places like Grimspound on Dartmoor, this was a massive stone wall (Butler 1991: 143–5), but on the chalk of southern England significantly smaller enclosures could be bounded by a considerable ditch. These stand out from the slighter compounds associated with the remaining settlements of this date. Such enclosures are by no means common, and for a long time they were thought to have been intended for livestock. That was based on the apparent absence of domestic structures inside them, but re-excavation of one of the type sites, South Lodge Camp, has shown that the post holes of wooden houses were missed by the original excavator (Barrett, Bradley, and Green 1991: 144–53). In fact it contained a pair of circular buildings like those on other Middle Bronze Age sites. Its main distinguishing feature was the enclosure ditch which was excavated two metres into the bedrock. This earthwork was approximately square and conformed to the layout of an existing group of fields. Perhaps more important, it may have been built as occupation was coming to an end. A comparable sequence was identified on a nearby site at Down Farm, Woodcutts, where the final phase of activity was marked by the demolition of two of the

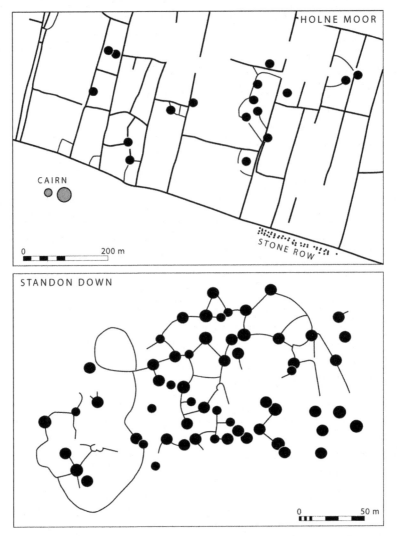

Figure 4.6. (Upper) Co-axial field and houses on Holne Moor, Dartmoor. (Lower) Irregular field plots and houses on Standon Down, Dartmoor. Information from Fleming (1988).

round houses and their replacement by a massive rectangular building whose closest parallels are among the long houses of The Netherlands (ibid., 183–211). This is one of a small group of rectangular structures recognised during recent years. A very similar long house has been identified at Barleycroft in the Fenland (Evans and Knight 1996). Again it is associated with an enclosure and a co-axial field system (Fig. 4.7).

The second unusual feature of the Dartmoor landscape was the creation of large territories based on the valleys radiating out from the higher ground (Fleming 1988). This is like the system postulated for the North York Moors during the Earlier Bronze Age (Spratt 1993: 116–20), but in that case it was

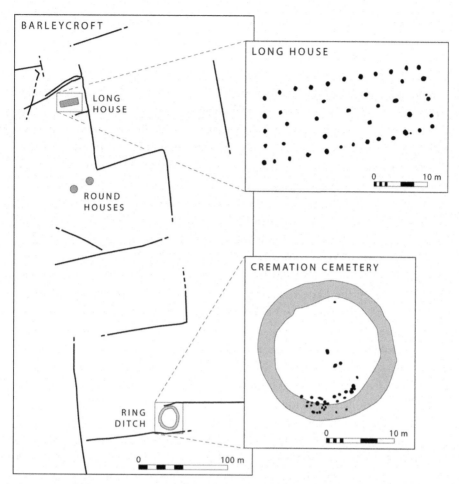

Figure 4.7. Plan of part of a co-axial field system at Barleycroft, East Anglia, showing the positions of two round houses, a long house, and a cremation cemetery. Insets provide more detailed plans of the rectangular building and the cemetery. Plan courtesy of Chris Evans, Cambridge Archaeological Unit.

represented by a distribution of round barrows rather than a continuous barrier. Very similar systems have been identified in other parts of Britain, but their chronology is uncertain. They were usually defined by linear ditches, and there are a few cases in which they seem to have been integrated with enclosures or field systems established during the Middle Bronze Age. On the other hand, this development is more often associated with the Late Bronze Age and even the Iron Age (Bradley, Entwistle, and Raymond 1994), and for that reason it will be considered in more detail in a later section of this chapter. These early beginnings are important mainly because they emphasise that the evolution of local landscapes may have moved at different paces from one region to another.

That is especially true outside lowland England. One of the most remarkable results of recent fieldwork has been to show that the distribution of enclosed

landscapes was confined to the south and east. Co-axial field systems are ubiquitous on the chalk and the river gravels, extending in a broad swathe along
the North Sea coastline from the Welland valley to the north as far as Kent to
the south. They are uncommon over large parts of the midlands but probably
extend along the English Channel as far west as Devon or Cornwall (Bradley
and Yates in press). Beyond that restricted area, settlements may take a similar
form, but do not seem to have been associated with ditched fields. It may be
that these landscapes were characterised by more ephemeral boundaries, but
it also seems as if the density of settlements was lower. Those that have been
discovered show the same range of variation as the examples considered so
far. Some were small groups of round houses and others were associated with
earthwork enclosures. Although longer boundary earthworks are known in
these areas, none so far has been dated to this early phase.

Such contrasts extend to northern England, Wales, and Scotland, but they
may prove to be more apparent than real. One reason is that there have been
fewer developer-funded excavations here. That is important as small open
settlements are most likely to be found in large stripped areas and will rarely
be discovered by more modest site evaluations. That is amply demonstrated
by large scale fieldwork in West Yorkshire (Roberts, Burgess, and Berg 2001:
49–54, 258–60) and by current work at Kintore in northeast Scotland where a
continuous sequence of round houses, extending from the Earlier Bronze Age
to the Iron Age, has been identified in excavation (Cook and Dunbar 2004).
Although the evidence is limited, it already suggests that in northern Britain
and in Ireland the houses and settlements of this period had more in common
with those of the Earlier Bronze Age than their counterparts in the south. A
serious problem is that the clearest ceramic sequence is in lowland England,
and in other areas the coarseware associated with such sites is very difficult to
define. Only the routine application of radiocarbon dating is likely to improve
the situation. That is certainly what is happening in Ireland, where round
houses of this period are being identified in developer-funded excavations. This
evidence may well take a distinctive form, for recent excavation at Corrstown
on the north coast has revealed an extraordinary complex of forty Middle
Bronze Age houses (Conway, Gahan, and Rathbone 2005). It remains to be
seen whether this will happen more extensively, although it may be relevant
that large settlements of similar date are being discovered in the Western Isles
(Parker Pearson, Sharples, and Symonds 2004: chapter 5).

Another development in Ireland was the production of a wide variety of gold
ornaments, including discs, neck rings, and torcs, during the thirteenth and
twelfth centuries BC (G. Eogan 1994: chapter 4). They were surely made from
native metal and form part of a more extensive tradition which is represented
along the Atlantic coast from Portugal to northwest France. The products of the
Irish industry are also found in Britain, with distinct concentrations in Wales,
the Severn estuary, and southern England. They also suggest close connections

between northern Ireland and northeast Scotland. A few of these artefacts have been found in graves, but most of them were deposited in hoards and often in bogs. It is not clear how their production was related to the settlement sites of this period, but their chronology may overlap with the development of the fortified enclosures in Ireland, discussed later in this chapter. For example, there are finds of gold from Haughey's Fort, which was in use by 1100 BC (Mallory 1995).

The mortuary rituals of the Middle Bronze Age pose many problems (Fig. 4.8). From the Yorkshire Wolds to the English Channel coast, crema-tion cemeteries are quite easy to identify because they are associated with readily recognised styles of pottery. The same is true in the southwest, but beyond these areas the ceramic evidence is so unsatisfactory that at different times the same kinds of vessels have been attributed to every phase from the Neolithic to the Iron Age.

It was not until 1972 that it was possible to link a Middle Bronze Age settlement with its cemetery (Holden 1972). A group of cremations associated with a small round barrow was discovered close to the excavated site at Itford Hill in Sussex. The connection between them was confirmed when it was realised that a sherd associated with one of the houses fitted a broken vessel associated with the burials (Holden 1972). Subsequent fieldwork has shown that cemeteries of this kind are regularly associated with settlement sites, and there are other burials among the dwellings themselves (Brück 1995). The main groups of cremations are usually located behind the living area but within about two hundred metres (Bradley 1981). This hypothesis has been tested by excavation and is supported by radiocarbon dating.

The links between these settlements and their cemeteries extend to other features. It is sometimes claimed that the pottery associated with Earlier Bronze Age burials was rather different from that employed in settlements. That is controversial (Healy 1995), and it was certainly not true during this phase as the ceramics associated with cremation cemeteries are indistinguishable in type, fabric, and decoration from those used in the houses. In the same way, the occasional metal items found with cremation cemeteries are of the same types as the artefacts deposited in settlements, often when individual structures were built or went out of use. There are even cases in which the layout of an individual cemetery reflects that of the domestic buildings. Newly constructed barrows were of about the same size as the houses of the same period, and sometimes both kinds of structure had an entrance to the south or southeast. It was often on this side of the mound that the main group of burials was concentrated. In such cases it seems as if the settlement and its cemetery were mirror images of one another (Bradley 1998b: 148–58). The distribution of cremations can often be divided into a series of separate clusters, although it is impossible to say whether these represented individual households (Ellison 1980). Certainly, it is clear that these deposits did not exclude any section of the population; the cremations include men, women, and children. What is really striking is that so little was done to distinguish one burial from another. There is little sign of the complex spatial organisation that typifies the cemeteries of the Earlier Bronze Age. Rather, it seems as if social distinctions were being suppressed.

In certain cases it even appears that the burials were organised according to a similar principle to the houses. For example, at Kimpton in Wessex the successive clusters of cremation burials resemble the sequence of dwellings within a settlement (Dacre and Ellison 1981). Similarly, at a number of places in the Thames Estuary the burials were associated with groups of small ring ditches rather like the individual buildings found on an occupation site (N. Brown 2000). This was a practice that may have continued on a reduced scale during the Late Bronze Age. Yet another configuration has been identified at Bromfield in the West Midlands where the burials describe an enormous arc, rather like one section of a circular enclosure (Stanford 1982). Another possibility is that the cemetery formed around a barrow which has since disappeared.

Until recently, it would have been difficult to discuss the northern and western British equivalents of these practices. That was partly because of the problems posed by the pottery of this period, but also because there were few radiocarbon dates. The situation has improved considerably as a result of new excavations. The direct dating of cremated bone from older projects has made a special contribution to Scottish and Irish archaeology (Sheridan 2003c).

For a long time it had seemed likely that the practice of cremation burial, which was such a feature of the Earlier Bronze Age, continued into later prehistory, although the evidence for this interpretation was very limited. Cremation pyres had been identified at the settlements of Gwithian in southwest England (C. Thomas 1958) and Cladh Hallan in the Hebrides (Parker Pearson, Sharples, and Symonds 2004: fig. 29). In Wales standing stones were erected on the sites of earlier houses and could also be associated with cremation burials (G. Williams 1988). Otherwise the evidence was difficult to evaluate. There have been three crucial developments. The first has been a campaign of dating human remains from reliable contexts. This has produced unexpected evidence that during the Later Bronze Age a whole variety of Scottish monuments were reused, often as cemeteries or pyres. These are monuments built during the Later Neolithic or the Earlier Bronze Age periods, including stone circles, ring cairns, and Clava Cairns. There seems to have been a peak of activity during the Middle Bronze Age, but it continued into the Late Bronze Age too (Sheridan 2003c). A similar development has been identified at some of the henges of northeast England, which appear to have been reused at about this time (Gibson 2002b).

The second result is equally challenging, for it has shown that the rather nondescript pottery associated with these developments ('flat-rimmed ware')

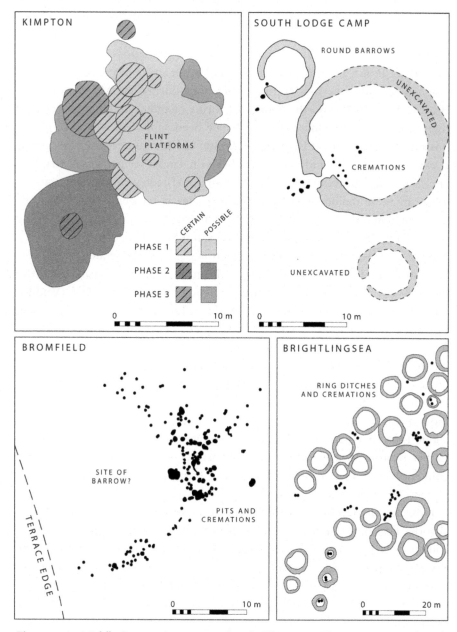

Figure 4.8. Middle Bronze Age cemeteries. At Kimpton, Wessex, cremation burials were associated with a sequence of flint platforms. At South Lodge Camp, Wessex, they were associated with small round barrows, each with an entrance on one side. At Bromfield, in the English midlands, urned and unurned cremations were arranged in an arc forming a sector of an enclosure about twenty-five metres in diameter, and at Brightlingsea in the Thames Estuary they were associated with a dense distribution of small ring ditches. Information from Dacre and Ellison (1981), Barrett, Bradley, and Green (1991), Stanford (1982), and N. Brown (2000).

had a finite currency. It was not in use for as long as had once been supposed, and in most areas it was made between about 1500 and 800 BC. That is important because it suggests that still more monuments were reused as cemeteries during this phase. It also raises the possibility that other structures which had been assigned to earlier periods were actually built during the Middle and Late Bronze Ages. In the north, traditional forms of public monument retained their importance for longer than had once been supposed. A ring of pits or posts in the settlement at Billown on the Isle of Man is interpreted as a shrine (Darvill 2002: 10–15), and even in southern England it seems possible that post circles and timber avenues remained important (Bradley and Sheridan 2005). There are fewer radiocarbon dates from Irish sites, but it seems possible that the same happened there. In Scotland it is clear that stone circles were still being built during the Later Bronze Age (Bradley and Sheridan 2005).

Such evidence suggests a close connection between the sequences in Scotland and Ireland. There is a striking resemblance between the smallest Scottish 'henges' and a series of Irish earthworks known as 'ring barrows' (Waddell 1998: 173). These are not really burial mounds but circular enclosures defined by an external bank and a wide internal ditch. Sometimes there is evidence for an eastern entrance that seems to have been blocked. The British monuments, which are mainly in the north of Scotland, have very similar features, but at present none is adequately dated. In Ireland, the situation is slightly more encouraging, and it is clear that these sites are among the principal mortuary monuments of the Later Bronze Age and, indeed, the Early Iron Age. Until about 1300 BC there were burials with grave goods similar to those of the Earlier Bronze Age, but after that time barrows and other monuments rarely contained more than a token collection of burnt bones from the pyre. As in Britain, the treatment of the dead seems to have changed.

How are the developments in the landscape related to the deposits of metalwork? The most important point is that some of the types of artefacts which had previously been placed in graves were deposited in other locations. During the Middle Bronze Age ornaments were often buried in hoards, either in dry ground or in bogs. The evidence is unsatisfactory, but it is clear that some of these collections were accompanied by bones, but they do not seem to have been formal burials. Detailed analysis of the associated artefacts suggests that they were sets of personal equipment. Different items were worn to different extents, raising the possibility that they had been accumulated during the course of people's lives and may even have been deposited when they died (R. Taylor 1994: 101). Something similar happened with the bronze weapons of this period. Most of the daggers are found in Wessex barrows, but their direct successors were usually deposited in water. The Thames has produced the largest number of examples (York 2002), but in Ireland there is another concentration of these finds in the Shannon (Bourke 2001).

It must be more than a coincidence that as elaborate artefacts disappear from the funerary record, they occur with increasing frequency in other contexts.

The connection between these deposits is especially obvious in the case of daggers, dirks, and rapiers (Gerloff 1975; Burgess and Gerloff 1981). The dagger had been one of the main artefacts associated with Earlier Bronze Age burials, and it is generally agreed that it provided the prototype for these other weapons. Most of the daggers have been found in graves, but the latest examples are also discovered in rivers (Gerloff 1975). The two groups of finds have mutually exclusive distributions. Those associated with barrows are mostly from Wessex; the river finds are from the Thames. Very few dirks and rapiers are associated with human burials, and the number of river finds increases sharply. Thus the rate of consumption increased as barrow building was coming to an end (Bradley 1998a: 140–1).

On one level this evidence suggests that the cemeteries provide a misleading impression of Middle Bronze Age society. Overt distinctions may have been suppressed in the mortuary rite (although nothing is known about the rituals taking place around the pyre), and it seems as if the dead were denied the conspicuous memorials that had been provided for earlier generations. Now the mounds were smaller, and many sites lacked them entirely. One possibility is that only part of the population was buried there, whilst the people who had access to elaborate metalwork were commemorated at a different location and in a different way. Another possibility is that the finery traditionally associated with the dead was removed from contact with their bodies and deposited somewhere else. If so, then it may have been the structure of the mortuary rites that altered, rather than the structure of society.

It is difficult to decide between these models, and each of them may be more appropriate in different areas. For example, barrow building was drastically curtailed about 1200 BC in lowland England but continued in Ireland as late as the Iron Age (Waddell 1998; Grogan 2004; J. Eogan 2004). Similarly, there are flat cemeteries in the English midlands, but in the north of Scotland stone circles and related monuments were still used at this time. One point is quite clear. In southern Britain, the embellishment of barrow cemeteries had reached its limit by the end of the Earlier Bronze Age. One way of considering the problem is to suggest that these earthworks were no longer an effective way of communicating relationships with the dead. Individual cemeteries had perhaps become too complex or arcane for their message to be understood, and new ways of expressing these ideas developed.

Maybe the obligations expressed by Earlier Bronze Age funerary practices were finally coming under pressure. After a long period in which the same places had been used for celebrating the dead, the social order could have been under strain, for the main deposits of rich metalwork were certainly changing their distributions. For all the biases created by antiquarian excavation, the richest artefact assemblages of the Earlier Bronze Age come from Wessex. In the following period they are in the Thames Valley and the Fenland. These were surely centres of political power as the raw material had to be imported from the Continent.

But is there any evidence that the deposits of fine metalwork were associated with the dead? It is not enough to say that their immediate predecessors had been found in graves, for cemeteries were still being created during the Middle Bronze Age. There are two arguments that might support this hypothesis. The first concerns the treatment of the corpse. Although cremation was certainly the main burial rite, there is evidence for a few inhumation burials during this period, and also for smaller deposits of human remains (Brück 1995). These are rarely dated because they are seldom associated with artefacts. In recent years it has become clear that unburnt bones, mainly skulls, are found in rivers or in other watery locations, usually in the same locations as the weapons. This raises many problems – the skulls may have been separated from the other parts of the body as a result of taphonomic processes (Turner, Gonzales, and Ohman 2002); both weapons and human remains may have been brought together by the action of the river – but it happens too often to be entirely coincidental. That is particularly true of the skulls from the River Thames, some of which have radiocarbon dates in the Later Bronze Age (Bradley and Gordon 1988). This may be evidence for some kind of 'river burial'. Again it could have developed out of an existing practice, as there are Earlier Bronze Age skeletons associated with artefacts from wet deposits in the Fenland (Healy and Housley 1992). Indeed, round barrows were sometimes built on islands within major rivers (T. Brown 2003).

The second argument must also be rather tentative, but recent analysis of the weapons from British and Irish rivers has shown that they had obviously been used in combat over a significant period before they were deposited (York 2002). These objects had not been made as votive offerings, and they were only discarded at the end of a lengthy history. That might mirror the lives of those who had used them.

SUBSEQUENT DEVELOPMENTS: THE LATE BRONZE AGE (1100–800 BC)

Although this chapter treats the Middle and Late Bronze Ages together, there were important developments from the twelfth century BC. Most of these grew directly out of existing processes of change. There is no need to postulate a major crisis at this time.

In particular, the new practice of depositing metalwork in rivers continued unabated. It may even have intensified, although in England its geographical focus changed from an emphasis on the Fenland to a greater concern with the Thames. There was more continuity in the use of other British and Irish rivers. In some respects the deposition of weaponry underwent a subtle modification. Throughout the Later Bronze Age it is clear that these artefacts had been used in combat and that some of them had been repaired or resharpened long before they were taken out of circulation. At the same time,

detailed study of the metalwork from the Thames shows that they were normally disabled before they were committed to the water. The frequency of
deliberately damaged items increased steadily through time, whilst the proportion of artefacts showing signs of use remained at a constant level (York
2002). It was not easy to damage some of the finest swords and spears without
considerable effort. Some of these weapons had also been burnt, and it seems
possible that they had been present on a cremation pyre (Bridgford 1998).
They include examples from Duddingston Loch in Edinburgh which were
associated with human bones (Callender 1922). Late Bronze Age swords and
spearheads have also been found in rivers together with unburnt skulls, but it
is difficult to interpret their relationship to one another (Bradley and Gordon
1988).

The deposition of weaponry may have become more of a public event and
could have involved a greater spectacle than before. One reason for suggesting
this is the amount of damage inflicted on many of the weapons. Another is that
there is an increasing number of sites where such deposits seem to be directly
associated with timber structures in rivers and similar settings. Some of these
were conceived on a massive scale, and where they have been excavated in
recent years they turn out to be associated not only with finds of metalwork
but also with ceramic vessels, human remains, and animal bones. They were
clearly laid down with a certain formality. Thus entire pots could be placed
beside upright timbers (Bell, Caseldine, and Neumann 2000: chapter 5); human
and animal remains might have different distributions from one another (Pryor
2001: 427–9); wooden ard tips could be included among the offerings (T. Allen,
pers. comm.); and the faunal remains may have an unusual composition, with
an emphasis on horses and dogs that has no counterpart in the settlement sites
of the same period (Bradley 2005b: 172).

The wooden structures are difficult to explain. Some of them were considerable undertakings. A great causeway at Flag Fen in eastern England linked a
platform built in open water to two areas of settled land (Pryor 2001: 421–7).
Bones were deposited on one side of this alignment, and items of metalwork
on the other. Although this was an unusually elaborate construction, there
are signs of similar features elsewhere in southern and eastern England. It is
difficult to decide whether they were provided simply as a stage for public ceremonies or whether they might have played a more practical role as well. For
instance, Middle *and* Late Bronze Age finds are associated with the remains of
wooden bridges, jetties, or causeways at a number of places in England (they
belong to both phases as such structures were sometimes long-lived). They
include Testwood in southern Wessex (Falkner 2004), Shinewater in southeast
England (Greatorix 2003), Greylake in the Somerset Levels (Brunning 1997),
and two sites along the River Thames, one at Vauxhall (Sidell et al. 2002:
29–30), and the other at Eton Rowing Lake where several of these structures have been identified (T. Allen 2002). Not all these sites are associated

with weapons. They do occur in most instances, but at Eton the river contained pottery and human bones, and Greylake was associated with a broken axehead and human remains. Chris Evans (2002) has suggested that similar deposits were made at other places where people travelled across water, and it certainly seems as if major deposits of metalwork were associated with the routes leading to the Isle of Ely. There are also cases in which deposits of weapons have been found with the remains of log boats (C. Phillips 1941). Some of the richest collections of metalwork come from the River Shannon in Ireland, where they are often associated with fords (Bourke 2001). The very act of crossing the water might have been conceived as a rite of passage.

That is still more obvious where platforms were built in the water itself, or where small islands became a focus for human activity. The causeway at Flag Fen provided access to one of these sites (Fig. 4.9). The platform had a distinctive character for it was made out of reused timbers. These showed little sign of wear, and the wood had not always been selected for its structural qualities or for its ability to sustain a long period of use. It had originally been employed in substantial rectangular buildings very different from the circular dwellings of the same period. Such constructions must surely have played a specialised role, and that may be why they lasted for such a short period before they were dismantled (Pryor 2001: chapter 7).

In some respects the platform at Flag Fen might be compared with the occupation of small islands during the Late Bronze Age. Two examples have been excavated in recent years, at Runnymede Bridge and Wallingford, both in the Thames (Needham 1991; Needham and Spence 1996; Cromarty et al. 2005). In each case an island seems to have been delimited by vertical piles driven into the river bed. At Runnymede the site was located at a confluence between the Thames and one of its tributaries and formed only part of a larger complex with an enclosed settlement nearby. Both these islands were in a river that has produced many finds of weapons, but there is no direct association between them, and those from Wallingford seem to be earlier in date than the finds from the excavation.

Little is known about the structures built on these sites, although it is interesting that at Runnymede they seem to have included rectangular buildings quite different from the round houses found with the enclosure on dry land (Needham 1992). The feature that links this site with that at Wallingford is the presence of a midden (Cromarty et al. 2005). Runnymede Bridge also provides evidence of metalworking. In neither case could animals have been raised on the islands themselves, so the presence of large quantities of faunal remains suggests that feasts were taking place there. A possible link with river finds is the burial of a human skull (Needham 1992: pl. 2).

Another comparison is with the artificial islands known as crannogs, although there is no evidence that structures of this kind were built in Britain

Figure 4.9. Part of the timber platform at Flag Fen, East Anglia. Photograph courtesy of Francis Pryor.

before the Iron Age. On the other hand, a recent study of the Irish evidence suggests a different situation. Christina Fredengren has undertaken a survey of the evidence from Loch Gara in the west of the country (Fig. 4.10) and has compared her results with those of older fieldwork. At three of the sites that she studied structural timbers were dated by radiocarbon. In each case the results fall between 930 and 800 BC and clearly relate to activity towards the end of the Bronze Age (Fredengren 2002: chapter 9). That is consistent with the results of earlier excavations on this kind of monument which also place them in the Late Bronze Age.

Such crannogs may have played many different roles, and the same must surely apply to the wooden platforms that were built in areas of blanket bog (A. O'Sullivan 1998: 69–96). Their characteristics overlap, and a number of prehistoric crannogs may actually have been built around small natural islands. They were generally composed of brushwood and large quantities of stones, and despite the good conditions of preservation the structural evidence from these sites can be surprisingly meagre. They were apparently bounded by a wooden barrier, and it is often assumed that they included the sites of houses, although the main evidence is that of hearths. In some cases they would have been under water for part of the year and cannot have been inhabited continuously (Fredengren 2002: chapter 9). The two timber platforms at Ballinderry were more substantial undertakings (Fig. 4.10). One of them had a foundation of parallel beams, but again the nature of their superstructure is not clear (Newman 1997b). They seem to have been connected by a path, and something similar has been found at Killymoon, where a platform associated with a small gold hoard is linked to an earthwork enclosure on dry land (Hurl 1995).

The contents of these sites are dominated by burnt stone and animal bones, perhaps suggesting that, among other activities, they were used for cooking and consuming food; there was even a flesh hook among the finds from Ballinderry. Other associations of the crannogs are more distinctive and perhaps compare with the British finds mentioned earlier. A number of these structures are associated with items of fine metalwork of kinds which are rarely, if ever, found in settlements on land. This is unlikely to reflect the unusual preservation conditions, for some of these artefacts seem to have been formal deposits. At Rathtinaun, for instance, a number of them had been deposited together just beyond the limits of the platform (Raftery 1994: 32–5). They were inside a wooden box and included bronze rings, amber beads, a pair of tweezers, a pin, and boar's tusks. This is particularly interesting as other Bronze Age crannogs have produced finds of rings, as well as swords. A surprising number of these sites also contained the moulds for making weapons (Fredengren 2002: chapter 9).

By their very nature the crannogs were located in open water, and it seems clear that they formed a focus for further deposits. These are of two main kinds, and both of them recall the discoveries from Irish and British rivers. There are a considerable number of bronze weapons, especially swords (G. Eogan 1965). That is hardly surprising since these kinds of artefacts were apparently being made on sites like Rathtinaun (Raftery 1994: 32–5) and Lough Eskragh (B. Williams 1978). There were also significant numbers of human skulls. They have not been dated by radiocarbon, but their discovery is significant for two reasons. First, their presence does not raise the taphonomic problems that affect the finds from fast-flowing rivers. Most of these come from the still waters of lakes, and are found in the same areas as the artificial islands. Secondly, further skulls come from stratified contexts within the structure of the crannogs themselves.

If weapons seem to have been discarded according to specific conventions, it would be wrong to suppose that their main function was as votive offerings. Their deposition is sometimes thought of in terms of a kind of ritualised warfare, but that may impose a modern antipathy to violence on the past. There is sufficient evidence to show that these weapons had been used. That is most apparent from the damage that they had sustained in the course of their history (York 2002). There are also a small number of instances in which human remains show obvious signs of wounds, but the skulls recovered from the Thames did not exhibit similar damage.

Another indication of the importance of conflict during the Later Bronze Age is the earliest evidence of fortifications. This needs to be treated rather cautiously for the terminology used by archaeologists can easily be misleading. Near to some of the English weapon finds are the circular earthworks described as 'ring forts' on analogy with post-Roman monuments of similar appearance in Ireland (Needham and Ambers 1994). A better term would be 'ringwork',

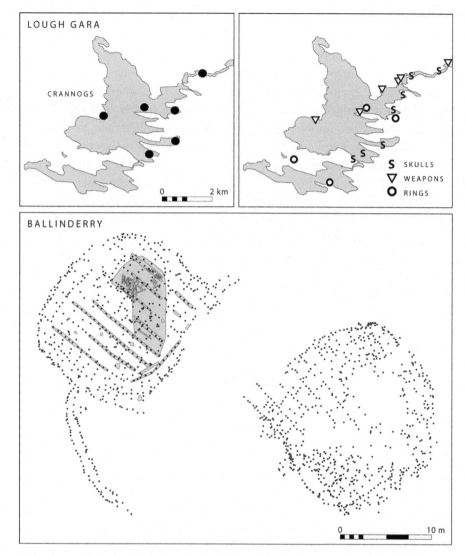

Figure 4.10. (Upper) The distribution of Late Bronze Age crannogs in Lough Gara in the west of Ireland and the findspots of skulls, weapons, and rings from watery contexts. (Lower) Two timber structures, perhaps joined by a wooden path, at Ballinderry, Irish Midlands. Information from Fredengren (2002) and Newman (1997b).

for it makes fewer assumptions. These sites are a recent discovery and were first investigated because they looked like henges. Others have been discovered in the course of developer-funded fieldwork or have been recognised through retrospective analysis of already excavated sites (Fig. 4.11).

Why did it take so long to identify them? In some ways they provide an object lesson in the dangers of air photograph interpretation. Because they have a similar ground plan to Neolithic henges, it was tempting to link them to an established class of monument. That was understandable in the case of

Springfield Lyons which is located beside a causewayed enclosure (N. Brown 2001); the same relationship has been observed at two sites in Kent (Dyson, Shand, and Stevens 2000). The features that first attracted attention were the circular layout of these monuments, the presence of one or two main entrances (although other members of this group actually have interrupted ditches), and hints that at their centre there was a circular timber building. Before their chronology was resolved, John Collis (1977) described them as 'Iron Age henges'. Now it is known that they were built and used between about 1100 and 700 BC. Most examples fall in the centuries between 1000 and 800 BC, but at least two sites may be significantly earlier than that: the inner enclosure at Thwing which dates from the Middle Bronze Age and resembles an older henge (Manby, King, and Vyner 2003, 65–7), and a palisaded enclosure of similar age at Worcester (Griffin et al. 2002).

Later work has modified some of these clear distinctions. Not all the enclosures are precisely circular, nor was there necessarily one central building inside them. Some of these sites had internal ramparts with a vertical timber face reinforced by upright posts, yet the earliest enclosure at Thwing had an external bank like a Late Neolithic monument. Even so, several members of this group are remarkably similar to one another. Rams Hill on the northern margin of the Wessex chalk has a timbered rampart of almost exactly the same kind as a recently discovered example at Taplow in the Middle Thames (Bradley and Ellison 1975; T. Allen, pers. comm.). It also has a distinctive entrance structure that it shares with Thwing on the Yorkshire Wolds (Manby, King, and Vyner 2003: fig. 28). Similarly, the earthwork monument at South Hornchurch is the same size and shape as two wooden enclosures on the same site (Guttmann and Last 2000), and there are other excavated examples in the Thames Estuary and the Severn Valley. The unusually large round houses found within several ringworks sometimes occur as freestanding structures, notably at Bancroft in the south midlands (Williams and Zeepfat 1994: 21–40).

One result of the expansion of fieldwork in the last few years is that the number of ringworks has increased and their distribution has extended from the North Sea coastline inland as least as far as Wessex. Similarly, it is clear that their earthworks normally formed part of a more extensive landscape, including further houses and a field system (N. Brown 2001; Manning and Moore 2003). For a long time it has been accepted that Bronze Age ringworks provided an important focus for public events, including the provision of offerings. Excavation outside one such monument at Carshalton shows that these activities may have extended into the surrounding area. Here there were a number of unusual deposits and a small semicircular enclosure associated with a horse skull (Proctor 2002). Similar features have also been identified on a settlement site in the Cotswolds (D. Mullin, pers. comm.).

It seems possible to interpret the ringworks in more than one way. They may have been elite residences, cut off by earthworks from the surrounding area

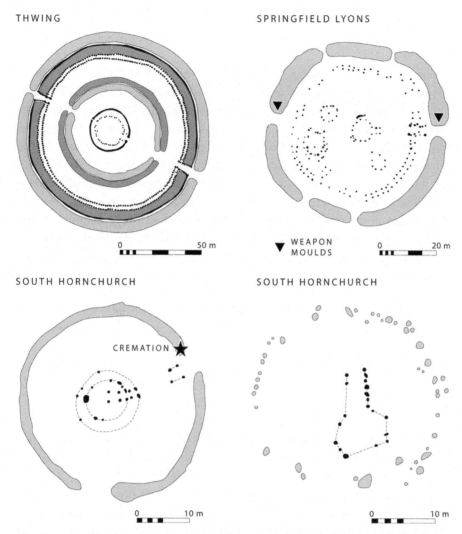

THWING

SPRINGFIELD LYONS

0   50 m

▼ WEAPON
   MOULDS

0   20 m

SOUTH HORNCHURCH

SOUTH HORNCHURCH

CREMATION ★

0   10 m

0   10 m

Figure 4.11. Three Late Bronze Age ringworks and associated deposits. The inner enclosure at Thwing, northeast England, was the first to be built. There are weapon moulds in the main entrances at Springfield Lyons and a cremation in a similar position at South Hornchurch (both sites are in the Thames Estuary). There was also a circular post-built enclosure at South Hornchurch of similar proportions to the ringwork. Information from Manby, King, and Vyner (2003), Buckley and Hedges (1987), and Guttmann and Last (2000).

and possibly protected from attack. One argument in favour of this hypothesis is that, like Irish crannogs, these sites are associated with weapon production. Both the entrances to the enclosure at Springfield Lyons contained clay moulds for making swords (Buckley and Hedges 1987). Another possibility is that they were public buildings and employed in a similar fashion to the henges with which they had been confused. Some of them contain large deposits of animal bones and fine pottery which may result from feasting. The finds include ceramic sets suitable for the service of food and drink, and a number of sites in southeast England produce perforated clay slabs which may have been used in cooking.

The local setting of these earthworks is revealing, too. David Yates (2001) has argued that they generally occur in regions with large co-axial field systems and major deposits of metalwork, whether these are dry land hoards like those around the enclosures at Springfield Lyons (Buckley and Hedges 1987) and Great Baddow (Brown and Lavender 1994), or weapons like those in the Thames near to the sites at Taplow and Wittenham Clumps (York 2002). They conform to a still more general pattern, for the distribution of the field systems is strikingly similar to that of weapons in southern English rivers. It is certainly true that from the twelfth century BC the lowland landscape assumed a quite uniform character. Some of its typical features had already developed before that time, including co-axial field systems, droveways and occasional metal hoards, but now there is a more consistent structure to the ways in which these areas were used.

The settlements themselves were becoming more diverse. They were no longer restricted to small groups of houses but, like the Middle Bronze Age site at Corrstown (Conway, Gahan, and Rathbone 2004), could extend over a considerable area. Most of these sites were entirely open, but now the dwellings within them were frequently superimposed. They were associated with a similar range of ancillary structures – granaries, storehouses, pits, ponds, and occasional rectangular buildings – but they may have been occupied more intensively or over longer periods. Many were new creations in the Late Bronze Age. They are found with large co-axial field systems in the same way as earlier settlement sites, and many produce finds of carbonised grain.

A number of the fields established during the Middle Bronze Age had gone out of use by this time, and on the Wessex chalk they were supplemented and often slighted by long linear earthworks which define the limits of a series of territories (Bradley, Entwistle, and Raymond 1994: chapter 7). These usually extended from the rivers onto the higher ground, but in other cases they followed the upper limits of fertile valleys in a similar manner to the Dartmoor reaves (Fig. 4.12). Their interpretation has always been controversial, although it seems to be agreed that most of these developments began during the Late Bronze Age. Such earthworks were once described as 'ranch boundaries' on the assumption that cattle raising became more important at this time. That idea has been revived by Barry Cunliffe (2004), but other fieldworkers have suggested that there may have been a greater emphasis on sheep, an interpretation which is supported by faunal remains from the local settlements (McOmish 1996). Another possibility is that land holding was reorganised around a series of enclosed 'estates', each of which contained a variety of different resources, extending from grazing land on the flood plains, through arable land on the valley sides to summer pasture on the high downland. Recent fieldwork on

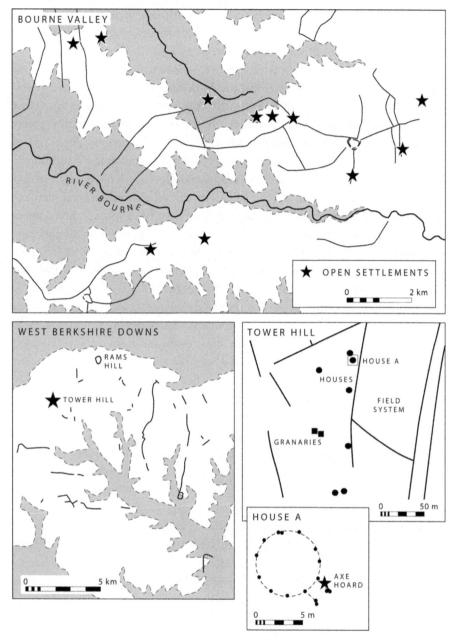

Figure 4.12. Linear land boundaries in the Bourne Valley and on the Berkshire Downs, Wessex, showing the positions of the ringwork at Rams Hill and a series of open settlements. Insets show the distribution of houses and granaries within one of these settlements at Tower Hill and the plan of House A which was associated with a hoard of metalwork. Information from Bradley, Entwistle, and Raymond (1993) and Miles et al. (2003).

Salisbury Plain suggests that each of these territories included the position of at least one large open settlement (M. Fulford, pers. comm.). There is an excavated example on Dunch Hill (Andrews 2006).

It is not known whether this was part of a more general development, but something similar did take place on the Yorkshire Wolds. In this case less is known about the location of Late Bronze Age settlements, and field systems of this period have not been identified. On the other hand, one of the points where several of these territories converged was the defended enclosure of Thwing (Manby, King, and Vyner 2003: 70–8). This occupied a prominent hilltop, but the main role of the ditched boundaries may have been to define a series of territories based on the valleys in this area. Another vital element was water, and some of the linear ditches may have been intended to control access to springs (Fenton-Thomas 2003: chapter 3). Something similar may have happened in lowland areas where long linear earthworks cut off bends in major rivers like the Thames. Although they are usually assigned to the Iron Age, a few are associated with radiocarbon dates that fall within this period.

There is no reason to suppose that the open settlements associated with these land boundaries were any different from those discovered with co-axial field systems on the lower ground, although a few examples seem to be subdivided by fence lines, and others may even have been bounded by hedges. The recent expansion of developer-funded excavations has helped put these sites in context. It is clear that they contain a number of specialised deposits which recall those of the Neolithic period. They include offerings of pottery, grain, and animal remains which were connected with houses, pits, waterholes, the entrances of enclosures and buildings, and even the foundations of granaries (Guttmann and Last 2000: 354). They were not a completely new development, but their frequency was certainly increasing. The deposits found in ponds and wells are especially revealing for they emphasise the special importance of these places. In one case a pond even contained a bronze weapon similar to those found in rivers. Less is known about the open settlements in other parts of Britain and Ireland, although their sites are gradually being discovered in excavation. There is little to suggest that they changed their form from the Middle Bronze Age, and in many areas the structures of these two periods can be told apart only by radiocarbon dating. Certainly, the distribution of co-axial field systems did not extend any further than it had done before, and few occupation sites were enclosed until the Early Iron Age.

It is normally supposed that Late Bronze Age settlements did not have cemeteries in the way that their Middle Bronze Age predecessors had done in lowland England, but that is not altogether true (Fig. 4.13). Flat cemeteries have been identified in increasing numbers by developer-funded projects in Ireland; their positions were sometimes indicated by marker posts. Some of the settlements in England were actually built over the remains of existing urnfields, whilst a number of small ring ditches have been identified on the edges of living areas or field systems in the south. Most were associated with

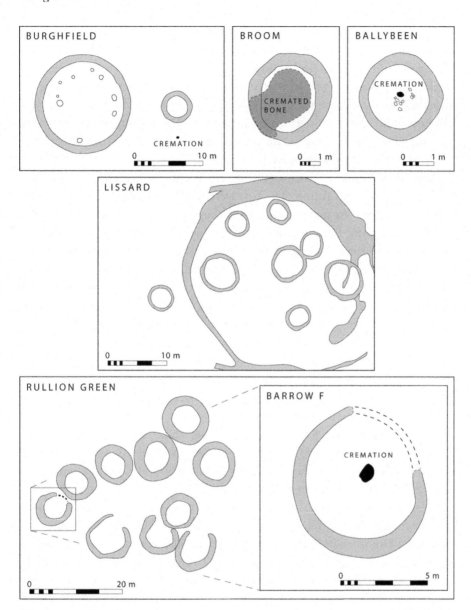

Figure 4.13. Late Bronze Age mortuary monuments. Cremations were associated with the excavated ring ditches at Burghfield (Kennet Valley), Broom (English Midlands), Ballybeen (northern Ireland), and Rullion Green (southern Scotland). The excavated site at Lissard, southwest Ireland, may be of similar character but remains undated. The ring ditch at Broom was associated with the remains of bronze cauldrons. Information from Bradley et al. (1980), Palmer (1999), Mallory (1984), Watkins (1984, 1985), and Ó'Riordáin (1936).

a single cremation, and at one site in the English midlands an unusual burial found with one of these monuments was accompanied by the remains of several cauldrons (Palmer 1999b: 36–56). These miniature round barrows had not been recognised until recently and their distribution has still to be worked out, but it appears to extend across both islands. Another practice that has been identified for the first time is the deposition of small quantities of cremated human bone in pits within the settlement itself (Brück 1995). It began in the Middle Bronze Age, and this phenomenon has now been traced across a wide area from Kent to the Severn Valley. Detailed analysis of the contents of these features suggests that they were no more than token deposits of material selected from a pyre (Bishop and Bagwell 2005: 47). That implies that the burning of human bodies may have been more common than archaeologists had supposed and that most of the remains were not preserved.

Two other features are associated with settlement sites, but until recently they had been treated in isolation. The first were the deposits of bronze metalwork known as hoards. As mentioned earlier, they were often associated with the activities of smiths, but it seems doubtful whether they were simply stores of finished items or raw material. It seems more likely that they represent a deliberate offering of part of the stock of metal which had been processed near the site (Bradley 2005b: chapter 5). There were also small hoards of ornaments or weapons which may have been connected with particular individuals. Recent fieldwork is shedding light on the places where this happened. Although some sites could have been genuinely isolated, others were clearly on the edge of settlements and have been found by the open area excavation during recent years. Perhaps the clearest example of this is at Bradley Fen in eastern England. Here a series of single finds of spearheads had been placed along the boundary between a field system and the edge of the wetland. Outside the enclosed area was a hoard (Fig. 4.14). Similar evidence comes from field survey in southern England which has investigated the findspots of other collections of metalwork. These were originally studied for their associated artefacts, but the new work established that they had been deposited beside streams and just outside settlement sites dating from this period (Dunkin 2001). Other finds are associated with occupied hilltops. There was a major deposit of metalwork outside the settlement at Dinorben in North Wales (Gardner and Savory 1964: 1), and below the open site at South Cadbury in southwest England there was a remarkable deposit of a shield (Coles et al. 1999). Similar considerations apply to a number of caves in Britain and Ireland. These often produce unusual assemblages of artefacts. They are found with human skulls at Covesea in northern Scotland (I. Shepherd 1987).

Some collections of metalwork were close to a curious group of monuments which are usually known as burnt mounds (Buckley ed. 1990). They have a lengthy history, for the oldest of them belong to the Neolithic period and others are associated with Beaker pottery, although radiocarbon dating suggests that most examples formed during the Later Bronze Age. As their name suggests, these are simply mounds of fire-cracked stones, although excavated examples are usually associated with a trough and sometimes with a small building. They are normally found beside streams and seem to result from a specific technology in which heated stones were employed to boil large amounts of water. It is less

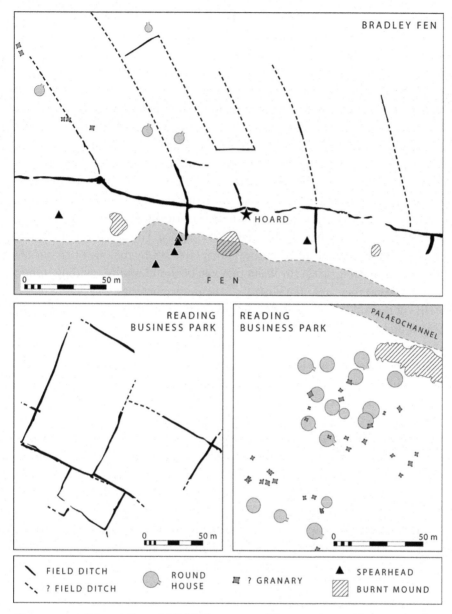

BRADLEY FEN

★ HOARD

0   50 m

F E N

READING
BUSINESS PARK

READING
BUSINESS PARK

PALAEOCHANNEL

0   50 m

0   50 m

FIELD DITCH

? FIELD DITCH

ROUND
HOUSE

? GRANARY

SPEARHEAD

BURNT MOUND

Figure 4.14. (Upper) Co-axial fields, houses, possible granaries, and burnt mounds at Bradley Fen, East Anglia, showing the findspots of individual spearheads and a metalwork hoard. Plan courtesy of Chris Evans and Mark Knight, Cambridge Archaeological unit. (Lower) Successive phases in the development of the settlement at Reading Business Park. The structures overlie part of an older field system. Information from Brossler, Early, and Allen (2004).

clear why this was done. One possibility is that these sites were used to cook joints of meat, yet very few animal bones are preserved at these locations. It seems more likely that the main objective was to create large amounts of steam, so that they may have been used like North American sweat lodges (Barfield and Hodder 1987). Again there is no clear evidence of this, although the small size of the structures associated with them might support this idea. They have few artefact associations, but they suggest that these sites may have played a part in specialised activities. They include fine metalwork, the moulds for making bronze weapons, and occasional human remains. One example at Drombeg in southwest Ireland was only fifty metres away from a stone circle of the same date (Fahy 1959, 1960). That does not mean that the burnt mounds themselves were used for making artefacts or for mortuary rituals. Rather, it suggests that they were in places where such activities took place. For that reason they may not have been accessible to everyone. Perhaps that is why they are often outside the settlements (Fig. 4.14). In Wales they can be found near to standing stones, and in Ireland they are often close to cremation cemeteries.

Burnt mounds are particularly common in the north and west and are probably found in their greatest numbers towards the east coast of Ireland and in the west of Wales. They are also a common feature of the Northern Isles where they accompany stone buildings (Hedges 1975). For a long time it was assumed that they were related to a mobile pattern of settlement. That was because the Irish examples were interpreted by reference to early medieval literary sources which suggested that they were where hunting parties cooked their prey (O'Kelly 1954). That is clearly anachronistic, and the extensive excavations occasioned by road building in Ireland suggests that these sites conform to the same basic pattern as their British counterparts. They are located outside, and in between, Later Bronze Age settlements, but here they seem to have been even more abundant.

Many of the recently excavated settlements in Ireland had been enclosed by a circular earthwork. The smallest of these were insubstantial structures which contained a single round house, but they really form a continuum which extends to some of the most impressive monuments created during this period. The only contrasts are the scale on which these enclosures were conceived and the material richness of their contents. Again a comparison with England seems appropriate, for the larger examples in Ireland bear a strong resemblance to the English ringworks.

The Irish evidence is all-too-little known. Nonetheless a number of famous settlement sites may belong to this tradition, and again they take the form of circular ditched or walled enclosures with a central house. Perhaps the best known of these are from Lough Gur (Grogan and Eogan 1987) where the features associated with 'Lough Gur Class II' pottery have been shown to date to the Later Bronze Age and not to the Neolithic, as had been thought by the excavator (Cleary 2003). This echoes the situation in Scotland with 'flat-rimmed ware' (Sheridan 2003c). There is evidence that specialised activities were taking place at Lough Gur. One of the enclosures provides evidence of metalworking, another includes a series of human burials, whilst the water of the lake beside the occupied area contains a number of weapons.

At the opposite end of the continuum are three other sites which are also very well known: Navan Fort, Downpatrick, and Rathgall. They share the same basic characteristic. They are circular enclosures which probably had a round house or other structure in the centre, but in each case they have some exceptional features. The enclosure at Navan Fort was rebuilt throughout the pre-Roman Iron Age and eventually the site became the capital of Ulster (Waterman 1997). Downpatrick was the findspot of an important hoard of gold ornaments (Proudfoot 1955), and Rathgall contains an exceptionally rich artefact assemblage, including metalwork, many mould fragments, and a number of imported glass beads (Raftery 1994: 58). There is also a series of cremation burials.

In some respects the Irish sites have an unusual character, for whilst they can be compared with enclosed settlements, they include other elements which suggest that they played a role in public ritual. That seems appropriate in the light of another recent project. For a long time The Grange embanked stone circle close to Lough Gur has been regarded as the most extensively excavated Neolithic henge in Ireland, but Helen Roche's recent reassessment has shown that it was actually built during the Late Bronze Age (Roche 2004). It is a circular enclosure with a recessed interior, an external bank, and a single entrance facing east. Human skull fragments were found inside the monument, which also included four small ring ditches that may well date from the same period. These recall the small burial enclosures at Rathgall, whilst another Late Bronze Age 'henge' at Johnstown South was associated with evidence of metalworking (Ó'Faoláin 2004: 186). A third site at Lugg contained a series of houses but had a large mound at its centre (Kilbride-Jones 1950). Before its true date became apparent, the excavator interpreted it as a henge. 'Embanked enclosures' with similar characteristics are often found near to burnt mounds.

The similarity between the Irish enclosures and the English ringworks is not so surprising, for both these groups of monuments occur in areas with important deposits of swords and spears. They have been studied by Margaret Ehrenberg (1989), who makes the interesting point that the contents of these two 'weapon zones' have the same composition and include the same kinds of artefacts. On that basis she suggests a close relationship between Late Bronze Age elites in the two islands. Not only were they associated with similar earthworks and deposits of metalwork, there may have been other links between these areas (Fig. 4.15). The gold ring with a cremation burial at Rathgall resembles one from a ringwork at Mucking in the Thames Estuary (Bond 1988), and the small circular enclosures associated with that site and The Grange may be related to those used in lowland England during the Late Bronze Age. If so, then other sites may also be relevant to the argument. The contents of Irish crannogs are very similar to those of the occupied islands and timber platforms used during this period, and so are the deposits found in rivers and lakes. A striking characteristic of this evidence is the emphasis on human skulls.

At the same time, the earthwork enclosure at Rathgall is only the innermost of three circuits defining the hilltop. This was not a major concern at the time of the original excavation, but in recent years a distinct group of trivallate hillforts has been identified in Ireland, the best dated of which is Haughey's Fort in the north which was used around 1100 BC (Fig. 4.16; Mallory 1995). Other sites have produced comparable dating evidence, including Dun Aonghasa (Cotter 1996) and Mooghaun (Grogan 1996). Again very similar elements seem to be involved. Dun Aonghasa was associated with weapon production, and an artificial pool outside Haughey's Fort was used for the deposition of sword moulds and human skull fragments (Lynn 1977). All these places were probably inhabited, at least on a temporary basis, and Mooghaun and Dun Aonghasa both include the remains of round houses. It is too soon to say when the occupation of hillforts began in Ireland, although it was clearly under way by the beginning of the Late Bronze Age, but recent work has shown that the Irish Iron Age was aceramic. The pottery attributed to that period is actually older than it seemed (Raftery 1995). It means that any site dated by such material may be earlier than was once supposed. This pattern may not be limited to Ireland. Another candidate, this time with only two ramparts, is South Barrule on the Isle of Man (Gelling 1972).

It seems as if the creation of some of these monuments was contemporary with the renewed production of gold artefacts in Ireland. There was a second phase of gold working in the tenth century BC, following a hiatus of between one and two hundred years (G. Eogan 1994: chapter 5). The scale of production had certainly increased, and so did the quantity of gold employed in individual artefacts and the extent to which the finished artefacts were deposited in bogs and similar locations. Again these objects had a wider currency and certain types have a distribution extending well beyond Ireland itself (Fig. 4.17). For example, one type of gold pennanular bracelet was distributed across the entire country as well as northern Scotland, whilst other distinctive forms resemble those in much more distant areas. Some types share features in common with artefacts produced in the Iberian peninsula and others suggest links with Scandinavia. There are even indications of regional styles within the island itself. One was in the northeast and was closely linked to Britain and the Nordic culture area; the other was around the River Shannon and seems to have had links to Spain and Portugal. That is not the only indication of regional developments at this time. In southwest Ireland the Late Bronze Age is characterised by a distinctive range of ceremonial monuments, including small stone circles (Fig. 4.18) and burials beneath conspicuous boulders (Walsh 1993; O'Brien 1992, 2004).

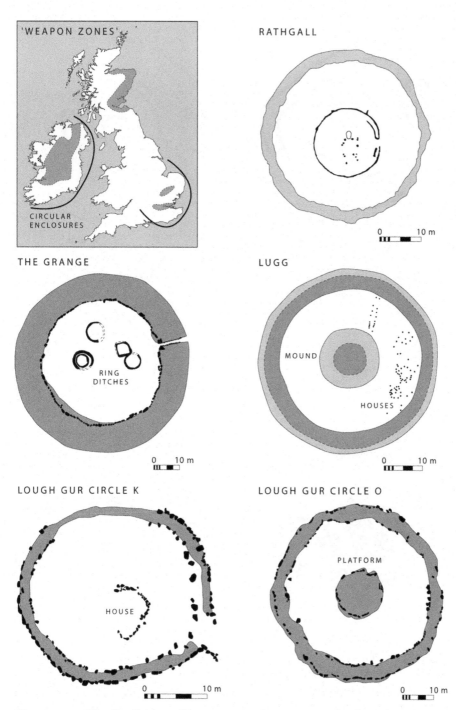

Figure 4.15. The distribution of 'weapon zones' in Britain and Ireland. The contour delimits the areas with the main concentrations of circular enclosures, and these are illustrated by five monuments in Ireland: Rathgall and Lugg in the east of the country, and The Grange and Lough Gur Circles K and O in the southwest. Lugg and The Grange have been interpreted as henge monuments and the other three sites as settlements. Information from Ehrenberg (1989), Raftery (1994), Kilbride-Jones (1950), Roche (2004), and Grogan and Eogan (1987).

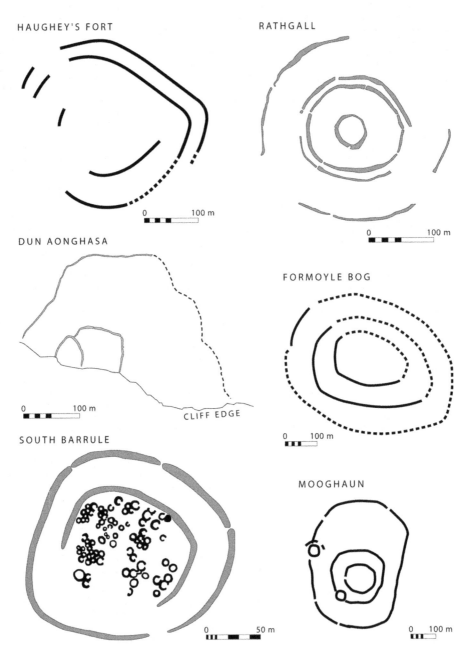

Figure 4.16. The plans of five defended enclosures with spaced walls or ramparts attributed to the Late Bronze Age in Ireland, compared with that of South Barrule on the Isle of Man. Information from Raftery (1994), Grogan (1996), Cotter (1996), and Gelling (1972).

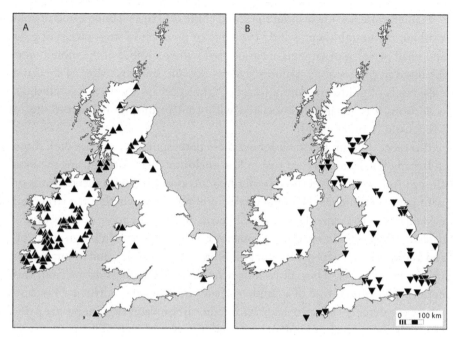

Figure 4.17. The distribution of two kinds of Late Bronze Age pennannular gold bracelets in the Late Bronze Age. A shows the distribution of the 'Irish type' and emphasises the close links between Ireland and northern Scotland. B illustrates the distribution of the 'British type' and emphasises the remaining part of Britain. Information from G. Eogan (1994).

Figure 4.18. The Late Bronze Age stone circle at Drombeg, southwest Ireland.

Rather more is known about the social context of this second period of gold working. Although there is little evidence of production sites, pieces of gold and small personal ornaments are associated with a number of the monuments discussed in this section: crannogs, ringworks, and hillforts. Most of the large collections of goldwork come from bogs, but perhaps the largest of all these collections was apparently associated with a burnt mound below the site of Mooghaun (Condit 1996).

It is more difficult to establish how these developments compare with those in Britain, but again it is clear that hilltop enclosures originated during the Late Bronze Age and that a series of other hills are associated with metal hoards or with large settlements. The difficulty is in establishing whether the structural evidence is of the same date as the defences. Among the most obvious candidates are three sites in southern Scotland: Castle Rock at Edinburgh (Driscoll and Yeoman 1997: 220–3), Eildon Hill North (Owen 1992), and Traprain Law (Armit et al. 2005). They all include artefacts and buildings dating from this period. The same is true of a number of sites in Wales and northwest England where the defences are associated with radiocarbon dates or with bronze artefacts. The best dated examples are probably Beeston Castle (Ellis 1993: 20–5) and the Breiddin (Musson 1991: 25–33). Again each provides evidence of domestic occupation, as well as food storage and craft production, but in no case is it absolutely clear that these locations were permanently occupied. In the south there are other signs that large hilltop enclosures were established in the Late Bronze Age, although their construction and use certainly continued during the transition to the Iron Age. These sites can be difficult to date because of a plateau in the radiocarbon calibration curve, but one clue to their wider relationships is provided by the early hillfort at Harting Beacon on the South Downs (Bedwin 1979). In its gateway was a pair of gold rings which can be compared with those from Rathgall and the Late Bronze Age ringwork at Mucking. Again they were associated with a human skull. As the first British hillforts extend into the Early Iron Age they are considered in more detail in Chapter Five.

SUMMARY: PRODUCTION, ALLIANCE AND EXCHANGE

Recent years have seen a massive increase in the amount of Later Bronze Age material available for study. It has also become more diverse. The final section of this chapter reflects on the significance of this evidence and provides an interpretation.

The first question to ask is whether the change from an Earlier to a Later Bronze Age represents a social collapse. There is no reason to take this view. It is true that there were certain tensions towards the middle of the second millennium BC – fluctuations in the supply of metals, changes of burial customs, the settlement of increasingly marginal land – but it is better to think in terms of transformation rather than a catastrophe. There is nothing to indicate that social distinctions had disappeared; rather, they were expressed in different ways, and what did lapse was the emphasis on mortuary monuments which had played such an important role before. Now the consumption of wealth focused not on the grave but on different locations such as rivers and lakes. The disappearance of mortuary monuments suggests a less stable society, perhaps one which placed less weight on genealogy.

There is a direct relationship between these Middle Bronze Age practices and an important change in the political geography of the prehistoric period, for now the main deposits of portable wealth were to be found in different areas. In Britain, they were most evident in those parts of lowland England where the landscape was transformed by the creation of co-axial field systems, although this evidence cannot be treated in isolation. Similar settlements can be found in regions where these boundaries do not appear, and there are other areas with major collections of artefacts of both bronze and gold. What is important is that the regions over which land holding was so radically reorganised are precisely those with the closest connections to Continental Europe, for this soon became the source of the metalwork used during this period. Surely it was the intensification of food production that made these changes possible, and one wonders whether hides and textiles were among the commodities exchanged for supplies of metal or finished artefacts. Grain was important too, and that is why this chapter has the title 'Ploughshares into Swords'. It is probable that long distance exchange was managed by a social elite, but the only evidence for its existence is provided by the bronzes, for there are no signs of specialised or high-status settlements at this time.

In Ireland, events took a rather different course. Again the inhabitants seem to have been dependent on foreign sources of bronze, but they had their own supplies of gold, and during the thirteenth and twelfth centuries BC they deployed them to spectacular effect, producing a series of personal ornaments of the highest quality. Some of the gold was exchanged with communities on the Continent, whilst the products that remained in the country were commonly deposited in bogs. Environmental evidence suggests that the land was used more intensively than before, but this process does not seem to have involved the creation of extensive field systems or territorial boundaries. It may be that relations with the European mainland took a different form, and it is certainly true that the most likely points of contact would have been along the Atlantic coastline and probably in Scandinavia.

It was during the Late Bronze Age that the settlement pattern became more diverse, and this was when a series of largely new kinds of field monuments first emerged in these islands: fortifications such as ringworks and the earliest hillforts; and wooden platforms, bridges, and crannogs in the wetlands. Despite the formal differences between these sites, they have much in common. Some of them are associated with metal production, especially the making of weapons, and they are very probably connected with feasting. They include large quantities of animal bones, fine pottery (where it was available), the residues of craft production, occasional items of gold, bronze metalwork, and human skulls. Although there is similar evidence from Continental Europe, the strongest connections may have been between the British and Irish 'weapon zones' identified by Ehrenberg (1989), and this may explain why these places have so much in common. There seems little doubt that they were used by a social elite and that members of that select group formed alliances with one another. Some connected people in the two islands, and others linked them to groups in Continental Europe. The close connection between production, alliance, and exchange is illustrated by the Late Bronze Age ringworks in eastern England. Almost all of these were located in areas with tracts of fields and large open settlements, and it can be no coincidence that the very same areas contain the largest number of weapon deposits, including material that had been imported across the English Channel. A different system might have prevailed in Ireland, where land boundaries of similar extent have still to be discovered, but here there must have been a similar relationship between status and the conspicuous consumption of wealth. In this case that included the fine goldwork produced towards the end of this period.

Those changes did not extend into every region, and it is important to remember that the settlement pattern in northern Britain shows much more continuity than it does in the south. Here there was a more gradual increase in the number and density of settlements and also in the evidence of personal wealth. This may provide the background to the appearance of the first hillforts or hilltop settlements, although the dating evidence is unsatisfactory. At the same time, it is clear that traditional forms of public monument had not gone out of use in the way that was once supposed. A variety of stone and earthwork enclosures may still have been constructed during the Late Bronze Age and represent the last stage in a sequence that had started in the Neolithic period. The same is true in Ireland, where it is clear that henges and ringworks, hillforts and stone circles were all used at the same time.

In many ways this interpretation is like conventional accounts of the Earlier Bronze Age. It presupposes that developments in these islands were largely dependent on outside sources of raw material and metal artefacts. That was not entirely likely when southwest Ireland was an important source of copper and Britain first developed bronze, but during the period considered here this model is much more plausible. Metal analysis has shown that an increasing proportion of the artefacts that circulated during the Later Bronze Age made use of ores whose ultimate source was in the copper mines of the Alps. Most of the metal had been recycled many times, but it is clear that much of the raw material had been imported across the English Channel. That surely provides a context for the recent discovery of a large Middle Bronze Age boat at Dover (P. Clark 2004) and for possible shipwrecks, including metalwork of the same period at Langton Bay and Salcombe (Muckelroy 1981). Ireland participated in the same process, but may have been integrated into a further exchange network extending along the Atlantic coastline to Iberia and the West Mediterranean.

These relationships seem to have been sustained for nearly seven hundred years, and there can be no doubt that the Later Bronze Age was a period of growing prosperity, even if it was sometimes characterised by conflict and competition. Only one element was vulnerable, precisely because it was outside local control. This was the supply of metalwork on which so many social relationships seem to have been based. If this came under pressure, the situation was liable to change. That is exactly what happened towards 800 BC, and over a comparatively short period of time the system seems to have collapsed. The reasons for this are complex and need to be treated in detail, but not only did these changes undermine the developments described throughout this chapter, they led to the emergence of a very different kind of society in the Iron Age. Both that crisis and its resolution are studied in Chapter Five.

CHAPTER 5

THE END OF PREHISTORY

FOREGROUND AND BACKGROUND

English common law is based on precedent. The results of any court case establish a principle that must be followed in the future. In theory the legal system should become increasingly rigid, but that is not what happens. Rather than considering themselves bound by previous rulings, judges institute subtle changes to the law. They do so by arguing that the details of particular cases are different from one another, so that what once appeared to be a point of general application actually applies in very specific circumstances (Figs. 5.1 and 5.2).

Prehistorians have taken a similar approach to the Three Age Model. This was devised in the nineteenth century when archaeologists believed that progress was based on technological innovation, so that stone gave way to bronze and bronze to iron. Since that time they have retained the terminology but have changed its connotations. These period divisions are not used in a consistent way. The Neolithic, for instance, is defined by its material culture but also by its economy and systems of belief. Recent work has tended to play down the distinction between that phase and the beginning of the Bronze Age. There are other problems as well. In this book two of the chapters begin halfway through the periods into which the sequence was organised. This procedure reflects the timing of fundamental changes in the prehistoric landscape. Archaeologists rely on precedent when they use the vocabulary of the Three Age system, but the distinguishing features of those different phases have changed completely.

The Iron Age is no exception, but this is not always apparent from the way in which it is studied. At the risk of oversimplification, there have been two main approaches to the period. One treats it as a self-contained entity, giving way to the Roman occupation of Britain. It can even emphasise a certain continuity between those two phases. A good example is Barry Cunliffe's *Iron Age Communities in Britain*, now in its fourth edition (Cunliffe 2005). The other approach envisages a longer sequence of change and interprets the distinctive features of the Iron Age as the outcome of processes which had started late in the second millennium BC. That is illustrated by Kristian Kristiansen's review of *Europe Before History* (Kristiansen 1998). What is called the Bronze Age 'background' in one account is central to the interpretation put forward in the other book.

That second approach is perhaps more satisfactory, and that is why this chapter begins with the closing years of what can still be called the 'Bronze Age'. It will end as these islands first came into contact with the peoples of the Classical world, since Martin Millett (1992) and John Creighton (2000, 2006) have shown that the Late Iron Age is better studied in relation to the Roman period, at least in England. The earliest use of iron was not a sudden event, nor did it depend on the technological progress favoured by Victorian writers. In fact it was probably precipitated by a shortage of metals of any kind. Indeed, it may be that the period around 800 BC is more aptly characterised by a reduced supply of bronze than by the adoption of an unfamiliar material.

Such developments are not well understood, but it seems as if copper of increasingly poor quality had been extracted as the supply of the most suitable Continental ores ran out (Sperber 1999). Some of the Alpine mines ceased operation, and new ones took their place, but the situation did not improve significantly. The metal supply came under yet more pressure and greater attempts were made to recycle the material that was still in circulation. These difficulties began about 1100 BC and became especially severe during the ninth century.

Other developments were taking place at about the same time. In the Mediterranean, complex societies were forming in Greece and Italy and needed regular metal supplies of their own. They were already using iron when a period of rapid social and economic change began around 800 BC. In Italy itself, the rise of new elites put pressure on the supply of metalwork from the north, and bronze seems to have been imported across the Alps (Kristiansen 1998: chapters 5 and 6). The artefacts of this period are very similar to those in Central Europe. This would have reduced the supply to other regions.

These developments in the Mediterranean did not take place in isolation, for the late eighth century BC also saw the establishment of a Phoenician trading network extending as far west as the Iberian peninsula, where it exploited established contacts along the Atlantic coast of Europe to obtain raw material (Aubet 2001). This axis assumed a greater importance as the circulation of metals became more difficult. The last metalwork of the Bronze Age was obtained by a different route from most of the objects of that period and placed a greater emphasis on the Atlantic coast (Ruiz-Gálvez Priego 1998). This change of geographical alignment proved to be short lived, for soon the process was curtailed, and the deposition of artefacts in hoards and rivers declined. In the end the system collapsed. The clearest indication that established practices had been abandoned is provided by the working of iron.

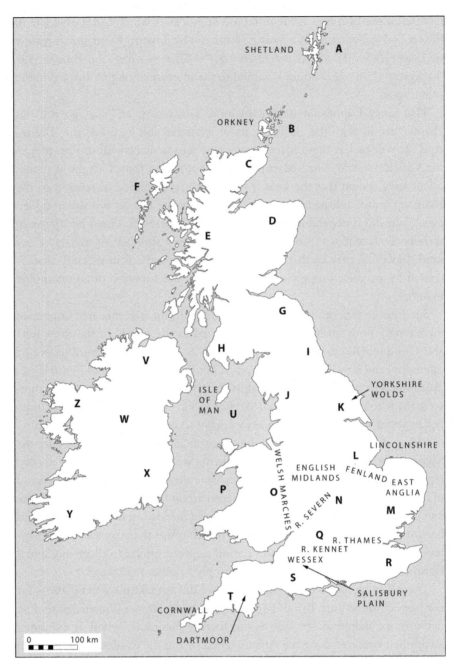

Figure 5.1. Places and regions mentioned in Chapter Five. For the purposes of this map Britain and Ireland have been divided into twenty-six areas, and the individual sites are listed according to these divisions. A: Shetland; B: Orkney (*Gurness, Mine Howe*); C: Northern Scotland; D: Northeast Scotland; E: Western Scotland; F: Outer Hebrides; G: Eastern and Central Scotland (on either side of the Firth of Forth) (*Newbridge*); H: Southwest Scotland; I: the English/Scottish borderland; J: Northwest England; K: Northeast England and the Peak District (*Garton Slack, Rudston, Thwing, Wetwang Slack*); L: Eastern England between the Humber and East

These developments affected both Britain and Ireland and can be illustrated in several different ways. There is evidence that bronze was being distributed in standard forms so that some of the latest axeheads were probably treated as ingots (Briard 1965: chapter 13). They contained so much lead that they could hardly have been used as tools, and in Brittany, where many of them had been made, it seems as if they conformed to standard weights. Discarded artefacts were increasingly recycled. This is most obvious from metal analysis, but it may also be reflected by the large number of 'scrap hoards' that were deposited during the ninth century BC. They certainly include fragments of many different kinds of objects, including tools, ornaments, and weapons, and some of them also contain traces of slag (Bradley 1988). Colin Burgess (1979) suggests that people were dumping surplus artefacts; by withdrawing so much material from circulation they might have forced its value to rise. The reasoning behind this hypothesis is anachronistic for it suggests a degree of coordination which would be possible only in the modern economy – in many ways the best comparison is with the operation of the stock exchange. It is equally unsatisfactory to suppose that supplies of bronze were concealed and lost during a political crisis, for the main evidence of that crisis is provided by the hoards themselves. That is a circular argument which leads to even more confusion. In fact it may be wrong to interpret these collections entirely in practical terms. Perhaps they were really offerings associated with the transformation of the raw material. That is certainly consistent with ethnographic accounts of metalworking in traditional societies (Budd and Taylor 1995).

One clue is provided by changes in the circulation of bronze artefacts which emphasised the importance of the Atlantic seaways. It is not clear whether there really was an 'Atlantic Bronze Age' (Jorge ed. 1998), but no one would deny that a growing number of metal items were exchanged or copied along the western rim of Europe, from Scotland and Ireland in the north, to Spain and Portugal in the south. Some of these connections even extended into the Mediterranean (Ruiz-Gálvez Priego 1998). Such links had always been important, especially in prehistoric Ireland, but now they seem to have assumed a greater prominence than before, and ultimately this network reached across

---

←

Figure 5.1 (*continued*) Anglia (*Fiskerton*); M: East Anglia (*Springfield Lyons, Wandlebury, West Harling*); N: the English Midlands (*Weekley*); O: The English/Welsh borderland (*The Breiddin, Dinorben, Wrekin*); P: West Wales from the southwest to Anglesey (*Dan Y Coed, Walesland Rath, Woodside*); Q: the Thames Valley, Cotswolds, and South Midlands (*Crickley Hill, Devil's Quoits, Gravelly Guy, Runnymede, Wallingford, Wittenham Clumps*); R: Southeast England; S: Wessex (*All Cannings Cross, Balksbury, Barbury Castle, East Chisenbury, Cleavel Point, Danebury, Fyfield Down, Hengistbury Head, Liddington Castle, Maiden Castle, Potterne, Quarley Hill, Sidbury, Silchester, Winklebury*); T: Southwest England (*Cadbury Castle, Glastonbury, Harlyn Bay, Meare*); U: the Isle of Man; V: Northern Ireland (*Corlea, Navan Fort*); W: from the Irish Midlands to the east coast; X: Southeast Ireland: Y: Southwest Ireland; Z: the Irish west coast.

southern and eastern England into Northern Europe. The latest bronze hoards seem to reflect the new alignment (R. Thomas 1989). Such evidence suggests that the inhabitants of these islands were drawing on different sources of supply.

Any relief was short-lived, however, and towards the end of the Late Bronze Age there are indications that people had started to experiment with iron production, using ores that could probably be discovered locally; only the techniques of working them were foreign. It is not clear quite when this process began, or how far iron was intended to take the place of bronze, but iron slag has been found in at least thirty contexts dating from the ninth century BC (Lawson 2000: 202), and there is evidence from a recently excavated settlement at Hartshill Quarry in the Kennet Valley that production may have begun even earlier (Collard 2005). At the same time, the new technology could be used to make composite tools in combination with bronze or could even be employed to produce traditional forms of artefact in a different material. This was certainly the case with socketed axes (Manning and Saunders 1972).

The deposition of metalwork became an important issue as bronze was supplemented, and to some extent replaced, by iron. The latest bronze hoards date from the Llyn Fawr industrial phase which runs from approximately 800 to 600 BC, and the quantity of river metalwork decreased sharply at that time. It happened throughout Britain and Ireland, but it can hardly suggest a shortage of both kinds of metal since exactly the same pattern is found in Continental Europe, where iron weapons were commonly deposited in graves (Gerdsen 1976). Indeed, it seems to have been important that the votive deposits should contain foreign material. That might apply to the styles of the objects themselves but more often reflects the metal from which they were made. Copper and tin did not occur in many of the areas with these artefacts, and this may have provided the source of their power. In that case locally produced iron would not have been an acceptable substitute. Although prehistorians treat bronze and iron as if they were equivalent to one another, people in the past may have categorised them in a very different way (Bradley 1998a: 150–4).

FROM POSSESSION TO DISPOSSESSION

Access to foreign metal had been of fundamental importance in Later Bronze Age society, so that these changes would have had drastic consequences. The crucial point was made by Gordon Childe more than sixty years ago (1942: 182–3). The production of bronze artefacts involved a combination of copper and tin, both of which had restricted distributions in prehistoric Europe. One problem lay in bringing these materials together, and another concerned the circulation of the finished products. Some of the densest concentrations of Late Bronze Age metalwork were in areas which lacked metal sources of their own. They included southern and eastern England. There are other regions where metalwork could have been produced locally but seems to have been imported.

Figure 5.2. Outline drawings of the artefact types mentioned in Chapter Five. A: iron socketed axe; B: dagger; C and D: iron swords; E: decorated sword scabbard; F: decorated bronze disc; G: horse harness; H: decorated rotary quern; I: decorated terret; J and K: pottery with La Tène style ornament.

Among them are Ireland, Scotland, and, most probably, Wales. Because high-quality artefacts were being introduced from distant areas, it would have been possible to control their circulation, and the same applies to the raw material out of which they were made. Access to such objects could have been restricted in two ways. It involved a process of long-distance travel by sea which might have been in the hands of a specialist group of traders, or of a social elite who controlled their activities. The skills needed to make the finest objects were not generally available, and again the activities of smiths may have come under political control. Some of their work was so demanding that they must have depended on a patron for support (Rowlands 1976). At the same time, it would be necessary to accumulate suitable commodities with which to participate in exchange. Although this process may well have involved the circulation of marriage partners, it could also have included the movement of textiles, hides, and, in Ireland, gold. For Childe, the long-distance movement of Bronze involved the creation of alliances and was a source of power.

Iron, on the other hand, is widely available and could have been locally produced in many parts of these islands. Unless the process took place on a large scale – and that is not evidenced before the production of 'currency bars' in the third century BC (Hingley 2005) – it would be difficult to control. Thus the virtual collapse of the long-distance circulation of bronze might have undermined the influence of an elite, but the first adoption of ironworking would not have offered an equivalent power base. For Childe, Iron Age society became more 'democratic'. It is possible to quarrel with the idea that the adoption of iron improved the quality of life, but there is certainly some evidence of social change.

This takes two main forms. There are the new developments that happened during the period of transition, and there are signs that older practices were abandoned. Both happened simultaneously between about 800 and 600 BC, but it will make the argument clearer if they are treated separately here.

This account starts with the new developments. One of the most dramatic discoveries of recent years is the identification of a series of large middens in southern Britain whose chronology appears to span the last years of the Bronze Age and the period of transition (Needham and Spence 1997). Ironically, the first of these to be investigated, All Cannings Cross in Wessex, was once treated as the type site for the Early Iron Age (Cunnington 1923). That was not because of the structural evidence from the excavation, which was meagre, but because of the extraordinary abundance of artefacts. The same applies to the sites recognised more recently, whose distribution extends from East Anglia to south Wales. They attract attention for several reasons. First, it is most unusual to find such enormous accumulations of cultural material, for in normal circumstances such deposits would have been removed from settlements and spread on cultivated land; this is confirmed by excavation of the eroded ploughsoil found on valley floors (Bell 1983). Indeed, the material was not left where it had accumulated but was allowed to build up into considerable mounds. That is quite exceptional. It happened at the recently published site of Potterne on the chalk of southern England (Lawson 2000) and at another site, East Chisenbury, which was identified as a standing earthwork (McOmish 1996). Similar deposits have been recognised at some of the Late Bronze Age sites discussed in Chapter Four, including the occupied islands at Wallingford and Runnymede Bridge (Cromarty et al. 2005; Needham and Spence 1996).

The middens themselves have an unusual composition. The sediments at Potterne include an extraordinary quantity of cattle dung, but there are also considerable amounts of bronze metalwork. The upper levels contain a small amount of iron slag (Lawson 2000: 166–73). There is an abundance of fine pottery and animal bones and small quantities of unburnt human bone. Runnymede Bridge has produced a rather similar assemblage, but here there is evidence that some of the faunal remains were carefully organised within the filling of the midden (Needham 1992). There are indications of craft production, including bronze working, the working of antler, spinning, and the production of textiles. In each case the sheer abundance of bones suggests that feasts were taking place, and this is particularly likely at Runnymede Bridge where the midden is located on an island in the River Thames (Needham and Spence 1995). Detailed study of the ceramics from Potterne suggests that the people who used that site had a wide range of contacts with other places (Lawson 2000: 166–73). The same is true of the metalwork from Runnymede Bridge.

Lastly, not all these sites show much evidence of structures contemporary with the accumulation of the midden. There is considerable uncertainty, for pits and postholes are difficult, if not impossible, to recognise within the dark soil of these deposits; the same problem affects research in the late levels of Roman towns in England (Courty, Goldberg, and Macphail 1989: chapter 15). It is certainly true that a range of timber buildings was identified at Runnymede Bridge and that the midden at Potterne overlay a Bronze Age occupation site. Even so, the only structural evidence found within some of these accumulations consists of small patches of cobbling, often rectangular in outline, various hearths, and the remains of ovens. It may be that in their final form such places were not settlements at all. They are readily accessible from the surrounding area, and it is tempting to compare them with the Middle Saxon 'productive sites' which raise many of the same problems (Pestell and Ulmschneider eds. 2003). These were often located in places that were easy to reach beside Roman roads, and they eventually became local centres, but their main characteristic is the exceptionally large collections of metalwork which are found together with evidence of craft production. Again their roles are very difficult to define. Some may have been high-status settlements, whilst others could have been the sites of markets or fairs. Given the unusual character of the excavated evidence, the same ideas provide the most plausible explanation of the prehistoric middens.

Occasionally they can be associated with other features. The midden at East Chisenbury overlay one side of an earthwork enclosure (Fig. 5.3; McOmish 1996). A similar deposit at Wittenhem Clumps in the Upper Thames was just outside an early hillfort notable for its deposits of human remains (T. Allen pers. comm.), and at Balksbury on the chalk of Wessex another midden, which included large amounts of cattle dung, was within a defended enclosure (Ellis and Rawlings 2001: 83). Again there was perhaps some evidence of feasting.

Balksbury is one of a group of earthwork enclosures which were built in southern England during this period. They are closely related to the Late Bronze Age hillforts discussed in Chapter Four, but some of them may be slightly later in date and are usually assigned to an Earliest Iron Age that extends from about 800 to 600 BC. They share certain features in common (Cunliffe 2005: 378–83). They are of considerable extent and often occupy the tops of particularly prominent hills. They are enclosed by surprisingly slight earth-works, and excavations inside them suggest that they were not intensively occupied. They provide evidence for a very limited number of dwellings, but the main structures were small square buildings which are usually interpreted as granaries or storehouses. They do not produce many artefacts. In the absence of more detailed information, it has been suggested that these places were used intermittently and perhaps on a seasonal basis. In that respect they have features in common with the midden sites.

In each case the evidence suggests that certain places were serving as focal points for a wider population in a way that had not happened since the Earlier Bronze Age. Indeed, they could have played a part in public events at which feasting was particularly important. In the early first millennium BC there was probably an added element, for these seem to have been places where people congregated for the purpose of production and exchange. The great accumu-lations of manure might not be there because large numbers of animals were collected for slaughter; surely there were also gatherings at which livestock were changing hands. Similarly, there is evidence that artefacts were being made, including fine metalwork. This is especially interesting as it had nor-mally taken place at more secluded locations, including Irish crannogs, Welsh hillforts, and some of the English ringworks, where it might have been easier to exercise control over its circulation. The new sites may have been places where people transacted communal business, but if so, this was a novel development and one which suggests that political organisation was changing. Perhaps the community was assuming greater authority at the expense of a weakened elite.

If these were new developments, other features of the landscape seem to have gone out of use. One characteristic of the Late Bronze Age landscape was the evidence of fortified ringworks (Needham and Ambers 1994). In most cases activity ended during the Bronze Age/Iron Age transition, and the same applies

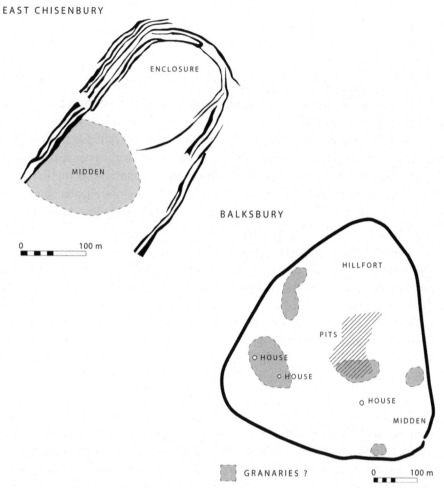

Figure 5.3. The middens at East Chisenbury and Balksbury, Wessex. The site at East Chisenbury is associated with an earthwork enclosure and that at Balksbury with a defended settlement. Information from McOmish, Field, and Brown (2002) and Ellis and Rawlings (2001).

to the building of Irish crannogs (Fredengren 2002). That may be significant as they have similar contents and both may have been of high status. Just as the deposition of fine metalwork in water seems to have diminished, these locations lost their special significance, and the same is true of most of the platforms and islands discussed in Chapter Four. It is a trend that applies to other sites in the English landscape, for the co-axial field systems which were such a feature of the Later Bronze Age were largely abandoned during this phase (Yates 2001). The significance of this change will be considered in due course; what matters here is that the associated settlements were normally deserted or moved to new positions at this time.

HOUSES AND ENCLOSURES

There are other signs of dislocation in the settlement pattern. Two features are particularly important.

The first is a gradual shift in the distribution of prehistoric activity. During the Later Bronze Age there was an extraordinary density of occupation sites along some of the rivers discharging into the North Sea. That is where many of the field systems were created and accounts for the siting of most of the ringworks. Perhaps more important, it is in this area that the principal deposits of fine metalwork occur: there are weapons and ornaments in the Fenland, and more artefacts are found in the Thames. The previous chapter suggested that these features were directly related to one another: elites based in the ringworks and perhaps at other settlements controlled the flow of metalwork and engaged in long-distance exchange. They were able to do so because of the surplus provided by cattle raising and crop cultivation, and it even seems possible that these people were commemorated in death by the bronze objects deposited in water.

During the Early Iron Age, however, the distribution of weapon deposits contracted until it was practically confined to the Middle Thames (Jope 1961). There is much less evidence for occupation sites in the areas that had played such a prominent role before, and instead there are more signs of activity in other regions. In the south, these included the midlands, the upper reaches of the Thames, and the southwestern peninsula. In the north, there was a similar increase in settlement sites, especially in the uplands on either side of the modern border between Scotland and England. This may also have happened in Wales, although the evidence is limited, but in Ireland, Iron Age settlements of any kind are very difficult to find. That is partly because pottery was not used during this period (Raftery 1995). The best chance way of discovering the 'missing' sites is by dating the ore roasting pits and grain drying kilns which are commonly found in fieldwork. A few of these date from this period. On the other hand, there was probably a reduction in the cultivated area or in the intensity with which the land was exploited. That is certainly suggested by pollen analysis (Weir 1995).

On one level the new settlements took distinctly regional forms, just as the ceramics of this period can be divided into a series of mutually exclusive style zones (Cunliffe 2005: 90–7). To some extent these contrasts may also be deceptive as Chapter Four showed that Late Bronze Age settlements are difficult to identify except by large scale excavation. That is because so many of them were open sites and may be hard to recognise by other means. That is particularly true outside the distribution of regular field systems. Iron Age settlements, on the other hand, were sometimes enclosed by a palisade or more often by a bank and ditch (R. Thomas 1997). That was certainly the case in England, Scotland, and Wales, and it may have happened in Ireland, where aerial photography is revealing a variety of crop mark enclosures which do not conform to the standard types of field monuments (G. Barrett 2002). Despite some promising indications from rescue archaeology, they remain largely undated.

Roger Thomas (1997) has offered an interesting discussion of this phenomenon. He makes two important points. The process of enclosure began at about the same time as the decline in the supply of bronze entering these islands from the Continent. The new sites were usually associated with agricultural production, and there is every reason to suppose that Iron Age activity had an even greater impact on the landscape than that of the previous period. Excavations at these enclosures support this interpretation. They provide evidence for stock raising and cereal growing on a substantial scale and include a whole range of agricultural facilities within their area, in particular the sites of raised granaries or storehouses, and silos for keeping grain over the winter. Such sites can produce large collections of carbonised cereals, and faunal remains, almost entirely of domesticates (Fowler 1983). Thomas suggests that with the decline in the circulation of prestigious metalwork people were placing a greater emphasis on food production. Such evidence is so widely distributed that it is hard to disagree.

At the same time the building of boundaries may have had a further significance. Like their Late Bronze Age predecessors, individual houses seem to have been subdivided on the axis of the porch, and particular activities took place at specific locations within the building (Fitzpatrick 1997). The landscape was also divided according to some simple conventions, but in this case it was occupied by a number of communities who seem to have emphasised the differences between them by monumentalising the outer limits of their settlements. To an increasing extent they also imbued those boundaries with a special significance by the deposition of human bones and other items. This is a special feature of the enclosure ditch and the area around the entrance (Hill 1995: chapter 8). Few of these enclosures could be defended against attack. Roger Thomas (1997) suggests that the inhabitants of these places were increasingly self-sufficient and that this might even be related to concerns over succession and the inheritance of land from one generation to the next. It is certainly true that, once founded, many of these settlements were occupied and rebuilt over a considerable period of time.

The forms of these enclosures have attracted less attention than their chronology, and yet they support a similar interpretation (Fig. 5.4). The dominant feature of the Late Bronze Age ringworks had been large round houses like those at Mucking, Springfield Lyons, and Thwing. These were generally located within a circular enclosure whose defences could be built on an extravagant scale. Such buildings were generally aligned on the gateway, but could be separated from it by a screen. Like the henge monuments of the Later Neolithic period, the entire structure gives the impression of one enormous house, and this is even more obvious at a transitional site like West Harling, where the

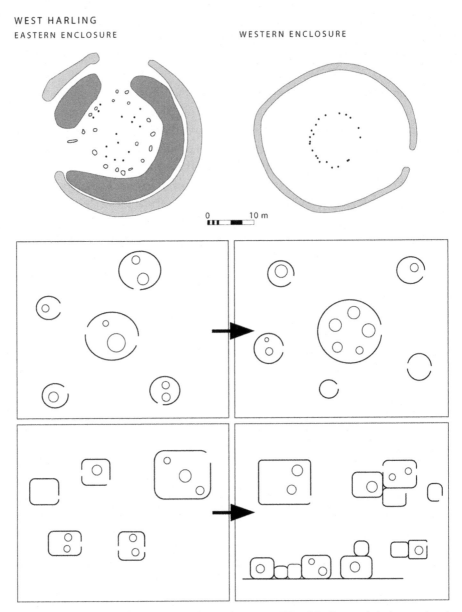

Figure 5.4. (Upper) The two circular enclosures at West Harling and their associated round houses, East Anglia. Information from Clark and Fell (1953). (Lower) Model suggesting the evolution over time of landscapes with circular and rectangular enclosures, respectively.

earthwork perimeter abutted the outer edge of such a building (Clark and Fell 1953).

Houses of similar size occur widely during the Early Iron Age, which runs from about 600 to 400 BC, but they are comparatively rare after that time. That is not to say that this was the standard form of dwelling. Rather, like the Late Bronze Age buildings that they resemble in so many respects, they were the largest examples in a wide range of timber structures. Their associations

Figure 5.5. An Iron Age round house under excavation at Yarnton in the Upper Thames Valley. Photograph courtesy of Gill Hey and Oxford Archaeology.

changed, too. Ringworks with their timbered ramparts were no longer built during the Early Iron Age, but large circular buildings could still be the dominant feature inside the new earthwork enclosures. Others occurred in some of the early hillforts discussed in a later section of this chapter.

What is less often considered is the importance of the circular or subcircular ground plan. This is not confined to the major houses but quite often extends to the earthwork perimeter as well. Again it is a format that applies to several different classes of monument: to palisaded enclosures, earthwork enclosures, and even to the organisation of many hillforts. It is by no means ubiquitous, but at its simplest it has two distinct elements. The perimeter is generally curvilinear, and it is frequently breached by an entrance to the east or south (Hill 1995: chapter 8). In both respects it resembles the plan of a round house. There can be some elaborations of this format. A second entrance may be provided on the opposite side of the circuit, but even this feature is shared with a number of large timber buildings, especially in northern Britain (D. Harding 2004: fig. 2.6). It is often argued that such buildings have their doorways to the south or east to allow the morning light to illuminate the interior, but the relationship between these houses and the position of the sun may have a cosmological significance as well, for such a practical argument can hardly explain why the same principle extended to the gateway to the settlement (Oswald 1997).

Not all the enclosures adopted this particular layout, nor were all settlements defined by a ditch or a palisade, but circular enclosures are far too common to have developed fortuitously. Others were roughly square or rectangular, but these variations usually follow regional lines. Thus circular enclosures are common in Wessex, or southwest England, for instance; rectilinear compounds are more often found in the east midlands and the Welsh Marches. One reason for these distinctions concerns the overall pattern of settlement. Like roundhouses, circular enclosures are usually set apart from one another. Rectilinear enclosures, however, can easily be joined together. Although many of them maintain their isolation, sometimes they are found in groups, as also happens in the Iron Age of northwest France (Arbousse Bastide 2000).

If there were practical advantages to a rectangular ground plan, why did so many communities in Britain choose to build circular enclosures? Was it to evoke connections with domestic architecture (Fig. 5.5)? The word 'house' usually refers to a residential building, but it can be used as a metaphor as well (Helms 2004). Thus the royal family in Britain is known as the House of Windsor. In this sense it relates not just to the place where they live but also to the social bonds that exist between them and distinguish them from other people. The term refers both to the members of an extended family and to a line of descent. One reason why the domestic building may have been such an important symbol during the Early Iron Age was that it stood for the integrity and independence of different communities. Perhaps that was less important in those regions where other kinds of enclosure were built. The question requires more research.

It is impossible to discuss the Irish evidence, but in most parts of Britain it is clear that large domestic buildings were gradually replaced by smaller circular structures. These are a particular feature of the Middle Iron Age, which ran from about 400 to 150 BC. For the most part they followed the same conventions as the earlier houses, but now it seem as if there were few, if any, significant differences of size between the individual dwellings. Indeed, they present such a uniform appearance that it seems almost as if any overt distinctions between them were suppressed. Like the buildings of the Late Bronze Age and Early Iron Age, they were normally replaced in exactly the same positions. Where this did not happen, successive structures overlapped, implying a set of conventions that were respected over the generations. Important thresholds within them could be marked by offerings of artefacts, animal bones, or even human remains (Bradley 2005b: 50–7). Again there seems to have been an emphasis on the continuity of the domestic group of the kind suggested by Roger Thomas (1997). At the same time, certain of the enclosures were reconstructed on an increasing scale. It is possible that the social distinctions that had been signified by domestic buildings now applied to the settlement as a whole. Perhaps the main differences of status were between the inhabitants of different sites and were expressed by the size and elaboration of the earthworks that enclosed them.

THE ORGANISATION OF THE LAND

Iron Age farming has always provided a major topic for research. Food remains are well preserved and many settlement sites have seen large-scale excavations. Surviving earthworks in England, Scotland, and Wales have all been the subject of field survey, and even the agricultural implements of this period have been studied in detail. The results of this endeavour have been tested by a series of experiments. These have been concerned not only with the practicalities of constructing Iron Age buildings but with raising livestock and cultivating crops. The Butser Ancient Farm on the chalk of southern England has been claimed as a working model of the prehistoric landscape (P. Reynolds 1979), and similar recreations of life in this period have provided the material for television programmes (Percival 1980).

As a result it might seem easy to characterise the archetypal Iron Age landscape, and exactly this assumption lay behind a series of important excavations on Fyfield and Overton Downs on the Wessex chalk (Fowler 2000). The results of that work were published recently and provide some indication of how far knowledge of this subject has changed. When the project was devised in the 1960s, it seemed important to investigate a series of Iron Age settlements, land boundaries and 'Celtic' fields which were located not far from a major hillfort. When the results of this project became available, those elements proved to be less closely related to one another than had originally been expected. The field systems which seemed to unite these different features actually dated from the Late Bronze Age and, like many others, had gone out of use in the Early Iron Age. One of the settlements was certainly integrated into this system of boundaries, but by the time it was established few of the plots were being used. Instead an open settlement was fitted into the surviving earthworks. Although it was accompanied by a small area of arable land, the system as a whole was derelict and may have been used as pasture. The project did not investigate the hillfort, Barbury Castle, but comparison with similar sites in the same region suggests that it would probably have included the remains of houses, granaries, and storage pits; this is indicated by its earthworks and by geophysical survey (Bowden 2005). Such monuments were closely integrated into the process of crop production, but may not have been linked with the use of regular field systems. How, then, was Iron Age agriculture organised?

Recent work by David Yates (2001) has shown that co-axial fields were established in lowland England during the Bronze Age. Chapter Four argued that they were first created on Dartmoor towards the end of the Earlier Bronze Age and that the same form of land organisation was adopted widely on the chalk and the river gravels of southern England during the later part of that period. Not all the systems initiated during the Middle Bronze Age remained in use for long, and new ones were certainly established in the Late Bronze Age. What is striking is that their distribution was limited to the region with the greatest density of metalwork deposits. It was also related to the areas with ringworks. Except in the Upper Thames, these systems went out of use during, or soon after, the transition to the Early Iron Age, and many of the associated settlements were abandoned. A second group of co-axial field systems was created towards the end of the Iron Age and covered a much larger area. That process continued into the Roman period and is not considered here (Fulford 1992). Not only were some of the relict field systems reused at that time, new ones were created. There is little sign of a similar development in Ireland.

In fact those changes should not have seemed so troubling, for some of the best recorded prehistoric landscapes are without surviving fields of any kind, even though there is evidence that crops were being grown. Perhaps the most obvious example is provided by the Yorkshire Wolds (Stoertz 1997). The problem needs to be approached in another way.

Certain points are clear. Environmental evidence shows that, unlike the situation in Ireland, the British landscape was largely open during the Iron Age and that it was being exploited on a large scale. There are signs of soil erosion caused by cultivation and excessive grazing, and carbonised cereals are virtually ubiquitous on excavated sites. So are the remains of domesticated animals (Fowler 1983). Many settlements in the south contain grain storage pits which sometimes preserve traces of their original contents, and where these do not occur there may be the foundations of timber granaries. The problem is not whether Iron Age people engaged in intensive mixed farming: it is how that activity was carried out on the ground. If Celtic fields went out of use, what does this imply for the nature of Iron Age society? If the older boundaries were no longer important, how was farming organised? That discussion must take in other elements: settlements, boundaries, and hillforts.

Chapter Four discussed the origin of the linear earthworks which divided up large tracts of the later prehistoric landscape. Many were poorly dated, but they seem to have originated during the early first millennium BC, and in central southern England they often cut across groups of coaxial fields in a way that would certainly have put them out of use (Bradley, Entwistle, and Raymond 1994; McOmish, Field, and Brown 2002: 56–67). The distribution of these boundary ditches was more extensive than that of field systems, and a second group of earthworks of Bronze Age origin has been studied in northeast England. One of its focal points was the great ringwork at Thwing (Stoertz 1997: fig. 42). Unlike the co-axial fields, these boundaries remained in use in the Iron Age. Indeed, more of them were built, and they occur across a much greater area. The simple banks and ditches that seem to characterise the earliest examples were increasingly supplemented by other kinds of feature, including multiple dykes and pit alignments.

Such changes happened in many areas, but they have been studied in particular detail on Salisbury Plain (Bradley, Entwistle, and Raymond 1994; McOmish, Field, and Brown 2002). Here large areas of co-axial fields had been established during the Middle and Late Bronze Ages. Some of their boundaries were aligned on older round barrows, and the original layout seems to have been associated with a number of small enclosures of the kind discussed in Chapter Four. During the Late Bronze Age a series of long linear earthworks was constructed which cut obliquely across many of the existing plots, meaning that some of them must have gone out of use. These ditches could also be orientated on older mounds. The new boundaries extended from the river valleys onto the high chalk plateaux and defined a series of elongated blocks of land, not unlike the parishes of the early medieval period. Each territory contained at least one

Figure 5.6. Linear ditches and associated settlements on the northern scarp of the Yorkshire Wolds, northeast England. They are associated with two hilltop enclosures, Staple Howe and Devil's Hill, and with a large open settlement on the lower ground. Information from Powlesland (1988).

open settlement, and beyond the limits of this system there were burnt mounds, sources of flint, and the findspot of a major metal hoard (Bradley, Entwistle, and Raymond 1994: 130–1). During the Early and Middle Iron Ages some of the earthworks were rebuilt, often on several occasions, and deposits of human bone and animal skulls were placed within them; similar material was associated with the boundaries of settlements. Certain earthworks were probably extended during this period and others were levelled (Bradley, Entwistle, and Raymond 1994). Curvilinear and rectilinear enclosures were built within these land blocks, whilst some of the points at which the separate territories converged became the sites of Iron Age hillforts. It was not until such monuments had gone out of use in the Late Iron Age that field systems were re-established on Salisbury Plain (ibid.: chapter 8).

A comparable process happened on the Yorkshire Wolds, where some of the boundaries were defined by lines of pits rather than ditches (Fig. 5.6).

Excavation at West Heslerton has shown that the land divisions long recognised on the chalk hills extended down into the Vale of Pickering to their north (Powelsland 1988). At least two of these territories were dominated by palisaded enclosures situated on prominent summits, whilst a large open settlement with round houses and raised granaries was identified on the lower ground. Another unenclosed settlement has been investigated in the valley known as Wetwang Slack (Dent 1982). This contained a similar range of structures distributed on one side of a prominent earthwork boundary which was maintained throughout the Iron Age. It is doubly important because a major cemetery developed there.

In Yorkshire and to some extent in Wessex, these linear earthworks coexisted with pit alignments, and there are even cases in which a discontinuous boundary was eventually replaced by a more substantial feature. In Lincolnshire and Yorkshire there was also a predilection for constructing several earthworks side by side (Boutwood 1998; Stoertz 1997). Such features are often very difficult to date as linear ditches might be recut many times. Pit alignments, on the other hand, had a more restricted currency and are easy to identify on air photographs (Wilson 1978). Their distribution extends across large areas of the English river gravels, into the Welsh borderland to the west and northwards into Scotland. It is unfortunate that so few of the boundaries have produced any artefacts, but what little dating evidence is available suggests that the earliest were built around the Bronze Age/Iron Age transition and the latest were probably constructed in the Middle Iron Age (Fig. 5.7). They are occasionally associated with human and animal burials and with deposits of quernstones and other artefacts. As so often, the chronology is more secure in regions with a well-defined pottery sequence and less precise in those areas where ceramics show less change or were little used. At present it is uncertain whether a similar boundary system developed in Iron Age Ireland.

Although these land divisions could have formed over a long period of time, they seem to have been employed in the same ways across a considerable area. They normally defined large blocks of land. Often the boundaries ran parallel to one another and at right angles to a river. Although the layout may have changed over time, the effect was to enclose substantial territories with a mixture of different resources extending from the floodplain onto the higher ground. A number of these units show some evidence of subdivision, but normally they are of similar extent to the land of a small modern farm. There are few signs of field systems within these enclosures, and what excavated evidence exists suggests that either they predate these boundaries or were created after those features had gone out of use (J. Taylor 1997). It does not seem likely that these different elements were contemporary with one another.

At the same time the large areas of land defined by these divisions might include the positions of one or more settlements, which varied considerably in their layout and their history. Some were established beside these boundaries

Figure 5.7. A pit alignment under excavation at the Cotswold Community Park in the Upper Thames Valley. Photograph courtesy of Gill Hey and Oxford Archaeology.

and could have been contemporary with them; others were located some distance away, but were situated within one of the blocks of land which they defined. It was unusual for any settlement to extend across such boundaries, and, when this happened, it was often because that feature had gone out of use. The settlements themselves might be open or enclosed and in many cases oscillated between these forms in the course of their history. Several settlements could be established within a single land unit, and where they were attached to the same boundary they have been described as 'clothesline enclosures'. Sometimes their use was quite short-lived, so that one occupation site replaced another, but just as often they coexisted. It is clear that the boundaries usually show a greater stability than the rather fluid pattern of activity within them.

There is some evidence to suggest that the individual settlements practised a specialised economy, but this is largely confined to a few regions, including Wessex (Cunliffe and Poole 2000a) and the Upper Thames (Lambrick and Allen 2004), and it is unlikely that these ditched territories had a single role. It is not possible to argue that they were reserved for grazing land. Rather, they seem to be associated with a mixed farming regime in which cultivation and the raising of livestock were both important. Nearly all the excavated settlements include large collections of faunal remains and are associated with carbonised cereals, raised granaries, and grain storage pits.

The main difference between the Bronze Age and Iron Age systems is that now there seem to have been no fixed boundaries within the separate land units; Celtic fields had virtually disappeared, although the sharp edges to the distribution of storage pits on sites in the Thames Valley suggests that more ephemeral boundaries did exist. They could have been established on the temporary basis, but they have left no trace behind. It is sometimes suggested that the landscape was broken up by hedges (Pollard 1996), but even these would have been bedded in a low earthwork if they were to flourish (Pryor 1998b: 87). At the same time, arable land needed to be protected from predators and the movement of livestock had to be controlled. Maybe this was achieved using a series of temporary divisions that could be changed on a regular basis.

A possible model is provided by Caesar's account of the early Germans (Thompson 1965: 10–11). Instead of being dominated by a social elite, decisions were made at a communal level and leaders were elected to serve on a temporary basis. Access to land was allocated every year, so that differences of wealth and power were reduced to a minimum. The distribution of agricultural produce may have been administered in the same way. This method had certain advantages, for it would be difficult to accumulate and control a surplus in the way that seems to have happened during other periods. This is simply an analogy since there was no direct connection between the inhabitants of Early Iron Age Britain and the people described by Roman writers, but it is very similar to George Lambrick's carefully researched reconstruction of the Iron Age landscape around Gravelly Guy in the Thames Valley (Lambrick and Allen 2004: chapter 12). It would certainly account for the surprising rarity of Early and Middle Iron Age field systems when they were used before and after that time; and it may also provide a reason why the houses within the settlements developed such a uniform character. If the Later Bronze Age had seen the growth of social distinctions, this phase illustrates their decline.

Figure 5.8. The defences of the major hillfort at Herefordshire Beacon, West Midlands.

It may also provide the background to the development of early hillforts in Britain; it is uncertain whether such monuments were in use over the same period in Ireland. They are widely distributed across the south and west. Barry Cunliffe dates them to the period between about 600 and 400 BC, and in some respects they follow a similar trend to the earthwork enclosures considered in the previous section (2005: 384–7). Some of the oldest examples, such as Crickley Hill (Dixon 1994) or Winklebury (K. Smith 1977), include unusually large round houses rather like those associated with Late Bronze Age ringworks, but the later buildings are smaller and are of roughly uniform size. If the first of these structures were used to express social distinctions, those differences had either disappeared or they were no longer emphasised. A second link concerns the 'defences' of these sites. They were built on a variety of different scales, and the more impressive examples often included ramparts that were reinforced with timber in the manner of an older site like Springfield Lyons (Buckley and Hedges 1987). The less-monumental examples were perhaps no different from other ditched enclosures. They have been identified as hillforts by their position in the landscape or because their earthworks have not been levelled by the plough, but, like the round houses of the Early Iron Age, such earthworks really form a continuum. That is not to deny that some of these places could have been attacked. A number of hillforts seem to have been destroyed by fire, particularly in western and northern Britain. These sites include Crickley Hill on the Cotswolds where the defences are associated with deposits of sling stones (Dixon 1994: 105 and 115–16).

Although Cunliffe distinguishes between 'early' and 'developed' hillforts, this is not based on major differences in their forms and associations but on their chronology and distribution. In general terms, the early hillforts were widely distributed, and some of them provide only limited evidence for the activities taking place inside them. The developed hillforts, whose history runs down to the second century BC, were fewer in number and in some areas may have been spaced at roughly equal intervals across the landscape. These sites generally provide more evidence of occupation (Cunliffe 2005: 388–96).

There were also some differences in their outward appearance (Fig. 5.8). The ramparts of the early hillforts were more likely to have a vertical outer face, supported by a stone wall or a setting of timbers, whilst later fortifications were often defined by a deep V-profile ditch and a steeply inclined bank so that a potential attacker was confronted by a continuous scree slope (Avery 1993). In the same way, the earlier sites often had two opposing entrances, whilst those used in later phases sometimes had only one which might be reinforced by a series of outworks (Cunliffe 2005: 365–74). Certain enclosures also increased their area at a late stage in their development.

How were these places related to the exploitation of the wider landscape? It has always been tempting to think of them as the power bases of a social elite, but it is difficult to find much evidence for that idea. In southern England a few of these sites, like Sidbury and Quarley Hill, were established at the meeting points of several of the territories defined by linear ditches (Bradley, Entwistle, and Raymond 1994; Cunliffe and Poole 2000a: chapter 4; Bowden 2005), and for the most part the artefacts associated with these places have a similar character to those found at other settlements in the same area. Perhaps these hillforts represented a more public expression of the same concerns as those sites. The main difference between these two categories is that in the hillforts certain activities were performed in a more ostentatious manner (Hill 1996). Thus the defences were sometimes constructed on an altogether larger scale than the domestic enclosures, yet there seems to have been as much emphasis on their appearance as there was on military architecture, and it is not always easy to see how they would have provided much defence against attack (Bowden and McOmish 1987). In the same way, hillforts in both the categories recognised by Cunliffe include an exceptionally large number of raised storehouses, which were probably used to hold grain (Gent 1983). These buildings were often the most conspicuous features of these sites, and in several areas, including the Wessex chalk and the Welsh Marches, they could be laid out in rows or organised on a grid. It may have been as important to display the harvested crop as it was to protect it (Fig. 5.9).

A number of recently excavated hillforts also contain specialised structures which have been interpreted as shrines, but their chronology varies from site to site. At Danebury they were used throughout the occupation (Cunliffe 1984: 83–7), yet at Cadbury Castle a similar building was not constructed until the use

MOEL Y GAER

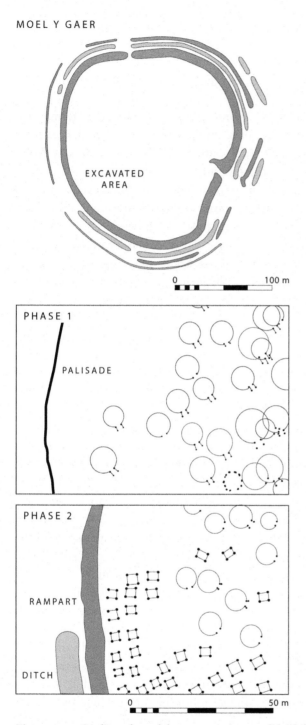

Figure 5.9. Outline plan of the excavated area of the hillfort at Moel Y Gaer, north Wales, showing the dense distribution of round houses and possible storehouses associated with successive phases of activity on the site. Information from Guilbert (1981).

of the hilltop was largely over, some time after the Roman Conquest (Barrett, Woodward, and Freeman 2000: 170–3). Before then, the same area had been used for the production and deposition of bronze metalwork and for a series of animal burials. Even these specialised buildings have parallels on other kinds of site.

The animal burials at Cadbury Castle recall the wide range of offerings that are associated with Iron Age settlements, although much of the evidence comes from a small number of regions: central southern England, the south midlands, East Anglia, northeast England, the Hebrides, and Orkney. Their main association seems to be with food production and the agricultural cycle, although they extend from the burial of selected artefacts to the treatment of the dead (Whimster 1981; Hill 1995; M. Williams 2003). Such deposits are found in a series of different contexts which may have changed their locations over time, but they are especially common in hillforts. Some were associated with the perimeters of these sites, and others with earthwork enclosures, land boundaries, and the edges of open settlements. Such deposits were directly linked with the storage of food, so they are found in grain silos in southern Britain or in souterrains in Orkney. The human remains reveal some striking patterns. In certain cases there were important differences between these groups, so that in the hillfort at Danebury the remains of adults were kept separate from those of the very young who were associated with the positions of the houses (Cunliffe and Poole 1991b: chapter 8). In the open settlement at Glastonbury adult skulls were distributed along the edge of the settled area, and the remains of children were found in the platforms where people lived (Coles and Minnit 1995: 17–24 and fig. 8.10). More might be learnt from excavation outside the settlements themselves as recent excavations in East Anglia, Wessex, and the Thames Valley have located small inhumation cemeteries (Hey, Bayliss, and Boyle 1999).

What distinguishes the sites known as hillforts from the other earthwork enclosures of the Early and Middle Iron Ages? Apart from their size and the labour devoted to their construction, there seem to be three important features. These monuments include a greater density of storage facilities than other sites. That applies not only to the raised granaries mentioned earlier but also to the evidence of pits. Given the comparatively limited number of houses inside the excavated hillforts, it seems unlikely that so much food was produced by the occupants of these sites (Gent 1993). Although the raised storehouses could have displayed food for consumption, the pits most likely held seed corn.

At the same time, there is more evidence for ritual practices in hill forts than there is in the settlements of the same period (Hill 1996). These focused on the process of crop production, and the main focus was the grain storage pit. They contained a series of deposits but may have been selected because of their links with the cycle of death and regeneration associated with the harvesting and keeping of grain. Such notions of fertility and renewal may have extended to the treatment of the dead.

Lastly, the houses inside some of the hillforts have a different character from many of those at other sites. They are often more ephemeral structures with light stake walling, and some were even built of turf. They were often rather smaller than their counterparts on other sites and may not have been inhabited on a permanent basis. That is also implied by the creation of building platforms inside the hillforts at the Wrekin (Stanford 1984) and Dinorben (Guilbert 1981), for they are not associated with the remains of any recognisable structures. The same idea is suggested by the insects preserved by a pond within the developed hillfort of the Breidddin on the Welsh border, for despite the presence of houses and granaries within this enclosure, the use of the site had little impact on the local environment (Buckland et al. 2001). Similarly, some of the storage pits inside the Wessex hillfort of Winklebury seem to have been left open over the winter, trapping a number of wild animals which must have been living on the site (K. Smith 1977: 111). In other cases there may have been more houses and other features outside the defences than there were within them, again suggesting that this space may have played a specialised role. That is certainly the implication of recent fieldwork at three of these sites: Wittenham Clumps in the Upper Thames valley (T. Allen pers. comm.), Wandlebury in eastern England (French 2004), and Cadbury Castle in the southwest (Tabor 2004).

The relationship between hillforts and ordinary settlements remains quite problematical. The defended sites contain rather slighter traces of domestic buildings, and yet they have a higher density of storehouses and pits. A few of them seem to have included shrines, whilst the proportion of special deposits exceeds that at other sites. They were closely associated with the agricultural cycle and the keeping of grain (M. Williams 2003). Large numbers of people obviously made use of these places, but it is not clear that they settled there on a permanent basis (Lock, Gosden, and Daly 2005: chapter 4). In many ways these were public monuments which reflected the concerns of people during this period and emphasised them on an impressive scale (Bradley 2005b: 168–77). Indeed, the very form of some of these hillforts still seems to echo the basic principle of the round house. They can adopt a roughly circular ground plan with an entrance that faces the rising sun; Danebury provides a good example. Such places may have been conceived as the houses of an entire community who could have used them in much the same way as an early medieval assembly (Pantos and Semple eds. 2003). Perhaps they were where communal business was transacted and important decisions were made. Again Caesar's description of the early Germans could be relevant to the argument. Such an arrangement would not have been unprecedented for it is also the interpretation suggested for the middens which are such a striking feature of the Late Bronze Age/Early Iron Age transition. It may have been through periodic meetings in such places that land and its products were distributed among the population. That did not require a permanent elite.

In fact the very term 'hillfort' is probably a misnomer. At times they may have served as fortifications, as places where resources were protected from attack, but they were also production sites and even a kind of theatre at which public events took place and the concerns of a farming people were played out in ritual and ceremonial. That may have changed only towards the end of their period of use.

If so, then it may be possible to suggest how some of the same activities could be organised at other kinds of site. In southwest England, for example, the wetland settlements of Glastonbury and Meare are associated with an extraordinary abundance of artefacts, in spite of their rather marginal location (Coles and Minnit 1995; J. Coles 1987). The authors of the most recent accounts of these two sites suggest that they acted rather like medieval fairs, as seasonal meeting places where goods were made and exchanged and where social transactions took place. The same interpretation might apply to other areas that were occupied on a discontinuous basis or where large numbers of people gathered for only part of the year, like the East Anglian Fens (Evans 2003) or the Severn Estuary (Bell, Caseldine, and Neumann 2000). A further possibility is that much older monuments were brought back into use by the wider community. One candidate is the henge monument of the Devil's Quoits in the Upper Thames Valley (Fig. 5.10). George Lambrick has suggested that it was surrounded by a large area of open pasture which was shared by the occupants of a number of different settlements (Lambrick and Allen 2004: chapter 12). Another example might be the Ferrybridge henge in northeast England. In this case the area outside the Neolithic monument was enclosed by a series of pit alignments associated with human burials, and a sword scabbard was deposited inside the ancient enclosure (Roberts 2005: 229–31). The activities that took place at the most famous hillforts may have happened in other places too.

VARIATIONS ON AN ORIGINAL THEME

If these features represent the main currents in the archaeology of the Iron Age, in some parts of Britain they were expressed in a very different way. Virtually nothing is known about Irish settlements of the late first millennium BC (Raftery 1994), but it is clear that those in western Britain possessed a distinctive character. This is not a unique feature of insular prehistory, for there are similar sites in a number of regions along the Atlantic seaboard of Europe, including Finistère, Galicia, and northern Portugal. In each case the settlement pattern was dominated by a dense distribution of small fortified enclosures (Cunliffe 2001a: 336–539). These were often circular constructions, but along the coast they could be supplemented by a distribution of promontory forts. These in Brittany are often compared with examples in southwest England.

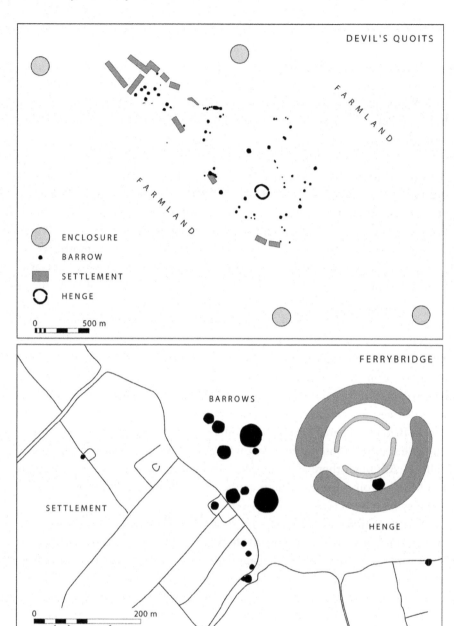

Figure 5.10. (Upper) The henge monument of Devil's Quoits, Upper Thames Valley, and the areas occupied by enclosures and open settlement in the Iron Age. (Lower) The henge monument at Ferrybridge, northeast England, compared with the distribution of Iron Age enclosures and land boundaries outside it. Information from Lambrick and Allen (2004) and Roberts (2005).

There are other links between the regions along the western limit of the Continent. In the Iberian peninsula the circular enclosures or *castros* were normally associated with round houses – it was only during the Roman period that they were replaced by rectangular buildings – and, where more impressive defences were built, they could be supplement by a chevaux de frise: a setting of upright stones so called because it was thought to impede attackers on horseback. Their distribution is revealing for, like that of the round houses, it focuses on Britain and Iberia. Examples are found on sites in north and west Wales, in eastern and southwest Scotland, and along the west coast of Ireland (Harbison 1972). Their overall chronology is uncertain, and individual examples could be earlier or later than the period considered here.

Several distinctive features characterise the earthwork enclosures of western Britain, including those of the Isle of Man. Most of them are fairly small, but individual examples can be massively defended. In southwest Wales the entrance is sometimes screened by monumental outworks (Fig. 5.11; Cunliffe 2005: chapter 13). They contain a relatively small number of circular houses as well as raised storage structures, but their relationship to one another is not consistent from one site to the next. At Walesland Rath the putative granaries lined the inner edge of the rampart, and the houses were in the middle of the enclosure (Wainwright 1971); at Woodside they were to the right of the gateway, and the dwellings were towards the rear of the enclosure; whilst at Dan Y Coed the positions of both groups of buildings overlapped (Williams and Mytum 1998). Another way of providing secure storage was by constructing a kind of cellar. In Cornwall, it took the form of a stone-lined trench, roofed by a series of lintels, and in this case it could be associated with an individual house (Christie 1978: 314–33). These features are called *souterrains* and occur also in Brittany. There is no obvious difference between the structures found on these sites and those in the larger enclosures which are usually described as hillforts. Although there are some signs of open settlements during the Early and Middle Iron Ages, enclosures are densely distributed across the landscape and may have been largely self sufficient.

Apart from differences of size – most of the enclosures are small – the main distinctions between them concern the scale of the surrounding earthworks. In west Wales and southwest England many of them conformed to a precisely circular ground plan, as if to echo the same principle as the round house. It was a tradition that was to last into the post-Roman period in Britain (Quinnell 2004), when it had its counterpart among early ring forts in Ireland. The latter normally contain circular buildings (M. Stout 1997), but these structures were quite similar to one another. The early medieval Irish laws show that it was the scale of the perimeter earthwork that was the main way of displaying status. It was carefully controlled, so that the number of concentric earthworks enclosing a settlement site might have been related to the social position of its occupants (Edwards 1990: 33). Perhaps a similar model would explain the evidence from western Britain in the pre-Roman period.

There were other regions with a dense distribution of small circular enclosures. These include the uplands of northern England and southern Scotland, where the field evidence can be exceptionally well preserved. The pattern

WOODSIDE

DAN-Y-COED

COLLFRYN

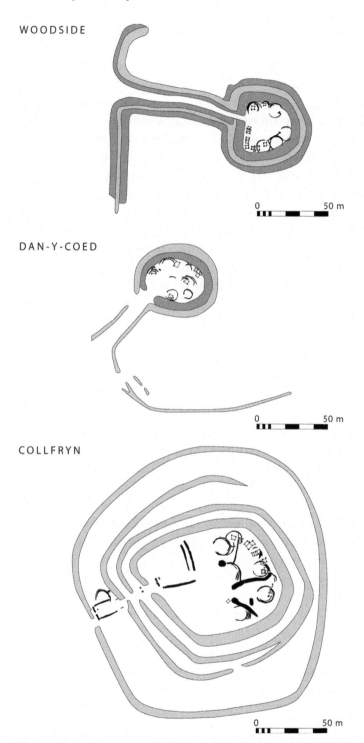

0   50 m

0   50 m

0   50 m

Figure 5.11. Two Iron Age enclosed settlements in southwest Wales (Woodside and Dan Y Coed) and a more elaborate enclosure in north Wales (Collfryn), showing the distribution of round houses and square storehouses or granaries. Information from Williams and Mytum (1998) and Britnell (1989).

extends further up the North Sea coast, but here there may have been a higher proportion of open sites (Armit and Ralston 2003). It is clear that the basic pattern goes back to the beginning of the Iron Age and that on either side of the border between England and Scotland individual sites might be rebuilt on an increasingly impressive scale, so that an enclosure could be defined first by a palisade, and then by a low earthwork (Fig. 5.12); some sites were eventually defended by a substantial rubble wall. The main feature inside these enclosures was the round house (Hingley 1992). These structures occurred in varying numbers, from a single example to a dense distribution of buildings, but some of them were as large as any dwellings occupied during this period. Individual settlements can be associated with plots of cultivated land which may have been worked by hand (Topping 1989), but there is no sign of any specialised storage structures. The upland enclosures have their counterparts on the lowland soils, but they are more difficult to interpret as few artefacts or food remains survive. The results of commercial excavation show that open sites also existed there. In central and northeast Scotland houses within these settlements were often associated with souterrains (Armit and Ralston 2003).

It is difficult to say whether the upland enclosures which have dominated the discussion were inhabited all year round. Many of them were in exposed places on the high ground and might have been inhospitable or inaccessible in winter. Moreover, the houses rarely show much sign of maintenance or repair, suggesting that they had not been occupied for long (Halliday 1999). The same problems affect the large hillforts of highland Britain (D. Harding 2004: 58–66). They are strongly defended, they were built in dominant positions, and they enclose the sites of many round houses, but it is difficult to see how they could have been inhabited continuously. They might have been used during the summer months when climatic conditions were more favourable, but in any case the sheer density of internal buildings is not consistent with the character of the local environment which might not have been capable of supporting a large population. Again it is tempting to suggest that these were aggregation sites, used on an occasional basis and possibly in the course of summer grazing. A number of these monuments adopted a curvilinear ground plan.

The tendency to build self-contained circular enclosures reached its apogee in western and northern Scotland, and especially in the Hebrides, Orkney, and Shetland (Fig. 5.12). Unfortunately some of the strongest patterning has been obscured by disagreements about terminology and chronology (Armit ed. 1990; Armit 1992; Parker Pearson and Sharples 1996: chapter 12; D. Harding 2004: chapter 5).

Again the circular archetype was very important and extended from individual dwellings to more monumental walled enclosures. All these features were conceived on an impressive scale. They vary from the crannogs built in open water to small circular compounds, and from relatively insubstantial dwellings to massive domestic buildings, the most impressive of which – the brochs of the Scottish mainland, the Western and Northern Isles – resemble towers (Armit

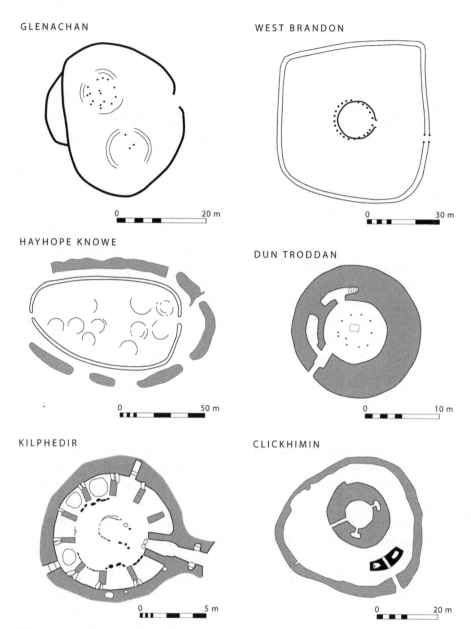

Figure 5.12. Outline plans of five Iron Age sites in Scotland and one (West Brandon) in northeast England. All illustrate the importance of the round house in its different forms. Dun Troddan is a broch, and the defences at Clickhimin enclose another structure of this type. Kilphedir is a wheelhouse. Glenachan, West Brandon, and Hayhope Knowe are bounded by single or double palisades. At Hayhope Knoll there is also an earthwork enclosure. Information from D. Harding (2004).

2003b). Some of these structures are isolated but quite densely distributed and were surely designed to impress, whilst others can be found inside defended enclosures which contain a variety of other buildings. Many of them were distributed along the coast where there were a number of promontory forts (Armit 1992).

Here is another case in which large round houses may have been an important settlement form from an early stage of the Iron Age. Ian Armit (2003b) has argued that structures ancestral to brochs were built as early as 600 BC and that during the Iron Age stone houses in Atlantic Scotland became increasingly complex in design. True brochs seem to have emerged about 200 BC. They are interpreted as defended high-status dwellings, characterised by such features as internal staircases and guard cells. They must have had more than one storey, and there can no longer be any doubt that they were roofed.

Some of the structural principles that characterise the brochs extend to other forms of defensive architecture: to some of the circular walled enclosures known as duns and even to the monumental gateways of a number of the promontory forts in Shetland (Hamilton 1968; D. Harding 2004: 137–50). Another key element is the way in which domestic structures were organised. In some brochs there seems to have been a communal space with a hearth located in the centre of the building. It was ringed by a range of compartments which were divided from one another by partitions projecting from the interior wall. In Shetland and the Hebrides, this principle was expressed on a smaller scale in the distinctive dwellings known as wheelhouses (Parker Pearson and Sharples 1999: chapter 12). A number of these were built after the broch themselves, and it has yet to be worked out how far their histories overlapped. In any case there are important contrasts between them. Wheelhouses were sometimes set into the ground, whereas brochs were conspicuous monuments, and on certain sites the domestic accomodation was probably at first floor level (Armit 2003b: chapter 3). Wheelhouses were sometimes associated with souterrains, but the connection between storage structures and individual dwellings is entirely different from the more centralised system illustrated by hillforts in southern Britain.

In many ways the Scottish sites combine the two of the key elements discussed so far, the enclosure and the round house, and sometimes they fused them together in a single structure (Parker Pearson and Sharples 1996). But a very different tradition remains to be defined. If the Atlantic round houses are conspicuous features of the northern landscape, the settlements of eastern England have left little trace, and most are known from air photography or from small-scale excavation. Others have been found as scatters of surface artefacts.

In his study of Iron Age Britain Barry Cunliffe suggests that the region between the Thames and the Humber was dominated by 'villages and open settlements' (2005: figs. 4.3 and 21.6). That pattern extended westwards as far as the zone of hillforts that follows the modern border between England and Wales. The division is not clear-cut, for earthwork enclosures are common in both the midlands and the Thames Estuary, and some hillforts occur in both those areas. Moreover, open settlements are among the largest occupation sites on the Yorkshire Wolds (Dent 1982; Powelsland 1988). Such regional divisions only describe broad tendencies in the evidence, but there is considerable variation. At the heart of this zone is East Anglia. Enclosed sites are not

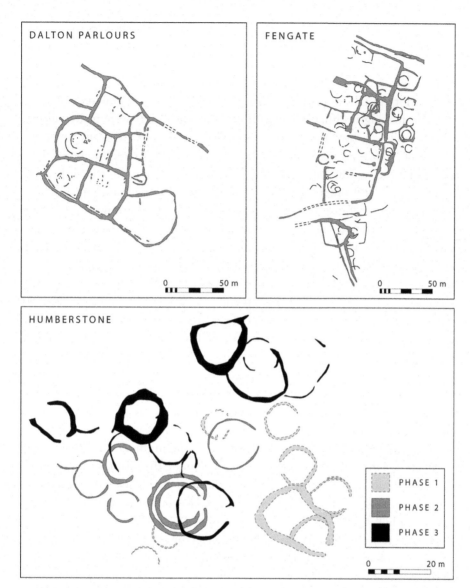

Figure 5.13. Three open settlements in eastern England. Dalton Parlours, northeast England, and Fengate, East Anglia, are characterised by conjoined enclosures, whilst the excavated area at Humberstone, East Midlands, shows shifts in the distribution of occupation in successive phases. Information from Wrathmell and Nicholson (1990), Pryor (1984), and Charles, Parkinson, and Foreman (2000).

particularly common here, and not all of them need have been settlements, as it is possible that they played a specialised role (Martin 1988). Although some standing earthworks have been identified as hillforts, there is little evidence that they were used intensively (Davies et al. 1991; Evans 2003). Instead, occupation sites extend over considerable areas, sometimes changing their centre of gravity over time (Fig. 5.13; Hill 1999). There were few fixed boundaries, although individual houses or small groups of houses might have been located in compounds within a more extensive living area. These houses were inter-spersed with granaries and storage pits. In some cases rectilinear compounds were built onto one another as the settled area increased: a process that would have been more difficult in a landscape of circular enclosures.

It is not clear how many of the structures were contemporary with one another, making it difficult to decide whether these sites were really villages. Nor is it obvious how much of the occupied area was in use at any one time. J. D. Hill (1999) has made an interesting comparison between some of these places and the 'wandering settlements' of the same date in Northern Europe, where houses and other structures were often abandoned and replaced after a limited period of use (Gerritsen 1999, 2000). Their positions often shifted, but over a restricted area so that the dwellings occupied during successive phases had mutually exclusive distributions. In eastern England that process could easily have generated the large areas of buildings, pits, and ditches that now survive. Some sites may be as much as ten hectares in extent. Another possibility is that certain of the settlements resulted from the amalgamation of smaller units as larger numbers of people elected to live together in one place and to give up such independence as they had once possessed. That would be the opposite of the situation on the chalk of southern England, and it is certainly suggested by the chronological evidence from East Anglia, where there were few large occupation sites during the Early Iron Age. The emergence of these settlements seems to be a later development, and the relationships between their separate elements may be expressed by the ways in which compounds and even individual dwellings were joined on to one another over time (Bradley 1984: 140). This may have been one way of defining the relationships between different groups of people. If the occupation sites served large communities in this way, it may explain why there was less need to coordinate activities through the use of hillforts.

In some respects this chapter has followed a conventional sequence, starting with some of the larger enclosures and hillforts, then turning to smaller sites in the north and west before finally considering the large open settlements of eastern England. That reflects the extent of current knowledge, where certain regions have been intensively excavated at the expense of others, but it may not reflect the actual situation in prehistory. For all the labour invested in their construction, the hillforts could have been a rather peripheral phenomenon, on the margin of a more prosperous and perhaps more expansive system with its emphasis on the North Sea coast. Perhaps it would be better to think in even broader geographical terms, so that the large open settlements of eastern England could be treated as the local equivalents of similar sites in Northern Europe (Hill 1999), whilst the enclosed sites of southern England might be compared with their counterparts in the north of France. The tradition of building small but monumental enclosures along the west coast of Britain could then be accepted as part of a still-wider phenomenon extending southwards

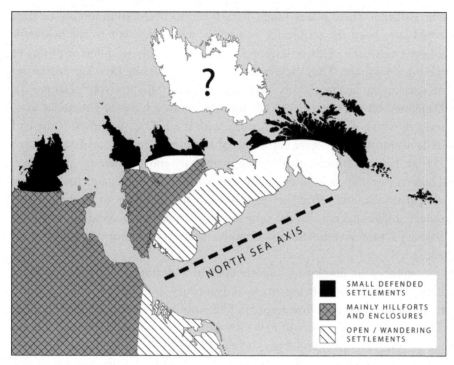

Figure 5.14. The character of Iron Age settlement in Britain and the near-Continent.

into Atlantic Europe (Cunliffe 2001a). That mental adjustment would involve turning the map of Britain on its side so that the North Sea became the dominant axis (Fig. 5.14). That would provide a corrective to accounts of this period which are conceived on too small a scale, but any new scheme will be incomplete until more is discovered about the Irish Iron Age.

AN END OF ISOLATION

It may be difficult to envisage such broad alignments, but they seem to be implied by the convergence of British and Irish archaeology with the prehistory of the European mainland. This involved two related processes. The first were changes in local patterns of settlement, whilst the second saw the renewal of relationships with the Continent. As part of that process activities in Ireland assumed a growing importance.

Cunliffe's interpretation of the hillforts of southern England suggested that there were gradual changes in the ways in which they were used. Although the details of his argument have proved controversial, there seems no doubt that some of his developed hillforts did assume new roles towards the end of their history (Cunliffe 2005: 388–96). One finding is of particular importance. Two of the largest projects carried out at these sites involved fieldwork in and around Danebury and Maiden Castle, each of which contained houses, pits, granaries, and a shrine. These places might have been occupied continuously or they could have been the setting for communal assemblies, but recent fieldwork suggests that each of these interpretations might apply to different phases in their development. Thus there is little sign of any Middle Iron Age enclosures or settlements in the vicinity of Maiden Castle (Sharples 1991: chapter 3). Danebury, on the other hand, was located amidst a series of settlement sites, most of which were used concurrently with the hillfort, but towards the end of its occupation they were apparently abandoned (Cunliffe and Poole 2000a: 181–2). It seems possible that people might have moved there for protection. There is certainly skeletal evidence that some of its inhabitants had suffered violent deaths, and other sites provide similar indications of warfare at this time. Cunliffe suggests that the same sequence took place around the hillfort of Barbury Castle, mentioned earlier in this chapter (Cunliffe 2005: 393; Bowden 2005).

A number of developed hillforts contain a distinctive assemblage. Sheet bronze artefacts were being made at Danebury and Maiden Castle during their later phases (Northover 1984). The same happened at Cadbury Castle. This is only one of a series of new associations. Swords are also found at these places (Piggott 1950), and from the third century BC, so are iron currency bars which are recorded from no fewer than seventeen of these sites (Hingley 2005). Another clue to the changing role of the last hillforts has been suggested by John Creighton, who draws attention to the increasing importance of the horse, both as a symbol of power displayed on the earliest pre-Conquest coins and for its use in warfare (2000: 15–17). Bronze horse bits are another artefact associated with the last use of southern English hillforts (Jope 2000: 152–60). Perhaps the roles of these sites had changed. Recent excavations have also found the remains of horses in a number of specialised deposits in eastern England.

Until the Middle Iron Age there was no sign of a regular burial rite in Iron Age Britain. In Ireland, the situation is equally confusing. Ring barrows may still have been used there, but few of their contents can be dated (Raftery 1994: 189). In southern England the remains of the dead were treated in other ways and were often associated with settlement boundaries or with storage pits (Hill 1995).

It was in the fourth century BC that formal cemeteries developed in at least two regions of England (Whimster 1981: chapters 3 and 4); others may have existed outside the settlements of this period, but they have not been recognised until recently (Hey, Bayliss, and Boyle 1999). Each of the burial traditions possessed a distinctly regional character, although in both cases bodies were laid out in the ground according to the same conventions as those in pits. On the other hand, each of these traditions was also linked with a different region of Europe.

The first of these groups is found in southwest England and has some features in common with Iron Age cemeteries in Brittany and the Channel Islands

Figure 5.15. An Iron Age vehicle burial at Ferrybridge, northeast England. Photograph courtesy of Alan Lupton and Oxford Archaeology North. Reproduced by permission of the Highways Agency.

(Whimster 1977; Whimster 1981: chapter 3; Burns, Cunliffe, and Sebire 1996). All these sites were located near to the sea and contained inhumation burials, which, unlike their Continental counterparts, assumed a crouched position. They were in use between the fourth century BC and the first century AD. There was one body to a grave, and they were usually associated with personal ornaments such as brooches, bracelets, and pins. One of the best known of these sites was at Harlyn Bay and may have been associated with a timber round house, but it is not clear whether this formed part of a settlement or whether it had played a more specialised role connected with the treatment of the dead. Three of the brooches from Harlyn Bay were probably imported from Spain (Whimster 1981: 60–9).

The distinctive Iron Age burials of the Yorkshire Wolds are much better known and have often been discussed because of their striking similarity to those found in Champage, the Ardennes, and the Middle Rhine (Dent 1982;

Stead 1991). Their currency is roughly similar to that of the cemeteries in southwest England. They probably originated during the fourth century BC, but may have gone out of use during the first century BC when settlements expanded over the sites of some of the graves.

These burials have been attributed to a unitary 'Arras Culture', but in some respects they are surprisingly diverse. The best known are a small series of vehicle burials, which may have occasional counterparts elsewhere in eastern and southern Britain (Fig. 5.15); another has recently been excavated at Newbridge on the outskirts of Edinburgh (Carter and Hunter 2003). They resemble their Continental counterparts in many ways, but again the details of the funeral rite are subtly different and so are the associated artefacts. The vehicles were usually dismantled and the bodies were laid out in the crouched position that characterises other mortuary traditions of the British Iron Age. Even the associated artefacts are British versions of European prototypes (Stead 1991).

The same applies to the barrow cemeteries in northeast England. They consist of dense concentration of square mounds, defined by a shallow ditch which allows these distinctive monuments to be recognised from the air. They developed over a long period of time but probably increased in number during the late third and second centuries BC. Again many of the burials were laid out according to a specifically British tradition, and they were accompanied by a small selection of personal ornaments which were generally insular versions of Continental forms (Stead 1991).

There is a further subgroup of Arras Culture graves which needs to be considered here, for in many respect it differs from the norm. These contained extended inhumation burials accompanied by weapons – swords and spears – and are a particular feature of the Makeshift cemetery at Rudston (Stead 1991: 6–15 and 185–208). They seem to be a late development within this local tradition and are probably related to a series of isolated 'warrior burials' found in other parts of these islands (Collis 1973). There are only a small number of them, and their distribution extends across lowland England with a distinct concentration in Wessex. Outlying examples of burials with swords are recorded from central Scotland, north Wales, and the east coast of Ireland (Fig. 5.16; Hunter 2005). They are important because they suggest that the symbolism of conflict and warfare was becoming more important during the later part of this period. That is surely confirmed by a series of small chalk sculptures found on the Yorkshire Wolds which depict warriors carrying swords (Stead 1988). Like the changing character of southern and western British hillforts, this evidence suggests that the egalitarian ethos of the earlier Iron Age was breaking down.

The most extensively excavated barrow cemetery in Yorkshire is at Garton and Wetwang Slacks (it has two names because it crosses a modern parish boundary). It was established beside a linear earthwork and was located on a site which already included a series of mortuary monuments of earlier

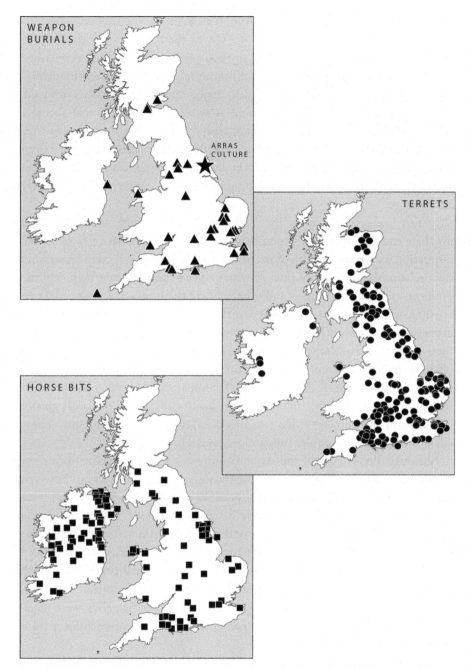

Figure 5.16. Distributions of weapon burials, terrets, and horse bits in the British and Irish Iron Ages. Information from Hunter (2005) and Jope (2000).

prehistoric date (Brewster 1981; Dent 1982). It is important because the ceme-tery developed alongside a large open settlement which contained the usual mixture of round houses, raised granaries, and storage pits. What is especially interesting is that there are few convincing signs of social divisions within the living area, even though the cemetery itself contained some exceptionally rich burials. There are certain anomalies – a few of the houses departed from the usual easterly alignment (Parker Pearson 1999); some of the buildings contained large deposits of animal bone of a kind more familiar in southern England – but it would be impossible to postulate major differences of status from the buildings in the settlement. Moreover, it is surely significant that the one region of Britain to posses a tradition of weapon graves does not seem to have included any hillforts of the same date. Even though the skeletal evidence from the cemeteries shows that certain individuals had engaged in combat (Dent 1983), there is no indication of anything that might be interpreted as military architecture.

In fact the evidence from the Yorkshire Wolds is quite anomalous, and nowhere more so than in the combination of square barrows of Continental inspiration with round houses of an entirely insular kind. It is hard to understand their relationship. There are cases in which square mounds were built over the positions of circular dwellings and others where these two types respected one another, suggesting that the houses of the dead were replaced by mortuary monuments, but both halves of the same complex seem to have maintained their distinctive character over time (Fig. 5.17; Dent 1982). Perhaps this is most obvious from the concentration of infant burials associated with certain of the houses at Garton Slack (Brewster 1981). Similar deposits are widespread in Iron Age Britain, and yet the burials of adults were carried out with greater formality in the cemetery that was located alongside the living area. These curious relationships require much more research.

Although the burials of the Arras Culture are rather different from their Continental counterparts, there was obviously a close relationship between them: so much so that it is perfectly possible that the Yorkshire Wolds were settled from overseas. The distinctive artefacts associated with some of the graves pose a more general problem, for they clearly form part of a much wider network that extended across large parts of Europe and takes its name from the Swiss site of La Tène (Raftery 1984; Jope 2000). The forms of the British artefacts were clearly inspired by those produced on the European mainland, but there is little to suggest that they were imports. Rather, they were made according to specifically local techniques and often show regional distinctions of their own.

If this observation applies to some of the grave goods of the Arras Culture, it is even more relevant to the archaeological sequence on the other side of the Irish Sea (Raftery 1984, 1994). Because pottery went out of use at the end of the Bronze Age, settlement sites have been very difficult to identify. So few have been investigated by excavation that it is understandable that most attention has focused on portable artefacts, particularly metalwork and querns. This approach is inescapable but it poses many problems. Most of the metalwork comes from votive deposits in rivers, bogs, and lakes, and a smaller

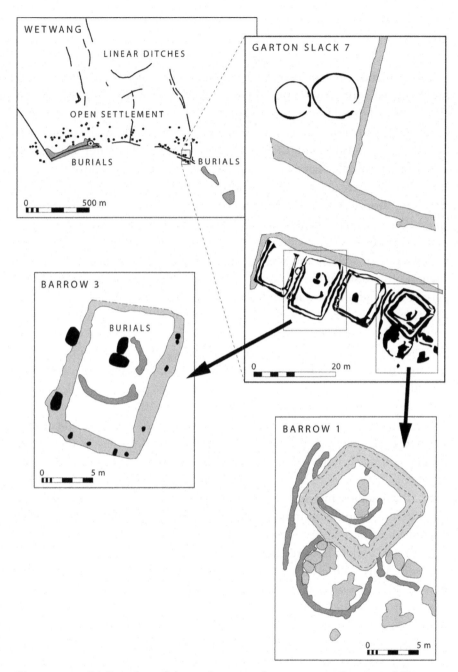

Figure 5.17. Outline plan of the settlement and cemetery at Garton and Wetwang Slacks, northeast England, with details showing the close relationship between round houses and square barrows. Information from Dent (1982) and Brewster (1981).

amount is found in hoards. It is rarely associated with burials, and only a few graves contain brooches or other ornaments which recall the La Tène style of decorated bronzes. The querns, on the other hand, are domestic artefacts and seem to be virtually indestructible, but even these could assume a special character. Again some of them seem to have been placed in bogs, whilst others were decorated in the same style as late pre-Roman metalwork: a style that also extends to a small series of decorated standing stones (Raftery 1984: 290–303).

This evidence presents two rather different problems. There are very few finds of metalwork between the end of the Irish Bronze Age and the adoption of new styles inspired by developments on the Continent from perhaps the third century BC. Either fine artefacts were no longer being made, or the tradition of depositing them had lapsed (Bradley 1998b: chapter 4). The latter seems more likely for it is a trend that can be recognised across much of northwest Europe. It is certainly preferable to the attempts that once were made to extend the Irish Late Bronze Age to cover any apparent gap in the sequence (Champion 1989). The second problem is that when the circulation of fine metalwork – or, more accurately, its use as offerings – began again, the evidence was confined to only part of Ireland and was entirely missing from the south. The same applies to the distribution of rotary querns which should date from the same period, although they are absent from an even larger area (Raftery 1994: 124). How are such anomalies to be explained? Perhaps the best solution is to focus on the supposedly mundane artefacts. They were obviously used for grinding grain and seem to have replaced the less efficient saddle querns, but the reasons for this change are rarely considered. Did this happen simply because they were more effective, or was it really because the new technology allowed the processing of larger amounts of food? In that case they could have played an important social role. Maybe they were most important in contexts that required large scale consumption, and that may be why a few of them were lavishly decorated. Indeed their distribution may overlap with that of La Tène metalwork because both were associated with the activities of an elite. In the south, the sequence may have continued as before. There could have been less role for conspicuous consumption and here a simpler way of treating cereals continued.

The metalwork of Iron Age Ireland raises similar issues to the artefacts associated with Arras Culture burials; and there are stylistic links between them. Very little of this material could have been imported directly from the Continent, and yet it conforms to the same basic styles of decoration as the metalwork found across large parts of Western Europe. The quality of these objects is quite exceptional and includes not only small personal items such as brooches and pins, but swords with decorated hilts and scabbards, spearheads, cauldrons, and horse harness. This must have been produced by specialists working for a patron and surely provides evidence for the growth of a new elite, whose concerns included riding, feasting, and warfare (Creighton 2000: chapter 1). Much of this material may have been used to communicate social status, but in the end it was employed in votive deposits. Irish archaeologists have sometimes asked themselves whether the appearance of so much wealth was the result of settlement from overseas, but the distinctly insular style of this material argues against that idea. Rather, it suggests that Ireland was increasingly integrated into a social network that extended into Continental Europe.

Much the same can be said about the fine metalwork produced in Britain, which Martyn Jope (2000) considered was made with increasing frequency from the third century BC. Unfortunately this has not played a major role in studies of the Iron Age. Instead many of the objects have been treated as 'Celtic art' and regarded as a specialist field in themselves. Apart from the relatively rare objects found in graves, these artefacts lack an obvious archaeological context for, like so many of their counterparts in Ireland, they are generally found in rivers rather than dry land (Fitzpatrick 1984). This evidence occurs in most parts of Britain and Ireland, but perhaps the best documented group comes from Fiskerton in the Witham Valley, where a timber causeway was associated with a large number of tools and weapons dating from this period (Field and Parker Pearson 2003). In certain respects such deposits recall Bronze Age sites like Flag Fen, but this case is subtly different, as similar material is sometimes found in graves.

The finest metalwork of the Iron Age is too often studied in isolation. That is unfortunate as it loses sight of some of the connections that have already been suggested in this chapter. In particular it overlooks the evidence for the production of these objects which has been identified during recent years. This shows that some of the finest metalwork – weapons, ornaments, and specialised equipment for feasting and horse riding – was produced not only in certain of the developed hillforts but also at a series of other settlements of the same period (Foster 1980). It provides a clue to the sheer scale on which such items were made, for it is obvious from the clay moulds that survive that many more fine objects were being manufactured than found their way into the archaeological record. That is hardly surprising, for exactly the same problem has been identified in the Later Bronze Age.

The La Tène style extended into other spheres and is represented by decorated pottery in several areas of Britain, including parts of East Anglia and the east midlands (Cunliffe 2005: 106–13), but it is not found in the same area as the Arras Culture burials (Rigby 2004). That is interesting, for the distribution of square barrows seems to extend into both these regions, although it avoids the southwest, where another ceramic style, Glastonbury Ware, has similar decoration. It is not clear whether these vessels played a specialised role, although they were particularly common in an enclosure at Weekley which seems to have been attached to a larger settlement with a different pottery assemblage. This enclosure was associated with a round house, with finds of three iron spears and with evidence of metalworking (Jackson and Dix 1987).

A small selection of other artefacts, often personal ornaments, have been identified in excavations, but many more as known as chance finds. Their distribution is very striking indeed (Jope 2000). The most elaborate metalwork, which is often described as parade armour, is mainly associated with the rivers discharging into the North Sea. The principal concentrations of surface finds echo this distinctive pattern and seem to be concentrated in the zone of large unenclosed settlements in eastern England. Although there are many exceptions, the best provenanced artefacts often come from sites of that kind, although very few examples have been excavated. They also include artefacts made of gold, whose use had lapsed since the Late Bronze Age. It seems increasingly likely that the large open settlements in this area provided the power base of an elite, but again there is a need for more research.

SUMMARY

It is difficult to sum up such a wide range of evidence, particularly when it comes from so many sources: the later use of hillforts in some areas; the evidence of burials in others; large open settlements with a range of distinctive surface finds; and the fine metalwork found in rivers. Even so, they lead to a similar conclusion.

This discussion began by considering the social impact of a diminishing supply of bronze from overseas. Access to this material had been one source of social power, and food production may well have been reorganised so that local leaders could participate in exchange. As those connections fell away, their political power was threatened and, with it, their ability to participate in long distance alliances. There followed a period of comparative isolation, in which internal social differences were less apparent and the community itself may have played a more important role. The house became the dominant symbol of this period, and its characteristic layout may have influenced the organisation of enclosures and fortifications. Control over agricultural land and its products seems to have been of central importance.

That egalitarian ethos was not to last, and from about the fourth century BC in parts of Britain there was a greater emphasis on certain individuals, expressed through the development of new burial rites. They were closely related to practice in Continental Europe, and that link was emphasised even more strongly from about the third century BC by the adoption of a new suite of fine metalwork of foreign inspiration, even if most of the products were of local manufacture. Although these special artefacts had rather different associations, a similar process affected much of Britain, and in particular the east coast, as well as the northern half of Ireland. The circulation of these objects suggests some new concerns: the display of personal wealth and adornment, feasting, horse riding and the use of wheeled vehicles, and, above all, the importance of armed conflict. The latter is surely expressed by the later burials of the Arras Culture and perhaps by the changing character of the major hillforts, and yet it was around the open settlements of the North Sea coast that much of the new wealth was concentrated. That may have been partly because there was greater scope for the expansion of population into this area, but perhaps it was also because the more open landscape presented fewer impediments than the dense network of enclosures and boundaries that was found further inland. Still more important, this was a zone with ready access to the sea and easy communications with Continental Europe. In that respect the new system that developed had much in common with the political geography of the Late Bronze Age.

Between the fourth and second centuries BC both Britain and Ireland were more closely integrated with the European mainland than had been the case for many years, and it is no accident that it was in this period, around 320 BC, that Pytheas made the famous voyage described in Chapter One. It seems clear that by then these islands already played a part in long-distance trade. It is sometimes claimed that it was the northward expansion of Roman power that provided the catalyst for changes in the insular sequence (Cunliffe 1988), but the chronological developments considered here suggest that it merely accelerated processes that were already under way. British society was very different when Julius Caesar first invaded lowland England in 55 BC, and between his second expedition and the Claudian Conquest nearly a century later a more profound economic and political transformation took place (Millett 1992; Creighton 2000, 2006). These processes tend to overshadow the more subtle developments that have been considered here, but it is to see events through the eyes of Classical writers to believe that it was the influence of Rome that was the only important issue. As Chapter One has demonstrated, those authorities knew little about the societies that they were describing, and could not understand the geography of the countries where those people lived.

That is not to underestimate the importance of trade with the Roman world, but it deserves a book in itself, and so do the intricate political relationships that developed between different areas before and after the Conquest of AD 43. Fortunately, such work is already available and rightly advances the view that the archaeology of the Late Iron Age is best studied in relation to a much longer process of interaction with Rome which did not even end with the withdrawal of her army from Britain in AD 410 (Millett 1992). There was considerable variation during this period of cultural contact, and it took too many guises for it to be considered here. Over four thousand years the archaeo-logical sequence had assumed very different forms, but now in quick succession societies in lowland Britain experienced the development of the state and even their incorporation into a foreign empire. These two islands were no longer inconceivable places on the very edge of the world. They had lost something of their mystery.

THE END OF PREHISTORY

Four brief vignettes will serve to illustrate the course of events, two of them in what was to be the heart of the Roman province of Britannia, and the other two well beyond its limits.

The first of these examples falls into the latter category. This is Navan Fort in northern Ireland (Waterman 1997). It is best known as the legendary capital of the kingdom of Ulster and the home of the gods of the underworld, but the archaeological sequence has much to add to what is known of its legendary associations. This was one of the Late Bronze Age ringworks discussed in Chapter Four, but, unlike the other examples, it remained in use throughout the pre-Roman Iron Age. During that period it consisted of a circular earthwork enclosure with a sequence of substantial round houses at its centre. It was not until the beginning of the first century BC that the scale of the monument increased significantly, and it may be no accident that during the later pre-Roman Iron Age there is unusual evidence for long-distance contacts along the Atlantic coastline. Excavation of the monument between 1961 and 1971 brought to light the skull of a barbary ape, which must have been introduced to the site from its natural habitat in Gibraltar or North Africa. Its authenticity is confirmed by radiocarbon dating. At the same time the landscape to the south of Navan Fort was subdivided by massive linear earthworks, part of a system of such features that seem to be contemporary with the royal centres in the north of the island (Raftery 1994: 83–97). A great timber road was built at Corlea during this phase (Raftery 1996: 418–22), and the entire hill at Navan was enclosed by an earthwork which resembled a Neolithic henge. Its Iron Age date was established by a recent excavation (Mallory 2000).

At the centre of this enclosure there was what may have been the largest round house ever constructed, a massive wooden building thirty-seven metres in diameter with a gigantic post at its centre (Fig. 5.18). According to dendrochronology the timber was felled in 95 or 94 BC. Unlike a domestic structure, it seems to have been entered from the west, the position of the setting sun. It seems likely that this was actually roofed, but it contained no hearth, nor were any domestic artefacts found inside it. No sooner had it been constructed than it its interior was packed with rubble and the outer wall was set on fire, then, once it had collapsed, it was buried beneath an enormous mound. Richard Warner (2000) is surely right when he suggests that the site was regarded as an entrance to the underworld and that this building was the house of the deities who dwelt there. The purely archaeological evidence is extraordinary, and this monument surely took the symbol of the circular building to its limits.

The second example is the broch of Gurness on the Mainland of Orkney (Figs. 5.19 and 5.20; Hedges 1987: Part 2). Its chronology is less well understood, but again it would be easy to overemphasise its geographical isolation. Not only did the Romans make a treaty with the inhabitants of Orkney, even that distant archipelago includes finds of Roman imports (Fitzpatrick 1989). Gurness is one of a series of monuments in the Northern Isles which have been interpreted as enclosed villages (D. Harding 2004: 116), for the broch itself is at the centre of what would once have been a circular enclosure with two concentric banks and ditches (part of the monument has been lost to coastal

NAVAN FORT
TIMBER BUILDING

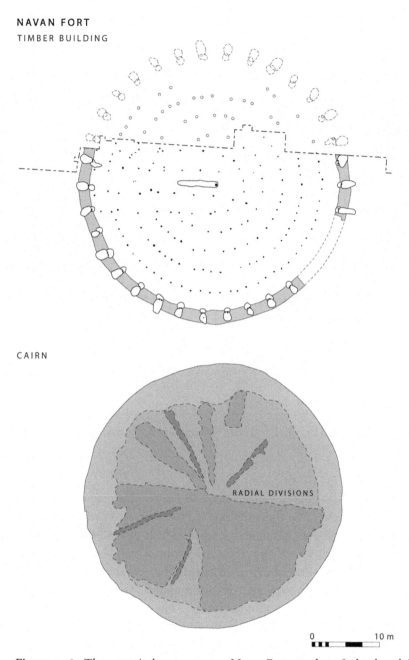

CAIRN

RADIAL DIVISIONS

0   10 m

Figure 5.18. The great timber structure at Navan Fort, northern Ireland, and the cairn that was built after its destruction by fire. Information from Waterman (1997).

erosion). Both the enclosure and the broch have their entrances to the east, and these are actually aligned on one another. In between the central structure and the earthwork perimeter was a whole series of other buildings, whose interpretation is far from clear; nor is the site record good enough to establish their sequence of development (McKie 1995). Even so, the plan has such a

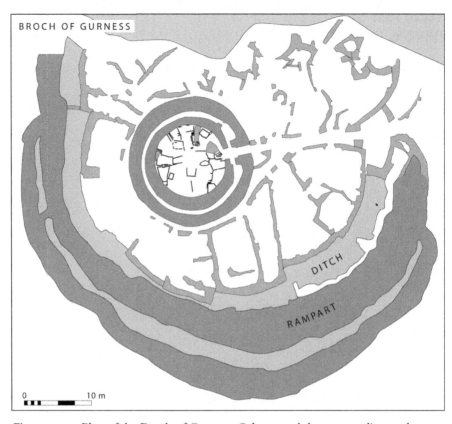

Figure 5.19. Plan of the Broch of Gurness, Orkney, and the surrounding settlement. Information from Hedges (1987).

unitary character that it was obviously conceived as a single design. Like other brochs, the monument at Gurness was divided between a central space with a hearth, and a series of compartments arranged radially around the inner wall. Within this building there was also a curious feature which was interpreted as a well. It was a complex structure reached down a flight of steps, but it may not have played an entirely practical role, as recent excavation at Mine Howe on the same island has investigated a similar feature. This was built at the centre of a large earthwork enclosure and was associated with evidence of metalworking and with deposits of human bone (Card and Downes 2003).

One feature of Gurness is quite remarkable, although a similar argument might apply to other broch villages in Orkney and Shetland. The basic plan of the site is a circle set within a larger circle. The interior of the central monument is subdivided by a series of radial divisions, and the same is true of the area in between its outer wall and the defensive earthworks which are occupied by a whole series of less imposing buildings. The effect is rather like that of a set of Chinese boxes, one inside the other, so that the entire complex could be interpreted as a single enormous dwelling. Like the timber building

Figure 5.20. The Broch of Gurness, Orkney.

at Navan Fort, it adopted the principle of the circular house and reproduced its features on a monumental scale.

Both those sites were beyond the periphery of the Roman Empire, but the last two examples were more closely integrated with Continental Europe. The first was Hengistbury Head, a defended promontory on the coast of the English Channel commanding the sheltered waters of Christchurch Harbour (Cunliffe 1987). The site was occupied throughout the Iron Age but played a major role in two distinct phases (Fig. 5.21). At the beginning of the period it seems to have been one of a series of coastal settlements which were actively engaged in overseas trade during the Bronze Age/Iron Age transition. During this phase the excavated part of the site was dominated by an unusually large round house, comparable to those further inland on the Wessex chalk. Hengistbury Head became even more important during the period in which southern Britain was again involved in regular contact with the mainland, and at this stage it seems to have acted as both a seaport and a production site. It enjoyed a wide range of contacts extending from Northern and Western France to southwest England, and it was through this site that metals were exported to the Continent and a variety of exotic commodities, chiefly wine, were introduced. Only a small part of the site has been excavated, but it seems possible that the internal area was reorganised at this time. There may have been a grid of square enclosures on Hengistbury Head, and the same is evidenced much more clearly at a nearby site that took its place, Cleavel Point on the shore of Poole Harbour (Sunter and Woodward 1987: 44–124). Not far away at Green Island a massive pier or jetty was built (Markey, Wilkes, and Darvill 2002). Southern Britain

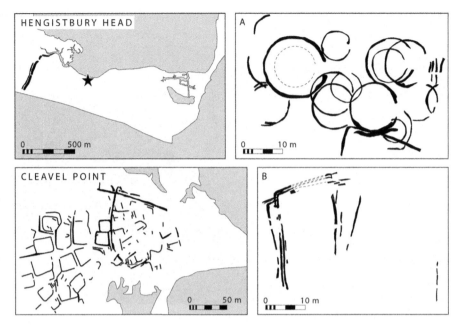

Figure 5.21. Two Iron Age coastal settlements. A and B show successive phases in the occupation of the excavated area at Hengistbury Head, Wessex. The second phase is compared with an outline plan of the Late Iron Age and Roman coastal settlement at Cleavel Point nearby. Information from Cunliffe (1987) and Sunter and Woodward (1987).

increasingly formed part of a wider network which extended well beyond that island.

The final example is Silchester, a royal capital of the Late Iron Age which was eventually replaced by a major Roman town (Fig. 5.22; Fulford and Timby 2000). It was bounded by a large earthwork enclosure. It enjoyed a wide range of outside contacts extending to the Continent and was engaged in craft production, including the minting of coins. These are features that occur on other major sites of this period, some of which are interpreted as royal residences. There were two main groups of Iron Age buildings, deeply buried beneath the Roman levels. The first consisted of the fragmentary remains of what were apparently circular houses of the kind that is discovered on practically any settlement of this period. The second group, which probably replaced them, consisted of rectangular buildings that were arranged in an orderly layout and conformed to a grid of metalled roads. There were also traces of a considerable palisaded enclosure which followed the same orientation. It dates from the early first century AD. The buildings were associated with a wide variety of artefacts which showed the close connections between the inhabitants of Silchester and the Roman world. These extended to particular forms of social behaviour, including the consumption of wine, to imported foodstuffs and to Classical notions of hygiene and bodily adornment.

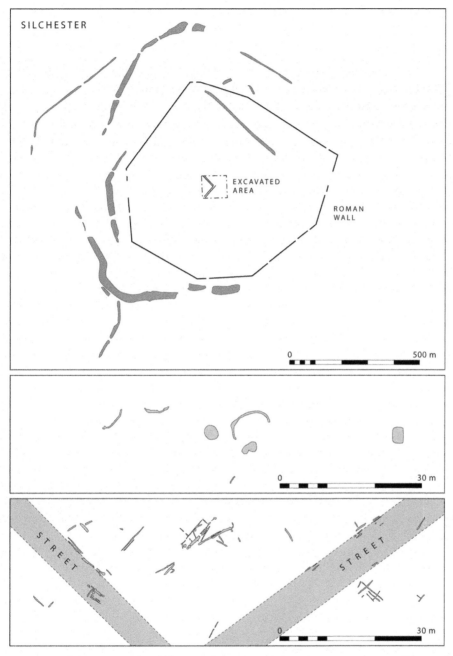

Figure 5.22. (Upper) The defences of the Iron Age and Roman site at Silchester, Wessex. (Lower) Successive pre-Roman structures in the excavated area. Information from Fulford and Timby (2000).

Similar buildings have been found at other sites in lowland England and seem to have been influenced by Roman prototypes, but Silchester is remarkable in two other ways. The site was little used before the Late Iron Age and has even been interpreted as a deliberate creation: a very different process from the gradual expansion of settlement that happened over much of southern England. At the same time, the best parallels for the rectangular houses and the grid of streets are not found in Britain but in the north of France (Pommepuy et al. 2000). It seems as if new practices and new forms of communal life were developing and that older ways of living were rejected.

That is surely the point at which to end this account. Prehistory and Roman archaeology flow into one another, but a transformation of this kind requires a new kind of study. It would be a fitting subject for another volume in this series.

BIBLIOGRAPHY

Aalen, F., Whelan, K. and Stout, M. 1997. *Atlas of the Irish Rural Landscape*. Cork: Cork University Press.

Albarella, U. and Serjeantson, D. 2002. A passion for pork: Meat consumption at the British Late Neolithic site of Durrington Walls. In P. Miracle and N. Milner (eds), *Consuming Passions and Patterns of Consumption*, 33–49. Cambridge: McDonald Institute for Archaeological Research.

Allen, M. 2005. Beaker settlement and environment on the chalk downs of southern England. *Proceedings of the Prehistoric Society* 71, 219–81.

Allen, M. and Gardiner, J. 2002. A sense of time: Cultural markers in the Mesolithic of southern England? In B. David and M. Wilson (eds.), *Inscribed Landscapes: Marking and Making Place*, 139–53. Honolulu: University of Hawai'i Press.

Allen, T. 2002. Eton College Rowing Course at Dorney. *Current Archaeology* 181, 20–5.

Allen, T., Barclay, A., and Landin-Whymark, H. 2004. Opening the wood, making the land: A study of a Neolithic landscape in the Dorney area of the Middle Thames Valley. In J. Cotton and D. Field (eds.), *Towards a New Stone Age. Aspects of the Neolithic in South-east England*, 82–98. London: Council for British Archaeology.

Andrews, P. 2006. A Middle to Late Bronze Age settlement on Dunch Hill, Tidworth. *Wiltshire Studies* 99, 51–78.

Annable, K. and Simpson, D. 1964. *Guide Catalogue to the Neolithic and Bronze Age Collections in Devizes Museum*. Devizes: Wiltshire Archaeological Society.

ApSimon, A. 1986. Chronological contexts for Irish megalithic tombs. *Journal of Irish Archaeology* 3, 5–15.

Aranyosi, E.F. 1999: Wasteful advertising and variation reduction: Darwinian models for the significance of non utilitarian architecture. *Journal of Anthropological Archaeology* 18, 356–75.

Arbousse Bastide, T. 2000. *Les structures de l'habitat rural protohistoriques dans le sud-ouest de l'Angleterre et le nord-ouest de la France*. Oxford: British Archaeological Reports (BAR International Series 847).

Arias, P. 1999. The origins of the Neolithic along the Atlantic coast of Continental Europe: A survey. *Journal of World Prehistory* 13, 403–64.

Armit, I. (ed.). 1990. *Beyond the Brochs: Changing Perspectives on the Scottish Iron Age*. Edinburgh: Edinburgh University Press.

Armit, I. 1992. *The Later Prehistory of the Western Isles of Scotland*. Oxford: British Archaeological Reports (BAR 221).

Armit, I. 2003a. The Drowners: Permanence and transience in the Hebridean Neolithic. In I. Armit, E. Murphy, E. Nelis, and D. Simpson (eds.), *Neolithic Settlement in Ireland and Western Britain,* 93–100. Oxford: Oxbow.

Armit, I. 2003b. *Towers in the North: The Brochs of Scotland*. Stroud: Tempus.

Armit, I., Dunwell, A., Hunter, F., and Nelis, E. 2005. Traprain Law: Archaeology from the ashes. *Past* 49, 1–4.

Armit, I. and Finlayson, B. 1992. Hunter-gatherers transformed: The transition to farming in northern and western Europe. *Antiquity* 66, 664–76.

Armit, I. and Ralston, I. 2003. The Iron Age. In K. Edwards and I. Ralston (eds.), *Scotland after the Ice Age*, 169–93. Edinburgh: Edinburgh University Press.

Ashbee, P. 1960. *The Bronze Age Round Barrow in Britain*. London: Phoenix House.

Ashmore, P. 1999. Radiocarbon dating: Avoiding errors by avoiding mixed samples. *Antiquity* 73, 124–30.

Atkinson, R. 1956. *Stonehenge*. Harmondsworth: Penguin.

Atkinson, R. 1979. *Stonehenge*. Revised edition. Harmondsworth: Penguin.

Aubet, M. E. 2001. *The Phoenicians and the West*. 2nd edition. Cambridge: Cambridge University Press.

Avery, M. 1993. *Hillfort Defences of Southern England*. Oxford: British Archaeological Reports (BAR 231).

Ballin-Smith, B. 1994. *Howe. Four Millennia of Orkney Prehistory*. Edinburgh: Society of Antiquaries of Scotland.

Barber, J. 1997. *The Archaeological Investigation of a Prehistoric Landscape: Excavations on Arran 1978–81*. Edinburgh: Scottish Trust for Archaeology for Research.

Barber, M., Field, D., and Topping, P. 1999. *The Neolithic Flint Mines of England*. London: English Heritage.

Barclay, A. 2002. Ceramic lives. In A. Woodward and J. D. Hill (eds.), *Prehistoric Britain: The Ceramic Basis*, 85–95. Oxford: Oxbow.

Barclay, A. and Bayliss, A. 1999. Cursus monuments and the radiocarbon problem. In A. Barclay and J. Harding (eds.), *Pathways and Ceremonies: The Cursus Monuments of Britain and Ireland*, 11–29. Oxford: Oxbow.

Barclay, A. and Halpin, C. 1999. *Excavations at Barrow Hills, Radley, Oxfordshire*. Oxford: Oxford Archaeological Unit.

Barclay, A. and Harding, J. (eds.). 1999. *Pathways and Ceremonies: The Cursus Monuments of Britain and Ireland*. Oxford: Oxbow.

Barclay, A. and Hey, G. 1999. Cattle, cursus monuments and the river: The development of ritual and domestic landscapes in the Upper Thames Valley. In A. Barclay and J. Harding (eds.), *Pathways and Ceremonies: The Cursus Monuments of Britain and Ireland*, 67–76. Oxford: Oxbow.

Barclay, A., Gray, M., and Lambrick, G. 1995. *Excavations at the Devil's Quoits, Oxfordshire*, Oxford: Oxford Archaeological Unit.

Barclay, G. 1996. Neolithic buildings in Scotland. In T. Darvill and J. Thomas (eds.), *Neolithic Houses in North-west Europe and Beyond*, 61–75. Oxford: Oxbow.

Barclay, G. 2001. 'Metropolitan' and 'parochial / core' and 'periphery': A historiography of the Neolithic of Scotland. *Proceedings of the Prehistoric Society* 35, 1–18.

Barclay, G., Brophy, K., and MacGregor, G. 2002. Claish, Stirling: An early Neolithic structure and its context. *Proceedings of the Society of Antiquaries of Scotland* 132, 65–137.

Barclay, G. and Maxwell, G. 1998. *The Cleaven Dyke and Littleour*. Edinburgh: Society of Antiquaries of Scotland.

Barclay, G. and Russell-White, C. 1993. Excavations in the ceremonial complex of the fourth to second millennium BC at Balfarg, Glenrothes, Fife. *Proceedings of the Society of Antiquaries of Scotland* 123, 43–210.

Barfield, L. and Hodder, M. 1987. Burnt mounds as saunas and the prehistory of bathing. *Antiquity* 61, 370–9.

Barnatt, J. 1989 *Stone Circles of Britain*. Oxford: British Archaeological Reports (BAR 215).

Barnatt, J. 1998. Monuments in the landscape: Thoughts from the Peak. In A. Gibson and D. Simpson (eds.), *Prehistoric Ritual and Religion*, 92–105. Stroud: Sutton.

Barnatt, J., Bevan, B., and Edmonds, M. 2002. Gardom's Edge – A landscape through time. *Antiquity* 76, 51–6.

Barnatt, J. and Collis, J. 1996. *Barrows in the Peak District: Recent Research*. Sheffield: J. R. Collis Publications.

Barnatt, J. and Edmonds, M. 2002. Places apart? Caves and monuments in Neolithic and Earlier Bronze Age Britain. *Cambridge Archaeological Journal* 12, 113–29.

Barrett, G. 2002. Flights of discovery: Archaeological air survey in Ireland 1989–2000. *Journal of Irish Archaeology* 11, 1–29.

Barrett, J. 1994. *Fragments From Antiquity*. Oxford: Blackwell.

Barrett, J. and Bradley, R. 1980. Preface: The ploughshare and the sword. In J. Barrett and R. Bradley (eds.), *Settlement and Society in the British Later Bronze Age*, 9–13. Oxford: British Archaeological Reports (BAR 83).

Barrett, J. and Bradley, R. (eds.). 1980. *Settlement and Society in the British Later Bronze Age*. Oxford: British Archaeological Reports (BAR 83).

Barrett, J., Bradley, R., and Green, M. 1991. *Landscape, Monuments and Society: The Prehistory of Cranborne Chase*. Cambridge: Cambridge University Press.

Barrett, J. and Fewster, K. 1998. Stonehenge: *Is the medium the message? Antiquity* 72, 847–52.

Barrett, J., Lewis, J., and Welsh, K. 2000. Perry Oaks – A history of inhabitation. *London Archaeologist* 9.7, 195–9.

Barrett, J., Woodward, A., and Freeman, P. 2000. *Cadbury Castle, Somerset: The Later Prehistoric and Early Historic Archaeology*. London: English Heritage.

Beckensall, S. 1999. *British Prehistoric Rock Art*. Stroud: Tempus.

Bedwin, O. 1979. The excavations at Harting Beacon, West Sussex: Second season, 1977. *Sussex Archaeological Collections* 117, 21–35.

Bell, M. 1983. Valley sediments as evidence of prehistoric land use on the South Downs. *Proceedings of the Prehistoric Society* 49, 119–50.

Bell, M., Caseldine, A., and Neumann, H. 2000. *Prehistoric Intertidal Archaeology in the Welsh Severn Estuary*. York: Council for British Archaeology.

Bell, M. and Walker, M. 2004. *Late Quaternary Environmental Change*. 2nd edition. London: Edward Arnold.

Bennett, P. and Williams, J. 1997. Monkton. *Current Archaeology* 151, 258–64.

Bergh, S. 1995. *Landscape of the Monuments*. Stockholm: Riksantikvarieämbet Arkeologiska Undersöknigar.

Besse, M. and Desideri, J. 2005. La diversidad Campaniforme: hábitats, sepulturas y cerámicas. In M. Rojo-Guerra, R. Garrido-Pena and I. García-Martínez de Lagrán (eds.), *El Campaniforme en la Península Ibérica y su contexto Europeo*, 61–105. Valladolid: Universidad de Valladolid.

Bishop, B. and Bagwell, M. 2005. *Iwade. Occupation of a North Kent Village from the Mesolithic to the Medieval Period*. London: Pre-Construct Archaeology.

Boast, R. 1995. 'Fine pots, pure pots, Beaker pots'. In I. Kinnes and G. Varndell (eds.), *Unbaked Urns of Rudely Shape*, 69–80. Oxford: Oxbow.

Bond, D. 1988. *Excavation at North Ring, Mucking, Essex: A Late Bronze Age enclosure*. East Anglian Archaeology 43.

Bonsall, C., Macklin, M., Anderson, E., and Payton, R. 2002. Climate change and the adoption of agriculture in north-west Europe. *European Journal of Archaeology* 5, 9–23.

Bourke, L. 2001. *Crossing the Rubicon: Bronze Age Metalwork from Irish Rivers*. Galway: Department of Archaeology, National University of Ireland, Galway.

Boutwood, Y. 1998. Prehistoric land boundaries in Lincolnshire and its fringes. In R. Bewley (ed.), *Lincolnshire's Archaeology from the Air*, 29–46. Lincoln: Society for Lincolnshire Archaeology and History.

Bowden, M. 2005. The middle Iron Age on the Marlborough Downs. In G. Brown, D. Field, and D. McOmish (eds.), *The Avebury Landscape, Aspects of the Field Archaeology of the Marlborough Downs*, 156–63. Oxford: Oxbow.

Bowden, M. and McOmish, D. 1987. The required barrier. *Scottish Archaeological Review* 4, 67–84.

Bowen, E. G. 1972. *Britain and the Western Seaways*. London: Thames and Hudson.

Bowen, H. C. 1970. *Ancient Fields*. Wakefield: S. R. Publishers.

Bradley, R. 1970. The excavation of a Beaker settlement at Belle Tout, East Sussex, England. *Proceedings of the Prehistoric Society* 36, 312–79.

Bradley, R. 1975. Maumbury Rings, Dorchester: The excavations of 1908–13. *Archaeologia* 105, 1–97.

Bradley, R. 1978. *The Prehistoric Settlement of Britain*. London: Routledge.

Bradley, R. 1981. 'Various styles of urn': Cemeteries and settlement in southern England c. 1400 – 1000 BC. In R. Chapman, I. Kinnes, and K. Randsborg (eds.), *The Archaeology of Death*, 93–104. Cambridge: Cambridge University Press.

Bradley, R. 1983. The bank barrows and related monuments of Dorset in the light of recent fieldwork. *Proceedings of the Dorset Natural History and Archaeological Society* 105, 15–20.

Bradley, R. 1984. *The Social Foundations of Prehistoric Britain*. Harlow: Longman.

Bradley, R. 1987. Flint technology and the character of Neolithic settlement. In A. Brown and M. Edmonds (eds.), *Lithic Analysis and Later British Prehistory*, 181–185. Oxford: British Archaeological Reports (BAR 162).

Bradley, R. 1988. Hoarding, recycling and the consumption of prehistoric metalwork:

Technological change in western Europe. *World Archaeology* 20, 249–260.

Bradley, R. 1991. The pattern of change in British prehistory. In T. Earle (ed.), *Chiefdoms: Power, Economy and Ideology*, 44–70. Cambridge: Cambridge University Press.

Bradley, R. 1992. The excavation of an oval barrow beside the Abingdon causewayed enclosure, Oxfordshire. *Proceedings of the Prehistoric Society* 58, 127–142.

Bradley, R. 1997. *Rock Art and the Prehistory of Atlantic Europe*. London: Routledge.

Bradley, R. 1998a. *The Passage of Arms*. 2nd edition. Oxford: Oxbow.

Bradley, R. 1998b. *The Significance of Monuments*. London: Routledge.

Bradley, R. 1998c. Ruined buildings, ruined stones: Enclosures, tombs and natural places in the Neolithic of South-West England. *World Archaeology* 30, 13–22.

Bradley, R. 1998 d. Stone circles and passage graves – A contested relationship. In A. Gibson and D. Simpson (eds.), *Prehistoric Ritual and Religion*, 2–13. Stroud: Sutton.

Bradley, R. 2000a. *The Good Stones. A New Investigation of the Clava Cairns*. Edinburgh: Society of Antiquaries of Scotland.

Bradley, R. 2000b. *An Archaeology of Natural Places*. London: Routledge.

Bradley, R. 2001. Orientations and origins: A symbolic dimension to the long house in Neolithic Europe. *Antiquity* 75, 50–6.

Bradley, R. 2005a. *The Moon and the Bonfire. An Investigation of Three Stone Circles in North-East Scotland*. Edinburgh: Society of Antiquaries of Scotland.

Bradley, R. 2005b. *Ritual and Domestic Life in Prehistoric Europe*. Abingdon: Routledge.

Bradley, R. in press. Bridging the two cultures – Commercial archaeology and research on prehistoric Britain. *Antiquaries Journal*.

Bradley, R., Barclay, A., Hey, G., and Lambrick, G. 1996. The earlier prehistory of the Oxford region in the light of recent research. *Oxoniensia* 61, 1–20.

Bradley, R. and Chambers, R. 1988. A new study of the cursus complex at Dorchester on Thames. *Oxford Journal of Archaeology* 7, 271–289.

Bradley, R. and Edmonds, M. 1993. *Interpreting the Axe Trade*. Cambridge: Cambridge University Press.

Bradley, R. and Ellison, A. 1975. *Rams Hill: A Bronze Age Defended Enclosure and its Landscape*. Oxford: British Archaeological Reports (BAR 19).

Bradley, R., Entwistle, R., and Raymond, F. 1994. *Prehistoric Land Divisions on Salisbury Plain*. London: English Heritage.

Bradley, R. and Gordon, K. 1988. Human skulls from the River Thames, their dating and significance. *Antiquity* 62, 503–509.

Bradley, R. and Hart, C. 1983. Prehistoric settlement in the Peak District during the third and second millennia BC: A preliminary analysis in the light of recent fieldwork. *Proceedings of the Prehistoric Society* 49, 177–93.

Bradley, R. and Holgate, R. 1984. The Neolithic sequence in the Upper Thames Valley. In R. Bradley and J. Gardiner (eds.), *Neolithic Studies*, 107–34. Oxford: British Archaeological Reports (BAR 133).

Bradley, R., Lobb, S., Richards, J., and Robinson, M. 1980. Two Late Bronze Age settlements on the Kennet gravels. Excavations at Aldermaston Wharf and Knight's Farm, Burghfield, Berkshire. *Proceedings of the Prehistoric Society* 46, 217–95.

Bradley, R., Phillips, T., Richards, C., and Webb, M. 2001. Decorating the houses of the dead. Incised and pecked motifs in Orkney chambered tombs. *Cambridge Archaeological Journal* 11, 45–67.

Bradley, R. and Sheridan, A. 2005. Croft Moraig and the chronology of stone circles. *Proceedings of the Prehistoric Society* 71, 269–81.

Bradley, R. and Yates, D (in press). After Celtic Fields: The social organisation of Iron Age agriculture. In C. Haselgrove and R. Pope (eds.), *The Earlier Iron Age in Britain and the Near Continent*. Oxford: Oxbow.

Brennan, M. 1983. *The Stars and the Stones. Ancient Art and Astronomy in Ireland*. London: Thames and Hudson.

Brennand, M. and Taylor, M. 2003. The survey and excavation of a Bronze Age timber circle at Holme-next-the Sea, Norfolk, 1998–9. *Proceedings of the Prehistoric Society* 69, 1–84.

Brewster, T. 1981. *The Excavation of Garton and Wetwang Slacks* (published in microfiche). London: Royal Commission on the Historical Monuments of England.

Brewster, T. 1984. *The Excavation of Whitegrounds Barrow, Burythorpe*. Wintringham: East Riding Archaeological Research Committee.

Briard, J. 1965. *Les depôts bretons du l'âge du bronze Atlantique*. Rennes: Laboratoire d'anthropologie préhistorique de la Faculté des Sciences de Rennes.

Bridgford, S. 1998. British Late Bronze Age swords: The metallographic evidence. In C. Mordant, M. Pernot, and V. Rychner (eds.), *L'atelier du bronzier en Europe, tome 2. Du miner au métal, du métal à l'objet*, 205–19. Paris: Éditions du comité des travaux historiques et scientifiques.

Brindley, A. and Lanting, J. 1990. Radiocarbon dates for Neolithic single burials. *Journal of Irish Archaeology* 5, 1–7.

Brindley, A. and Lanting. J. 1992. Radiocarbon dates from wedge tombs. *Journal of Irish Archaeology* 6, 19–26.

Britnell, B. 1982. The excavation of two round barrows at Trelystan, Powys. *Proceedings of the Prehistoric Society* 48, 133–201.

Britnell, B. 1989. The Collfryn hill slope enclosure, Llansantffraid, Deuddwr, Powys: Excavations 1980–82. *Proceedings of the Prehistoric Society* 55, 89–134.

Britnell, B. and Savory, H. 1984. *Gwernvale and Penywyrlod*. Bangor: Cambrian Archaeological Association.

Broodbank, C. 2000. *An Island Archaeology of the Early Cyclades*. Cambridge: Cambridge University Press.

Brophy, K. 2000. Water coincidence: Cursus monuments and rivers. In A. Ritchie (ed.), *Neolithic Orkney in its European Context*, 59–70. Cambridge: McDonald Institute for Archaeological Research.

Brophy, K. and Barclay, G. 2004. A rectilinear timber structure and post-ring at Carsie Mains, Meikleour, Perthshire. *Tayside and Fife Archaeological Journal* 10, 1–22.

Brossler, A., Early, R., and Allen, C. 2004. *Green Park, Phase 2 Excavations, 1995 – Neolithic and Bronze Age Sites*. Oxford: Oxford Archaeology.

Brown, N. 2000. *The Archaeology of Ardleigh, Essex*. East Anglian Archaeology 90.

Brown, N. 2001. The Bronze Age enclosure at Springfield Lyons in its landscape context. *Essex Archaeology and History* 32, 92–101.

Brown, N. and Lavender, N. 1994. Later Bronze Age sites at Great Baddow and settlement in the Chelmer Valley, Essex. *Essex Archaeology and History* 25, 3–13.

Brown, P. and Chappell, G. 2005. *Prehistoric Rock Art in the North York Moors*. Stroud: Tempus.

Brown, T. 1997. Clearances and clearings: Deforestation in Mesolithic / Neolithic Britain. *Oxford Journal of Archaeology* 16, 133–46.

Brown, T. 2003. Divisions of floodplain space and sites on riverine 'islands': Functional, ritual, social or liminal places? *Journal of Wetland Archaeology* 3, 3–15.

Brück, J. 1995. A place for the dead: The role of human remains in Late Bronze Age Britain. *Proceedings of the Prehistoric Society* 61, 245–77.

Brück, J. 1999. Houses, life cycles and deposition on Middle Bronze Age settlements in Southern England. *Proceedings of the Prehistoric Society* 65, 145–66.

Brück, J. 2004. Material metaphors. The relational construction of identity in Early Bronze Age burials in Ireland and Britain. *Journal of Social Archaeology* 4, 307–33.

Brun, P. 2004. Processes of stratification and state formation in Europe. In N. Matsumoto (ed.), *Cultural Diversity and the Archaeology of the 21st Century*, 110–21. Okayama: Society of Archaeological Studies.

Brunning, R. 1997. Two Bronze Age wooden structures in the Somerset Moors. *Newswarp* 22, 24–8.

Buckland, P., Parker Pearson, M., Wigley, A., and Girling, M. 2001. Is there anybody out there? A reconsideration of the environmental evidence from the Breiddin hillfort, Powys. *Antiquaries Journal* 81, 51–76.

Buckley, D. and Hedges, J. 1987. *The Bronze Age and Saxon settlements at Springfield Lyons, Essex: Interim Report*. Chelmsford: Essex County Council Archaeology Section.

Buckley, D., Hedges, J., and Brown, N. 2001. Excavations at the Neolithic cursus, Springfield, Essex, 1979–85. *Proceedings of the Prehistoric Society* 67, 101–62.

Buckley, R. and George, S. 2003. Archaeology in Leicestershire and Rutland 2002. *Transactions of the Leicestershire Antiquarian and Historical Society* 77, 125–56.

Buckley, V. (ed.). 1990 *Burnt Offerings*. Dublin: Wordwell.

Budd, P. and Taylor, T. 1995. The faerie smith meets the bronze industry: Magic versus science in the interpretation of prehistoric metal making. *World Archaeology* 27, 133–43.

Burenhult, G. 1980. *The Archaeological Excavation at Carrowmore, Co. Sligo, Ireland. Excavation Seasons 1977–79*. Stockholm: Stockholm University Institute of Archaeology.

Burenhult, G. 1984. *The Archaeology of Carrowmore: Environmental Archaeology and the Megalithic Tradition at Carrowmore, Co. Sligo, Ireland.* Stockholm: Stockholm University Theses and Papers in North-European Archaeology 14.

Burgess, C. 1979. A find from Boyton, Suffolk, and the end of the Bronze Age in Britain and Ireland. In C. Burgess and D. Coombs (eds.), *Bronze Age Hoards. Some Finds Old and New*, 269–82. Oxford: British Archaeological Reports (BAR 67).

Burgess, C. 1980. *The Age of Stonehenge.* London: Dent.

Burgess, C. 1985. Population, climate and upland settlement. In D. Spratt and C. Burgess (eds.), *Upland Settlement in Britain. The Second Millennium BC and After*, 195-230. Oxford: British Archaeological Reports (BAR 143).

Burgess, C. 1992. Discontinuity and dislocation in later prehistoric settlements from Atlantic Europe. In C. Mordant and A. Richard (eds.), *L'habitat et l'occupation du sol à l'Age du Bronze en Europe*, 21–40. Paris: Editions du Comité des Travaux historiques et scientifiques.

Burgess, C. 2001. Note to the Phoenix Press edition. In C. Burgess, *The Age of Stonehenge*, 2nd edition, 13–14. London: Phoenix Press.

Burgess, C. 2004. Forty-five years' researches in the chronology and ordering of the British Bronze Age: A personal memoir. In A. Gibson and A. Sheridan (eds.), *From Sickles to Circles*, 339–65. Stroud: Tempus.

Burgess, C. and Gerloff, S. 1981. *The Dirks and Rapiers of Great Britain and Ireland.* Munich: C.H. Beck.

Burgess, C. and Shennan, S. 1976. The Beaker phenomenon: Some suggestions. In C. Burgess and R, Miket (eds.), *Settlement and Economy in the Third and Second Millennia BC*, 309–31. Oxford: British Archaeological Reports (BAR 33).

Burl, A. 1981. By the light of the cinerary moon: Chambered tombs and the astronomy of death. In C. Ruggles and A. Whittle (eds.) *Astronomy and Society in Britain during the Period 4000 – 1500 BC*, 243–74. Oxford: British Archaeological Reports (BAR 88).

Burl, A. 1988. *Four-posters. Bronze Age Stone Circles of Western Europe.* Oxford: British Archaeological Reports (BAR 195).

Burl, A. 1993. *From Carnac to Callanish: The Prehistoric Stone Rows and Avenues of Britain, Ireland and Brittany.* New Haven: Yale University Press.

Burl, A. 1994. Long Meg and her Daughters, Little Salkeld. *Transactions of the Cumberland and Westmorland Antiquarian and Archaeological Society 94*, 1–11.

Burl, A. 2000 *The Stone Circles of Britain, Ireland and Brittany.* New Haven: Yale University Press.

Burns, B., Cunliffe, B., and Sebire, H. 1996. *Guernsey: An Island Community of the Atlantic Iron Age.* Oxford: Oxford University Committee for Archaeology.

Burrow, S. 1997. *The Neolithic Culture of the Isle of Man. A Study of the Sites and Pottery.* Oxford: British Archaeological Reports (BAR 263).

Bush, M. 1988. Early Mesolithic disturbance: A force on the landscape. *Journal of Archaeological Science 15*, 453–62.

Butler, J. 1991 *Dartmoor Atlas of Antiquities, Volume 1.* Exeter: Devon Books.

Butler, J. 1997. *Dartmoor Atlas of Antiquities, Volume 5.* Exeter: Devon Books.

Callender, J. 1922. Three hoards recently added to the national collection, with notes on the hoard from Duddingston Loch. *Proceedings of the Society of Antiquaries of Scotland 56*, 351–65.

Campbell, E. 2001. Were the Scots Irish? *Antiquity 75*, 285–92.

Card, N. and Downes, J. 2003. Mine Howe – The significance of space and place in the Iron Age. In J. Downes and A. Ritchie (eds.), *Sea Change: Orkney and Northern Europe in the Later Iron Age*, 11–19. Balgavie: The Pinkfoot Press.

Carsten, J. and Hugh-Jones, S.1995. Introduction. In J. Carsten and S. Hugh-Jones (eds.), *About the House: Lévi-Strauss and Beyond*, 1–46. Cambridge: Cambridge University Press.

Carter, S. and Hunter, F. 2003. An Iron Age chariot burial from Scotland. *Antiquity 77*, 531–5.

Carver, M. 2005. *Sutton Hoo. A Seventh-century Princely Burial Ground and its Context.* London: British Museum Press.

Case, H. 1966. Were the Beaker-people the first metallurgists in Ireland? *Palaeohistoria 12*, 140–77.

Case, H. 1973. A ritual site in north-east Ireland. In G. Daniel and P Kjaerum (eds.), *Megalithic Graves and Ritual*, 173–96. Moesgård: Jutland Archaeological Society.

Case, H. 1977. The Beaker Culture in Britain and Ireland. In R. Mercer (ed.), *Beakers in Britain and Europe,* 71–101. Oxford: British Archaeological Reports. (BAR Supplementary Series 26).

Case, H. 1995. Irish Beakers in their European context. In J. Waddell and E. Shee Twohig (eds.), *Ireland in the Bronze Age,* 14–29. Dublin: Stationery Office.

Case, H. 2004a. Beaker burial in Britain and Ireland. A role for the dead. In M. Besse and J. Desideri (eds.), *Graves and Funerary Rituals during the Late Neolithic and Early Bronze Age in Europe (2700 – 2000 BC),* 195–201. Oxford: British Archaeological Reports (BAR International Series 1284).

Case, H. 2004b. Bell Beaker and Corded Ware burial associations: A bottom-up rather than top-down approach. In A. Gibson and A. Sheridan (eds.), *From Sickles to Circles. Britain and Ireland at the Time of Stonehenge,* 106–15. Stroud: Tempus.

Champion, T. 1982. The myth of Iron Age invasions in Ireland. In B. Scott (ed.), *Studies on Early Ireland. Essays in Honour of M.V. Duignan,* 39–44. Belfast: Association of Young Irish Archaeologists.

Champion, T. 1989. From Bronze to Iron Age in Ireland. In M. L. S. Sørensen and R. Thomas (eds.), *The Bronze Age – Iron Age Transition in Europe,* 287–303. Oxford: British Archaeological Reports (BAR International Series 483).

Champion, T. 2004. Exotic materials in the Early Bronze Age of Southeastern Britain. In H. Roche, E. Grogan, J. Bradley, J. Coles, and B. Raftery (eds.), *From Megaliths to Metals,* 51–5. Oxford: Oxbow.

Chapman, A. 2004. Gayhurst. *Current Archaeology* 191, 510–11.

Chapman, H. 2005. Rethinking the 'cursus problem' – Investigating the Neolithic landscape archaeology of Rudston, East Yorkshire, UK, using GIS. *Proceedings of the Prehistoric Society* 71, 159–70.

Chappell, S. 1987. *Stone Axe Morphology and Distribution in Neolithic Britain.* Oxford: British Archaeological Reports (BAR 177).

Charles, B., Parkinson, A., and Foreman, S. 2000. A Bronze Age ditch and Iron Age settlement at Elms Farm, Humberstone, Leicester. *Transactions of the Leicestershire Archaeological and Historical Society* 74, 113–220.

Childe, V. G. 1942. *What Happened in History.* London: Penguin.

Childe, V. G. 1949. *Prehistoric Communities of the British Isles.* London: Chambers.

Childe, V. G. 1952. Old World prehistory: The Neolithic. In A. Kroeber (ed.), *Anthropology Today: An Encyclopedic Inventory,* 193–210. Chicago: Chicago University Press.

Christie, P. 1978. The excavation of an Iron Age souterrain and settlement at Carn Euny, Sancreed, Cornwall. *Proceedings of the Prehistoric Society* 44, 309–433.

Clare, T. 1978. Recent work on the Shap 'avenue'. *Transactions of the Cumberland and Westmorland Antiquarian and Archaeological Society* 78, 5–15

Clark, J. D. G. 1966. The invasion hypothesis in British archaeology. *Antiquity* 40, 172–89.

Clark, J. D. G. and Fell, C. 1953. The Early Iron Age site at Micklemoor Hill, West Harling, Norfolk, and its pottery. *Proceedings of the Prehistoric Society* 19, 1–40.

Clark, J. D. G., Higgs, E., and Longworth, I. 1960. Excavations at the Neolithic site of Hurst Fen, Mildenhall, Suffolk, 1954, 1957 and 1958. *Proceedings of the Prehistoric Society* 26, 202–45.

Clark, P. 2004. *The Dover Bronze Age Boat.* London: English Heritage.

Clarke, D. L. 1970. *Beaker Pottery of Great Britain and Ireland.* Cambridge: Cambridge University Press.

Clarke, D. L. 1976. The Beaker network – Social and economic models. In W. Pape and C. Strahm (eds.), *Glockenbechersymposion,* 459–77. Haarlem: Fibula-van Dishoek.

Clarke, D. V. and Sharples, N. 1990. Settlement and subsistence in the third millennium BC. In C. Renfrew (ed.), *The Prehistory of Orkney,* 54–82. Edinburgh: Edinburgh University Press.

Cleal, R. 2005. 'The small compass of a grave'? Early Bronze Age burial in and around Avebury and the Marlborough Downs. In G. Brown, D. Field, and D. McOmish (eds.), *The Avebury Landscape, Aspects of the Field Archaeology of the Marlborough Downs,* 115–32. Oxford: Oxbow.

Cleal, R., Walker, K., and Montague, R. 1995. *Stonehenge in its Landscape. Twentieth Century Excavations.* London: English Heritage.

Cleary, R. 2003. Enclosed Late Bronze Age habitation-site and boundary wall at Lough

Gur, Co, Limerick. *Proceedings of the Royal Irish Academy* 103C, 97–189.

Coles, B. 1998. Doggerland: A speculative survey. *Proceedings of the Prehistoric Society* 64, 45–81.

Coles, B. and Coles, J. 1986. *Sweet Track to Glastonbury*. London: Thames and Hudson.

Coles, J. 1987. *Meare Village East*. Exeter: Somerset Levels Project.

Coles, J. and Harding, A. 1979. *The Bronze Age in Europe*. London: Methuen.

Coles, J., Leach, P., Minnitt, S., Tabor, R. and Wilson, A. 1999. A Later Bronze Age Shield from South Cadbury, Somerset, England. *Antiquity* 73, 33–48.

Coles, J. and Minnitt, S. 1995. *'Industrious and Fairly Civilized'. The Glastonbury Lake Village*. Taunton: Somerset Levels Project and Somerset County Museum Service.

Coles, J. and Simpson, D. 1965. The excavation of a Neolithic round barrow at Pitnacree, Perthshire, Scotland. *Proceedings of the Prehistoric Society* 31, 34–57.

Coles, J. and Taylor, J. 1971. The Wessex Culture: A minimal view. *Antiquity* 45, 6–14.

Collard, M. 2005. Hartshill Quarry. The oldest ironworking site in Britain? *Current Archaeology* 195, 134–9.

Collis, J. 1973. Burials with weapons in Iron Age Britain. *Germania* 51, 121–33.

Collis, J. 1977. Iron Age henges? *Archaeologia Atlantica* 2, 55–63.

Condit, T. 1995. Avenues for research. *Archaeology Ireland* 9, 16–18.

Condit, T. 1996. Gold and fulachta fiadh – The Mooghaun find, 1854. *Archaeology Ireland* 10, 20–3.

Condit, T. and Simpson, D. 1998. Irish hengiform enclosures and related monuments: A review. In A. Gibson and D. Simpson (eds.), *Prehistoric Ritual and Religion*, 45–61. Stroud: Sutton.

Conneller, C. 2004. Becoming deer. Corporeal transformation at Star Carr. *Archaeological Dialogues* 11, 37–56.

Conway, M., Gahan, A., and Rathbone, S. 2005. Corrstown: A large Middle Bronze Age village. *Current Archaeology* 195, 120–3.

Cook, M. and Dunbar, L. 2004. Kintore. *Current Archaeology* 194, 84–9.

Cooney, G. 1998. Breaking stones, making places: The social landscape of axe production sites. In A. Gibson and D. Simpson (eds.), *Prehistoric Ritual and Religion*, 108–18. Stroud: Sutton.

Cooney, G. 2000. *Landscapes of Neolithic Ireland*. London: Routledge.

Cooney, G. and Grogan, E. 1994. *Irish prehistory – A social perspective*. Bray: Wordwell.

Copley, M., Berstan, R., Mukherjee, A., Dudd, S., Straker, V., Payne, S., and Evershed, R. 2005. Dairying in antiquity III: Evidence from absorbed lipid residues dating to the British Neolithic. *Journal of Archaeological Science* 32, 523–46.

Coppock, T. 1976a. *An Agricultural Atlas of England and Wales*. London: Faber and Faber.

Coppock, T. 1976b. *An Agricultural Atlas of Scotland*. Edinburgh: John Donald.

Costa, L., Strenke, F., and Woodman, P. 2005. Microlith to macrolith: The reasons behind the transformation of production in the Irish Mesolithic. *Antiquity* 79, 19–33.

Cotter, C. 1996. Western stone fort project: Interim report. *Discovery Programme Report* 4, 1–14.

Courty, M. A., Goldberg, P., and Macphail, R. 1989. *Soils and Micromorphology in Archaeology*. Cambridge: Cambridge University Press.

Cowie, T. G. 1993. A survey of the Neolithic pottery of eastern and central Scotland. *Proceedings of the Society of Antiquaries of Scotland* 123, 13–41.

Cowie, T. and Shepherd, I. 2003. The Bronze Age. In K. Edwards and I. Ralston (eds.), *Scotland after the Ice Age*, 151–68. Edinburgh: Edinburgh University Press.

Creighton, J. 2000. *Coins and Power in Late Iron Age Britain*. Cambridge: Cambridge University Press.

Creighton, J. 2006. *Britannia. The Creation of a Roman Province*. Abingdon: Routledge.

Cromarty, A. M., Barclay, A., Lambrick, G., and Robinson, M. 2005. *Late Bronze Age Ritual and Habitation on a Thames Eyot at Whitecross Farm, Wallingford*. Oxford: Oxford Archaeology.

Crone, A. 1993. Excavation and survey of subpeat features of Neolithic, Bronze Age and Iron Age date at Bharpa Carinish, North Uist, Scotland. *Proceedings of the Prehistoric Society* 59, 361–182.

Cummings, V. and Whittle, A. 2004. *Places of Special Virtue. Megaliths in the Neolithic Landscape of Wales*. Oxford: Oxbow.

Cunnington, M. 1923. *Early Iron Age Inhabited Site at All Cannings Cross Farm, Wiltshire*. Devizes: George Simpson.

Cunnington, M. 1929. *Woodhenge*. Devizes: George Simpson.

Cunliffe, B. 1984. *Danebury. An Iron Age Hillfort in Hampshire, Volume 1*. London: Council for British Archaeology.

Cunliffe, B. 1988. *Greeks, Romans and Barbarians. Spheres of Interaction*. London: Batsford.

Cunliffe, B. 2001a. *Facing the Ocean: The Atlantic and its Peoples 8000 BC – AD 1500*. Oxford: Oxford University Press.

Cunliffe, B. 2001b. *The Extraordinary Voyage of Pytheas the Greek*. London: Allen Lane.

Cunliffe, B. 2004. Wessex cowboys? *Oxford Journal of Archaeology* 23, 61–81.

Cunliffe, B. 2005. *Iron Age Communities in Britain*. 4th edition. Abingdon: Routledge.

Cunliffe, B. and Poole, C. 1991a. *Danebury. An Iron Age Hillfort in Hampshire, Volume 4*. London: Council for British Archaeology.

Cunliffe, B. and Poole, C. 1991b. *Danebury. An Iron Age Hillfort in Hampshire, Volume 5*. London: Council for British Archaeology.

Cunliffe, B. and Poole, C. 2000a. *The Danebury Environs Programme, Volume 1*. Oxford: Oxford University Committee for Archaeology.

Cunliffe, B. and Poole, C. 2000b. *The Danebury Environs Programme, Volume 2, part 4*. Oxford: Oxford University Committee for Archaeology.

Dacre, M. and Ellison, A. 1981. A Bronze Age urn cemetery at Kimpton, Hampshire. *Proceedings of the Prehistoric Society* 47, 147–203.

Dalland, M. 1999. Sand Fiold: The excavation of an exceptional cist in Orkney. *Proceedings of the Prehistoric Society* 65, 373–413.

Dark, P. and Gent, H. 2001. Pest and diseases of prehistoric crops: A yield 'honeymoon' for early grain crops in Europe? *Oxford Journal of Archaeology* 20, 59–78.

Darvill, T. 1996. Neolithic buildings in England, Wales and the Isle of Man. In T. Darvill and J. Thomas (eds.), *Neolithic Houses in North-west Europe and* Beyond, 77–111. Oxford: Oxbow.

Darvill, T. 2000. Neolithic Mann in context. In A. Ritchie (ed.), *Neolithic Orkney in its European Context*, 371–85. Cambridge: McDonald Institute for Archaeological Research.

Darvill, T. 2002. *Billown Neolithic Landscape Project, Isle of Man: Seventh Report 2002*. Bournemouth: Bournemouth University School of Conservation Sciences.

Darvill, T. 2004. *Long Barrows of the Cotswolds and Surrounding Areas*. Stroud: Tempus.

Darvill, T. and Wainwright, G. 2003. Stone circles, oval settings and henges in south-west Wales and beyond. *Antiquaries Journal* 83, 9–45.

David, A., Cole, M., Horsley, T., Linford, N., Linford, P., and Martin, L. 2004. A rival to Stonehenge? Geophysical survey at Stanton Drew, England. *Antiquity* 78, 341–58.

David, A. and Walker, E. 2004. Wales during the Mesolithic period. In A. Saville (ed.), *Mesolithic Scotland and its Neighbours*. Edinburgh: Society of Antiquaries of Scotland.

Davidson, J. and Henshall, A. 1989. *The Chambered Cairns of Orkney*. Edinburgh: Edinburgh University Press.

Davies, J., Gregory, T., Lawson, A., Pickett, R., and Rogerson, A. 1991. *The Hillforts of Norfolk*. East Anglian Archaeology 54.

Davies, M. 1946. The diffusion and distribution pattern of the megalithic monuments of the Irish Sea and North Channel coastlands. *Antiquaries Journal* 26, 38–60.

Davies, N. 1999. *The Isles: A History*. London: Macmillan.

Davis, S. and Payne, S. 1993. A barrow full of cattle skulls. *Antiquity* 67, 12–22.

Dennell, R. 1985. *European Economic Prehistory – A New Approach*. London: Academic Press.

Dent, J. 1982. Cemeteries and settlement patterns of the Iron Age on the Yorkshire Wolds. *Proceedings of the Prehistoric Society* 48, 437–457.

Dent, J. 1983. Weapons, wounds and war in the Iron Age. *Archaeological Journal* 140, 120–8.

de Valera, R. 1960. The court tombs of Ireland. *Proceedings of the Royal Irish Academy* 60C, 9–140.

Dixon, P. 1994. *Crickley Hill. The Hillfort Defences*. Nottingham: Department of Archaeology, University of Nottingham.

Downes, J. and Lamb, R. 2000. *Prehistoric Houses at Sunburgh in Shetland: Excavations at Sunburgh Airport 1967–74*. Oxford: Oxbow.

Driscoll, S. and Yeoman, P. 1997. *Excavations within Edinburgh Castle in 1988–91*. Edinburgh: Society of Antiquaries of Scotland.

Driscoll, S. 1998. Picts and prehistory: Cultural resource management in early medieval Scotland. *World Archaeology* 30, 142–58.

Dronfield, J. 1995. Subjective vision and the sources of Irish megalithic art. *Antiquity* 69, 539–49.

Dronfield, J. 1996. Entering alternative realities: Cognition, art and architecture in Irish passage tombs. *Cambridge Archaeological Journal* 6, 37–72.

Dunkin, D. 2001. Metalwork, burnt mounds and settlement on the West Sussex coastal plain: A contextual study. *Antiquity* 75, 261–2.

Durden, T. 1995. The production of specialised flintwork in the later Neolithic: A case study from the Yorkshire Wolds. *Proceedings of the Prehistoric Society* 61, 409–432.

Dutton, A. and Fasham, P. 1994. Prehistoric copper mining on the Great Orme, Llandudno, Gwynedd. *Proceedings of the Prehistoric Society* 60, 245–286.

Dyson, L., Shand, G., and Stevens, S. 2000. Causewayed enclosures [in Kent]. *Current Archaeology* 168, 470–2.

Earle, T. 1991. Property rights and the evolution of chiefdoms. In T. Earle (ed.), *Chiefdoms: Power, Economy and Ideology*, 71–99. Cambridge: Cambridge University Press.

Edmonds, M. 1999. *Ancestral Geographies of the Neolithic*. London: Routledge.

Edwards, K. 1998. Detection of human impact on the natural environment. In J. Bayley (ed.), *Science in Archaeology – An Agenda for the Future*, 69–88. London: English Heritage.

Edwards, N. 1990. *The Archaeology of Early Medieval Ireland*. London: Routledge.

Ehrenberg, M. 1989. The interpretation of regional variability in British and Irish metalwork. In H-Å. Nordström and A. Knape (eds.), *Bronze Age Studies*, 77–88. Stockholm: Statens Historiska Museum.

Ellis, C. 2004. *A Prehistoric Ritual Complex at Eynesbury, Cambridgeshire*. East Anglian Archaeology Occasional Paper 17.

Ellis, C. and Rawlings, M. 2001. Excavations at Balksbury Camp, Andover, 1995–97. *Proceedings of the Hampshire Field Club and Archaeological Society* 56, 21–94.

Ellis, P. (ed.). 1993. *Beeston Castle, Cheshire*. English Heritage.

Ellison, A. 1978. The Bronze Age of Sussex. In P. Drewett (ed.), *Archaeology in Sussex to AD 1500*, 30–7. London: Council for British Archaeology.

Ellison, A. 1980 Deverel Rimbury urn cemeteries: The evidence for social organisation. In J. Barrett and R. Bradley (eds.), *Settlement and Society in the British Later Bronze Age*, 115–26. Oxford: British Archaeological Reports (BAR 83).

Ellison, A. 1981. Towards a socio-economic model for the Middle Bronze Age in southern England. In I. Hodder, G. Isaac, and N. Hammond (eds.), *Pattern of the Past*, 413–36. Cambridge: Cambridge University Press.

Eogan, G. 1964. The Later Bronze Age in Ireland in the light of recent research. *Proceedings of the Prehistoric Society* 30, 268–351.

Eogan, G. 1965. *Catalogue of Irish Bronze Swords*. Dublin: Stationery Office.

Eogan, G. 1984. *Excavations at Knowth Volume 1*. Dublin: Royal Irish Academy.

Eogan, G. 1986. *Knowth and the Passage Tombs of Ireland*. London: Thames and Hudson.

Eogan, G. 1992. Scottish and Irish passage tombs: Some comparisons and contrasts. In N. Sharples and A. Sheridan (eds.), *Vessels for the Ancestors*, 120–7. Edinburgh: Edinburgh University Press.

Eogan, G. 1994. *The Accomplished Art: Gold and Gold-working in Britain and Ireland during the Bronze Age*. Oxford: Oxbow.

Eogan, G. 1997. Overlays and underlays: Aspects of megalithic art succession at Brugh na Bóinne, Ireland. In J. M. Bello Diéguez (ed.), *III Coloquio internacional de arte megalítico: Actas*, 217–34. A Coruña: Brigantium 10.

Eogan, G. 1998. Knowth before Knowth. *Antiquity* 72, 162–72.

Eogan, G. 1999. Megalithic art and society. *Proceedings of the Prehistoric Society* 65, 415–46.

Eogan, G. and Roche, H. 1997. *Excavations at Knowth, Volume 2*. Dublin: Royal Irish Academy.

Eogan, J. 2004. The construction of funerary monuments in the Irish Early Bronze Age: A review of the evidence. In H. Roche, E. Grogan, J. Bradley, J. Coles, and B. Raftery (eds.), *From Megaliths to Metals*, 56–60. Oxford: Oxbow.

Eriksen, P. 2004. Newgrange og den hvide mur. *Kuml* (2004), 45–77.

Evans, C. 2002. Metalwork and the 'cold claylands': Pre-Iron Age occupation on the Isle of Ely. In T. Lane and J. Coles (eds.), *Through Wet and Dry*, 33–53. Sleaford: Heritage Trust of Lincolnshire.

Evans, C. 2003. *Power and Island Communities: Excavations at Wardy Hill Ringwork, Coveney, Ely*. East Anglian Archaeology 103.

Evans, C. and Hodder, I. 2005. *A Woodland Archaeology. The Haddenham Project Volume 1.*

Cambridge: McDonald Institute for Archaeological Research.

Evans, C. and Knight, M. 1996. An Ouseside longhouse – Barleycroft Farm, Cambridgeshire. *Past* 23, 1–2.

Evans, C. and Knight, M. 2000. A fenland delta: Later prehistoric land-use in the lower Ouse Reaches. In M. Dawson (ed.), *Prehistoric, Roman and Post-Roman Landscapes in the Great Ouse Valley*, 87–106. York: Council for British Archaeology.

Evans, C. and Knight, M. 2001. The 'community of builders': The Barleycroft post alignments. In J. Brück (ed.), *Bronze Age Landscapes: Tradition and Transformation*, 83–98. Oxford: Oxbow.

Evans, C., Pollard, J., and Knight, M. 1999. Life in woods: Tree-throws, 'settlement' and forest cognition. *Oxford Journal of Archaeology* 18, 241–54.

Exon, S., Gaffney, V., Woodward, A., and Yorston, R. 2000. *Stonehenge Landscapes. Journeys through Real and Imagined Worlds*. Oxford: Archaeopress.

Fahy, E. 1959. A hut and cooking-place at Drombeg, Co. Cork. *Journal of the Cork Historical and Archaeological Society* 65, 1–17.

Fahy, E. 1960. A recumbent stone circle at Drombeg, Co. Cork. *Journal of the Cork Historical and Archaeological Society* 64, 1–27.

Falkner, N. 2004. Testwood Bridge. *Current Archaeology* 190, 428–9.

Fell, C. and Davis, R. V. 1988. The petrological identifications of stone implements from Cumbria. In T. Clough and W. Cummins (eds.), *Stone Axe Studies, Volume 2*, 71–7. London: Council for British Archaeology.

Fenton-Thomas, C. 2003. *Late Prehistoric and Early Historic Landscapes on the Yorkshire Chalk*. Oxford: British Archaeological Reports (BAR 350).

Fenwick, J. and Newman, C. 2002. Geomagnetic survey on the Hill of Tara, Co. Meath, 1989. *Discovery Programme Reports* 6, 1–17.

Field, D. 1998. Round barrows and the harmonious landscape: Placing Early Bronze Age burial mounds in south-east England. *Oxford Journal of Archaeology* 17, 309–26.

Field, D. 2001. Place and memory in Bronze Age Wessex. In J. Brück (ed.), *Bronze Age Landscapes. Tradition and Transformation*, 157–65. Oxford: Oxbow.

Field, N. and Parker Pearson, M. 2003. *Fiskerton: An Iron Age Timber Causeway with Iron Age and Roman Votive Offerings*. Oxford: Oxbow.

Fischer, A. 2002. Food for feasting? In A. Fischer and K. Kristiansen (eds.), *The Neolithicisation of Denmark: 150 Years of Debate*, 343–93. Sheffield: J. R. Collis Publications.

Fitzpatrick, A. 1984. The deposition of La Tène metalwork in watery contexts in Southern England. In B. Cunliffe and D. Miles (eds.), *Aspects of the Iron Age in Central Southern Britain*, 178–190. Oxford: Oxford University Committee for Archaeology.

Fitzpatrick, A. 1989. The submission of the Orkney islands to Claudius: New evidence? *Scottish Archaeological Review* 6, 24–33.

Fitzpatrick, A. 1997. Everyday life in Iron Age Wessex. In A. Gwilt and C. Haselgrove (eds.), *Reconstructing Iron Age Societies*, 73–86. Oxford: Oxbow.

Fitzpatrick, A. 2003. The Amesbury Archer. *Current Archaeology* 184, 146–52.

Fitzpatrick, A. 2005. A sacred circle on Boscombe Down. *Current Archaeology* 195, 106–7.

Fleming, A. 1988. *The Dartmoor Reaves*. London: Batsford.

Flemming, N. (ed.). 2004. *Submarine Prehistoric Archaeology of the North Sea*. York: Council for British Archaeology.

Foley, C. and MacDonagh, M. 1998. Copney stone circles – A County Tyrone enigma. *Archaeology Ireland* 12.1, 24–8.

Foster, J. 1980. *The Iron Age Moulds from Gussage All Saints*. London: British Museum.

Fowler, P. 1983. *The Farming of Prehistoric Britain*. Cambridge University Press.

Fowler, P. J. 2000. *Landscape Plotted and Pieced. Landscape History and Local Archaeology in Fyfield and Overton, Wiltshire*. London: Society of Antiquaries.

Fox, A. 1973. *South West England 3500 BC – AD 600*. Newton Abbot: David and Charles.

Fox, C. 1932. *The Personality of Britain*. Cardiff: National Museum of Wales.

Fredengren, C. 2002. *Crannogs*. Bray: Wordwell.

French, C. 1994. *Excavation of the Deeping St Nicholas Barrow Complex, South Lincolnshire*. Sleaford: Heritage Trust for Lincolnshire.

French, C. 2003. *Geoarchaeology in Action*. London: Routledge.

French, C. 2004. Evaluation, survey and excavation at Wandlebury ringwork. *Proceedings of the Cambridge Antiquarian Society* 93, 15–66.

French, C. and Pryor, F. 2005. *Archaeology and Environment of the Etton Landscape*. East Anglian Archaeology 109.

French, C. and Lewis, H. 2005. New perspectives on Holocene landscape development in the Southern English chalklands: The Upper Allen Valley, Cranborne Chase, Dorset. *Geoarchaeology* 20, 109–34.

French, C., Lewis, H., Allen, M., Scaife, R., and Green, M. 2003. Archaeological and palaeoenvironmental investigation of the Upper Allen Valley, Cranborne Chase, Dorset (1998–2000): A new model of earlier Holocene landscape development. *Proceedings of the Prehistoric Society* 69, 201–34.

French, C. and Pryor, F. 2005. *Archaeology and Environment of the Etton Landscape*. East Anglian Archaeology 109.

Fulford, M. 1992. Iron Age to Roman: A period of radical change on the gravels. In M. Fulford and E. Nichols (eds.), *Developing Landscapes of Lowland Britain*, 22–39. London: Society of Antiquaries.

Fulford, M. and Timby, J. 2000. *Late Iron Age and Roman Silchester: Excavation on the Site of the Forum-Basilica, 1977, 1980–86*. London: Society for the Promotion of Roman Studies. Brittania Monograph 15.

Gardiner, J. 1987. Excavations at Crouch Hill 1921, 1969. In B. Cunliffe, *Hengistbury Head, Dorset, Volume 1*, 40-7. Oxford: Oxford University Committee for Archaeology.

Gardiner, J. 1989. Flint procurement and Neolithic axe production on the South Downs: A reassessment. *Oxford Journal of Archaeology* 9, 119–140.

Gardner, W. and Savory, H. 1964. *Dinorben*. Cardiff: National Museum of Wales.

Garrow, D., Beadsmoore, E., and Knight, M. 2005. Pit clusters and the temporality of occupation: An Earlier Neolithic site at Kilverstone, Thetford, Norfolk. *Proceedings of the Prehistoric Society* 71, 139–57.

Garwood, P. 1999. Grooved Ware in Southern Britain. Chronology and implications. In R. Cleal and A. MacSween (eds.), *Grooved Ware in Britain and Ireland*, 143–76. Oxford: Oxbow.

Garwood, P. in press. Before the hills in order stood: Chronology, time and history in the interpretation of early Bronze Age round

barrows. In J. Last (ed.), *Beyond the Grave – New Perspectives on Barrows*. Oxford: Oxbow.

Gelling, P. 1972. The hill fort on South Barrule and its position in the Manx Iron Age. In C. Burgess and F. Lynch (eds.), *Prehistoric Man in Wales and the West*, 285–92. Bath: Adams and Dart.

Gent, H. 1983. Centralised storage in later prehistoric Britain. *Proceedings of the Prehistoric Society* 49, 243–67.

Gerdsen, H. 1976. *Studien zu den Schwertgräbern der älteren Hallstattzeit*. Mainz: von Zabern.

Gerloff, S. 1975. *The Early Bronze Age Daggers of Great Britain, with a Reconsideration of the Wessex Culture*. Munich: C.W. Beck. Prähistorishe Bronzefunde Abt. vi, Bd. 2.

Gerritsen, F. 1999. To build or to abandon. The cultural biography of late prehistoric houses and farmsteads in the southern Netherlands. *Archaeological Dialogues* 6.2, 78–114.

Gerritsen, F. 2000. The cultural biography of Iron Age houses and the long-term transformation of settlement patterns in the southern Netherlands. In C. Fabech and J. Ringtved (eds.), *Settlement and Landscape*, 139–48. Aarhus: Jutland Archaeological Society.

Gibson, A. 1982. *Beaker Domestic Sites*. Oxford: British Archaeological Reports (BAR 107).

Gibson, A. 1998. Hindwell and the Neolithic palisaded sites of Britain and Ireland. In A. Gibson and D. Simpson (eds.), *Prehistoric Ritual and Religion*, 68–79. Stroud: Sutton.

Gibson, A. 1999. *The Walton Basin Project*. York: Council for British Archaeology.

Gibson, A. 2002a. *Prehistoric Pottery in Britain and Ireland*. Stroud: Tempus.

Gibson, A. 2002b. A matter of pegs and labels: A review of some prehistoric pottery from the Milfield Basin. *Archaeologia Aeliana* 30, 175–80.

Gibson, A. 2004a. Round in circles. Timber circles, henges and stone circles: Some possible relationships and transformations. In R. Cleal and J. Pollard (eds.), *Monuments and Material Culture*, 70–81. East Knoyle: Hobnob Press.

Gibson, A. 2004b. Visibility and invisibility: Some thoughts on Neolithic and Bronze Age sites. In I. Shepherd and G. Barclay (eds.), *Scotland in Ancient Europe*, 155–69. Edinburgh: Society of Antiquaries of Scotland.

Gibson, A. 2005. *Stonehenge and Timber Circles*. 2nd edition. Stroud: Tempus.

Gibson, A. and Kinnes, I. 1997. On the urns of a dilemma: Radiocarbon and the Peterborough problem. *Oxford Journal of Archaeology* 16, 65–72.

Gibson, A. and McCormick, A. 1985. Archaeology at Grendon Quarry, Part 1: Neolithic and Bronze Age sites excavated in 1974–75. *Northamptonshire Archaeology* 125, 292–67.

Gillings, M. and Pollard, J. 1999. Non-portable stone artefacts and contexts of meaning: The tale of Grey Weather (www.museums.ncl.ac.uk/Avebury/stone4.htm). *World Archaeology* 31, 179–93.

Girling, M. and Greig, J. 1985. A first fossil record for *Scolytus scolytus* (F.) (Elm Bark beetle): Its occurrence in elm decline deposits from London and its implications for the Neolithic elm decline. *Journal of Archaeological Science* 12, 347–51.

Greatorix, C. 2003. Living on the margins? The Late Bronze Age landscape of the Willingdon Levels. In D. Rudling (ed.), *The Archaeology of Sussex to AD 2000*, 89–100. Brighton: University of Sussex, Centre for Continuing Education.

Green, H. S. 1974. Early Bronze Age burial, territory and population in Milton Keynes, Buckinghamshire, and the Great Ouse Valley. *Archaeological Journal* 131, 75–139.

Green, M. 2000. *A Landscape Revealed. 10,000 Years on a Chalkland Farm.* Stroud: Tempus.

Greenwell, W. 1877. *British Barrows.* Oxford: Clarendon Press.

Greig, M., Greig, C., Shepherd, A., and Shepherd, I. 1989. A Beaker cist from Chapleden, Tore of Troup, Banff and Buchan District. *Proceedings of the Society of Antiquaries of Scotland* 119, 73–81.

Griffin, S., Dalwood, H., Hurst, D., and Pearson, E. 2002. Excavations at the Perdiswell Park and Ride, Droitwich Road, Worcester. *Transactions of the Worcestershire Archaeological Society* 18, 1–24.

Grogan, E. 1996a. Neolithic houses in Ireland. In T. Darvill and J. Thomas (eds.), *Neolithic Houses in Northwest Europe and Beyond*, 41–60. Oxford: Oxbow.

Grogan, E. 1996b. North Munster Project. *Discovery Programme Reports* 4, 26–46.

Grogan, E. 2004a. The implications of the Irish Neolithic houses. In I. Shepherd and G. Barclay (eds.), *Scotland in Ancient Europe*, 103–14.

Edinburgh: Society of Antiquaries of Scotland.

Grogan, E. 2004b. Middle Bronze Age burial traditions in Ireland. In H. Roche, E. Grogan, J. Bradley, J. Coles, and B. Raftery (eds.), *From Megaliths to Metals*, 61–71. Oxford: Oxbow.

Grogan, E. and Eogan, G. 1987. Lough Gur excavations by Seán P. O' Riordáin: Further Beaker and Neolithic habitations at Knockadoon. *Proceedings of the Royal Irish Academy* 87C, 299–506.

Guilbert, G. 1981. Hill-fort functions and populations: A sceptical view. In G. Guilbert (ed.), *Hill-Fort Studies*, 104–21. Leicester: Leicester University Press.

Guttmann, E. 2005. Midden cultivation in prehistoric Britain: Arable crops in gardens. *World Archaeology* 37, 224–39.

Guttmann, E. and Last, J. 2000. A Late Bronze Age landscape at South Hornchurch, Essex. *Proceedings of the Prehistoric Society* 66, 319–59.

Haggarty, A. 1991. Machrie Moor, Arran: Recent excavations of two stone circles. *Proceedings of the Society of Antiquaries of Scotland* 58: 51–94.

Hall, D. and Coles, J. 1994. *Fenland Survey: An Essay in Landscape and Persistence.* London: English Heritage.

Halliday, S. 1999. Hut-circle settlements in the Scottish landscape. *Northern Archaeology* 18, 49–65.

Hamilton, J. 1968. *Excavations at Clickhimin, Shetland.* Edinburgh: HMSO.

Harbison, P. 1972. Wooden and stone chevaux-de-frise in Central and Western Europe. *Proceedings of the Prehistoric Society* 37, 195–225.

Harbison, P. and Laing, L. 1974. *Some Iron Age Mediterranean Imports in England.* Oxford: British Archaeological Reports (BAR 5).

Harding, A. 1987. *Henge Monuments and Related Monuments of Britain.* Oxford: British Archaeological Reports (BAR 175).

Harding, A. 2000. *European Societies in the Bronze Age.* Cambridge: Cambridge University Press.

Harding, D. 2004. *The Iron Age in Northern Britain.* London: Routledge.

Harding, J. 1995. Social histories and regional perspectives in the Neolithic of Lowland England. *Proceedings of the Prehistoric Society* 61, 117–6.

Harding, J. 1996. Reconsidering the Neolithic round barrows of eastern Yorkshire. *Northern Archaeology* 14, 67–78.

Harding, J. 2000. Later Neolithic ceremonial centres, ritual and pilgrimage: The monument complex at Thornborough, North Yorkshire. In A. Ritchie (ed.), *Neolithic Orkney in its European Context*, 31–46. Cambridge: McDonald Institute for Archaeological Research.

Harding, J. 2003. *Henge Monuments of the British Isles*. Stroud: Tempus.

Harrison, R. 1980. *The Beaker Folk*. London: Thames and Hudson.

Hartwell, B. 1998. The Ballynahatty complex. In A. Gibson and D. Simpson (eds.), *Prehistoric Ritual and Religion*. Stroud: Sutton.

Haughton, C. and Powelsland, D. 1999. *West Heslerton. The Anglian Cemetery, Volume 1*. Yedingham: Landscape Research Centre.

Healy, F. 1987. Prediction or prejudice? The relationship between field survey and excavation. In A. Brown and M. Edmonds (eds.), *Lithic Analysis and Later British Prehistory*, 9–18. Oxford: British Archaeological Reports (BAR 162).

Healy, F. 1988. *The Anglo-Saxon Cemetery at Spong Hill, North Elmham, Part VI: Occupation during the Seventh to Second Millennia BC*. East Anglian Archaeology 39.

Healy, F. 1995. Pits, pots and peat: Ceramics and settlement in East Anglia. In I. Kinnes and G. Varndell (eds.), *'Unbaked Urns of Rudely Shape.' Essays on British and Irish Pottery for Ian Longworth*, 173–84. Oxford: Oxbow.

Healy, F. 2004. Hambledon Hill and its implications. In R. Cleal and J. Pollard (eds.), *Monuments and Material Culture*, 15–38. East Knoyle: Hobnob Press.

Healy, F. and Harding, J. in press. *Raunds Area Project. The Neolithic and Bronze Age Landscapes of West Cotton, Stanwick and Irthlingborough, Northamptonshire*. London: English Heritage.

Healy, F. and Housley, R. 1992. Nancy was not alone: Human skeletons of the Early Bronze Age from the Norfolk peat fen. *Antiquity* 66, 948–55.

Hedges, J. 1975. Excavation of two Orcadian burnt mounds at Liddle and Beaquoy. *Proceedings of the Society of Antiquaries of Scotland* 106, 39–98.

Hedges, J. 1987. *Bu, Gurness and the Brochs of Orkney. Part 2: Gurness*. Oxford: British Archaeological Reports (BAR 163).

Helms, M. 1998. *Ulysses' Sail: An Ethnographic Odyssey of Power, Knowledge and Geographical Distance*. Princeton: Princeton University Press.

Helms, M. 2004. Tangible materiality and cosmological others in the development of sedentism. In E. DeMarrais, C. Gosden, and C. Renfrew (eds.), *Rethinking Materiality. The Engagement of Mind with the Material World*, 117–27. Cambridge: McDonald Institute for Archaeological Research.

Hemp. W. 1930. The chambered tomb of Bryn Celli Ddu. *Archaeologia* 80, 179–214.

Henley, C. 2004. Falling off the edge of the Irish Sea: Clettraval and the two-faced Neolithic of the Outer Hebrides. In V. Cummings and C. Fowler (eds.), *The Neolithic of the Irish Sea*, 64–71. Oxford: Oxbow.

Henley, C. 2005. Choreographed monumentality: Creating the centre of other worlds at the monument complex of Callanish, western Lewis. In V. Cummings and A. Pannett (eds.), *Set in Stone. New Approaches to Neolithic Monuments in Scotland*, 95–106. Oxford: Oxbow.

Henshall, A. 1963. *The Chambered Tombs of Scotland. Volume 1*. Edinburgh: Edinburgh University Press.

Henshall, A. 2004. Scottish passage-graves: Some confusions and conclusions. In A. Gibson and A. Sheridan (eds.), *From Sickles to Circles. Britain and Ireland at the Time of Stonehenge*, 78–91. Stroud: Tempus.

Herity, M. and Eogan, G, 1977. *Ireland in Prehistory*. London: Routledge.

Herne, A. 1986. A time and place for the Grimston bowl. In J. Barrett and I. Kinnes (eds.), *The Archaeology of Context in the Neolithic and Bronze Age: Recent Trends*, 9–21. Sheffield: Sheffield University Department of Prehistory and Archaeology.

Hey, G., Baylis, A., and Boyle, A. 1999. Iron Age inhumation burials at Yarnton, Oxfordshire. *Antiquity* 73, 551–62.

Hill, J. D. 1995. *Ritual and Rubbish in the Iron Age of Wessex*. Oxford: British Archaeological Reports (BAR 242).

Hill, J. D. 1996. Hillforts and the Iron Age of Wessex. In T. Champion and J. Collis (eds.), *The Iron Age in Britain and Ireland: Recent Trends*, 95–116. Sheffield: J. R. Collis Publications.

Hill, J. D. 1999. Settlement, landscape and regionality: Norfolk and Suffolk in the pre-Roman Iron Age of Britain and beyond. In J. Davies and T. Williamson (eds.), *Land of the*

Iceni. The Iron Age in Northern East Anglia, 185–207. Norwich: University of East Anglia Centre of East Anglian Studies.

Hingley, R. 1992. Society in Scotland from 700 BC to AD 200. *Proceedings of the Society of Antiquaries of Scotland* 122, 7–53.

Hingley, R. 2005. Iron Age 'currency bars' in Britain: items of exchange in liminal contexts? In C. Haselgrove and D. Wigg-Wolf (eds.), *Iron Age Coinage and Ritual Practices*, 183–205. Mainz: von Zabern.

Hodder, I. 1982a. Towards a contextual approach to prehistoric exchange. In J. Ericson and T. Earle (eds.), *Contexts for Prehistoric Exchange*, 199–211. New York: Academic Press.

Hodder, I. 1982b. *Symbols in Action: Ethnoarchaeological Studies of Material Culture*. Cambridge: Cambridge University Press.

Hodder, I. 1990. *The Domestication of Europe*. Oxford: Blackwell

Holden, E. 1972. A Bronze Age cemetery-barrow on Itford Hill, Beddingham, Sussex. *Sussex Archaeological Collections* 110, 70–117.

Howard, H. 1981. In the wake of distribution: Towards an integrated approach to ceramic studies in prehistoric Britain. In H. Howard and E. Morris (eds.), *Production and Distribution: A Ceramic Viewpoint*, 1–30. Oxford: British Archaeological Reports (BAR International Series 120).

Hughes, G. 2000. *The Lockington Gold Hoard: An Early Bronze Age Barrow in Leicestershire*. Oxford: Oxbow.

Hunter, F. 2005. The image of the warrior in the British Iron Age – Coin iconography in context. In C. Haselgrove and D. Wigg-Wolf (eds.), *Iron Age Coinage and Ritual Practices*, 43–67. Mainz: von Zabern.

Hunter, J. and MacSween, A. 1991. A sequence for the Orcadian Neolithic. *Antiquity* 65, 911–14.

Huntley, B. and Birks, H. 1983. *An Atlas of Past and Present Pollen Maps for Europe, 0–13,000 Years Ago*. Cambridge: Cambridge University Press.

Hurl, D. 1995. Killymoon – New light on the Late Bronze Age. *Archaeology Ireland* 9, 24–7.

Innes, J., Rowley-Conwy, P. , and Blackford, J. 2003. The start of the Mesolithic – Neolithic transition in north-west Europe – The palynological contribution. *Antiquity* 82 projectgall//297.html.

Jackson, D. and Dix, B. 1987. Late Iron Age and Roman settlement at Weekley, Northants. *Northamptonshire Archaeology* 21, 41–93.

Jacobi, R. 1976. Britain inside and outside Mesolithic Europe. *Proceedings of the Prehistoric Society* 42, 67–84.

Johnston, D. 1997. Biggar Common, 1987–93: An early prehistoric funerary and domestic landscape in Clydesdale, South Lanarkshire. *Proceedings of the Society of Antiquaries of Scotland* 127, 185–253.

Johnston, R. 2000. Dying, becoming and being in the field. In J. Harding and R. Johnston (eds.), *Northern Pasts*, 57–70. Oxford: British Archaeological Report (BAR 302).

Johnston, R. 2005. Pattern without a plan: Rethinking the Bronze Age coaxial field systems on Dartmoor, south-west England. *Oxford Journal of Archaeology* 24, 1–21.

Jones, A. 1999. The Excavation of a Later Bronze Age Structure at Callestick. *Cornish Archaeology* 38, 1–55.

Jones, C. 1998. The discovery and dating of the prehistoric landscape of Roughan Hill in Co. Clare. *Journal of Irish Archaeology* 9, 27–44.

Jones, C. 2004. *The Burren and the Aran Islands. Exploring the Archaeology*. Cork: The Collins Press.

Jones, C. in press. Coasts, mountains, rivers and bogs. Using the landscape to explore regionality in Ireland. In G. Barclay and K. Brophy (eds.), *Cores and Peripheries? The Nature of the Regional Neolithics in Britain and Ireland*. Oxford: Oxbow.

Jones, D. 1998. Long barrows and Neolithic elongated enclosures in Lincolnshire: An assessment of the air photographic evidence. *Proceedings of the Prehistoric Society* 64, 83–114.

Jope, E. M. 1961. Daggers of the Early Iron Age in Britain. *Proceedings of the Prehistoric Society* 27, 307–43.

Jope, E. M. 2000. *Early Celtic Art in the British Isles*. Oxford: Clarendon Press.

Jorge, S. O. (ed.), 1998 *Existe uma idade do bronze Atlantico?* Lisbon: Instituto Português de Arqueologia.

Kendrick, J. 1995. Excavation of a Neolithic enclosure and Iron Age settlement at Douglasmuir, Angus. *Proceedings of the Society of Antiquaries of Scotland* 125, 29–67.

Kilbride-Jones, H. 1950. The excavation of a composite Early Iron Age monument with 'henge' features at Lugg, Co. Dublin. *Proceedings of the Royal Irish Academy* 53C, 311–32.

Kinnes, I. 1979. *Round Barrows and Ring Ditches in the British Neolithic.* London: British Museum.

Kinnes, I. 1992. *Non-megalithic Long Barrows and Allied Structures in the British Neolithic.* London: British Museum

Kinnes, I. 2004. 'A truth universally acknowledged': Some more thoughts on Neolithic round barrows. In A. Gibson and A. Sheridan (eds.), *From Sickles to Circles. Britain and Ireland at the Time of Stonehenge,* 106–15. Stroud: Tempus.

Kinnes, I., Gibson, A., Ambers, J., Bowman, S., Leese, M., and Boast, R. 1991. Radiocarbon dating and British Beakers: The British Museum programme. *Scottish Archaeological Review* 8, 35–68.

Kinnes, I. and Longworth, I. 1985. *Catalogue of the Excavated Prehistoric and Romano-British Material in the Greenwell Collection.* London: British Museum Press.

Kinnes, I., Schadla-Hall, T., Chadwick, P., and Dean, P. 1983. Duggleby Howe reconsidered. *Archaeological Journal* 140, 83–108.

Kirch, P. 2000. *On the Road of the Winds: An Archaeological History of the Pacific Islands Before European Contact.* Berkeley: University of California Press.

Knight, M. 2000. Henge to house – Post-circles in a Neolithic and Bronze Age landscape at King's Dyke West, Whittlesey, Cambridgeshire. *Past* 34, 3–4.

Kristiansen, K. 1998. *Europe Before History.* Cambridge: Cambridge University Press.

Kunst, M. 2001. Invasion? Fashion? Social rank? Considerations concerning the Bell Beaker phenomenon in Copper Age fortifications of the Iberian Peninsula. In F. Nicolis (ed.), *Bell Beakers Today,* 81–90. Trento: Provincia Autonoma de Trento.

Ladle, L. and Woodward, A. 2003. A Middle Bronze Age house and burnt mound at Bestwall, Wareham, Dorset: An interim report. *Proceedings of the Prehistoric Society* 69, 265–77.

Ladle, L. and Woodward, A. in press. *Excavations at Bestwall Quarry, Wareham 1992-2005. Volume 1: The Prehistoric Landscape.* London: English Heritage.

Lambrick, G. and Allen, T. 2004. *Gravelly Guy, Stanton Harcourt, Oxfordshire. The Development of a Prehistoric and Romano-British Community.* Oxford: Oxford Archaeology.

Lanting, J. and Van der Waals, J. D. 1972. British Beakers as seen from the Continent. *Helinium* 12, 20–46.

Lanting, J., Mook, W., and Van der Waals, J. D. 1976. Beaker Culture relations in the Lower Rhine Basin. In W. Pape and C. Strahm (eds.), *Glockenbechersymposion,* 1–80. Haarlem: Fibula-van Dishoek.

Last, J. 1998. Books of Life: Biography and memory in a Bronze Age barrow. *Oxford Journal of Archaeology* 17, 43–53.

Lawson, A. 2000. *Potterne 1982–5: Animal Husbandry in Later Prehistoric Wessex.* Salisbury: Trust for Wessex Archaeology.

Legge, A. 1981. Aspects of cattle husbandry. In R. Mercer (ed.), *Farming Practice in British Prehistory,* 169–81. Edinburgh: Edinburgh University Press.

Lelong, O. and Pollard, T. 1998. The excavation and survey of prehistoric enclosures at Blackshouse Burn, Lanarkshire. *Proceedings of the Society of Antiquaries of Scotland* 128, 13–53.

Lévi-Strauss, C. 1983. *The Way of the Masks.* London: Cape.

Lewis, A. 1998. The Bronze Age mines of the Great Orme and other sites in the British Isles and beyond. In C. Mordant, M. Pernot, and V. Rychner (eds.), *L'atelier du bronzier en Europe. Tome 2,* 45–58. Paris: Editions du comite des travaux historiques et scientifiques.

Lewis-Williams, D. and Dowson, T. 1993. On vision and power in the Neolithic: Evidence from the decorated monuments. *Current Anthropology* 34, 55–65.

Lewis-Williams, D. and Pearce, D. 2005. *Inside the Neolithic Mind.* London: Thames and Hudson.

Lloyd Morgan, C. 1887. The stones of Stanton Drew: Their source and origin. *Proceedings of the Somerset Archaeological Society* 33, 37–50.

Lock, G., Gosden, C., and Daly, P. 2005. *Segsbury Camp. Excavations in 1996 and 1997 at an Iron Age Hillfort on the Oxfordshire Ridgeway.* Oxford: Oxford University Committee for Archaeology.

Logue, P. 2003. Excavations at Thornhill, Co. Londonderry. In I. Armit, E. Murphy, E. Nelis, and D. Simpson (eds.), *Neolithic Settlement in Ireland and Western Britain,* 149–55. Oxford: Oxbow.

Louwe Koojimans, L. 1976. Local developments in a borderland. A survey of the Neolithic of the Lower Rhine. *Oudheidkundige Mededelingen* 57, 227–97.

Loveday, R. 1998. Double entrance henges – Routes to the past? In A. Gibson and D. Simpson (eds.), *Prehistoric Ritual and Religion*, 14–31. Stroud: Sutton.

Lynch, F. 1967. Barclodiad y Gawres: Comparative notes on the decorated stones. *Archaeologia Cambrensis* 116, 1–22.

Lynch, F. 1971. Report on the re-excavation of two Bronze Age cairns in Anglesey: Bedd Branwen and Treiowerth. *Archaeologia Cambrensis* 120, 11–83.

Lynch, F. 1979. Ring cairns: Their design and purpose. *Ulster Journal of Archaeology* 42, 1–19.

Lynch, F. 1993. *Excavations in the Brenig Valley*. Bangor: Cambrian Archaeological Association.

Lynch, F., Aldhouse-Green, S., and Davies, J. 2000. *Prehistoric Wales*. Stroud: Sutton.

Lynch, F. and Musson, C. 2001. A prehistoric and early medieval complex at Llandegai, near Bangor, North Wales. *Archaeologia Cambrensis* 150, 17–142.

Lynn, C. 1977. Trial excavations at the King's Stables, Tray Townland, County Armagh. *Ulster Journal of Archaeology* 40: 42–62.

McAvoy, F. 2000. The development of the Neolithic monument complex at Godmanchester, Cambridgeshire. In M. Dawson (ed.), *Prehistoric, Roman and Post-Roman Landscapes of the Great Ouse Valley*, 51–6. York: Council for British Archaeology.

MacCartan, S. 2004. The Mesolithic in the Isle of Man: An island perspective. In A. Saville (ed.), *Mesolithic Scotland and its Neighbours*. 271–83. Edinburgh: Society of Antiquaries of Scotland.

McCarthy, M. 2000. Prehistoric settlement in northern Cumbria. In J. Harding and R. Johnston (eds.), *Northern Pasts*, 131–40. Oxford: British Archaeological Reports (BAR 302).

McCullagh, R. and Tipping, R. 1998. *The Lairg Project 1988–1996. The Evolution of an Archaeological Landscape in Northern Scotland*. Edinburgh: Scottish Trust for Archaeological Research.

MacDonagh, M. 2005. Valley bottom and hilltop: 6,000 years of settlement along the route of the N4 Sligo Inner Relief Road. In J. O'Sullivan and M. Stanley (eds.), *Recent Archaeological Discoveries on National Road Schemes 2004*, 9–23. Dublin: National Roads Authority.

McGrail, S. 1997. *Studies in Maritime Archaeology*. Oxford: British Archaeological Reports (BAR 256).

McKie, E. 1995. Gurness and Midhowe brochs in Orkney: Some problems of misinterpretation. *Archaeological Journal* 151, 98–157.

McOmish, D. 1996. East Chisenbury: Ritual and rubbish at the British Bronze Age-Iron Age transition, *Antiquity* 70, 68–76.

McOmish, D., Field, D., and Brown, G. 2002. *The Field Archaeology of the Salisbury Plain Training Area*. Swindon: English Heritage.

McSparron, C. 2003. The excavation of a Neolithic house and other structures at Enagh, County Derry. *Ulster Journal of Archaeology* 62, 1–15.

Malim, T. 1999. Cursuses and related monuments of the Cambridgeshire Ouse. In A. Barclay and J. Harding (eds.), *Pathways and Ceremonies: The Cursus Monuments of Britain and Ireland*, 77–85. Oxford: Oxbow.

Mallory, J. 1984. The Long Stone, Ballybeen, Dundonald, County Down. *Ulster Journal of Archaeology* 47, 1–4.

Mallory, J. 1995. Haughey's Fort in the Navan complex of the Late Bronze Age. In J. Waddell and E. Shee Twohig (eds.), *Ireland in the Bronze Age*, 73–86. Dublin: Stationery Office.

Mallory, J. 2000. Excavation of the Navan ditch. *Emainia* 18, 21–35.

Manby, T. 1988. The Neolithic of eastern Yorkshire. In T. Manby (ed.), *Archaeology in Eastern Yorkshire*, 35–88. Sheffield: Sheffield University Department of Archaeology.

Manby, T., King, A., and Vyner, B. 2003. The Neolithic and Early Bronze Age: A time of early agriculture. In T. Manby, S. Moorhouse, and P. Ottaway (eds.), *The Archaeology of Yorkshire*, 35–116. Leeds: Yorkshire Archaeological Society.

Manning, A. and Moore, C. 2003. A Late Bronze Age site at Springfield Park, Chelmsford. *Essex Archaeology and History* 34, 19–35.

Manning. W. and Saunders, C. 1972. A socketed iron axe from Maids Moreton, Buckinghamshire, with a note on the type. *Antiquaries Journal* 52, 276–92.

Marcigny, C. and Ghesquière, E. 2003. *L'île de Tatihou (Manche) à l'âge du Bronze*. Paris: Editions de la maison des sciences de l'homme.

Markey, M., Wilkes, E., and Darvill, T. 2002. Poole Harbour: An Iron Age port. *Current Archaeology* 181, 7–11.

Martin, E. 1988. *Burgh: The Iron Age and Roman Enclosure*. East Anglian Archaeology 40.

Martin, E. and Murphy, P. 1988. West Row Fen, Mildenhall, Suffolk: A Bronze Age fen-edge settlement. *Antiquity* 62, 353–8.

Masters, L. 1983 Chambered tombs and non-megalithic barrows in Britain. In C. Renfrew (ed.), *The Megalithic Tombs of Western Europe*, 97–112. London: Thames and Hudson.

Meillassoux, C. 1972. From reproduction to production. *Economy and Society* 1, 93–105.

Melton, N. and Nicholson, R. 2004. The Mesolithic in the Northern Isles: The preliminary evaluation of an oyster midden at West Voe, Sunburgh, Shetland, UK. *Antiquity* 78 ProjGall/229.html.

Mercer, R. 1981a. Excavations at Carn Brea, Illogan, Cornwall 1970–73. *Cornish Archaeology* 20, 1–204.

Mercer, R. 1981b. The excavation of a late Neolithic henge-type enclosure at Balfarg, Markinch, Fife, Scotland. *Proceedings of the Society of Antiquaries of Scotland* 111, 63–171.

Mercer, R. 1981c. *Grimes Graves, Norfolk, Excavations 1971–2, Vols. 1 & 2*. London: HMSO.

Mercer, R. 1997. The excavation of a Neolithic enclosure complex at Helman Tor, Lostwithiel, Cornwall. *Cornish Archaeology* 36, 5–63.

Miles, D., Palmer, S., Lock, G., Gosden, C., and Cromarty, A. M. 2003. *Uffington White Horse and its Landscape*. Oxford: Oxford Archaeology.

Millett, M. 1992. *The Romanization of Britain*. Cambridge: Cambridge University Press.

Mitchell, F. 1992. Notes on some non-local cobbles at the entrances to the passage graves at Newgrange and Knowth, County Meath. *Journal of the Royal Society of Antiquaries of Ireland* 122, 128–45.

Mizoguchi, K. 1992. A historiography of a linear barrow cemetery: A structurationist's point of view. *Archaeological Review From Cambridge* 11.1, 39–49.

Mizoguchi, K. 1993. Time in the reproduction of mortuary practices. *World Archaeology* 25, 223–235.

Moffet, L., Robinson, M., and Straker, V. 1989. Cereals, fruits and nuts: Charred plant remains from Neolithic sites in England and Wales and the Neolithic economy. In A. Milles, D.

Williams and N. Gardner (eds.), *The Beginnings of Agriculture*, 243–61. Oxford: British Archaeological Reports (BAR International Series 496).

Molloy, K. and O' Connell, M. 1995. Palaeoecological investigations towards the reconstruction of environment and land use changes during prehistory at Céide Fields, western Ireland. *Probleme der Küstenforschung im südlichen Nordseegebiet* 23, 187–225.

Moloney, C., Holbrey, R., Wheelhouse, P., and Roberts, I. 2003. *Catterick Racecourse North Yorkshire. The Reuse and Adaptation of a Monument from Prehistoric to Anglian Times*. Morley: West Yorkshire Archaeology Service.

Moore, D. 2004. Hostilities in Early Neolithic Ireland: Trouble with the new neighbours – The evidence from Ballyharry, County Antrim. In A. Gibson and A. Sheridan (eds.), *From Sickles to Circles. Britain and Ireland at the time of Stonehenge*, 142–54. Stroud: Tempus.

Mordant, C. 1998. Emergence d'une architecture funéraraire monumentale (vallées de la Seine et de l'Yonne). In J. Guilaine (ed.), *Sépultures d'occident et genèses des mégalithes*, 73–88. Paris: Editions Errance.

Mount, C. 1994. Aspects of ritual deposition in the late Neolithic and Beaker periods at Newgrange, Co. Meath. *Proceedings of the Prehistoric Society* 60, 433–443.

Mount, C. 1997. Adolf Mahr's excavation of an Early Bronze Age cemetery at Keenoge, County Meath. *Proceedings of the Royal Irish Academy* 97C, 1–68.

Muckelroy, K. 1981. Middle Bronze Age trade between Britain and Europe: A maritime perspective. *Proceedings of the Prehistoric Society* 47, 275–297.

Musson, C. 1991. *The Breiddin Hillfort*. York: Council for British Artchaeology.

Myers, A. 1987. All shot to pieces? Inter-assemblage variability, lithic analysis and Mesolithic assemblage types. In A. Brown and M. Edmonds (eds.), *Lithic Analysis and Later British Prehistory*, 137–53. Oxford: British Archaeological Reports (BAR 162).

Nebelsick, L. 2000. Rent asunder: Ritual violence in Late Bronze Age hoards. In C. Pare (ed.), *Metals Make the World Go Round. The Supply and Circulation of Metals in Bronze Age Europe*, 160–75. Oxford: Oxbow.

Needham, S. and Ambers, J. 1994. Redating Rams Hill and reconsidering Bronze Age enclosures. *Proceedings of the Prehistoric Society* 60, 225–43.

Needham, S. 1988. Selective deposition in the British Early Bronze Age. *World Archaeology* 20, 229–248.

Needham, S. 1991. *Excavation and Salvage at Runnymede Bridge 1978: The Late Bronze Age Waterfront Site*. London: British Museum Press.

Needham, S. 1992. The structure of settlement and ritual in the Late Bronze Age of south-east England. In C. Mordant and A. Richard (eds.), *L'habitat et l'occupation du sol à l'Age du Bronze en Europe*, 49–69. Paris: Editions du comité des travaux historiques et scientifiques.

Needham, S. 1996. Chronology and periodisation in the British Bronze Age. *Acta Archaeologica* 67, 121–46.

Needham, S. 2000 Power pulses across a cultural divide: Cosmologically driven acquisition between Armorica and Wessex. *Proceedings of the Prehistoric Society* 66, 151–207.

Needham, S. 2004. Migdale-Marnoch: Sunburst of Scottish metallurgy. In I. Shepherd and G. Barclay (eds.), *Scotland in Ancient Europe*, 217–45. Edinburgh: Society of Antiquaries of Scotland.

Needham, S. 2005. Transforming Beaker culture in North West Europe: Processes of fission and fusion. *Proceedings of the Prehistoric Society* 71, 171–217.

Needham, S., Bronk Ramsay, C., Coombs, D., Cartwright, C., and Pettitt, P. 1998. An independent chronology of British Bronze Age metalwork: The results of the Oxford Radiocarbon Accelerator Programme. *Archaeological Journal* 154, 55–107.

Needham, S. and Spence, T. 1996. *Refuse and Disposal at Area 16 East, Runnymede*. London: British Museum Press.

Needham, S. and Spence, T. 1997. Refuse and the formation of middens. *Antiquity* 71, 77–90.

Newman, C. 1997a. *Tara. An Archaeological Survey*. Dublin: The Discovery Programme.

Newman, C. 1997b. Ballinderry Crannog No. 2, Co. Offaly: The later Bronze Age. *Journal of Irish Archaeology* 8, 91–100.

Newman, C. 1999. Notes on four cursus-like monuments in County Meath, Ireland. In A. Barclay and J. Harding (eds.), *Pathways and Ceremonies: The Cursus Monuments of Britain and Ireland*, 141–7. Oxford: Oxbow.

Niblett, R. 2001. A Neolithic dug-out from a multi-period site near St Albans, Herts, England. *International Journal of Nautical Archaeology* 30, 155–95.

Northover, P. 1982. The exploration of the long-distance movement of bronze in Bronze and Early Iron Age Europe. *Bulletin of the London University Institute of Archaeology* 19, 45–72.

Northover, P. 1984. Iron Age bronze metallurgy in Central Southern England. In B. Cunliffe and D. Miles (eds.), *Aspects of the Iron Age in Central Southern Britain*, 126–145. Oxford: Oxford University Committee for Archaeology.

Nowakowski, J. 2001. Leaving home in the Cornish Bronze Age: Insights into planned abandonment processes. In J. Brück (ed.), *Bronze Age Landscapes. Tradition and Transformation*, 139–48. Oxford: Oxbow.

Nowakowski, J. 2006. Life and Death in a Cornish Valley. *British Archaeology* 89, 12–17.

O'Brien, W. 1992. Boulder burials: A Later Bronze Age megalith tradition in south-west Ireland. *Journal of the Cork Historical and Archaeological Society* 97, 11–35.

O'Brien, W. 1999. *Sacred Ground. Megalithic Tombs in Coastal South-west Ireland*. Galway: National University of Ireland.

O'Brien, W. 2004a. *Ross Island. Mining, Metal and Society in Early Ireland*. Galway: Department of Archaeology, National University of Ireland, Galway.

O'Brien, W. 2004b. (Con)fusion of tradition? The circle henge in Ireland. In A. Gibson and A. Sheridan (eds.), *From Sickles to Circles. Britain and Ireland at the Time of Stonehenge*, 323–38. Stroud: Tempus.

O'Connell, M. and Molloy, K. 2001. Farming and woodland dynamics in Ireland during the Neolithic. *Proceedings of the Royal Irish Academy* 101B, 99–128.

Ó'Drisceoil 2001. Balgatheran Site 4. In I. Bennett (ed.), *Excvavations 2001: Summary Accounts of Archaeological Excavations in Ireland*, 255–7. Bray: Wordwell.

Ó'Faoláin, S. 2004. *Bronze Artefact Production in Late Bronze Age Ireland*. Oxford: British Archaeological Reports (BAR 382).

Ó' Floinn, R. 1992. A Neolithic cave burial in Limerick. *Archaeology Ireland* 20, 19–22.

O'Kelly, M. 1954. Excavations and experiments in ancient Irish cooking-places. *Journal of the*

Royal Society of Antiquaries of Ireland 84, 105–55.

O'Kelly, M. 1958. A wedge-shaped gallery grave at Island, Co. Cork. *Journal of the Royal Society of Antiquaries of Ireland* 88, 1–23.

O'Kelly, M. 1982. *Newgrange: Archaeology, Art and Legend*. London: Thames and Hudson.

O'Kelly, M., Cleary, R., and Lehane, D. 1983. *Newgrange, Co. Meath: The Late Neolithic/ Beaker Period settlement*. Oxford: British Archaeological Reports (BAR International Series 190).

Ó'Nualláin, S. 1972. A Neolithic house at Ballyglass near Ballycastle, Co. Mayo. *Journal of the Royal Society of Antiquaries of Ireland* 102, 49–57.

Ó'Nualláin, S. 1998. Excavation of the small court cairn and associated hut sites at Ballyglass, near Ballycastle, Co. Mayo. *Proceedings of the Royal Irish Academy* 98C, 125–75.

Ó'Ríordáin, S. 1936. Excavations at Lissard, Co. Limerick and other sites in the locality. *Journal of the Royal Society of Antiquaries of Ireland* 66, 173–85.

O'Sullivan, A. 1998. *The Archaeology of Lake Settlement in Ireland*. Dublin: Royal Irish Academy.

O'Sullivan, M. 2004. Little and large. Comparing Knockroe with Knowth. In H. Roche, E. Grogan, J. Bradley, J. Coles, and B. Raftery (eds.), *From Megaliths to Metals*, 44–50. Oxford: Oxbow.

O'Sullivan, M. 2005. *Duma na nGiall, Tara. The Mound of the Hostages*. Bray: Wordwell.

Oswald, A. 1997. A doorway on the past: Practical and mystic concerns in the orientation of roundhouse doorways. In A. Gwilt and C. Haselgrove (eds.), *Reconstructing Iron Age Societies*, 87–95. Oxford: Oxbow.

Oswald, A., Dyer, C., and Barber, M. 2001. *The Creation of Monuments. Neolithic Causewayed Enclosures in the British Isles*. Swindon: English Heritage.

Owen, O. 1992. Eildon Hill North. In J. Rideout, O. Owen, and E. Halpin, *Hillforts of Southern Scotland*, 21–71. Edinburgh: AOC (Scotland).

Palmer, S. 1999a. Church Lawford. *West Midlands Archaeology* 42, 103–5.

Palmer, S. 1999b. Archaeological excavations in the Arrow Valley, Warwickshire. *Transactions of the Birmingham and Warwickshire Archaeological Society* 103, 1–231.

Pantos, A. and Semple, S. (eds.) 2003. *Assembly Places and Practices in Medieval Europe*. Dublin: Four Courts Press.

Pare, C. 2000. Bronze and the Bronze Age. In C. Pare (ed.), *Metals Make the World Go Round: The Supply and Circulation of Metals in Bronze Age Europe*, 1–38. Oxford: Oxbow.

Parker, A., Goudie, A., Anderson, A., Robinson, M., and Bonsall, C. 2002. A review of the mid-Holocene elm decline in the British Isles. *Progress in Physical Geography* 26, 1–45.

Parker Pearson, M. 1999. Food, sex and death: Cosmologies in the British Iron Age with special reference to east Yorkshire. *Cambridge Archaeological Journal* 9, 43–69.

Parker Pearson, M., Pollard, J., Richards, C., Thomas, J., Tilley, C., Welham, K. and Albarella, U. 2006. Materializing Stonehenge. The Stonehenge Riverside Project and New Discoveries. *Journal of Material Culture* 11, 227–61.

Parker Pearson, M. and Ramilsonina. 1998. Stonehenge for the ancestors: The stones pass on the message. *Antiquity* 72, 308–26.

Parker Pearson, M. and Sharples, N. 1999. *Between Land and Sea: Excavations at Dun Vulan, South, Uist*. Sheffield: Sheffield Academic Press.

Parker Pearson, M., Sharples, N., and Symonds, J. 2004. *South Uist: Archaeology and History of a Hebridean Island*. Stroud: Tempus.

Patrick, J. 1975. Megalithic exegesis: A comment. *Irish Archaeological Research Forum* 11.2, 9–14.

Pearson, T. and Topping, P. 2002. Rethinking the Carrock Fell enclosure. In G. Varndell and P. Topping (eds.), *Enclosures in Neolithic Europe*, 121–7. Oxford: Oxbow.

Percival, J. 1980. *Living in the Past*. London: BBC.

Pestell, T. and Ulmschneider, K. (eds.). 2003. *Markets in Early Medieval Europe: Trading and Productive Sites, 650 – 850*. Maccesfield: Windgather.

Peters, F. 2000. Two traditions of Bronze Age burial in the Stonehenge landscape. *Oxford Journal of Archaeology* 19, 343–58.

Petersen, F. 1972. Traditions of multiple burial in Later Neolithic and Early Bronze Age England. *Archaeological Journal* 129, 22–55.

Pétrequin, P., Cassen, S., Croutsch, C., and Errera, M. 2002. La valorisation sociale des longues haches dans l'Europe Néolithique. In

J. Guilaine (ed.), *Materiaux, productions, circulations du Néolithique á l'Age du Bronze,* 67–98. Paris: Editions Errance.

Phillips, C. W. 1941. Some recent finds from the Trent near Nottingham. *Antiquaries Journal* 21, 133–43.

Phillips, T. 2002. *Landscapes of the Living, Landscapes of the Dead.* Oxford: British Archaeological Reports (BAR 328).

Phillips, T. and Watson. A. 2000. The living and the dead in northern Scotland 3500 – 2000 BC. *Antiquity* 74, 786–92.

Pierpoint, S. 1980. *Social Patterns in Yorkshire Prehistory 3500 – 750 BC.* Oxford: British Archaeological Reports (BAR 74).

Piggott, S. 1938. The Early Bronze Age in Wessex. *Proceedings of the Prehistoric Society* 4, 52–106.

Piggott, S. 1950. Swords and scabbards of the British Early Iron Age. *Proceedings of the Prehistoric Society* 16, 1–28.

Pilcher, J. 1969. Archaeology, palaeoecology and C 14 dating of the Beaghmore stone circles. *Ulster Journal of Archaeology* 32, 73–91.

Pitts, M. 2001. Excavating the Sanctuary: New investigations on Overton Hill, Avebury. *Wiltshire Archaeological Magazine* 94, 1–23.

Pollard, J. 1992 The Sanctuary, Overton Hill: A re-examination. *Proceedings of the Prehistoric Society* 58, 213–26.

Pollard, J. 1996. Iron Age riverside pit alignments at St Ives, Cambridgeshire. *Proceedings of the Prehistoric Society* 62, 93–115.

Pollard, J. 2004. The art of decay and the transformation of substance. In C. Renfrew, C. Gosden, and E. DeMarrais (eds.), *Substance, Memory, Display. Archaeology and Art,* 47–62. Cambridge: McDonald Institute for Archaeological Research.

Pollard, J. and Reynolds, A. 2002. *Avebury. The Biography of a Landscape.* Stroud: Tempus.

Pommepuy, C., Auxette, G., Desenne, S., Gransar, F., and Henon, B. 2000. Des enclos à l'âge du fer dans la vallée de l'Aisne: Le monde des vivants et le monde des morts. *Revue Archéologique de Picardie* 2000 1/2, 197–216.

Powell, A. 2005. The language of lineage: Reading Irish court tomb design. *European Journal of Archaeology* 8, 9–28.

Powelsland, D. 1988. Staple Howe in its landscape. In T. Manby (ed.), *Archaeology in Eastern Yorkshire,* 101–8. Sheffield: Sheffield University Department of Archaeology.

Powelsland, D., Haughton, C., and Hanson, J. 1986. Excavations at Heslerton, North Yorkshire 1978 – 82. *Archaeological Journal* 143, 53–173.

Proctor, J. 2002. Late Bronze Age / Early Iron Age placed deposits from Westcroft Road, Carshalton: Their meaning and interpretation. *Surrey Archaeological Collections* 89, 65–103.

Proudfoot, V. B. 1955. *The Downpatrick Gold Find: A Hoard of Gold Objects from Cathedral Hill, Downpatrick.* Belfast: HMSO.

Pryor, F. 1984. *Excavations at Fengate, Peterborough, England: The Fourth Report.* Northampton: Northamptonshire Archaeological Society.

Pryor, F. 1998a. *Etton. Excavations at a Neolithic Causewayed Enclosure near Maxey, Cambridgeshire 1982–7.* London: English Heritage.

Pryor, F. 1998b. *Farmers in Prehistoric Britain.* Stroud: Tempus.

Pryor, F. 2001. *The Flag Fen Basin: Archaeology and Environment of a Fenland Landscape.* London: English Heritage.

Pryor, F., French, C., Crowther, D., Gurney, D., Simpson, G., and Taylor, M. 1985. *Archaeology and Environment in the Lower Welland Valley.* East Anglian Archaeology 27.

Purcell, A. 2002. Excavation of the Neolithic houses at Corbally, Kilcullen, Co. Kildare. *Journal of Irish Archaeology* 11, 77–97.

Quinnell, H. 2004. *Tregurthy: Excavations at Tregurthy Round, St Austell, Cornwall.* Truro: Cornwall County Council.

Raftery, B. 1974. A prehistoric burial mound at Baunogenasraid, Co, Carlow. *Proceedings of the Royal Irish Academy* 74C, 277–312.

Raftery, B. 1984. *La Tène in Ireland: Problems of Origins and Chronology.* Marburg: Vorgeschichtlichen Seminar Marburg.

Raftery, B. 1994. *Pagan Celtic Ireland.* London: Thames and Hudson.

Raftery, B. 1995. The conundrum of Irish Iron Age pottery. In B. Raftery, V. Megaw, and V. Rigby (eds.), *Sites and Sights of the Iron Age,* 149–56. Oxford: Oxbow.

Raftery, B. 1996. *Trackway Excavations in the Mountdillon Bogs, Co. Longford, 1985–91.* Dublin: Department of Archaeology, University College Dublin.

Renfrew, C. 1973a. Monuments, mobilisation and social organisation in Neolithic Wessex. In

Renfrew, C. (ed.), The *Explanation of Culture Change,* 539–58. London: Duckworth.

Renfrew, C. 1973b. *Before Civilization. The Radiocarbon Revolution and Prehistoric Europe.* London: Cape.

Renfrew, C. 1979. *Investigations in Orkney.* London: Society of Antiquaries.

Renfrew, C. 2000. The auld hoose spaeks: Society and life in Stone Age Orkney. In A. Ritchie (ed.), *Neolithic Orkney in its European Context,* 1–20. Cambridge: McDonald Institute for Archaeological Research.

Reynolds, N. 1978. Dark Age timber halls and the background to excavation at Balbridie. *Scottish Archaeological Forum* 10, 41–60.

Reynolds, P. 1979. *Iron Age Farm.* London: British Museum Publications.

Richards, C. 1988. Altered images: A re-examination of Neolithic mortuary practices in Orkney. In J. Barrett and I. Kinnes (eds.), *The Archaeology of Context in the Neolithic and Bronze Age: Recent Trends,* 42–56. Sheffield: Sheffield University Department of Archaeology and Prehistory.

Richards, C. 1991. Skara Brae: Revisiting a Neolithic village in Orkney. In W. Hanson and E. Slater (eds.) *Scottish Archaeology: New Perspectives,* 24–43. Aberdeen: Aberdeen University Press.

Richards, C. 1992. Doorways into another world: The Orkney-Cromarty chambered tombs. In N. Sharples and A. Sheridan (eds.), *Vessels for the Ancestors,* 62–76. Edinburgh: Edinburgh University Press.

Richards, C. 1996a. Henges and water: Towards a cosmological understanding of monumentality and landscape in Late Neolithic Britain. *Journal of Material Culture* 1, 313–36.

Richards, C. 1996b. Monuments as landscape. Creating the centre of the world in Neolithic Orkney. *World Archaeology* 28, 190–208.

Richards, C. 2004a. Labouring with monuments: Constructing the dolmen at Carreg Samson, south-west Wales. In V. Cummings and C. Fowler (eds.), *The Neolithic of the Irish Sea,* 72–80. Oxford: Oxbow.

Richards, C. 2004b. *Dwelling among the Monuments.* Cambridge: McDonald Institute for Archaeological Research.

Richards, C. 2004c. A choreography of construction: Monuments, mobilization and social organisation in Neolithic Orkney. In J. Cherry, C. Scarre, and S. Shennan (eds.), *Explaining Social Change,* 103–13. Cambridge: McDonald Institute for Archaeological Research.

Richards, C. and Thomas, J. 1984. Ritual activity and structured deposition in later Neolithic Wessex. In R. Bradley and J. Gardiner (eds.), *Neolithic Studies,* 189–218. Oxford: British Archaeological Reports (BAR 133).

Richards, J. 1990. *The Stonehenge Environs Project.* London: Historic Buildings and Monuments Commission.

Richards, M. 2000. Human consumption of plant foods in the British Neolithic. Direct evidence from bone stable isotopes. In A. Fairbairn (ed.), *Plants in Neolithic Britain and Beyond,* 123–35. Oxford: Oxbow.

Richards, M. 2003. Explaining the dietary isotope evidence for the rapid adoption of the Neolithic in Britain. In M. Parker Pearson (ed.), *Food, Culture and Identity in the Neolithic and Early Bronze Age,* 31–6. Oxford: British Archaeological Reports (BAR International Series 1117).

Richards, M. 2004. The Early Neolithic in Britain: New insights from biomolecular archaeology. In I. Shepherd and G. Barclay (eds.) *Scotland in Ancient Europe,* 83–90. Edinburgh: Society of Antiquaries of Scotland.

Rigby, V. 2004. *Pots in Pits. The British Museum Yorkshire Settlements Project 1988–92.* East Riding Archaeologist 11.

Ritchie, A. 1983. The excavation of a Neolithic farmstead at Knap of Howar, Papa Westray, Orkney. *Proceedings of the Society of Antiquaries of Scotland* 113, 189–218.

Ritchie, A. 2004. The use of human and faunal remains in chambered cairns in Orkney. In A. Gibson and A. Sheridan (eds.), *From Sickles to Circles. Britain and Ireland at the Time of Stonehenge,* 92–105. Stroud: Tempus.

Ritchie, G. 1974. Excavation of a stone circle and cairn at Balbirnie, Fife. *Archaeological Journal* 131, 1–32.

Ritchie, G. 1976. The Stones of Stenness, Orkney. *Proceedings of the Society of Antiquaries of Scotland* 107, 1–60.

Ritchie, G. 1998. The Ring of Brodgar, Orkney. In C. Ruggles (ed.), *Records in Stone,* 337–50. Cambridge: Cambridge University Press.

Ritchie, J. 1920. The stone circle at Broomend of Crichie. *Proceedings of the Society of Antiquaries of Scotland* 53, 20–8.

Rivet, A. L. F. and Smith., C. 1979. *The Place-names of Roman Britain*. London: Batsford.

Roberts, I., Burgess, A., and Berg, D. 2001. *A New Link to the Past. The Archaeological Landscape of the M1-A1 Link Road*. Morley: West Yorkshire Archaeology Service.

Roberts, I. 2005. *Ferrybridge Henge: The Ritual Landscape*. Morley: West Yorkshire Archaeology Service.

Robinson, M. 2000. Further consideration of Neolithic charred cereals, fruits and nuts. In A. Fairbairn (ed.), *Plants in Neolithic Britain and Beyond*, 85–90. Oxford: Oxbow.

Roche, H. 2004. The dating of the embanked stone circle at Grange, Co. Limerick. In H. Roche, E. Grogan, J. Bradley, J. Coles, and B. Raftery (eds.), *From Megaliths to Metals*, 109–16. Oxford: Oxbow.

Rohl, B. and Needham, S. 1998. *The Circulation of Metal in the British Bronze Age: The Application of Lead Isotope Analysis*. London: British Museum.

Rowlands, M. 1976. *The Production and Distribution of Metalwork in the Middle Bronze Age in Southern England*. Oxford: British Archaeological Reports (BAR 31).

Rowlands, M. 1980. Kinship, alliance and exchange in the European Bronze Age. In J. Barrett and R. Bradley (eds.), *Settlement and Society in the British Later Bronze Age*, 15–59. Oxford: British Archaeological Reports (BAR 83).

Rowley-Conwy, P. 2003. No fixed abode? Nomadism in the northwest European Neolithic. In G. Burenhult (ed.), *Stones and Bones*, 115–43. Oxford: British Archaeological Reports (BAR International Series 1201).

Rowley-Conwy, P. 2004. How the west was lost. A reconsideration of agricultural origins in Britain, Ireland and Southern Scandinavia. *Current Anthropology* 45 supplement, S83–S113.

Roymans, N. and Kortelag, N. 1999. Urn-field symbolism, ancestors and the land in the Lower Rhine region. In F. Theuws and N. Roymans (eds.), *Land and Ancestors*, 33–61. Amsterdam: Amsterdam University Press.

Ruggles, C. 1999. *Astronomy in Prehistoric Britain and Ireland*. New Haven (CT): Yale University Press.

Ruiz-Gálvez Priego, M. 1998. *La Europa atlántica en la Edad del Bronce*. Barcelona: Crítica.

Sahlins, M. 1974. *Stone Age Economics*. London: Tavistock Publications.

Salanova, L. 2002. Fabrication et circulation des céramiques campaniformes. In J. Guilaine (ed.), *Materiaux, productions, circulations du Néolithique á l'Age du Bronze*, 151–66. Paris: Editions Errance.

Saville, A. 1990. *Hazleton North*. London: English Heritage.

Saville, A. 1994. A Skaill knife from Skara Brae, Orkney. *Proceedings of the Society of Antiquaries of Scotland* 124, 103–11.

Saville, A. 2002. Lithic artefacts from Neolithic causewayed enclosures: Character and meaning. In G. Varndell and P. Topping (eds.), *Enclosures in Neolithic Europe*, 91–105. Oxford: Oxbow.

Savory, H. 1956. Excavation of the Pipton, long cairn. *Archaeologia Cambrensis* 105, 7–48.

Scarre, C. 1992. The early Neolithic of western France and megalithic origins in Atlantic Europe. *Oxford Journal of Archaeology* 11, 121–54.

Schulting, R. and Wysocki. M. 2005. 'In the chambered tombs were found cleft skulls . . .' An assessment of the evidence for cranial trauma in the British Neolithic. *Proceedings of the Prehistoric Society* 71, 107–38.

Scott, J. G. 1989. The stone circle at Temple Wood, Kilmartin, Argyll. *Glasgow Archaeological Journal* 15, 53–124.

Shanks, M. and Tilley, C. 1982. Ideology, symbolic power and ritual communication: A reinterpretation of Neolithic mortuary practices. In I. Hodder (ed.), *Symbolic and Structural Archaeology* 129–54. Cambridge: Cambridge University Press.

Sharples, N. 1984. Excavations at Pierowall Quarry, Westray, Orkney. *Proceedings of the Society of Antiquaries of Scotland* 114, 75–125.

Sharples, N. 1985. Individual and community: The changing role of megaliths in the Orcadian Neolithic. *Proceedings of the Prehistoric Society* 51, 59–74.

Sharples, N. 1991. *Maiden Castle: Excavation and Field Survey 1985–6*. London: English Heritage.

Shee Twohig, E. 1981 *The Megalithic Art of Western Europe*. Oxford: Clarendon Press.

Shennan, I. and Andrews, J. eds. 2000. *Holocene Land-Sea Interaction and Environmental Change around the North Sea*. London: Geological Society.

Shennan, S. 1995. *Bronze Age Copper Producers of the Eastern Alps: Excavations at St. Veit-Klinglberg*. Bonn: Habelt.

Shepherd, A. 2000. Skara Brae. Expressing identity in a Neolithic community. In A. Ritchie (ed.), *Neolithic Orkney in its European Context*, 139–58. Cambridge: McDonald Institute for Archaeological Research.

Shepherd, I. 1987. The early peoples. In D. Omand (ed.), *The Grampian Book,* 19–30. Golspie: The Northern Times.

Sheridan, A. 1986. Megaliths and megalomania: An account and interpretation of the development of passage tombs in Ireland. *Journal of Irish Archaeology* 3, 17–30.

Sheridan, A. 2003a. French Connections 1: Spreading the marmites thinly. In I. Armit, E. Murphy, E. Nelis, and D. Simpson (eds.), *Neolithic Settlement in Ireland and Western Britain*, 3–17. Oxford: Oxbow.

Sheridan, A. 2003b. Ireland's earliest 'passage tombs': A French connection? In G. Burenhult (ed.), *Stones and Bones*, 9–25. Oxford: British Archaeological Reports (BAR International Series 1201).

Sheridan, A. 2003c. New dates for Scottish cinerary urns: Results from the National Museums of Scotland Dating Cremated Bones Project. In A. Gibson (ed), *Prehistoric Pottery: People, Pattern and Purpose*, 201–26. Oxford: British Archaeological Reports (BAR International Series 1156).

Sheridan, A. 2004a. Going round in circles? Understanding the Irish Grooved Ware 'complex' in its wider context. In H. Roche, E. Grogan, J. Bradley, J. Coles, and B. Raftery (eds.), *From Megaliths to Metals*, 26–37. Oxford: Oxbow.

Sheridan, A. 2004b. Scottish Food Vessel chronology revisited. In A. Gibson and A. Sheridan (eds.), *From Sickles to Circles. Britain and Ireland at the Time of Stonehenge*, 243–69. Stroud: Tempus.

Sheridan, A., Kochman, W., and Aranauskas, R. 2003. The grave goods from the knowes of Trottie, Orkney: Reconsideration and replication. In J. Downes and A. Ritchie (eds.), *Sea Change; Orkney and Northern Europe in the later Iron Age AD 300–800*, 176–88. Balgavies: The Blackfoot Press.

Sheridan, A. and Shortland, A. 2004. '. . . beads that have given rise to so much dogmatism, controversy and rash speculation': Faience in

Early Bronze Age Britain and Ireland. In I. Shepherd and G. Barclay (eds.), *Scotland in Ancient Europe*, 263–79. Edinburgh: Society of Antiquaries of Scotland.

Sherratt, A. 1996. Why Wessex? The Avon route and river transport in later British prehistory. *Oxford Journal of Archaeology* 15, 211–234.

Sherratt, A. 1997. *Economy and Society in Prehistoric Europe*. Edinburgh; Edinburgh University Press.

Sidell, J., Cotton, J., Rayner, L., and Wheeler, L. 2002. *The Prehistory and Topography of Southwark and Lambeth*. London: Museum of London.

Simmons, I. 1996. *The Environmental Impact of Later Mesolithic Cultures*. Edinburgh: Edinburgh University Press.

Simpson, D. 1993. Stone artefacts from the Lower Bann Valley. *Ulster Journal of Archaeology* 56, 31–43.

Simpson, D. and Thawley, J. 1972. Single Grave art in Britain. *Scottish Archaeological Forum* 4, 81–104.

Simpson,D., Weir, D., and Wilkinson, J. 1992. Excavations at Dun Ruadh, Crouck, Co. Tyrone. *Ulster Journal of Archaeology* 55, 36–47.

Simpson, G. 1981. Excavations in Field OS 124, Maxey, Cambridgeshire. *Northamptonshire Archaeology* 16, 34–64.

Smith, I. 1979. The chronology of British stone implements. In T. Clough and W. Cummins (eds.), *Stone Axe Studies 2*, 13–22. London: Council for British Archaeology.

Smith, K. 1977. The excavation of Winkelbury Camp, Basingstoke. *Proceedings of the Prehistoric Society* 43, 31–129.

Smith, K., Coppen, G., Wainwright, G., and Beckett, S. 1981. The Shaugh Moor Project: Third report. *Proceedings of the Prehistoric Society* 47, 205–73.

Smith, R., Healy, F., Allen, M., Morris, E., Barnes, I., and Woodward, P. 1997. *Excavations along the Route of the Dorchester By-pass, Dorset, 1986–8*. Salisbury: Wessex Archaeology.

Speak, S. and Burgess, C. 1999. Meldon Bridge: A centre of the third millennium BC in Peebleshire. *Proceedings of the Society of Antiquaries of Scotland* 129, 1–118.

Sperber, L. 1999. Crises in Western European metal supply during the Late Bronze Age: From bronze to iron. In K. Demakapoulou, C. Eluère, J. Jensen, A. Jockenhövel, and J.

P. Mohen (eds.), *Gods and Heroes of the European Bronze Age*, 48–51. London: Thames and Hudson.

Spikins, P. 2002. *Prehistoric People of the Pennines.* Morley: West Yorkshire Archaeology Service.

Spratt, D. 1993. *Prehistoric and Roman Archaeology of North-East Yorkshire*. London: Council for British Archaeology.

Stanford, S. 1982. Bromfield, Shropshire – Neolithic, Beaker and Bronze Age sites. *Proceedings of the Prehistoric Society* 48, 279–320.

Stanford, S. 1984. The Wrekin: Excavations, 1973. *Archaeological Journal* 141, 61–90.

Startin, B. and Bradley, R. 1981. Some notes on work organisation and society in prehistoric Wessex. In C. Ruggles and A. Whittle (eds.), *Astronomy and Society in the Period 4000 – 1500 BC*, 289–96. Oxford: British Archaeological Reports (BAR 88).

Stead, I. 1988. Chalk figurines of the Parisi. *Antiquaries Journal* 68, 9–29.

Stead, I. 1991. *Iron Age Cemeteries in East Yorkshire*. London: English Heritage.

Stoertz, C. 1997. *Ancient Landscapes of the Yorkshire Wolds*. Swindon: Royal Commission on the Historical Monuments of England.

Stone, J. F. S. and Young, W. 1948. Two pits of Grooved Ware date near Woodhenge. *Wiltshire Archaeological Magazine* 52, 287–304.

Stout, G. 1991. Embanked enclosures of the Boyne region. *Proceedings of the Royal Irish Academy* 91C, 254–84.

Stout, M. 1997. *The Irish Ringfort*. Dublin: Four Courts Press.

Suddaby, I. 2003. The excavation of two Late Bronze Age roundhouses at Ballypriorbeg, County Antrim. *Ulster Journal of Archaeology* 62, 45–91.

Sunter, N. and Woodward, P. 1987. *Romano-British Industries in Purbeck*. Dorchester: Dorset Natural History and Archaeological Society.

Sweet, R. 2004. *Antiquaries. The Discovery of the Past in Eighteenth Century Britain*. London: Hambledon.

Sweetman, D. 1976. An earthen enclosure at Monknewtown, Co. Meath. *Proceedings of the Royal Irish Academy* 76C, 25–72.

Sweetman, D. 1985. A Late Neolithic / Early Bronze Age pit circle at Newgrange, Co. Meath. *Proceedings of the Royal Irish Academy* 81C, 195–221.

Sweetman, D. 1987. Excavation of a Late Neolithic / Early Bronze Age site at Newgrange, Co. Meath. *Proceedings of the Royal Irish Academy* 87C, 283–98.

Tabor, R. 2004. Cadbury Castle: Prehistoric pottery distributions in the surrounding landscape. *Proceedings of the Somerset Archaeological and Natural History Society* 147, 29–40.

Tavener, N. 1996. Evidence of Neolithic activity near Marton-le-Moor, North Yorkshire. *Northern Archaeology* 14, 183–7.

Taylor, J. 1970. Lunulae reconsidered. *Proceedings of the Prehistoric Society* 36, 38–81.

Taylor, J. 1997. Space and place: Some thoughts on Iron Age and Romano-British landscapes. In A. Gwilt and C. Haselgrove (eds.), *Reconstructing Iron Age Societies*, 192–204. Oxford: Oxbow Monograph 71.

Taylor, J. 2000. The ancient Irish in Classical ethnography. *Emainia* 18, 45–8.

Taylor, R. 1994. *Hoards of the Bronze Age in Southern Britain*. Oxford: British Archaeological Reports (BAR 228).

Thomas, C. 1958. *Gwithian: Ten Years Work.* Gwithian: privately published.

Thomas, J. 1988. Neolithic explanations revisited: The Mesolithic-Neolithic transition in Britain and south Scandinavia. *Proceedings of the Prehistoric Society* 54, 59–66.

Thomas, J. 1996a. Neolithic houses in mainland Britain and Ireland – A sceptical view. In T. Darvill and J. Thomas (eds.), *Neolithic Houses in Northwest Europe and Beyond*, 1–12. Oxford: Oxbow.

Thomas, J. 1996b. *Time, Culture and Identity.* London: Routledge.

Thomas, J. 1999. *Understanding the Neolithic.* London: Routledge.

Thomas, J. 2004a. Identity, power and material culture in Neolithic Britain. In N. Matsumoto (ed.), *Cultural Diversity and the Archaeology of the 21st Century*, 166–79. Okayama: Society of Archaeological Studies.

Thomas, J. 2004b. The Later Neolithic architectural repertoire: The case of the Dunragit complex. In R. Cleal and J. Pollard (eds.), *Monuments and Material Culture*, 98–108. East Knoyle: Hobnob Press.

Thomas, K. 1982. Neolithic enclosures and woodland habitats on the South Downs in Sussex, England. In M. Bell and S. Limbrey (eds.), *Aspects of Woodland Ecology*, 147–170. Oxford: British Archaeological Reports (BAR International Series 146).

Thomas, N. 2005. *Snail Down, Wiltshire.* Devizes: Wiltshire Archaeological and Natural History Society.

Thomas, R. 1989. The Bronze Age – Iron Age transition in Southern England. In M. L. S. Sørensen and R. Thomas (eds.), *The Bronze Age – Iron Age Transition in Europe*, 263–86. Oxford: British Archaeological Reports (BAR International Series 483).

Thomas, R. 1997. Land, kinship relations and the rise of enclosed settlements in first millennium BC Britain. *Oxford Journal of Archaeology* 16, 211–18.

Thomas, R. 1999. Rise and fall: The deposition of Bronze Age weapons in the Thames Valley and the Fenland. In A. Harding (ed.), *Experiment and Design. Archaeological Studies in Honour of John Coles*, 116–22. Oxford: Oxbow.

Thompson, E. A. 1965. *The Early Germans.* Oxford: Clarendon Press.

Thorpe, R., Williams-Thorpe, O., Jenkins, D., and Watson, J. 1991. The geological sources and transport of the bluestones of Stonehenge, Wiltshire, UK. *Proceedings of the Prehistoric Society* 57.2, 103–58.

Tilley,C. 1994. *A Phenomenology of Landscape.* Oxford: Berg.

Timberlake, S. 2001. Mining and prospecting for metals in Early Bronze Age Britain: Making claims within the archaeological landscape. In J. Brück (ed.), *Bronze Age Landscapes. Tradition and Transformation*, 179–92. Oxford: Oxbow.

Timberlake, S. 2002. Ancient prospection for metals and modern prospection for ancient mines – The evidence for Bronze Age mining in the British Isles. In M. Baretelheim, E. Pernicke, and R. Krause (eds.), *Die Anfänge der Metallurgie in der alten Welt*, 327–57. Rahden: Marie Leidorf.

Tipping 1994a. The form and fate of Scotland's woodlands. *Proceedings of the Society of Antiquaries of Scotland* 124, 1–54.

Tipping, R. 1994b. 'Ritual' floral tributes in the Scottish Bronze Age – Palynological evidence. *Journal of Archaeological Science* 21, 133–9.

Tipping, R. 2002. Climatic variability and 'marginal' settlement in British upland landscapes: A re-examination. *Landscapes* 3.2, 10–28.

Toms, H. S. 1925. Bronze Age or earlier lynchets. *Proceedings of the Dorset Natural History and Archaeological Society* 46, 88–100.

Topping, P. 1989. Early cultivation in Northumberland and the Borders. *Proceedings of the Prehistoric Society* 55, 161–179.

Topping, P. 1992. The Penrith henges: A survey by the Royal Commission on the Historical Monuments of England. *Proceedings of the Prehistoric Society* 58, 249–64.

Topping, P. 1996. Structure and ritual in the Neolithic house. In T. Darvill and J. Thomas (eds.), *Neolithic Houses in Northwest Europe and Beyond*, 1–12. Oxford: Oxbow.

Tresset, A. 2003. French Connections 2: Of cows and men. In I. Armit, E. Murphy, E. Nelis, and D. Simpson (eds.), *Neolithic Settlement in Ireland and Western Britain*, 18–30. Oxford: Oxbow.

Tuckwell, A. 1975. Patterns of burial orientation in the round barrows of East Yorkshire. *Bulletin of the London University Institute of Archaeology* 12, 95–123.

Turner, A., Gonzales, S., and Ohman, J. 2002. Prehistoric human and ungulate remains from Preston Docks, Lancashire, UK: Problems of river finds. *Journal of Archaeological Science* 29, 423–33.

Van de Noort, R. 2003. An ancient seascape: The social context of seafaring in the Early Bronze Age. *World Archaeology* 35, 404–15.

Varndell, G. and Needham, S. 2002. New gold cup from Kent. *Past* 41, 2–4.

Vatcher, F. 1961. The excavation of a long mortuary enclosure on Normanton Down, Wiltshire. *Proceedings of the Prehistoric Society* 27, 160–73.

Vera, F. 2000. *Grazing Ecology and Forest History.* Wallingford: CAB International.

von Brunn, W. A. 1959. *Bronzezeitliche Hortfunde, Teil 1.* Berlin: Akademie Verlag.

Vyner, B. 1984. The excavation of a Neolithic cairn at Street House, Loftus, Cleveland. *Proceedings of the Prehistoric Society* 50, 151–95.

Waddell, J. 1978. The invasion hypothesis in Irish prehistory. *Antiquity* 52, 121–8.

Waddell, J. 1990. *The Bronze Age Burials of Ireland.* Galway: Galway University Press.

Waddell, J. 1992. The Irish Sea in prehistory. *Journal of Irish Archaeology* 6, 29–40.

Waddell, J. 1998. *The Prehistoric Archaeology of Ireland.* Galway: Galway University Press.

Waddell, J. 2005. *Foundation Myths. The Beginnings of Irish Archaeology.* Bray: Wordwell.

Wailes, B. 1982. The Irish 'royal' sites in history and archaeology. *Cambridge Medieval Celtic Studies* 3, 1–29.

Wainwright, G. 1969. A review of henge monuments in the light of recent research. *Proceedings of the Prehistoric Society* 35, 112–33.

Wainwright, G. 1971. The excavation of a fortified settlement at Walesland Rath, Pembrokeshire. *Britannia* 2, 48–108.

Wainwright, G. 1979. *Mount Pleasant.* London: Society of Antiquaries of London.

Wainwright, G. and Longworth, I. 1971. *Durrington Walls.* London: Society of Antiquaries of London.

Walker, K. and Farwell, D. 2000. *Twyford Down, Hampshire. Archaeological Investigations 1990–93.* Winchester: Hampshire Field Club and Archaeological Society.

Walsh, P. 1993. In circle and row: Bronze Age ceremonial monuments. In E. Shee Twohig and M. Ronayne (eds.), *Past Perceptions: The Prehistoric Archaeology of South-West Ireland,* 101–13. Cork: Cork University Press.

Warner, R. 2000. Keeping out the Otherworld: The internal ditch at Navan and other Iron Age 'hengiform' enclosures. *Emainia* 18, 39–44.

Warren, H. 1921. Excavations at the stone-axe factory at Graig Llwyd, Penmaenmawr. *Journal of the Royal Anthropological Institute* 51, 165–99.

Waterman, D. 1997. *Excavations at Navan Fort 1961–71.* Belfast: The Stationery Office.

Watkins, T. 1984. *Rullion Green 1983.* Edinburgh: Edinburgh University Department of Archaeology.

Watkins, T. 1985. *Rullion Green. Report on the 1985 Season of Excavations.* Edinburgh: Edinburgh University Department of Archaeology.

Watson, A. 2001. Composing Avebury. *World Archaeology* 33, 296–314.

Watson, A. 2004. Making space for monuments: Notes on the representation of experience. In C. Renfrew, C. Gosden, and E. DeMarrais (eds.), *Substance, Memory, Display. Archaeology and Art,* 79–96. Cambridge: McDonald Institute for Archaeological Research.

Watson, A. and Bradley, R. in press. On the edge of England: Cumbria as a Neolithic region. In G. Barclay and K. Brophy (eds.), *Cores and Peripheries? The Nature of the Regional Neolithics in Britain and Ireland.* Oxford: Oxbow.

Watson, A. and Keating, D. 1999. Architecture and sound: An acoustical analysis of megalithic monuments in Britain. *Antiquity* 73, 325–36.

Weir, D. 1995. A palynological study of landscape and agricultural development in County Louth from the second millennium BC to the first millennium AD. *Discovery Programme Reports* 2, 77–126.

Weisberger, G. (ed.). 1981. *5000 Jahre Feuersteinbergbau.* Bochum: Deutschens Bergbau-Museum.

Whimster, R. 1977. Harlyn Bay reconsidered: The excavations of 1900–1905 in the light of recent work. *Cornish Archaeology* 16, 61–88.

Whimster, R. 1981. *Burial Practices in Iron Age Britain.* Oxford: British Archaeological Reports (BAR 90).

Whitley, J. 2002. Too many ancestors. *Antiquity* 76, 119–26.

Whittle, A. 1978. Resources and population in the British Neolithic. *Antiquity* 52, 34–41.

Whittle, A. 1986. *Scord of Brouster.* Oxford: Oxford University Committee for Archaeology.

Whittle, A. 1996 *Europe in the Neolithic. The Creation of New Worlds.* Cambridge: Cambridge University Press.

Whittle, A. 1997. *Sacred Mound, Holy Rings. Silbury Hill and the West Kennet Palisade Enclosures.* Oxford: Oxbow.

Whittle, A. 2004. Stones that float to the sky: Portal dolmens and their landscape of memory and myth. In V. Cummings and C. Fowler (eds.), *The Neolithic of the Irish Sea,* 81–90. Oxford: Oxbow.

Whittle, A., Atkinson, R., Chambers, R., and Thomas, N. 1992. Excavations in the Neolithic and Bronze Age complex at Dorchester-on-Thames, Oxfordshire, 1947–52 and 1981. *Proceedings of the Prehistoric Society* 58, 143–201.

Whittle, A., Pollard, J., and Grigson, C. 1999. *The Harmony of Symbols: The Windmill Hill Causewayed Enclosure, Wiltshire.* Oxford: Oxbow.

Whittle, A. and Wysocki, M. 1998. Parc le Breos Cwm transepted long cairn, Gower, West Glamorgan: Date, contents and context. *Proceedings of the Prehistoric Society* 64, 139–82.

Wickham-Jones, C. 1990. *Rhum: Mesolithic and Later Sites at Kinloch. Excavations 1984–86.* Edinburgh: Society of Antiquaries of Scotland.

Williams, B. 1978. Excavations at Lough Eskragh, County Tyrone. *Ulster Journal of Archaeology* 41, 37–48.

Williams, G. 1984. A henge monument at Ffynnon Newydd, Natgaredig. *Bulletin of the Board of Celtic Studies* 31, 177–90.

Williams, G. 1988. *The Standing Stones of Wales and South-West England*. Oxford: British Archaeological Reports (BAR 197).

Williams, G. and Mytum, H. 1998. *Llawhaden, Dyfed. Excavations on a Group of Small Defended Enclosures, 1980–4*. Oxford: British Archaeological Reports (BAR 275).

Williams, M. 2003. Growing metaphors: The agricultural cycle as metaphor in the later prehistoric period of Britain and North-Western Europe. *Journal of Social Archaeology* 3, 223–55.

Williams, R. and Zeepfat, R. 1994. *Bancroft. A Late Bronze Age / Iron Age Settlement, Roman Villa and Temple-Mausoleum*. Aylesbury: Buckinghamshire Archaeological Society.

Wilson, D. R. 1978. Pit alignments: Function and distribution. In H.C. Bowen and P. Fowler (eds.), *Early Land Allotment in the British Isles*, 3–5. Oxford: British Archaeological Reports (BAR 48).

Woodman, P. 2004. Some problems and perspectives: reviewing aspects of the Mesolithic period in Ireland. In A. Saville (ed.), *Mesolithic Scotland and its Neighbours*, 285–97. Edinburgh: Society of Antiquaries of Scotland.

Woodman, P., Finlay, N., and Anderson, E. 1999. *Excavations at Ferriter's Cove 1983–95*. Bray: Wordwell.

Woodward, A. 2000. *British Barrows: A Matter of Life and Death*. Stroud: Tempus.

Woodward, A. 2002. Beads and Beakers: Heirlooms and relics in the British Early Bronze Age. *Antiquity* 76, 1140–7.

Woodward, P., Davies, S. and Graham, A. 1993. *Excavations at Greyhound Yard, Dorchester*. Dorchester: Dorset Archaeological Society.

Wrathmell, S. and Nicholson, A. 1990. *Dalton Parlours: Iron Age Settlement and Roman Villa*. Wakefield: West Yorkshire Archaeology Service.

Wysocki, M. and Whittle, A. 2000. Directionality, lifestyle and rites. New biological and archaeological evidence from British earlier Neolithic assemblages. *Antiquity* 74, 591–601.

Yates, D. 1999. Bronze Age field systems in the Thames Valley. *Oxford Journal of Archaeology* 18, 157–70.

Yates, D. 2001. Bronze Age agricultural intensification in the Thames Valley and Estuary. In J. Brück (ed.), *Bronze Age Landscapes. Tradition and Transformation*, 65–82. Oxford: Oxbow.

York, J. 2002. The life cycle of Bronze Age metalwork from the Thames. *Oxford Journal of Archaeology* 21, 77–92.

Young, R. and Simmons, R. 1997. Marginality and the nature of later prehistoric settlement in the north of England. *Landscape Studies* 17, 9–16.

Zvelebil, M. and Rowley-Conwy, P. 1986. Foragers and farmers in Atlantic Europe. In M. Zvelebil (ed.), *Hunters in Transition*, 67–93. Cambridge: Cambridge University Press.

INDEX

Abingdon, 82
Achnacreebeag, 50
aerial photography
  impact of, 154
  Irish archaeology and, 154
  of monuments, 166
  of pit alignments, 244
The Age of Stonehenge (Burgess), 25
agriculture
  evidence of, 32
  introduction of, 30
  in Ireland, 38
  during Iron Age, 237, 240–241, 246
  societies and, 84
  on Yorkshire Wolds, 242
All Cannings Cross, 232
amber, distribution of, 155–156
Amesbury, 142, 150
Anglesey
  decorated passage tombs of, 118
  Neolithic Ireland impact on, 120
animal burials. *See also* burials
  at Cadbury Castle, 250
Arbor Low, 130, 136
  artefacts at, 135–136
archaeology. *See also* landscape archaeology; social
    archaeology
  of Britain and Ireland, 6
  ethnography and, 126
  Ireland *vs.* Scotland, 116
  language of, 24
  of Mediterranean, 7
  of megaliths, 6
  Neolithic, 30, 39
  of Polynesia, 7
  of Stonehenge, 5
architecture. *See also* monumental architecture
  of Britain and Ireland,
  landscapes and, 106
  Mycenaean, 156
  social practices and, 105

Arminghall, 130
Arran, 43
  monuments on, 6
Arras Culture, 264
  burials of, 266, 270
artefacts. *See also* gold artefacts; grave artefacts;
    Neolithic artefacts; portable artefacts
  at Arbor Low, 135–136
  Brittany *vs.* southern England, 155
  bronze, 146
  burial of, 44
  distribution of, 37, 96–97
  exchange of, 24
  flint, 124
  at Glastonbury, 252
  grave goods, 148
  ground stone, 27
  at Knowth, 106
  of Later Neolithic period, 78
  at Maumbury Rings, 127
  at Meare, 252
  metal, 91
  movement of, 134–135
  at Newgrange, 106
  recycling of, 229
  single burials and, 158
  social archaeology and, 25
  timber structures *vs.* stone monuments,
    126
  at Woodhenge, 124
Ascott-under-Wychwood, 50
Atkinson, Richard, 23, 139
Atlantic Bronze Age, 1, 229
Aubrey, John, 7
Auchenlaich, long mound, 62
Aunjetitz Culture
  burials of, 155
  growth of, 156–157
Avebury, 6, 16, 125
  construction of, 128
  Stonehenge *vs.*, 160

Aveline's Hole, 32
axes. *See also* stone axes
    copper *vs.* stone, 152
    deposits of, 148
    on Mesolithic sites, 30
    movement across Europe of, 37
    production of, 37

Balfarg, 64, 130
Balksbury, midden at, 234
Ballinderry, timber platforms at, 205
Balloy, 86
Ballyglass, 50, 53
Ballynahatty
    cairns over postholes at, 124
    Giant's Ring at, 113
    Orkney structures and, 118
    wooden structures at, 114
Bancroft, 208
bank barrow, at Stanwell, 64
Barbury Castle, 241, 262
Barclodiad Y Gawres, 118, 121–122
Barelycroft, 194
Barnack, burial analysis of, 162
Barnhouse, 95, 108
    Later Neolithic Village at, 110
Barrett, J., 178, 179
barrows. *See also* Druids' Barrows; Kings' barrows;
        long barrows; ring barrows; round barrows;
        square barrows
    of Bronze Age, 154
    forms of, 176
    individual burial mounds *vs.*, 161
    in Wessex, 166
Beaghmore, stone settings at, 175
Beaker pottery, 80, 147, 169
    adoption of, 152
    burnt mounds and, 214
    Continental Europe, 144–145
    Corded Ware and, 143
    distribution of, 142
    Grooved Ware and, 147, 152–153
    land divisions and, 150
    metalwork and, 143, 146–147
    radiocarbon dates for, 143
    wedge tombs and, 147
Bedd Branwen, cairn at, 161
Beeston Castle, 222
Bell Beakers. *See* Beaker pottery; Irish Beakers
Belle Tout, 151
Bergh, Stefan, 103, 106
Bestwall Quarry, 190
Bharpa Carinish, 50
Biggar Common, 89
Billown, 43, 200
Blackshouse Burn, 128
Blanuaran of Clava, 174
bluestones, of Stonehenge, 140

Bonsall, Clive, 36
Boyne Valley, 6, 94
    circular enclosures in, 113
    passage tombs of, 101
    raw materials in, 103
Bradley Fen, 214
Breckland, 171
Breiddin, 251
Brenig, 169
bridges, 184
Britain
    cultural integrity of, 22
    Highland and Lowland Zones of, 12–14
    hillforts of, 256
    Late Bronze Age hilltop enclosures in, 222
    megalithic art in, 118
    monuments of, 16
    natural environment of, 16
    Roman occupation of, 1, 2, 226, 271
    settlement of, 13, 58
Britain and Ireland
    archaeology of, 6
    architecture of,
    Continental Europe and, 7, 22, 153, 157, 166, 224,
        261, 271
    cursuses in, 68–69
    geography of, 1, 15
    isolation of, 8–10
    land use in, 14–15
    Late Bronze Age elites in, 217
    mapping of, 2
    Mesolithic burials in, 84
    monuments of, 4
    natural resources of, 6
    Neolithic period in, 27, 44
    as self-contained entities, 24–25
    settlement of, 2, 35
    waterways of, 16–20
    weapon zones of, 224
British and Irish Mesolithic, Northern European *vs.*,
    32
British and Irish Neolithic
    monumental architecture of, 86
    sources of, 35
British isles
    landscape archaeology of, 7
    original names of, 2
    Ptolemy's map of, 3
British Later Bronze Age (Barrett and Bradley), 178
British Museum, radiocarbon dating by, 144
Brittany
    ceramic tradition of, 29
    promontory forts of, 252
    souterrains of, 254
brochs
    emergence of, 258
    Gurness, 272–275
Bromfield, 198

bronze
  artefacts, 146
  in Britain, 152, 176
  copper use *vs.*, 146
  Ireland's sources of, 223
  long distance movement of, 232
  supply of, 186, 229, 270
  use of, 156
Bronze Age. *See also* Atlantic Bronze Age; Early
    Bronze Age; Irish Bronze Age; Late Bronze Age;
    Middle Bronze Age
  barrows of, 154
  burials, 168
  crannogs of, 206
  earthworks of, 242
  metalwork of, 186, 227
  middens of, 251
  mortuary monuments during, 223
  social collapse during, 222
  in southern England, 23
The Bronze Age in Europe (Coles and Harding), 178
bronze weapons
  in crannogs, 206
  deposition of, 200
Broomend of Crichie, 168
Brown, Tony, 36
Brun, Patrice, 4
Burgess, Colin, 25, 179, 229
burials. *See also* animal burials; cremation burials;
    graves; river burial
  adult *vs.* child, 159
  of Arras Culture, 266, 270
  deposition of, 91
  during Iron Age, 262
  male *vs.* female, 162
  metal sources and, 156
  settlement sites near, 185
  with swords, 264
burnt mounds, 216
  Beaker pottery and, 214
  metalwork at, 214
  of Neolithic period, 214
Butser Ancient Farm, 241

Cadbury Castle, 248, 251, 262
  animal burials at, 250
Cairnpapple, 130
cairns. *See also* court cairns; field cairns; long mounds;
    ring cairns; stalled cairns
  at Ballynahatty, 124
Calanais, 118
Callestick, 190
Campbell, Ewan, 24
Carinated Bowls, 29
Carlisle, monument group near, 134
Carn Brea, 70, 73, 74
carpentry techniques, during English Neolithic,
  44

Carrowkeel, 95, 116
  cemetery at, 101
  pottery at, 102
Carrowmore, 50, 52
  passage tombs at, 99
  radiocarbon dates from, 100
Carshalton, 208
Carsie Mains, 62
  Scottish hall at, 65
Carsten, Janet, 59
carved designs, 102
Case, Humphrey, 60, 143, 146
Castle Rock, 222
Catholme, radial post lines at, 124
Catterick
  henge at, 134
  Peterborough Ware at, 136
causewayed enclosures, 69–77
  of Continental Europe, 86
  long barrows and, 75–77
  Long Meg and her Daughters, 136
  open settlements *vs.*, 72
caves, remains in, 161
Céide Fields, radiocarbon dating of, 43
Celtic art, metalwork, 269
cemeteries. *See also* cremation cemeteries
  alignment of, 164
  flat, 212
  formal, 262
  Iron Age, 262
  of Late Bronze Age, 212
  linear, 176
  living areas and, 168
  mounds distribution of, 161
  Rudston, 264
  settlements and, 197
ceramics. *See also* pottery
  Brittany tradition of, 29
  domestic *vs.* grave, 150
  lowlands sequence in, 196
  of Middle Neolithic period, 38
cereal cultivation, evidence for, 192
ceremonial sites
  Grooved Ware and, 134
  Later Neolithic, 122
  Neolithic, 36
  in open grassland, 97
chambered tombs, Neolithic, 38
Champion, Timothy, 24
Chappell, Sylvia, 4
Childe, Gordon, 23, 27, 230
circular dwellings, enclosures
  in Boyne Valley, 113
  earliest, 96
  in Iberian peninsula, 253
Cladh Hallan
  cremation pyres at, 198
  domestic dwellings at, 192

Claish, 42, 62
Clark, Grahame, 24, 143
Clarke, David, 144
Claudian Conquest, 271
Clava Cairns, 169, 174, 175
Cleal, Rosamund, 160
Cleaval Point, 275
Cleaven Dyke, 64
climate change, settlement and, 172, 179
Coles, J., 178
collective burial, Neolithic practice of, 162
Collis, John, 208
colonisation
    of Britain and Ireland, 9–10, 35
    of Isle of Man, 8
    by sea, 36
connections
    between British isles and European mainland, 157
    between monuments, 117, 120, 133
    between new construction and older earthwork,
        133
Conquer Barrow, at Mount Pleasant, 131
Continental Europe. *See also* Northern Europe
    axes across, 37
    Beaker material in, 144–145
    Britain and Ireland and, 7, 22, 153, 157, 166, 224,
        261, 271
    causewayed enclosures of, 86
    deposition of metalwork in, 185
    earthwork enclosures in, 34
    funeral rites in, 264
    Ireland and, 269
    iron weapons in, 230
    long mounds in, 69
    longhouses of, 40
    metalwork from, 223
    passage tombs in, 99
Cooney, Gabriel, 84
copper
    bronze use *vs.*, 146
    in Ireland, 157
copper mining, 176
    in Alps, 224
    in Ireland, 146
    at Ross Island, 146–147
    in south-west Ireland, 156
    in Wales, 172
    in western Ireland, 172
Corbally, Neolithic houses at, 40
Corded Ware, Bell Beakers and, 143
Cornish tin, 156, 157
Cornwall, secure storage in, 254
Corrstown
    excavation at, 196
    Middle Bronze Age site at, 210
Cotswolds, rotunda graves of, 49
court cairns, of Ireland, 52–54
Court Hill, 73

crannogs, 204, 235
    of Bronze Age, 206
Creighton, John, 227, 262
cremation burials, 60–61, 161, 198, 202
cremation cemeteries
    location of, 197
    metalwork in, 185, 197
    at Itford Hill, 197
    ring cairns and, 185
    standing stones at, 198
    in uplands, 185
cremation pyres, 198
Crickley Hill, 73, 247
Crossiecrown, settlement at, 110
Crouch Hill, 133
Cummings, Vicki, 38
Cunliffe, Barry, 210, 226, 247, 258, 261–262
cup marks, monument decoration with,
        175
currency bars, production of, 232
cursuses, 62
    along Thames, 68
    Britain *vs.* Ireland, 68–69
    distribution of, 68
    Later Neolithic monuments and, 136
    origins of, 68
    Thornborough, 83
Cuween Hill, 110

daggers, in Early Bronze Age burials, 201
dairy economy, of Early Neolithic, 46
Dallington, 83
Dalriada, 24
Dan Y Coed, 254
Danebury, 248, 251, 261
    adult *vs.* children's remains at, 250
Dark, Petra, 43
Dartmoor, 169, 184, 210
    in Early Bronze Age, 188
    field systems of, 187
    landscape of, 194
    livestock of, 192
Davies, Margaret, 19
Davies, Norman, 11
decorative stones, 108
Dee, River, 14
Devil's Quoits, 150, 252
Dieskau, 160
Dinorben, 214
    building platforms at, 251
domestic dwellings
    of Later Neolithic Orkney, 108
    of Later Neolithic period, 94
    in lowland Britain, 190
    in Mesolithic period, 32
    in Neolithic Ireland, 29
    in Orkney, 192
    ring cairns and, 170

rituals centered on, 41
wells and, 190
domesticated animals
introduction of, 44
during Iron Age, 242
in Neolithic Ireland, 29
of Neolithic period, 34
settlement patterns and, 30
use of, 32
Dorchester on Thames, human remains at, 127–128
Dorset Cursus, 65, 81
Dorset Ridgeway, burial concentrations, 154
Dover, Middle Bronze Age boat at, 224
Down Farm, 193
Downpatrick, 217
gold ornament hoard at, 217
Dowth, 102
Drombeg, 216
Dronfield, Jeremy, 104
Druids' Barrows, 159
Duddingston Loch, 203
Duggleby Howe, 83
Neolithic round barrow at, 128
Dun Aonghasa, 218
Dun Ruadh, 114
Dunch Hill, 210–212
Dunragit, 130
Grooved Ware at, 130
mound on entrance axis at, 131
Durrington Walls, 128, 133
Grooved Ware and, 120
Northern Circle at, 123, 140
pottery distribution at, 124
Stonehenge and, 138, 141
dwellings. *See also* domestic dwellings; houses
of Early Iron Age, 238–239
inside hillforts, 251
of Middle Bronze Age, 190

Earle, Timothy, 4
Early Bronze Age
Dartmoor in, 188
funeral practices of, 201
in Wessex, 166
Early Bronze Age burials
contents of, 155
daggers in, 201
pottery associated with, 197
Early Iron Age
in East Anglia, 260
field systems of, 241
ground plans of settlements, 239–240
houses of, 238–239
ringworks of, 239
weapon deposit distribution of, 236
Early Neolithic
dairy economy of, 46
land use during, 43

occupation sites of, 96
pottery of, 38
regional differences in, 41
earthwork(s)
as aggregation sites, 87
of Bronze Age, 242
graves and, 164
henges and, 139
territory definition by, 210
in Wessex, 166
in Yorkshire Wolds, 166, 244
earthwork enclosures. *See also* enclosures
on European Continent, 34
of Isle of Man, 254
of Middle Neolithic period, 38
mounds and, 131
sequence of, 130
earthwork monuments, timber enclosures *vs.*, 128
East Anglia
Early Iron Age occupation sites of, 260
settlements in, 258
East Anglian Fens, 252
East Chisenbury, 233
midden at, 234
Ehrenberg, Margaret, 217, 224
Eildon Hill North, 222
Eilean Domhnuill, 41, 50
Elm Decline, chronological marker of, 33
enclosures
beginnings of, 237
in Scotland, 258
England
Bronze Age in, 23
Neolithic buildings in, 43
pit deposits in, 43
Roman towns in, 233
English barrows, organisation of, 161
English Channel
flint mines near, 37
formation of, 8, 10
sea routes across, 19–20
tin movement across, 156
English ringworks
Irish enclosures *vs.*, 217
of Late Bronze Age, 224
Eogan, George, 102, 178
Eriksen, Palle, 102
ethnography, archaeology and, 126
Eton Rowing Lake, structures at, 203
Etton, 73, 76
monument enclosures at, 71–72
Europe Before History (Kristiansen), 227
Europe, prehistoric. *See also* Continental Europe
society in, 4
Evans, Chris, 204
Eynesbury, 82

faience beads, Mycenaeans trade of, 156

farming
    appearance of, 30, 35
    Neolithic development of, 27
    spread of, 30
Fen Edge, 133
Fenland, weapons and ornaments in, 236
Ferriter's Cove, 32
Ferrybridge, 122
    henge at, 252
field archaeology, 38
field cairns, mortuary monuments and, 170
Field, David, 189
field systems
    Celtic vs. English, 187
    co-axial, 196, 210, 212, 223, 235
    on Dartmoor, 187
    dwelling groups and, 192
    of Early Iron Age, 241
    of Iron Age, 241, 246
    in lowland river valleys, 192
    monuments and, 188
    on Salisbury Plain, 242
    settlements and, 188
    workforces for, 188
Finistère, 252
Fiskerton, 269
Flag Fen, 269
    causeway at, 203, 204
Flagstones, 82
flat-rimmed ware, 217
flint, 133
    Grand Pressigny, 143
    mines, 37
food production, 98. See also agriculture
forests, 16
Fornham All Saints, 73, 77
fortifications. See also hillforts
    of Late Bronze Age, 206
    ringworks, 234
Fourknocks, 102
Fox, Cyril, 15, 23
Fredengren, Christina, 205
funeral rites, 270
    Continental Europe vs. British Iron Age, 264
    of Early Bronze Age, 201
    during Late Bronze Age, 186
    significance of, 116
    structure of, 201
Fyfield, 241
Fylingdales Moor, rock art on, 117

Galicia, 252
Garton, Slack, 264
Garwood, Paul, 160, 164
Gayhurst, 154, 162
Gent, Henry, 43
geography
    of Britain and Ireland, 1, 15

    of Ireland, 14
    names and, 10
Gerloff, Sabine, 155
Giant's Ring, at Ballynahatty, 113
Gibson, Alex, 122, 130, 150
Glastonbury
    adult vs. children's remains at, 250
    artefacts at, 252
Glastonbury Ware, 269
gold
    in Ireland, 156
    Irish export of, 176, 223
gold artefacts, 148
    distribution of, 218
    from Haughey's Fort, 197
    in Ireland, 196
    Irish renewed production of, 218
    at Ringlemere, 154
gold ornaments
    at Downpatrick, 217
    in individual burials, 158
    in Ireland, 196
    at Lockington, 154
    at Rathgall, 217
Grand Pressigny flint, 143
Grange, 217
grave artefacts, Brittany vs. southern England, 155
Gravelly Guy, Iron Age landscape around, 246
graves. See also Scottish graves
    of Arras Culture, 264
    British vs. Irish, 160
    earthworks and, 164
    exotic items in, 160
    flat, 161
    large, 161
    richer vs. poorer, 159
    siting of, 162
    social distinctions and, 160, 186
    of women and children, 160, 162
Great Baddow, 210
Great Orme, 172, 176, 186
Great Ouse valley, 68
Greece, tholos tombs of, 156
Green Island, pier at, 275
Greyhound Yard, 128
Greylake, 203
Grimes Graves, mining at, 133
Grimspound, 193
Grooved Ware, 96, 108
    Beaker pottery and, 147, 152–153
    distribution of, 134
    at Dunragit, 130
    Durrington Walls and, 120
    insular tradition of, 142
    in Ireland, 114–116
    origin of, 116
    styles of, 134
    Unstan bowls and, 116

ground plans
  of Early Iron Age settlements, 239–240
  of Middle Iron Age settlements, 240
Gulf Stream, impact of, 15
Gurness, broch of, 272–275
Gwernvale, 50
Gwithian
  cremation pyres at, 198
  land divisions at, 189
  spade cultivation at, 192

Haddenham, 48
Hambledon Hill, 72, 73, 75
Harding, A., 178
Harding, Jan, 136
Harlyn Bay, 263
Hartshill Quarry, 230
Haughey's Fort, 218
  gold finds from, 197
Hawley, Colonel, 139
Hazelton North, 50
Hebrides, Iron Age towers of, 7
Hekla, volcanic eruption of, 179
Helman Tor, 70
Helms, Mary, 59, 157
Hembury, 73
henges. *See also* Seahenge; Stonehenge
  at Catterick, 134
  earthworks and, 139
  at Ferrybridge, 252
  of Ireland, 114
  Irish *vs.* British, 114
  Iron Age, 208
  locations of, 134
  at Mayburgh, 134
  north-east England *vs.* upper Thames valley, 133
  on older structures, 136
  ring barrows and, 200
hengiform enclosures, 80–81
  round barrows *vs.*, 78–79
Hengistbury Head, 275
Henshall, Audrey, 110
Highland and Lowland Zones, of Britain, 12–14
Hill, J. D., 260
hillforts, 16, 17
  categories of, 247–248
  changing role of, 262
  community activities at, 260
  defined, 251–252
  development of, 247
  of highland Britain, 256
  houses inside, 251
  in Ireland, 218
  of Iron Age, 243
  peripheral phenomenon of, 260
  rituals at, 250
  settlements and, 251
  of southern England, 261

  specialized structures in, 248
hilltop settlements
  first appearance of, 224
  of Late Bronze Age, 222
Hindwell, 130
hoards, of metalwork, 185, 214
Hodder, Ian, 4
houses. *See also* large round houses
  English *vs.* Ireland, 61
  in Ireland, 60
  Neolithic, 27
Howe, 110
Hugh-Jones, Stephen, 59
human diet, during Neolithic period, 46
human remains
  at Dorchester on Thames, 127–128
  monuments and, 84, 175
  pit circles and, 127
  settlements and, 84, 214
  at Stonehenge, 141
Humber Estuary, open-water vessel remains from,
    157
Husbands Bosworth, 76

Iberian peninsula
  castros of, 253
  circular dwellings, enclosures in, 253
  monuments in, 99
  passage tombs in, 99
individual burials, adoption of, 89
invasion hypothesis, 24, 143
Ireland. *See also* Iron Age Ireland; Mesolithic Ireland
  agriculture in, 38
  archaeology of, 116
  Bronze age burials in, 168
  bronze sources of, 223
  colonisation of, 9–10, 35
  Continental Europe and, 269
  copper in, 156, 157, 172
  court cairns of, 52–54
  earliest settlements of, 8
  early ring forts in, 254
  geography of, 14
  gold artefacts in, 196, 218
  Grooved Ware in, 114–116
  henges of, 114
  hillforts in, 218
  houses in, 60
  Iron Age in, 244, 252
  megalithic monuments in, 6, 30
  metalwork in, 152
  Neolithic period in, 6, 29, 86, 120
  origin myth of, 24
  ring forts in, 254
  treatment of the dead in, 59–61
  wedge tombs in, 161
Irish archaeology
  aerial photography and, 154

Irish Beakers
　　Knowth and, 147
　　Newgrange and, 147
Irish Bronze Age
　　metalwork of, 268
　　two-fold division of, 178
Irish Neolithic
　　mortuary monuments of, 50
　　settlements of, 42, 50
iron
　　availability of, 232
　　social change and, 232
Iron Age. *See also* Early Iron Age; Iron Age Ireland;
　　　Middle Iron Age
　　agriculture production during, 237, 240–241, 246
　　cemeteries of, 262
　　domesticated animals during, 242
　　field systems of, 241, 246
　　funeral rites in, 264
　　henges, 208
　　hillforts of, 243
　　in Ireland, 244, 252
　　large round houses of, 258
　　metalwork of, 269
　　period approaches to, 226
　　pottery use during, 236
　　regular burial in, 262
　　settlements of, 236, 244–246, 254
　　soil erosion during, 242
　　Yorkshire burials, 263
Iron Age Communities in Britain (Cunliffe), 226
Iron Age Ireland, metalwork of, 268
iron weapons, in Continental Europe, 230
Isbister, walled enclosure construction at, 110
Isle of Ely, 204
Isle of Man, 7
　　Billown, 43
　　colonisation of, 8
　　earthwork enclosures of, 254
Italy, metalwork supply impact of, 227
Itford Hill
　　cremations at, 197
　　village at, 190

Jacobi, Roger, 10
Johnston, Robert, 170
Johnstown South, Late Bronze henge at, 217
Jones, Carleton, 17
Jope, Martyn, 269
Julius Caesar, invasion of England by, 1

Keenoge, 162
kerbstones, decorated, 103
Killymoon, platform at, 205
Kiltierney, 118
Kimpton, 198
Kings' Barrows, 159
Kintore, round houses at, 196
Knap of Howar, 41, 52
Knocknarea, 95

tomb exterior at, 106
Knockroe
　　decorated tomb at, 106
　　passages at, 104
Knowth, 69, 102, 112, 120
　　artefacts at, 106
　　carved designs at, 102
　　Irish Beakers and, 147
　　layout of, 104
　　pottery at, 94
　　structural sequence at, 94–95
Kristiansen, Kristian, 227

La Tène, 266–267
　　decorated pottery, 269
　　metalwork, 268
Lake District mountains, 37
Lambay Island, 7
　　stone from, 133
Lambrick, George, 246
land use
　　Britain *vs.* Ireland, 14–15
　　during Early Neolithic, 43
　　monuments and, 176
　　seasonal, 184
　　in uplands, 172
landscape(s)
　　Dartmoor, 194
　　enclosed, 195–196
　　lowland, 183
　　monumental architecture and, 106
　　of North York Moors, 194
landscape archaeology, of British isles, 7
Langton Bay, shipwreck at, 225
large round houses. *See also* round houses
　　of Iron Age, 258
　　of Late Bronze Age ringworks, 237
Last, Jonathan, 162
Late Bronze Age, 202–222
　　access to foreign metal in, 230
　　cemeteries of, 212
　　characteristics of, 181–187
　　elites of, 217
　　English ringworks of, 224
　　field monuments of, 223
　　fortifications of, 206
　　fortified ringworks of, 234
　　funeral rites during, 186
　　hilltop enclosures in, 222
　　iron production in, 230
　　large round houses of, 237
　　lowland landscapes of, 183
　　metalwork of, 186, 230
　　ores of, 224
　　prosperity of, 225
　　regional developments of, 218
　　ringwork of, 237
　　in Scotland, 200
　　settlements of, 181, 223, 236
　　small island occupation during, 204

social collapse during, 186
soils in, 183
study of, 222
terminology of, 181
Yorkshire Wolds settlements of, 212
Later Mesolithic period
Britain *vs.* Northern European, 35
social complexity in, 35
Later Neolithic
artefacts of, 78
domestic dwellings of, 94
monuments and cursuses of, 136
Lawford, 133
Lebor Gabála Érren, 24
Lévi-Strauss, 59
Lincolnshire, 57
earthwork construction in, 244
linear cemeteries, around Stonehenge, 176
linear monuments, 78
Linearbandkeramik, 40
Linkardstown cists, 80
Littleour, 62, 64
livestock
on Dartmoor, 192
importance of, 192
trade of, 234
Llandegai, 118
Llyn Fawr, industrial phase, 230
Loch Gara, 205
Lockington, gold ornaments at, 154
long barrows
causewayed enclosures and, 75–77
classification of, 54–55
first development of, 86
Long Meg and her Daughters
causewayed enclosure and, 136
monolith decoration at, 120
long mounds
of Neolithic period, 34
round barrows *vs.*, 52
longhouses, of Continental Europe, 40
Longstone Rath, henge at, 114
Lough Gur, 147, 216
Loughcrew, 101
lowlands
ceramic sequence in, 196
domestic dwellings in, 190
Late Bronze Age and, 183
Lugg, 217
lunula, 148

Macalister, Robert, 24
Maeshowe, 6, 110
Barclodiad Y Gawres *vs.*, 121–122
Boyne Valley impact on, 117
pillars at, 110–112
tomb at, 99, 109, 116
Maiden Castle, 6, 77, 261
marine resources, during Mesolithic period,
33

Maumbury Rings, 126
artefact distribution at, 127
Maxey, 76, 83
Mayburgh
henge monument at, 134
stone axe at, 134
Meare, artefacts at, 252
Mediterranean
archaeology of, 7
society formation in, 227
Medway, River, 14
Megale Britannia, 3
megalithic art
in Britain, 118
motifs in, 134
states of consciousness and, 104, 108
in Western Europe, 6
megaliths
archaeology of, 6
in Ireland, 30
Meldon Bridge, 130
Mercer, Roger, 123
Mesolithic Ireland, material culture of, 10
Mesolithic period. *See also* Later Mesolithic period
British and Irish *vs.* Northern European, 32
burials in, 84
domestic buildings in, 32
marine resources use in, 33
occupation sites of, 10, 29
Scandanavian model of, 32
Scottish, 15
settlement pattern in, 32
social practices in, 32, 35
Mesolithic sites, pottery and imported axes on,
30
metal, artefacts, 91
metal, movement of, 157
metal sources, 227
burials and, 156
metalwork, 91, 154, 202
adoption of, 156
Beaker pottery and, 143, 146–147
in Britain, 269
of Bronze Age, 186, 227
at burnt mounds, 214
Celtic art and, 269
chronology of, 179
Continental Europe and, 185, 223
with the dead, 185
distribution of, 176, 268
earliest Irish, 146
hoards of, 185, 214
imported, 186, 230
introduction of, 142
in Ireland, 152
of Irish Bronze Age, 268
of Iron Age, 269
of Iron Age Ireland, 268
Italian supply impact on, 227
La Tène, 268

metalwork (*cont.*)
  during Late Bronze Age, 186, 230
  for prehistoric people, 179
  process protocols of, 187
  river deposits of, 202
  from River Shannon, 204
  at Runnymede Bridge, 204, 233
  supply of, 225
  from Thames, 203
  transformation of, 187
metalwork deposits
  in north-east Scotland, 157
  in rivers, 202
microliths, in Northern England, 34
middens, 233–234
  at Balksbury, 234
  of Bronze Age, 251
  at East Chisenbury, 234
  shell, 37
  in southern Britain, 232
  in Thames Valley, 43
  at Wallingford, 204
Middle Bronze Age, 187–202
  dwellings of, 190
  mortuary rituals of, 197
Middle Iron Age, ground plans of settlements, 240
Middle Neolithic period
  ceramics of, 38
  earthwork enclosures of, 38
  mortuary monuments of, 38
Midhowe, 106
  walled enclosure at, 110
Mikra Britannia, 3
Mildenhall, 170
Millett, Martin, 227
Mine Howe, 274
mines. *See also* copper mining
  in mainland Europe, 185
Mizoguchi, Koji, 162, 166
Monknewtown, 113
Monkton, 164
monoliths, visual relationships and, 112
monumental architecture, 132–137
  of British and Irish Neolithic, 86
  curvilinear decoration of, 106
  landscape and, 106
  of Neolithic period, 34
  social impact of, 128
monuments, 4, 39, 57–58. *See also* mortuary
      monuments
  aerial photography of, 166
  alignment of, 157–158
  of Britain, 16
  closing of, 152
  community competition and, 142
  connections between, 117, 120, 133
  construction scale of, 122
  cup marks on, 175
  distribution of, 47

  earthwork perimeters of, 122
  field systems and, 188
  groupings of, 132
  houses and, 50
  of Iberian peninsula, 99
  land use and, 176
  large *vs.* small, 132
  of Late Bronze Age, 218
  location selection of, 17, 134
  materials and, 140
  mortuary rituals and, 174
  of Neolithic period, 7, 27
  origin myths and, 87
  private aspects of, 106
  rebuilding of, 73
  remains of dead and, 84, 175
  settlements and, 175
  siting of, 67, 136–137
  size of, 132
  of southern Britain, 122
  spatial relationships between, 166
  structural stages of, 164
  of uplands, 172
  use of turf in, 168
Mooghaun, 218
Moore, Dermot, 61
Moray Firth, 174
mortuary monuments
  Bronze Age disappearance of, 223
  distribution of, 160
  field cairns and, 170
  habitation evidence towards, 175
  of Irish Neolithic, 50
  of Middle Neolithic period, 38
  in Neolithic Ireland, 29
  in northern England, 29
mortuary rituals
  of Middle Bronze Age, 197
  monuments and, 174
mounds. *See also* burnt mounds; long mounds;
      oval mounds
  burnt, 214
  Dunragit, 131
  earthwork enclosures and, 131
Mount Pleasant, 128
  adoption of Beaker pottery at, 152
  Conquer Barrow at, 131
  post setting at, 124
  pottery at, 152
Mucking, 237
  ringwork at, 217
Mycenaeans
  faience bead trading of, 156
  Stonehenge and, 156

natural environment
  during post-glacial period, 15–16
  during Scottish Mesolithic, 15
Navan Fort, 6, 217, 272

Needham, Stuart, 91, 148, 152, 157, 178
Neolithic artefacts
    origins for, 34
    radiocarbon dates for, 33
Neolithic houses
    Ireland *vs.* England, 38
    in Orkney, 95
Neolithic Ireland, 6, 29, 86
    domestic buildings in, 29
    domesticated animals in, 29
    megaliths of, 6
    mortuary monuments in, 29
Neolithic monuments, burning down of,
    58
Neolithic period
    archaeology of, 30, 39
    in Britain and Ireland, 27, 44
    burnt mounds of, 214
    ceremonial monuments of, 36
    chambered tombs in, 38
    collective burial during, 162
    Continental Europe *vs.* Britain and Ireland,
        86
    continuity *vs.* disruption in, 84
    definitions of, 27–29
    domesticated animals of, 29, 34
    environmental record of, 33
    houses in, 27, 59
    human diet during, 46
    land clearance, timber working during, 37
    long mounds of, 34
    models of, 30
    monumental architecture of, 34
    monuments of, 7, 27
    in Northern Europe, 30
    settlement during, 38, 42, 171
Neolithic Revolution, 27
Neolithic settlements, in Ireland, 42
New Forest, 171
Newbridge, 264
Newgrange, 6
    artefacts at, 106
    carved designs at, 102
    entrance passage at, 104
    Irish Beakers and, 147
    modifications of, 102
    tomb at, 102
    view into, 132
North Mains, Scottish henge at, 130
North York Moors, 171
    landscape of, 194
Northern Britain
    elongated timber, earthwork monuments in, 64
    wooden halls in, 62
Northern Circle, at Durrington Walls, 123, 140
Northern Circle, Grooved Ware and, 138
Northern Europe
    Neolithic period in, 30
    'wandering settlements' of, 260

occupation sites, Mesolithic *vs.* Neolithic, 29
open grassland, ceremonial centers in, 97
origin myths, monuments and, 87
Orkney, 7, 39, 50, 95, 99, 106, 168
    Ballynahatty and, 118
    Boyne passage tombs impact on, 116
    ceramic tradition in, 134
    chambered tombs in, 106
    domestic dwellings in, 108, 192
    monuments on, 6
    settlement of, 8
Outer Hebrides, settlement of, 8
oval mounds, round, long barrows and, 82
Overton Down, 241

palisade enclosures. *See* earthwork enclosures
passage tombs
    of Boyne Valley, 101
    at Carrowmore, 99
    chronology of, 99
    contents of, 102
    in Continental Europe, 99
    distinctive features of, 98
    of Iberian peninsula, 99
    Irish, 99–101
    layout of, 104
    Maeshowe type, 99
    at Newgrange, 112–113
    restrictions of access to, 104
    use of, 104
Pearson, Parker, M., 126, 141, 175
Pennines, 171
period frameworks, 91
    Iron Age, 226
    metal technology and, 146
    settlement patterns and, 179
    terminology of, 226
The Personality of Britain (Fox), 15, 23
Peterborough Ware, 78, 81, 89, 94, 136
Petersen, F., 162
Pierowall, 110
Piggot, Stuart, 23, 155
Pike O' Stickle, stone from, 133
pit deposits
    alignment of, 244
    in Britain, 59
    in England, 43
    formality of, 133
    human remains in, 127
plant species, Britain *vs.* Ireland, 8
political autonomy, of Wales and Scotland, 11
political boundaries, 10
Polynesia, archaeology of, 7
portable artefacts, movement of, 157
portal dolmens, 49
Portugal, fortified enclosures of, 252
post settings, location of, 122
Potterne, 232–233
    ceramics from, 233

pottery. *See also* Beaker pottery; ceramics; Grooved
    Ware
    carbonised grain in, 41
    at Carrowkeel, 102
    at Durrington Walls, 124
    in Early Bronze age burials, 197
    of Early Neolithic, 38
    in graves, 142
    during Iron Age, 236
    at Knowth, 94
    La Tène style of, 269
    Lough Gur Class II, 216
    on Mesolithic sites, 30
    metalwork and, 146–147
    at Mount Pleasant, 152
    regional styles of, 29
    use of, 266
Powell, Andrew, 54
prehistoric Britain, Continental Europe *vs.*, 10
Prehistoric Communities of the British Isles (Childe), 23
prehistoric period, political geography of, 223
Ptolemy, British Isles map of, 3

Quanterness
    excavation at, 108
    tomb at, 110
Quoyness, 110

radiocarbon dating
    of Beaker pottery, 143
    by British Museum, 144
    of Neolithic artefacts, 33
Radley, 164
Ramilsonina, 126, 141, 175
Rams Hill, 208
Ramsgate, 76
Rathgall, 217
    gold ring at, 217
Rathtinaun, 206
Rathlin Island, 7
Raunds, 81, 154, 168
raw materials, southern Britain export of, 157
regional divisions, 91
Renfrew, Colin, 4, 108, 136
Richards, Colin, 51, 109, 112
Richards, Michael, 75
ring barrows, henges and, 200
ring cairns
    cremation cemeteries and, 185
    domestic dwellings and, 170
ring forts
    in Ireland, 254
    of Late Bronze Age, 206
Ring of Bookan, 112
Ring of Brodgar, 112, 126
    mace heads near, 136
Ringlemere, gold vessel from, 154
ringworks. *See also* English ringworks; fortifications
    distribution of, 208

of Early Iron Age, 239
    interpretation of, 208
    of Late Bronze Age, 206
    public focus of, 208
rituals. *See also* funeral rites
    in domestic buildings, 41
    at hillforts *vs.* settlements, 250
    of Middle Bronze Age, 197
    monuments and, 174
    mortuary, 174, 197
    at Star Carr, 32
river burial, evidence for, 202
River Shannon, metalwork from, 204
Robin Hood's Ball, 76
Roche, Helen, 114, 217
rock carvings, distribution of, 97
Roman Conquest, 1, 2, 226, 271
Ross Island, copper mining at, 146–147
rotary querns, distribution of, 268
Roughan Hill, 169
round barrows
    antiquarians on, 158
    hengiform enclosures *vs.*, 78–79
    individual burials in, 89
    long mounds *vs.*, 52
    replacement by urnfields of, 184
    reuse of, 186
    of Yorkshire Wolds, 80
Rowlands, Michael, 4
Rowley-Conwy, Peter, 32
Rudston, 65
    cemetery at, 264
Runnymede Bridge, 204
    metalwork from, 204, 233
    timber buildings at, 233
Rybury, 73

Salcombe, shipwreck at, 225
Salisbury Plain, 159
    burial concentrations on, 154
    coaxial field systems on, 242
Scandanavia, Mesolithic period of, 32
Scotland
    archaeology of, 116
    Earlier Neolithic halls in, 64
    earliest settlements in, 8
    enclosures and round houses in, 258
    Late Bronze Age in, 200
    metalwork deposits of, 157
    political autonomy of, 11
Scottish graves, flowers in, 159
Scottish Mesolithic, natural environment during, 15
sea routes, prehistoric, 19–20
Seahenge, timber setting of, 123
settlement(s). *See also* hilltop settlements
    Bronze *vs.* Iron Age, 246
    burials near, 185
    cemeteries and, 197
    climate change and, 172, 179

field systems and, 188
high status, 193
hillforts and, 251
human remains and, 84, 214
of Irish Neolithic, 50
of Iron Age, 236, 244–246, 254
of Late Bronze Age, 181, 236
in Mesolithic period, 32
monuments and, 175
during Neolithic period, 38, 42, 171
of Orkney, 8
Outer Hebrides, 8
over urnfields, 212
regional forms of, 236
sustainability of, 177
tombs and, 110, 112
in uplands, 172
on Yorkshire Wolds, 258
settlement patterns
in Britain, 13, 58
dislocation in, 236
domesticated animals and, 30
interpretations of, 97
of Late Bronze Age, 223
in Neolithic period, 42
northern *vs.* southern Britain, 224
period divisions and, 179
Severn, River, 14, 252
Shanks, Michael, 4
Shannon, bronze weapons deposits in, 200
Sharples, Niall, 110
Sheridan, Alison, 101, 105, 116
Sherratt, Andrew, 17
Shetland, 7, 43
oval stone-built houses in,
settlement of, 8
Shinewater, 203
Silbury Hill, 131
Silchester, 276–278
single burials
definition of, 158–159
early fieldwork and, 158
Skara Brae, 95, 108
smiths
political control of, 232
social position of, 187
Snail Down, 164
field boundaries at, 151
social practices, 37
architectural form and, 105
development of, 31
evidence of, 32
graves and, 160, 186
iron and, 232
in Mesolithic period, 32, 35
travel and, 157
soils
during Iron Age, 242
in Late Bronze Age, 183

under monuments, 130
Solway, River, 14
Somerset Levels, 29, 36
souterrains, 254
South Cadbury, shield deposit at, 214
South Hornchurch, earthwork monument at, 208
South Lodge Camp, 190
post holes at, 193
South Uist, 170
southern Britain
Bronze Age in, 23
middens of, 232
monuments of, 122
Spratt, Don, 169
Springfield Lyons, 65, 208, 209–210, 237, 247
square barrows, round houses and, 266
stalled cairn, at Midhowe, 106
Stanton Drew, 123
materials for, 126
Stanwell, bank barrow at, 64
Star Carr, ritual activity at, 32
Station Stones, location of, 139
stone axes
distribution of, 133
at Mayburgh, 134
movement of, 134–135
exchange of, 74–75
Stonehall, 40, 41
excavated houses at, 110
Stonehenge, 6, 168
archaeology of, 5
Avebury *vs.*, 160
bluestones of, 140
burials near, 160
concentric pits at, 138
cursus, 138
design of, 1, 23
Durrington Walls and, 138, 141
enclosures at, 82, 138
human remains at, 141
interior isolation of, 139
labor demand of, 141
landscape of, 138
layout of, 141, 176
linear cemeteries around, 176
materials of, 140
Mycenaean architecture and, 156
raw materials of,
second phase dates for, 138
Station Stones at, 139
timber to stone at, 139
timbers at, 86, 138
uniqueness of, 137
Stones of Stenness, 112, 126
Stukeley, William, 7, 159
Sun, tomb alignment with, 118
surface remains, documentation of, 7
Sutton Hoo, 151
swords, burials with, 264

Taplow, 208
Tara, passage tomb at, 168
Taverso Tuick, 110
Temple Wood, 118
Testwood, 203
textile production, 192
Thames
    bronze weapon deposits in, 200
    cursuses along, 68
    metalwork from, 203
    paths, platforms, causeways and, 184
    weapons in, 6
Thames Estuary, burials in, 198
Thames Valley, open air middens in, 43
the dead
    metalwork and, 185
    remains at monuments of, 84
    treatment in England of, 59–61
    treatment in Ireland of, 59–61
Thomas, Julian, 35, 38, 44
Thomas, Roger, 237
Thornborough
    cursus at, 83
    lithic materials at, 136
Three Age Model, 26, 226
Thwing, 208, 212, 237, 242
Tievebulliagh, stone from, 133
Tilley, Christopher, 4
timber circles
    at Balfarg, 123
    internal organisation of, 123
    stone settings and, 124
timber enclosures, earthwork monuments *vs.*,
        128
timber monuments, 86, 170
    stone replacement of, 125
Timberlake, Simon, 172
tin
    Cornish, 156
    cross-Channel movement of, 156
    sources of, 157
tombs. *See also* passage tombs; wedge tombs
    domestic buildings and, 59
    genealogy of, 54
    of Neolithic period, 38
    settlement links to, 110–112
    Sun's alignment with, 118
tools, deposition of, 186
Traprain Law, 222
travel, social power and, 157
treatment of the dead, England *vs.* Ireland, 59–
        61
tumuli. *See* round barrows
Tumulus Culture, Urnfield Culture *vs.*, 178
Twyford Down, 189

Ulaid, 10
Unstan bowls, 106
    Grooved Ware and, 116

uplands
    cremation cemeteries in, 185
    enclosure occupation in, 256
    land use in, 172
    monuments of, 172
    settlement evidence from, 172
    specialized monuments of, 172
Urnfield Culture, Tumulus Culture *vs.*, 178
urnfields
    replacement of round barrows by, 184
    settlements over, 212

Vauxhall, structures at, 203

Wales
    copper mining in, 172
    political autonomy of, 11
Walesland Rath, 254
Wallingford, 204
Wandlebury, 251
Warner, Richard, 272
waterways, of Britain and Ireland, 16–20
Watson, Aaron, 136
Weald, 171
weapons
    in Britain and Ireland, 224
    in Continental Europe, 230
    deposition of, 186
    Early Iron Age distribution of, 236
    of Late Bronze Age, 202
    in Thames, 6, 200
wedge tombs
    Beaker pottery and, 147
    in western Ireland, 161
Weekley, 269
wells, ponds
    deposits in, 212
    domestic dwellings and, 190
Wessex
    archaeological influence of, 153
    Early Bronze Age, 166
    earthwork barrows in, 166
    monuments in, 161
West Cotton, 83
West Harling, 237
West Heslerton, 244
West Kennet, 130
West Row Fen, 170
West Whittlesey, 170
Western Europe, megalithic art in, 6
Wetwang Slack, 244, 264
Whitegrounds, 89
Whitehorse Stone, 44
Whitley, James, 84
Whittle, Alasdair, 38, 49
Wideford Hill, passage grave at, 110
Windmill Hill, 69, 72
Winklebury, 247
    storage pits inside, 251

Wittenhem Clumps, 234, 251
wooden halls, in northern Britain, 62
wooden paths, 184
wooden structures, stone replacement of,
    132
Woodhenge, 130
    artefact distribution at, 124
    timber setting at, 123
woodland, use of, 36
Woodside, 254
Wrekin, building platforms at, 251
Wyke Down, artefact distribution at, 126

Yarnton, 44
Yates, David, 210, 241
Yorkshire Wolds, 52, 266
    agriculture on, 242
    burial concentrations on, 154
    chalk sculptures of, 264
    earthworks on, 166, 244
    Iron Age burials of, 263
    land divisions of, 243
    Late Bronze Age settlements of, 212
    open settlements of, 258
    round barrows of, 80